GENERALS OF
the ARDENNES

DEDICATION

This book is respectfully dedicated to two authentic heroes of the Battle of the Bulge and their comrades in arms:

EUGENE H. GARRETT
AND THE MEN OF B BATTERY
285TH FA OBSERVATION BATTALION
BAUGNEZ CROSSROADS, MALMÉDY, BELGIUM
17 DECEMBER 1944

Down in a row the brave tin-soldiers fall...

Robert Graves, *Recalling War*

COLONEL ROY U. CLAY, USA (RET.)
AND THE MEN OF THE
275TH ARMORED FIELD ARTILLERY BATTALION
ST. VITH, BELGIUM
16-23 DECEMBER 1944

Then shells and bullets swept the icy woods.

Louis Simpson, *The Battle*

Generals of
the Ardennes
AMERICAN LEADERSHIP
IN THE BATTLE OF THE BULGE

by
J.D. Morelock

University Press of the Pacific
Honolulu, Hawaii

Generals of the Ardennes:
American Leadership in the Battle of the Bulge

by
Jerry D. Morelock

With an Introduction by
Martin Blumenson

ISBN: 1-4102-0395-6

Copyright © 2003 by University Press of the Pacific

Reprinted from the 1994 edition

University Press of the Pacific
Honolulu, Hawaii
http://www.universitypressofthepacific.com

CONTENTS

ILLUSTRATIONS

MAPS

FOREWORD

Generals of the Ardennes is not a conventional history of the Battle of the Bulge, but a study of US command leadership at different levels during that fiery December of 1944 when a German offensive against the center of the American lines threatened to split the massed Allied Armies. It shows how US commanders from Eisenhower himself down through Army Group, Army, Corps, and Division commanders met the heavy burdens of leadership in the crucible of that bloody winter. It does so by presenting five case studies:

- Eisenhower's role as coalition commander overseeing the defense and counterattack;
- Bradley's direction of the 12th Army Group during the crisis;
- Lieutenant General William Simpson's contribution as his Ninth Army helped defeat the German onslaught;
- Major General Troy Middleton's stand with the VIII Corps in the center of the fighting; and
- Major General Alan Jones and Brigadier General Bruce Clarke dealing with the enormous challenges, uncertainties, and confusion that characterized the battle at "the point of the spear."

In each instance, the author, Colonel J. D. Morelock, answers two questions—What characteristics of leadership did these six generals display, and how did they affect the overall battle? His frank and objective answers are based on extensive documentary research and personal interviews with participants in the Battle. He also summarizes the careers of the six principals to show the formative influences that at least partially explain their characteristics of battle leadership.

Amid the countless books in many languages that tell and retell the history of the Battle of the Bulge, this one is unique in its focus on American generalship during those

epic and decisive weeks that turned the tide of World War II
in Europe. For that reason, it stands as both a significant
history and an important document for the study of
command and control.

Paul G. Cergan
Lieutenant General ,USA
President, National Defense
University

ACKNOWLEDGMENTS

The genesis of this book was an idea by Lieutenant Colonel Boyd M. "Mac" Harris while he was assigned to the Center for Army Leadership at Fort Leavenworth, KS, in 1983. Mac had just completed writing the Army's principal field manual on military leadership, which was directed at battalion level and below. It was Mac's creation to use illustrative case studies of historical examples in that manual, to help drive home the lessons of combat leadership. He was then just beginning to write a new field manual, this time aimed at the brigade level and higher, and approached me to support that effort by investigating, researching and writing illustrative case studies of some of our World War II senior leaders. The research for those cases studies introduced me to the wartime careers and battle leadership demonstrated by Dwight D. Eisenhower, Omar N. Bradley, William H. Simpson, Troy H. Middleton, Bruce C. Clarke, and other outstanding American commanders of that time. Sadly, Mac's untimely death in October 1983 cut short his efforts on the manual and robbed the Army of an original and innovative thinker on leadership and command. Without Mac's inspiration, this study would not have been possible.

During initial research I met three veterans of the Battle of the Bulge whose generous assistance proved invaluable in completing this book. General Bruce C. Clarke spent countless hours sharing his experiences of that battle and willingly opened his personal files and correspondence to me. Clarke's lifelong study of commandership and leadership produced a wealth of material that provided a rich source of personal and professional experiences. Colonel Roy U. Clay unselfishly provided much detailed information about 275th Armored Field Artillery's key role in the defense of St. Vith, including his candid observations on the situation leading to the surrender of the 422nd and 423rd Infantry Regiments on the Schnee Eifel, the greatest US capitulation of the European war. COL Clay's inspirational example stands as a model of what a battle leader ought to be. Mr. Eugene Garrett, who served in Battery B, 285th Field Artillery Observation Battalion, survived the Battle of the Bulge's most horrifying and infamous incident—the Malmedy Massacre. Silenced for many years by the grief and horror of this war crime, Mr. Garrett nonetheless shared his terrible experience with the author and the members of my artillery battalion to help instruct and train a new generation of soldiers. In so doing, Mr. Garrett contributed unique knowledge and insight about how Americans fought the battle and imparted an appreciation of what that terrible combat was actually like. Leaders such as these three men make one proud to serve in the same military.

I was especially fortunate to receive the guidance, encouragement, and assistance of several outstanding historians during preparation of this book. Dr. Robert H. Berlin, historian for the Army's School of Advanced Military Studies at Fort Leavenworth, generously provided his candid, critical analysis of early drafts and shared his extensive knowledge of World War II combat leaders. General Bill Stofft, Lieutenant Colonel Roger Cirillo, and Dr. Glenn Robertson all provided inspiration and assistance during the early days of the research for these case studies and never wavered in their support of this project. The manuscript also greatly benefitted from a careful and knowledgeable reading by Captain Peter Mansoor, who contributed many useful, insightful, and informed suggestions. Professor Martin Blumenson, Patton scholar and author of a volume of the official history of the war, very willingly shared his ideas, opinions, and observations about World War II command and leadership with the author. Discussions with Professor Blumenson proved extremely helpful in completing chapter seven. Any errors of fact or judgment, however, are the author's alone.

This book would not have been possible without the outstanding support and unwavering commitment of Dr. Fred Kiley, Director, Research Directorate, National Defense University, and members of his staff, especially Lt.Col. John Clements, Deputy Director, and Mary Sommerville, editor.

Their enthusiasm, perseverance, energy, diligence, and patience were indispensable in preparing this volume for publication.

Finally, I thank my family for their patience and understanding. Never was benign neglect more appreciated than during the preparation of this book.

INTRODUCTION

J. D. Morelock has used the Battle of the Bulge in World War II to assess the professional military skills and personal leadership characteristics of selected American officers operating on the six top echelons of command: Dwight D. Eisenhower at the supreme Allied command level; Omar N. Bradley at army group; William H. Simpson at army; Troy H. Middleton at corps; Alan W. Jones at division; and Bruce C. Clarke at combat command. How they performed during the reaction to the powerful German Ardennes counteroffensive of December 1944, probably the greatest pitched battle fought in the European Theater of Operations by United States forces, is the subject of Morelock's investigation and analysis.

The general officers Morelock has chosen to look at are instructive. Coming from different backgrounds, they display a remarkable range of activity. Each one illustrates the system for selection and advancement of leaders during the interwar period—or lack of a system—that brought him to the top of the profession of arms in the United States Army of the Second World War.

Morelock's procedure is the same in each of the several case studies. After narrating and discussing each commander's career up to the time of the German attack, he describes their actions in the ensuing combat and weighs their decisions. He then summarizes the effectiveness of their leadership.

The result is a fascinating read in military history. Most of the commanders of World War II have fled from our memories. The mere passage of time since that global conflict and also the emergence of newer heroes in our more recent wars have pushed these relatively ancient commanders from our minds. All too soon, any recollection of the battlefield performance of our Second World War commanders—the good along with the bad—will be gone. It is good to be reminded, as Morelock has done, of their exploits and failures.

But Morelock's work is more than a guided tour of the past; it is, by extension and inference, a practical exercise in personnel selection. Morelock has illustrated a basic question for all military institutions: how can an army in peacetime select and prepare the leaders for the next war? Those whose task it is to determine and groom the top warriors of the succeeding generations will find much of value in Colonel Morelock's study.

MARTIN BLUMENSON

Professor Martin Blumenson *has held the King Chair at the Naval War College, the Johnson Chair at the Army War College, and the Mark Clark Chair at The Citadel. Professor Blumenson is the author of 15 books, including* The United States Army in World War II. European Theater of Operations: Breakout and Pursuit, *a volume in the official history of the war;* The Patton Papers; Patton: The Man Behind the Legend; *and* Mark Clark.

PREFACE

In the almost 50 years since the Ardennes offensive blasted an enormous bulge in the American line and threatened to split the Allied armies in two,[1] the characterization of the battle leadership demonstrated by the senior American commanders who stopped and then turned back this German thrust has swung like a pendulum between hero worship and scorn. During the heady days immediately following the Allied victory over Nazi Germany and imperial Japan, the victorious American commanders were feted and honored as genuine military geniuses who had out-generaled the best the enemy had to offer. Memoirs thrown together from the daily diaries kept by wartime aides-de-camp were quickly published and became bestsellers.[2] Patton, who died suddenly and at the pinnacle of his fame and glory, achieved the status of military icon, with his eccentric leadership style (but not his genius) often imitated by later generations.

Yet more recently, the sharpened pens of some revisionist historians have rewritten the earlier accounts and re-interpreted the leadership performance of the senior Americans. The impetus for this later trend came from our former British Allies who, stung by the seeming unfairness of standing alone against Hitler only to be rewarded ultimately by seeing their Empire crumble and their country reduced to second-rate status, lashed out in frustration and envy at senior Americans.[3] They resented the men they viewed as military amateurs who bumbled through a global war principally on the strength of the world's greatest economy and received credit for masterminding the defeat of German military professionals.

These views eventually spread across the Atlantic and were picked up by historians (and politicians) in this country. Even such respected military writers and historians as Martin van Creveld and Martin Blumenson joined in. Van Creveld's conclusions that "the American officer corps of World War II was less than mediocre...(and was) often guilty of bad leadership" are typical.[4] Blumenson, Patton scholar and author of a volume of the US Army's official history of the war, has recently questioned the overall quality of American senior leaders, calling them "bland and plodding" and damning their leadership as "workmanlike rather than bold, prudent rather than daring," satisfied with the safe rather than the imaginative way.[5] Our World War II leaders, Blumenson writes, "displayed serious flaws in conception and execution," and were "unable to adapt and adjust to the new requirements of leadership."[6]

Given this wide spread of opinions of senior American leaders over the years, what judgment can be made today about their actual performance? Would a study of their conduct of one of the supreme leadership challenges of the war in Europe—the Battle of the Bulge—reveal the senior American commanders to be exceptional men of military legend? Or do their Ardennes actions merit Blumenson's and van Creveld's stinging criticisms?

The reality, it seems, lies between these two conflicting opinions. Like most military operations throughout the history of warfare, the Ardennes was characterized by failures in leadership as well as successes, and the leadership demonstrated by the Americans is not excepted. The facts are more complex and bear scrutiny, even after 50 years. Eisenhower and Patton weren't the only heroes, and even they made mistakes. Battle analysis is always a learning experience, as is any close review of leadership and command.

Much has been assumed about American leadership during World War II and the Battle of the Bulge, and many of these assumptions are either wrong, gross oversimplifications, or misinterpretations of what actually occurred. In the postwar glow of victory, the facts were often lost in the general feeling of superiority held by the victorious Allies. British military historian and theorist Sir Basil Liddell Hart recognized this tendency when he warned:

Everything in war looks different at the time from what it looks in the clearer light that comes after the war. Nothing looks so different as the form of the leaders.

> The public picture of them at the time is not only an unreal one, but changes with the tide of success.[7]

During the half-century since the Ardennes struggle ended, much of the leadership demonstrated by American commanders at crucial points in the fighting has become lost in the legends created from this greatest of US battles. General George S. Patton, Jr., did not win the battle alone, however important his army's dramatic change of direction to relieve the defenders of beleaguered Bastogne. If our collective memories of the Battle of the Bulge contain only Patton and General Dwight D. Eisenhower, we cheat future generations out of a rich heritage of combat leadership history. These case studies aim to bring out the critical role played by several important and outstanding but little-known commanders whose leadership significantly affected the battle's outcome. Men such as General William Simpson, Major General Troy Middleton, and Brigadier General Bruce C. Clarke should have their names burned into our collective memory along with the more famous ones like Patton, Eisenhower, and General Omar Bradley. Historians Martin Blumenson and James L. Stokesbury have provided an apt comment as well as a fitting tribute to these commanders when they wrote:

> The highly developed art of generalship that emerged in World War II spawned many great commanders, but the struggle was so immense in scope that all but a very few have been virtually forgotten. Some soldiers who receive a footnote in the history of World War II would have been the subjects of legends in the days before men could write.[8]

History is a great teacher, but only if we choose to study its implications with honesty. In this book, five case studies focus on how selected senior US commanders influenced the conduct of the Ardennes offensive—the Battle of the Bulge—in December 1944. Each case study illuminates the demonstrated leadership of the senior leaders by answering two central questions:

- What *characteristics* of leadership were displayed?
- How did they *affect* the overall battle?

The principal thrust of the case studies is not to retell the story of the battle. That has already been done in many excellent histories. Rather, the leadership studies in this book seek to use the battle's story to describe the command decisions, actions, and leadership impact of several American commanders who led the desperate struggle in the Ardennes. This review analyzes the American brand of battle leadership in World War II and how it affected this battle and the war.

NOTES

1. Hugh M. Cole, *The United States Army in World War II. European Theater of Operations. The Ardennes: The Battle of the Bulge* (Washington, DC: Office of the Chief of Military History/GPO, 1965), 650; Charles B. MacDonald, *A Time for Trumpets: The Untold Story of the Battle of the Bulge* (New York: William Morrow, 1984), 618; Jacques Nobécourt, *Hitler's Last Gamble* (New York: Schocken Books, 1967). This largest battle on the western front in northwest Europe eventually involved over a million men (600,000 Americans) from the opening guns on 16 December 1944 until the "bulge" in the Allied line was straightened out at the end of January 1945. About 20 percent of them became casualties. The critical phase of the battle from the US perspective was the December fighting, which included the defense of St.-Vith, the saving of the "northern shoulder" on the Elsenborn Ridge, the siege of Bastogne, and the defeat of the German Seventh Army's attack. Nobécourt describes the battle as "Hitler's last bluff...the final act of a great political adventure both on the German and on the Allied side."

2. Dwight D. Eisenhower, *Crusade in Europe* (Garden City: Doubleday, 1948); Omar N. Bradley, *A Soldier's Story* (New York: Henry Holt and Company, 1951); Basil H. Liddell Hart, *The Other Side of the Hill* (London: Cassell and Company, 1951), 10; Nobécourt, Last Gamble, 255. Ike's and Bradley's memoirs of their World War II experiences are probably the best known examples of the postwar publications. Liddell Hart warned readers of such memoirs that "it must be recognized that the writers of autobiographies are usually more concerned with their own

interests and the service of their own reputations than with the service of history." DeGaulle commented when Eisenhower's book was published, "However eminent the authors of memoirs may be, each has his own view of the truth."

3. Arthur Bryant, *Triumph in the West* (New York: Doubleday and Company, 1959); Chester Wilmot, *The Struggle for Europe* (New York: Harper and Brothers, 1952); Bernard Law Montgomery, *The Memoirs of Field-Marshal the Viscount Montgomery of Alamein, K.G.* (New York: Signet Books, 1958); Martin Blumenson, "Eisenhower Then and Now: Fireside Reflections," *Parameters 21* (Summer 1991): 27. The Bryant and Wilmot books are replete with examples of British Chief of Staff Alanbrooke's and Montgomery's disdain for all the top American generals. Montgomery's memoirs, of course, point out how he could have won the war quickly if he had only been given the resources. Blumenson's article contains a typical quote by Field Marshal Alexander regarding American soldiers and their leaders: "They simply do not know their jobs as soldiers. They are soft, green, and quite untrained. There is no policy and no plan...no firm direction or centralized control from above....(The Americans are) quite useless."

4. Martin van Creveld, *Fighting Power: German and U.S. Army Performance, 1939-1945* (Westport, CT: Greenwood Press, 1982), 168. Van Creveld bases much of his argument on effectiveness in battle on a "Combat Effectiveness Table" of 78 WWII engagements between Americans and Germans prepared by writer-historian Trevor Dupuy. An attempt to quantify effectiveness using a mathematical model, it purports to show Germans as being significantly more effective fighters (in defense as well as offense) throughout the war. However, the majority of engagements are taken from the Italian campaign, where the terrain was as much an enemy to the Allies as the Germans were. The battles examined in northwest Europe are taken, principally, from the miserable, rain-soaked battles of attrition in the Lorraine campaign. The table excludes, for the most part, the July-August battles in France, and, according to van Creveld, excludes prisoners from casualty counts (no reason is given for excluding what is routinely considered an important category of battle casualties). The table does not include any battle after 7 December 1944; therefore, the Battle of the Bulge and subsequent fighting in the Rhineland and central Germany are omitted. The value of such a "systems analysis" approach and using a table to compare different units, different commanders, and entirely different

tactical and strategic situations seems dubious. As historian Martin Blumenson once stated, "Each battle is unique."

5.   Martin Blumenson, "America's World War II Leaders in Europe: Some Thoughts," *Parameters 19* (December 1989): 3. Blumenson exempts Patton from the general criticism, referring to him as "a notable exception."

6.   Ibid.

7.   Liddell Hart, 15.

8.   Martin Blumenson and James L. Stokesbury, *Masters of the Art of Command* (Boston:Houghton-Mifflin, 1975).

GENERALS OF
the ARDENNES

An American soldier walks along a deserted road in the Luxembourg area of the Ardennes.

1. American Forces in the Ardennes, 1944-45

The powerful German Ardennes offensive, launched in the early morning hours of 16 December 1944, was the greatest single battle ever fought by the American Army.[1] At the Battle of the Bulge's end a month later, it had become, in the words of historian Charles B. MacDonald who had fought in it, "the greatest single victory in US history."[2]

Born of desperation, Hitler's last gamble struck a thinly held sector of the Allied line with a strength and fury that no one on the Allied side thought possible at this stage of the war. Expecting the battlewise enemy commanders to husband their remaining mobile forces for defense against the upcoming Allied invasion of Germany itself, Allied leaders failed to realize that Hitler had taken absolute control of the war's prosecution.[3] In October, the Nazi dictator presented his plan for an Ardennes counterstroke to Field Marshal von Rundstedt, commander of the western armies. Hoping to achieve the same success as the brilliant Ardennes attack against the French in May 1940, Hitler used "the same basic pattern as the 1940 masterpiece."[4] Devised to split the Allied line in two at its weakest point, the offensive's aim was to isolate the British forces in the north from the American forces in the south. Hitler optimistically hoped this would allow his forces to annihilate the British Army or, failing that, at least put Germany in a good position to sign separate peace agreements with the Allies, avoiding a disastrous and humiliating unconditional surrender.[5]

The two principal German commanders charged with the responsibility of carrying out this massive counteroffensive were Sepp Dietrich (SS General and Hitler's crony from the old Munich days)[6] and Hasso von Manteuffel (called "the

3

Ardennes Region (Belgium and Luxumbourg)

Panzer General" for his successes with armored formations).
Von Manteuffel outlined the offensive's purpose and overall
scheme of maneuver in a postwar interview:

> The object defined [by Hitler's plan] was to achieve a
> decisive victory in the West by throwing in two panzer
> armies—the 6th under Dietrich, and the 5th under me.
> The 6th was to strike north-east, cross the Meuse beyond
> Liége and Huy, and drive for Antwerp. It had the main
> role, and main strength. My army was to advance along a
> more curving line, cross the Meuse between Namur and
> Dinant, and push toward Brussels—to cover the flank.[7]

Anchoring the offensive's left flank were the infantry
forces of General Erich Brandenberger's Seventh Army.[8]
None of these German commanders cared much for the plan
or had any serious conviction that Hitler's goal of capturing
Antwerp would succeed. However, they were sworn by
Hitler to attempt to carry out the plan to the best of their
abilities, and they were too professional not to try to make
it work.[9] It would be the last time in the war that the
German Army would be on the attack, so commanders and
soldiers alike desperately wanted to make the most of this
final opportunity.

The brunt of this surprise offensive was borne by Major
General Troy H. Middleton's understrength, overextended
VIII Corps. Comprising slightly more than three divisions,
the VIII Corps held a frontage more than three times wider
than that of a "normal" corps. Each US division was
expected to defend a sector of about 26 miles, which made
any effort to conduct a cohesive defense impossible.[10] The
length of the line and thinness of his defenses forced
Middleton to forego any thought of maintaining a mobile
reserve to plug gaps in an emergency. If attacked,
Middleton's beleaguered troops would have to rely on help
from outside the Ardennes.

Complicating Middleton's task was the condition of his
troops. Two of his divisions were still recovering from their
devastation in the bloody Huertgen Forest fighting of the
previous 3 months, and the third had no combat experience.[11]
(A fourth unit, the 9th Armored Division, was assigned to

(SOURCE DEPT OF ARMY, US ARMY ARMOR SCHOOL, *THE BATTLE AT ST VITH, BELGIUM, 17-23 DECEMBER 1944*)

Allied and German Troop Dispositions, 15 December 1944

VIII Corps, but one of its combat commands was attached to the neighboring V Corps.) The 68,822 troops of VIII Corps were supported by 242 tanks and 394 pieces of corps and divisional artillery.[12]

At 0530 hours on 16 December 1944, nearly 200,000 German troops attacked Middleton's sector all along his 80-mile front. Supported by 1,900 pieces of heavy artillery and almost 1,000 tanks, the German forces, with surprise on their side and heavily outnumbering the American defenders, made dramatic gains.[13] Allied leadership reacted quickly, however, to regain control of the battle, and in the first few hours after the attack began, reinforcements were rushing to the threatened sector. By the end of January 1945, over 600,000 US forces were involved in stopping, then reversing, the German tide.[14]

The price paid to achieve this "greatest victory" was terribly high, with casualty figures massive on both sides in this bitter, confused fighting. Allied forces lost nearly 80,000 men to all causes—all but 1,400 were American. Bradley's 12th Army Group believed it suffered over 50,000 casualties (40,000 infantrymen) in the first week of the battle. German records are incomplete; estimates of German casualties range from 90,000 to 120,000. The higher figure is probably closer to the truth, because German railroad records indicate that, in December alone, they evacuated nearly 70,000 wounded from the Ardennes area.[15] When killed in action, captured, and missing are added, the figure must be staggering.

The Allied concentration of forces in the Ardennes region at the conclusion of the battle helped shape the nature of the Allies' final assault on Germany. American and British Armies would continue to advance on multiple axes into the heart of the Reich—and Montgomery's hopes of leading a "single thrust" to Berlin were ended for good.[16]

Hitler's Ardennes offensive consumed Germany's last remaining reserves of mobile forces in the west, leaving the devastated Reich without the means to resist the Allies' final attacks. Once the Rhine barrier was pierced, Allied armies roamed freely through Germany against only crumbling resistance. Begun as Hitler's last attempt to salvage part of his collapsing empire, the Battle of the Bulge sped up

Germany's final collapse and shortened the war.[17]

To these immediate effects on the outcome of the war must be added the long-term effects the Ardennes fighting has had over the psyche of the American Army. This battle produced some of the greatest and longest enduring legends in US Army history. Despite the appearance of myth-dispelling works by noted historians, including Russell Weigley, Charles B. MacDonald, Forrest Pogue, Hugh Cole, Stephen Ambrose, and John and David Eisenhower,[18] the legends persist. Many people, including senior Army leaders, still equate the entire battle with the siege of Bastogne, and believe Patton won the battle single handedly. More than one generation of Army leaders has grown up on "lessons learned" from a battle never fully understood by those preaching the lessons. Perhaps it's time to examine closely the battle leadership demonstrated by US senior commanders during the Ardennes offensive.

SETTING THE STAGE: THE US ARMY IN EUROPE

By 1944 the US Army had evolved into a superbly equipped, highly mobile force of 89 divisions, formed from 1,292 battalions of infantry, armor, artillery, and other combat arms. Ground combat soldiers aggregated 2,300,000 out of the Army's total strength of 7,004,000.[19] Although both the Germans and Russians mobilized more manpower, the American blend of industrial might and nearly complete motorization proved sufficient for its worldwide task. The US Army spearheaded the Allied drive to defeat the war-weary German forces in northwest Europe while simultaneously helping naval and marine forces tighten the noose around the Japanese empire in the Pacific. Indeed, early projections of American troop requirements were continually revised downward.[20]

Sixty-one divisions, organized into five armies totaling fifteen corps, were eventually needed in northwest Europe, their ranks filled with 1,700,000 ground combat troops by V-E Day.[21]

The brunt of the fighting across France and Germany in 1944-45 was borne by Bradley's 12th Army Group, which included General Courtney Hodges' "grimly intense" First

Army, Patton's "noisy and bumptious" Third Army, and Simpson's "breezy" Ninth Army.[22] Flanked by Montgomery's 21 Army Group to the north and General Jake Devers' 6th Army Group to the south, Bradley's soldiers drove from the beaches of Normandy in northwest France to the banks of the Elbe River in central Germany in 11 months of hard fighting.

In early June 1944, the Allied armies attacked across the English Channel to establish a beachhead on Europe. By early August, they had broken out of the Normandy lodgment and begun an unprecedented sweep across France that took them to the border of Germany by October. Surviving a violent, unexpected German counteroffensive in the Ardennes in December, the Allies breached the Rhine in several places in March 1945. In April and early May, the Western armies raced across Germany and met the advancing Russians at the Elbe River. Eisenhower's "Crusade in Europe" ended at midnight on 8 May 1945. America's cost for this European crusade was 104,812 dead and 377,748 wounded.[23]

Although far from totally perfect in organization, equipment, and doctrine, the American Army's accomplishments nevertheless bear tribute to the remarkable resilience, industry, ingenuity, and leadership of this unique Nation. Starting virtually from scratch in 1940, the Army was created—really improvised—during an incredibly short period to produce a war-winning organization.[24]

There were several reasons why this "improvisational" army proved to be ultimately successful on the battlefield against a foe that was usually more experienced, frequently more skillfully handled, and sometimes better equipped. One overwhelming advantage was in the American Army's exceptional mobility. The decision to motorize the Army almost totally led to combat situations where US units moving quickly over poor roads demonstrated a degree of mobility through motor transport that European armies could only dream about.[25]

Another advantage was its streamlined organization (we might call it "modularizing" today), which simplified command and control, eased the problem of repair and maintenance, and facilitated worldwide deployment. The use of a common organization throughout the Army, with the number of "specialized units" kept to a minimum, made training and equipping easier and encouraged the development and implementation of common doctrine.[26]

To all of this must be added ingenuity—inventiveness, mechanical ability, and initiative—with which to capitalize on the overwhelming American industrial capacity spewing forth a seemingly inexhaustible flood of arms, ammunition, and materiel.[27]

But, improvisation or not, the American Army of 1944-45, armed and equipped by the most robust industrial base in the world, and led by competent senior leaders·who learned their trade on the battlefields of Europe, proved to be an outstanding general-purpose combat force.

ORGANIZATION

From the robust but ponderous "square" division of World War I, General Lesley McNair, Chief of Staff of General Headquarters until 1942 and thereafter Command of Army Ground Forces, fashioned a more mobile, leaner, "triangular" division as the building block for the US Army of World War II. Based upon echelons of three (that is, units such as battalions and regiments), this organization was influenced by the concepts of pooling, motorization, and standardization.[28]

McNair had a passion for leanness and flexibility, which led to his adoption of a basic unit configuration that would include only those elements which would always be needed by that unit. Other resources would be maintained in a centralized "pool" to be attached to the division whenever necessary. McNair thought that "what a unit needed only occasionally should be held in a reserve pool under higher headquarters."[29] Specialized units, such a reconnaissance, antiaircraft, and tank elements, were kept in corps- and army-level pools, to be "loaned" to combat divisions when necessary. In practice, however, this concept had mixed results. While it was extremely successful for maximizing the employment of the generous field artillery assets available to divisions and corps, it was less successful with pools of other arms. For example, it was discovered that infantry divisions needed permanent assignment of tank units to ensure any consistent success in combat.[30]

McNair's more successful innovation was the motorization of the US Army. His decision to supply most formations generously with motor transport and eliminate all horse-drawn transport was one of the most important of the war when its impact on the battlefield is measured.[31] The mobility of the American Army, demonstrated time and again from North Africa to central Europe, continually amazed opposing commanders and often made up for inappropriate tactics or sloppy leadership.

In addition to added speed, flexibility, and mobility in combat, motorization had the benefit of requiring fewer critical shipping assets to support it across an ocean. Fodder for draught animals was a major shipping headache to Allied logisticians during World War I and accounted for an incredibly huge amount of cargo space. Supplies for motor transport required much less maritime support.[32]

Although the US combat division was not "officially" a "motorized" unit, McNair had done away with all horse-drawn transport. All artillery and heavy equipment was towed by truck or tractor. When this comparative abundance of motor transport is considered, the division was nearly totally motorized.[33] The addition of six quartermaster truck companies could complete the motorization of an infantry division, but most units found such attachments unnecessary. American divisions posted advances of over 30 miles a day by piling "its infantry on its howitzers, tanks and tank destroyers."[34] The mobility gained by this concept was the US Army's most dominant characteristic in the campaigns in northwest Europe in 1944-45.

A third concept, standardization, developed from McNair's conviction that a standardized, general purpose force was a more efficient utilization of America's resources. Such an organization, modified only as deemed necessary by the local theater commander, would prove a more effective and flexible organization than an army containing any number of highly specialized, and possibly wasteful, units.[35]

This was a definite advantage in the planning cell, on the

training ground, and, most of all, on the battlefield. Compare this American standardization with the situation in the German Army of the same time where "the German Army...had a variety of divisions not conforming to standard tables of organization."[36] The potential chaos produced by such diversity of organization could have a disastrous impact on supply, maintenance, and training, as well as on the German commander's tactical control during a battle.

Standardization of US units also facilitated the Army's ability to maximize the continuous flow of war supplies to the fighting front and allow the resulting combat power to be more effectively brought to bear on the enemy. The concept allowed logisticians to customize supplies in "units of fire"—the basic load of ammunition for a "type" battalion for 1 day's combat.[37] By facilitating this flow, the streamlining of US formations permitted the more efficient transformation of combat potential into combat power.

Of the 89 divisions that eventually emerged from these concepts, 66 were infantry divisions. The National Guard provided 18 of these infantry divisions with 10 Guard divisions serving in northwest Europe by V-E Day.[38] The World War II US Army infantry division comprised a base force of three infantry regiments, a division artillery, an engineer battalion, and the division trains (organic supply units).[39] Forty-two of these infantry divisions formed the bulk of the American Army in northwest Europe in 1944-45.[40]

Despite the official continuance of the "pooling" concept, each infantry division commander in Europe by 1945 controlled considerably more than their authorized basic strength of 15,000 troops. Division commanders often had more units in a "permanently attached" status within their divisions than they had organic formations.[41]

Supplementing the sturdy infantry divisions in Europe were the speed and power of 15 armored divisions.[42] The US armored divisions were basically of two types: an earlier, "heavy" armored division of two tank regiments and one infantry regiment, and a later "combat command" armored division with equal numbers of tank, infantry, and field artillery battalions. Initial organization of US armored units

(1940-42) produced the "heavy" three-regiment model. Troop strength numbered over 14,000, with about 5,000 men in tank units, 2,300 in armored infantry units, and 2,100 in field artillery units.[43] Although this organization seems strong in tank forces, many of the unit's 390 tanks were light, reconnaissance tanks—worthless in armored combat against the powerful German panzers.[44] After this type of division's many deficiencies were made painfully apparent in combat against Axis armored formations in North Africa in 1942-43, US armored divisions were reorganized.[45] By 1944, the majority of American armored formations had been redesigned into the "combat command" model; not by coincidence, this streamlining allowed McNair to create more units with the manpower savings. Only two units, the 2nd and 3rd US Armored Divisions, retained the older "heavy" configuration.[46] American armored divisions were able to field 200 percent more armored fighting vehicles than their German panzer division counterparts while using only 85 percent of the authorized manpower strength.[47]

From 1944-45, the US Army fought the war in Europe with these basic organizations (plus a few specialized units, such as the airborne divisions). That it proved adequate to the task is a recognition of the vision of men like McNair and the adaptability of the Army's combat leaders.

EQUIPMENT

The equipment used by American infantrymen, tankers, and artillerymen reflected both the strengths and weaknesses of an organization whose guiding principles were mobility, flexibility, and standardization.[48] Blessed with an excellent infantry rifle and superior artillery, the US Army compensated for an inferior tank by capitalizing on its inherent mobility and greater numbers.

The American infantryman was issued the finest shoulder weapon of World War II, the .30-caliber, semi-automatic M1 Garand that, compared to the German rifleman's bolt-operated Mauser 98K, was superior in all respects. In other infantry weapons, however, the American soldier was not as fortunate. In fact, much of the M1's advantage in firepower was overcome by the liberal German issue of machine pistols to its soldiers.[49] US machine guns also were embarrassingly outclassed by the German light and heavy machine guns. The German MG 34 and MG 42 were well-designed weapons that could fire 850 and 1,200 rounds per minute.[50] The best the ponderous US M1919 Browning could manage was 500 rounds per minute.[51]

In infantry support weapons, the Germans possessed an advantage in their 120-mm mortar, and the superb German antitank cannons clearly outmatched their US equivalents.[52] The Germans also held the advantage in rocket-launched antitank weapons. The infantryman's problem, however, was minor compared to that confronting the American tanker.

By the time of the Normandy invasion in June 1944, the US main battle tank, the 33-ton M4 Sherman with its short-barrelled 75-mm gun, was clearly inferior to the German PzKw V Panther tank and the monstrous PzKw VI Tiger. However, it equalled or surpassed the PzKw IV, still the most numerous German tank. Although the Sherman possessed a few advantages over the better German tanks, US tankers had to rely ultimately on greater numbers in tank encounters.[53]

The situation for US tankers was frequently worsened by the German "stiffening of the panzers by detachments of fifty-six ton and eventually larger" Tiger tanks—huge monsters mounting the universally feared 88-mm gun.[54] American tank destroyers could defeat most German tank armor with well-placed shots. However, because tank destroyers lacked their own armor protection, they were generally failures in their intended role of seeking out enemy tanks, striking them with their high-velocity guns, and destroying them.[55]

In late 1944, American tank designers finally produced an armored vehicle capable of slugging it out on equal terms with the best German tanks (M26 "Pershing"), but it was designed too late in the war to influence armored combat significantly.

The area where the Americans could clearly and consistently outdo the Germans was in field artillery. Available in abundant supply and usually well stocked with ammunition, American artillery weapons were linked by a superior fire control system that facilitated the massing of fires at the critical point.[56] Although the tank had now joined the infantry-artillery team to form a combined arms triad, artillery remained "the outstanding element in the American arsenal."[57] Much as it had in World War I, massed, coordinated field artillery support continued to provide the weight of combat power required to smash an opening in the enemy's defenses, then pin enemy forces down while tanks and infantry exploited the breakthrough.

Excellent communications equipment tied together the entire system of guns, fire direction center, and observers that could produce an enormous volume of fire in an incredibly short period of time. Even a single forward observer could "request and receive the fires of all batteries within range of a target in a single concentrated barrage."[58] The effect of massing the fires of the entire artillery battalion, or even of several battalions, upon a single target was awesome to behold and devastating to endure. The Germans grew to fear and respect American artillery and gave this branch much credit for Allied gains. "On all fronts artillery caused more than half the casualties of World War II battles; but the artillery was the American Army's special strong suit."[59]

In addition to an excellent rifle and superior artillery, the United States was nearly unchallenged in tactical air support. Despite an early lead in both quality of aircraft and tactics and techniques for close support of ground troops, the Luftwaffe had been overtaken by the US Army Air Forces in each of these areas by fall 1944, although air-ground teamwork sometimes misfired.

Along with these advantages, as well as other American technological developments that progressed throughout the war, was the overwhelming quantity of US equipment that flooded northern Europe during the last year of the war.[60] American industrial production, untouched and unthreatened by enemy attack, continued to pour forth a stream of rugged, serviceable equipment against which the Germans could ultimately achieve only brief, localized successes.

DOCTRINE

American Army doctrine for conducting the campaigns in northern Europe in 1944-45 was not unlike that used in the last days of the First World War. Indeed, "infantry assault doctrine of World War II was based on the covering fire tactics of the final phase of World War I."[61] Russell Weigley explained:

> ...twelve-man rifle squad had a two man scout section [Able], a four man fire section [Baker], which included the squad's [Browning] automatic rifle, and a five man maneuver-and-assault section [Charlie]. Customarily, the squad leader would advance with Able to locate the enemy. He would then signal his assistant leader in Baker to fire, according to whatever plan the situation suggested. Thereupon, he would join Charlie for the maneuver to exploit the cover laid down by Baker's fire.[62]

In actual combat, it was not uncommon for the squad leader to be pinned down with the forward elements, causing the resulting uncoordinated assault to bog down and fall apart.[63] One remedy was the habitual assignment of tanks to any sizable infantry formation. This allowed the tanks to engage the enemy strongpoints and centers of resistance, while the infantry protected the tanks by destroying antitank weapons and enemy infantry.[64] The 102nd Infantry Division reported that, in the Rhineland and later during the drive into central Germany, "the usual method of attack across the open ground was for the infantry and tanks to work closely together." This tactic called for "small groups of infantrymen [to be] assigned to each tank with instructions never to desert it and to coordinate their actions with that of the tank." The 102nd's unit history recorded, "This system worked to perfection."[65]

Armored units, as well as infantry formations, discovered that tanks unsupported by infantry were as vulnerable as infantrymen trying to force strongpoints without armored assistance. The 4th Armored Division relied heavily upon coordinated tank-infantry attacks during its sweep across France in summer 1944 and found this tactic essential in forcing any gains at all in the difficult Lorraine campaign.[66] In the mud and misery of Lorraine during fall 1944, the 4th's slow progress was achieved only by sending small teams of tanks supported by infantry forward "to deal with a strongpoint of enemy resistance which was holding up the advance of the main body or to clean out a village or to hold high ground to safeguard [an] advance."[67] Restricted by the weather, German mines, and a stubborn enemy to advancing on a "one tank front," the footsoldiers and tankers were nearly impotent without each other's support.

Another method of advance used by all types of units was known as the "marching fire offensive," in many ways similar to the massive troop assaults of the First World War.[68] But "marching fire" was perceived by the infantrymen and tankers who were expected to employ it as leading to more casualties among the advancing American troops than the standard "fire and maneuver" assault—thereby making them reluctant to employ it.[69]

Moving beyond the small unit level up to the division, the doctrine was simple but effective. "Regimental combat teams" (in the infantry divisions) or "combat commands" (in the armored divisions) were established as the basic maneuver element. The regimental combat team/combat command "afforded a method of decentralizing control during fast moving situations."[70] The base for the regimental combat team was an infantry regiment of three infantry battalions. The combat team took its numerical designation from the regiment's number.[71] To this base was added an artillery battalion; a combat engineer platoon; a tank company; and other supporting units, such as tank destroyers, signal, medical, and ordnance. In theory, these regimental combat teams would be dispatched to accomplish some appropriate task in semi-autonomy. In practice, the division commander usually exercised tighter control over his teams in order to apply better the full power of the division against the enemy. Thus the division, not the regimental combat team, became the standard tactical element and focus of combat.[72]

The combat command of the armored division was similar in theory, but was formed on a triumvirate of a tank battalion, an infantry battalion, and a field artillery battalion (as well as supporting units). All these formations emphasized the preferred doctrine of using firepower, normally artillery, instead of manpower. The generous US allocation of ammunition was unknown to the German Army's artillery by this stage of the war. Mostly horse drawn and always short on ammunition, the German soldier's artillery support was deficient in every category.[73]

In favorable weather, close air support added to the destruction the American Army could bring down on the German defenses. Fighter-bombers (or Jagdbombers, known to Germans as the dreaded "Jabos") had supplemented ground-based firepower as "aerial artillery" since the beginning of the war and by 1944 were important components of American fighting doctrine.[74] Roaming the skies nearly unopposed after the German disasters in the summer of 1944, they were normally assigned to circle behind the front lines waiting for the call from forward ground units to deliver their lethal close support. Dependent upon weather and reliable communications, coordination between the air and ground units improved steadily as the war progressed.[75] Additionally, the Army air forces were employed to interdict any enemy forces or supplies moving toward Allied forces, to delay the habitual German counterattack, to strike forces already in contact, and generally to disrupt the enemy through aggressive attacks on roads, rail, towns, and river traffic.[76]

This seemingly lavish use of firepower proved to be the cornerstone of US doctrine in northern Europe during the campaigns of 1944-45. An example of such free use of ammunition can be seen in one infantry division's ammunition expenditures during a time of relative supply austerity. In fewer than 10 days of attack in the Rhineland, the division expended 24,000 rounds of 105-mm (artillery) ammunition, 8,184 rounds of 60-mm mortar ammunition, and 1,712,550 rounds of small arms ammunition—more than 1,007 tons.[77] This high volume of fire from a seemingly inexhaustible supply of weapons was able to make the American Army's unspectacular but sound doctrine unbeatable by the German Army of 1944-45.

LEADERSHIP

The American officers who led the US Army in Europe during the last 2 years of the war constituted a core of about 15,000 prewar regular officers to which had been added nearly 750,000 wartime officers.[78] In a typical infantry regiment, one found the colonel, his executive officer, and one of the three battalion commanders were prewar Regular Army. The other two battalion commanders were a National Guardsman and a reserve officer. "Probably two-thirds of the company commanders were OCS graduates; the other one-third consisted of Guardsmen with a few reservists."[79] Thus, the burden of small unit leadership at the tactical level was borne, for the most part, by officers who had been commissioned after the beginning of the war—men who were not products of the prewar Army staff and school system.

But above regimental level, at the division and higher headquarters echelon that "demanded leadership and managerial qualities of an exceptional kind,"[80] the majority of commanding officers were Regular Army soldiers. That these officers, who were "exceptional in their skills, as well as character and decisiveness,"[81] performed well is a tribute to the Army staff and school system and to the judgment of the men who selected them. Weigley observed:

> Even those officers of high rank who enjoyed a fairly large scope for the exercise of their individual abilities reflected the qualities of the pre-war staff and school system. For most of them had long since been selected by their chiefs and by the instructors in the schools as men who would exercise the highest responsibilities if war should come.[82]

By the time of the Ardennes offensive in December 1944, senior American leaders in Europe had learned important lessons about command in combat and "gained invaluable experience in battlefield management."[83] During the early campaigns in North Africa, Sicily, and Italy, US senior leaders were given a crash course in modern warfare by an enemy who had honed his skills on numerous battlefields for 4 or more years before engaging the inexperienced Americans. Complicating matters was the additional strain of fighting with the Allies.

The Allied Supreme Command, and Eisenhower in particular, learned hard lessons on the value of aggressiveness and team play in the very first test of coalition warfare in Tunisia (November 1942 to May 1943). The abysmally poor performance of the US II Corps and of its commander, General Lloyd Fredendall, demonstrated to Eisenhower that, although prewar "friendship counted for much,"[84] it must not interfere with the relief of any officer who proved indecisive or an early failure. Ike and his senior commanders learned to be quick in relieving subordinates, and they exercised this option with increasing frequency in subsequent campaigns.[85]

Also important to Eisenhower was the concept of "team play." Ike demanded a spirit of cooperation in all his subordinate commanders and learned that his success as coalition warfare commander depended on achieving and maintaining consensus among the Allies. Throughout his exercise of Supreme Command, Ike was an "ally" first and an "American" second. Despite resistance from Patton, Bradley, and, eventually, General George C. Marshall, Eisenhower remained faithful to the principle of Allied unity to the end of the war—thereby becoming the most successful practitioner of coalition warfare in history.[86] Demanding and receiving cooperation among his Allied subordinates was not always easy, but the fact that his subordinates complied is a recognition of Eisenhower's influence as much as it is a statement of the officers' professionalism.

The campaigns in northern Europe in 1944-45 were clearly marked by Eisenhower's influence and leadership, and he shaped their conduct and outcome. In addition to setting an example for his subordinates to follow, Ike personally selected division, corps, and Army commanders from names supplied by Marshall and McNair (although he often sought the advice of Bradley or SHAEF Chief of Staff, Lieutenant General Walter Bedell Smith).[87]

Marshall facilitated this process by agreeing that Eisenhower "need take no commander unless he had full confidence in him."[88] Subordinate commanders had little latitude in selecting their respective subordinates. For example, Simpson, Ninth Army commander, was allowed to select three officers for his corps commanders from a list of only four names previously approved by Eisenhower.[89]

Eisenhower visited his field commanders frequently but "did not interfere with their conduct of operations...usually content[ing] himself with giving [them] a pat on the back and telling them to keep up the good work."[90] General Raymond S. McLain, XIX Corps commander, has written his opinion of how far down the ranks Eisenhower's influence was projected when he wrote, "As a corps commander, I frequently felt his personal influence, and I know, too, that my division commanders and even some of my regimental and battalion commanders, on occasion, also felt his personal presence and influence."[91] The extent of this influence can also be gauged by the celerity with which corps and army commanders relieved their division commanders for timidity, early failure, or "seriously lacking aggressiveness in [their] leadership"—all traits stressed by the Supreme Commander.[92]

The leadership climate established and set by the Supreme Commander in Europe during the final 2 years of the war was characterized by an attitude of aggressiveness at the senior American levels and Allied cooperation, the latter constantly sought by Eisenhower. That this climate produced satisfactory results is attributable, in no small part, to "the 12,000-13,000 officers of the old Army (who) had succeeded in preparing themselves mentally for the transition [to war] to a greater extent than the observer of mounted parades and maneuvers...might have suspected."[93] The American Army's staff and school system had proved its worth in the ultimate test.[94] Ike and his senior commanders learned their lessons well.

THE ENEMY

The army the Allies faced in the last 2 years of the war was not the powerful, confident force that had beaten France in 6 weeks and had stormed to the gates of Moscow during a furious summer of lightning warfare. Five years of constant war had drained Germany's manpower reserves to a dangerous level and had severely strained combat leadership and other vital resources—but the German Army was far from beaten. Thanks to excellent officers, a core of hardened, battlewise veterans and the focusing of Germany's celebrated efficiency into maximizing the potential of the remaining resources of personnel and equipment, the Reich fought on.[95]

Qualitatively, the German Army may still have been the best in the world, even at that late stage of the war. The liberal issue of automatic weapons allowed the German division to maintain "superior firepower [small arms] over its American rival despite having about 1,200 fewer combat infantrymen." Technologically superior equipment (especially tanks, machine guns, and antitank weapons) helped the German soldier compensate for his country's inability to match the overwhelming Allied production rates. And German officers and noncommissioned officers provided leadership that was tough, experienced, and characterized by "superior professional skill."[96]

These advantages, however, could not compensate for all the disadvantages that had accumulated by this stage in the war, nor could they avoid ultimate defeat. The odds were too great to do anything but postpone the inevitable results of attrition: above all other problems, the German Army faced an ever-shrinking manpower pool.

Unceasing warfare on several fronts had seriously depleted the German reserves of personnel, but in just the period June through August 1944, the German armed forces lost almost a million men out of a total ground force of 3 million. Yet, by reducing the authorized levels of existing divisions and stripping training and other specialized units, 25 new Volksgrenadier divisions appeared on the Western Front alone beginning in September. Nearly 1.5 million new men were called up to fill the depleted Wehrmacht ranks during the same periord.[97] Prodigious as this effort seems, Germany accomplished this rather remarkable feat only by calling up those men previously exempt from service.

Service schools were stripped of demonstration units in 1944, and the school cadres themselves followed them to the front in 1945. All men between the ages of 16 and 60 were eligible to serve in the Volkssturm, a militia-type organization usually poorly trained and poorly equipped. These units were thrown in late in the war and seldom had heavy weapons.[98] A final source of manpower was wounded or disabled veterans, the so-called "stomach soldiers" who were being called back to active service. By these expedient measures Germany was able to fill its depleted ranks, but deficiencies in training and combat preparation took a toll.[99]

Keeping these units supplied with equipment during the final months of the war was also a serious problem. Although German production figures imply that production of war materials was not as devastated by Allied air strikes as was assumed by Allied planners, production could by no measure meet the demands of all fronts.[100] In mid-1944, at the height of availability, total stocks of German tanks were approximately 5,000. On the eve of the Ardennes offensive, the Germans had about half that number available in the west, most of which were committed to the attack. About 45 percent of these were the excellent PzKw V "Panther" and the PzKw VI "Tiger" tanks. The remainder consisted of the inferior PzKw IV.[101] These numbers declined dramatically and consistently and German forces were usually overwhelmingly outnumbered by Allied armored fighting vehicles.

Tank strength within German panzer divisions also declined steadily over the course of the war, especially in the last 2 years. To compensate, the Germans either decreased the number of tanks in a company or reduced the number of companies in a battalion (or battalions in a regiment).[102]

A continuing problem for the German Army was its "astonishing dependence on horse transport."[103] The inventors of the blitzkrieg continued to rely heavily on the horse as the means for moving supplies and equipment, and German resistance and morale suffered when they compared their "hobbled" army to the superior mobility of the American divisions racing across Europe.[104] Weigley notes, "As the [US] infantrymen promptly demonstrated in combat...the mounting of infantry everywhere conceivable on the division's trucks and artillery vehicles and the attached tanks [allowed the division to] readily move on wheels and tracked vehicles. No other army in the world was so mobile."[105] The German Army of 1944-45 could not match this speed and efficiency.

As the Allies pressed ever closer to Germany and eventually entered the Reich, the German Army relied increasingly on fortifications to stem the advance. After the drive across France and the bloody battles in Lorraine, the Germans forced the Allies to breach the so-called Siegfried Line—the vaunted Westwall.

These defenses were never completed as originally planned because of France's rapid collapse in the spring of 1940, so the final months of 1944 brought on a feverish spurt of activity to strengthen them before the Allies attacked. This belt of intertwined fortifications extended nearly 500 miles from Switzerland to Holland and consisted of "a system of large and small pillboxes and bunkers with three to seven foot walls...protected by interlocking fields of fire and reinforced by minefields, fences and lines of obstacles."[106] Supplementing these defenses were antitank ditches, machine gun nests, and the ubiquitous concrete "dragon's teeth"—the line's most characteristic feature. German engineers took advantage of the rugged terrain in many sectors of the line, using streams and ravines as antitank ditches and flooding low-lying areas to prevent passage.[107] Bunkers of reinforced concrete formed the principal strongpoints of the Siegfried Line.

The Allied assault to break through the Siegfried Line, although interrupted by the German Ardennes offensive, cost an estimated 140,000 Allied casualties and consumed several months—an extremely high price for the small amount of territory gained.[108] That was exactly the purpose of the fortifications, and the German defenders used them skillfully to offset their numerical disadvantage in forces.

The Germans were also skillful at organizing strong defenses around towns and villages, as a way to capitalize upon the concealment and cover offered by the sturdy European buildings and urban areas. Isolated farms and small villages allowed the German defenders to establish strongpoints with excellent fields of fire and good observation across the open, cultivated countryside. Organizing "community diggings," they supplemented deliberate fortifications with thousands of trenches and antitank ditches. By establishing belts of such fortifications and trenches around towns, they made thousands of miniature forts, and each village or farm became a potential strongpoint.[109] As the Allies closed in and crossed the borders of Germany itself, such defenses multiplied, spurred on by the desperation of defending home and family.

Eventually, however, the German Army was forced out of even these fortifications by the Allied advance. Unable to muster sufficient mobile forces to properly defend the Rhine, the last great barrier to the Allied drive into central Germany, the Germans fought the last month of the war in hastily prepared positions as best they could. Finally, its last major field force in western Germany trapped in the Ruhr industrial area by the advancing American columns, the German Army began to surrender in ever-increasing numbers.[110] The German Army finally died as an effective fighting force along the banks of the Elbe River, fleeing the advancing Russians in a last, frenzied attempt to surrender to the Western Allies.

CAMPAIGNS IN NORTHWEST EUROPE, 1944-45

From the initial landings in Normandy on 6 June 1944, until the German incursion in the Ardennes was finally eliminated the following February, the US Army, chiefly the forces of Bradley's 12th Army Group, established a secure lodgment in Normandy, destroyed German resistance in France, and then survived the major counteroffensive in the Ardennes. In so doing, it accomplished the principal strategic successes of establishing the Normandy lodgment and racing across France to close on the German border.[111] Less than 3 months after winning the Battle of the Bulge, the Allies had linked up with the Russians in central Germany and conquered a devastated Reich.

Following the landings of the US V and VII Corps on D-Day, the Allies began pouring in men and supplies, building up the beachhead as fast as possible. The Allies put ashore 314,000 men, 41,000 vehicles, and 116,000 tons of supplies by 19 June. After several weeks of bitter fighting among the hedgerows of the bocages (woodlands), Allied forces were able to break out of the Cotentin Peninsula as a result of Bradley's COBRA carpet-bombing breakthrough scheme near St.-Lô on 25 July.[112] The next month brought a remarkable change from the static warfare near the beachhead and saw Allied forces (principally the US First and Third Armies) racing across France.

The Supreme Command's historian, Forrest Pogue, described the dash across France that summer:

> In four weeks the battle of stalemate in the bocage had changed to one of great mobility as the Allied forces searched out the enemy along the Loire and toward Brest, encircled and destroyed thousands of German troops in a great enveloping movement at Falaise, and dashed to the Seine to cut off the Germans and threaten Paris...the speed with which the drives were executed and with which the enemy opposition collapsed west of the Seine followed from the unexpected opportunities which Allied commanders had turned to their advantage.[113]

While the First and Third Armies drove eastward, the newly activated Ninth Army assumed responsibility for the VIII Corps' reduction and capture of the fortified port city of Brest on the Brittany Peninsula. Thousands of casualties resulted and great quantities of supplies were used, but ultimately no usable port facilities remained. The decision to capture this stoutly defended citadel, however, has been sharply criticized as detracting from the destruction of the main German forces farther east. Historian Martin Blumenson commented that "If [the Allied leaders] could have seen the bitter battle about to develop at Brest, their decision to take that port would have been a mistake."[114]

Stiffening German resistance and lengthening Allied supply lines caused the swift eastward advance of the Allied armies across France to slow considerably by the end of summer 1944. By mid-September the First Army had swept through Belgium and Luxembourg, and the Third Army had entered Lorraine, driving to the Metz and Nancy areas. By this time, Devers' 6th Army Group had invaded southern France and fallen in on Bradley's right flank. Lieutenant General Alexander Patch's Seventh Army had driven northward over 300 miles since landing on the beaches of southern France, helping to clear that country of German forces.[115]

Montgomery's 21 Army Group, consisting of British and Canadian forces, anchored the Allied left flank on the English Channel and Holland. Finally clearing the port of Antwerp after desperate German resistance in the Scheldt Estuary approaches, Montgomery's forces opened up badly needed port facilities to the supply-constrained Allies.[116] In September, Montgomery had tried unsuccessfully to establish a bridgehead across the lower Rhine at Arnhem. The resulting MARKET-GARDEN fiasco did more, perhaps, than any single event to cause Eisenhower to maintain the so-called "broad front" strategy of advancing on multiple axes. Certainly, if Montgomery had been successful in putting his British Second Army across the last major natural obstacle to a drive into Germany, and therefore "in a suitable position to be able to develop operations against the north face of the Ruhr,"[117] the Field Marshal's forces would surely have led the Allied main effort. Failing at Arnhem, however, the 21 Army Group prepared for the difficult fighting in the Rhineland followed by deliberate preparations for forcing the Rhine.[118]

From mid-September until the Germans launched their surprise offensive in the Ardennes on 16 December 1944, the Allied armies waged a bloody battle of attrition from Holland in the north, south to Switzerland. A determined enemy and miserable weather combined to cause a relatively modest advance to the Siegfried Line, this system of fortifications being breached only in the Aachen area. By fall 1944, General Simpson's Ninth Army had been inserted into the Allied line north of First Army and south of Field Marshal Montgomery's 21 Army Group. These battles of attrition in October, November, and into December:

> ...were based on the belief that Hitler's forces were still disintegrating and that some lucky push might find a soft spot in the opposing lines which would permit the Allies to advance to the Rhine before the dead of winter. Later, when it became evident that the Germans had reorganized their forces and had succeeded in manning the Westwall fortifications against the Allied offensive, General

Eisenhower refused to accept a static policy for the winter, feeling that even minor advances were better than completely defensive tactics.[119]

These "minor advances" included the disastrous Huertgen Forest campaign in which four of the attacking American divisions were nearly destroyed and 33,000 of the 120,000 US troops involved became casualties. Begun as an attempt by Major General J. Lawton Collins' VII Corps to "jump" the Siegfried Line on the run, it ended in bloody, frustrating, and fruitless assaults to capture the critical Roer River dams.[120] Two of the shattered divisions, the 4th and 28th Infantry Divisions, were moved to a quiet area of the front to recover—the Ardennes. Allied attention remained diverted elsewhere until, on 16 December 1944, the surprise German offensive riveted SHAEF's focus on the Ardennes.

NOTES

1.   Charles B. MacDonald, *A Time for Trumpets: The Untold Story of the Battle of the Bulge* (New York: William Morrow, 1984), 1, 618; Hugh M. Cole, *The United States Army in World War II. European Theater of Operations. The Ardennes: The Battle of the Bulge* (Washington, DC: Office of the Chief of Military History/ GPO, 1965), 650; David Eggenberger, *An Encyclopedia of Battles* (New York: Dover Publications, 1985). MacDonald writes that eventually 600,000 Americans were involved in the Ardennes fighting, "including 29 divisions, 6 mechanized cavalry groups, and the equivalent of 3 separate regiments." British forces involved totaled about 55,000. The attacking Germans probably used close to 500,000 troops (28 divisions and 3 brigades). American casualties were about 80,000 (the British lost 1,400), and German casualties were at least 100,000 (but probably much more). The number of troops involved by both sides places this Western Front battle on a nearly equal level with the enormous Russo-German encounters on the vast Eastern Front, including Stalingrad (November 1942-February 1943), in which the Germans lost about 300,000 men, and the giant tank battle at Kursk (July 1943), which cost the Germans 100,000 casualties. Russian casualty figures, as with everything in Stalin's paranoic empire, were never revealed but were undoubtedly enormous. Recently declassified records for the now-defunct Soviet Union indicate one million Russians died at Stalingrad, 13,500 of whom were shot by the

Soviets for "cowardice." American losses in the Ardennes offensive represented nearly 10 percent of total US losses for all of World War II (294,000 killed and 671,000 wounded in all theaters). US participation of 600,000 in the Ardennes offensive dwarfs the American involvement in most other famous American battles, including: Yorktown, 1781 (8,800 Americans allied with 7,800 French); New Orleans, 1815 (5,000); Chapultepec, 1847 (7,200); Gettysburg, 1863 (150,000 total Union and Confederate); and Desert Storm, 1991 (about 500,000).

2. MacDonald, A Time for Trumpets, 1.

3. B.H. Liddell Hart, The Other Side of the Hill (London: Cassell, 1951), 108-110, 468-469; Russell F. Weigley, Eisenhower's Lieutenants: The Campaigns of France and Germany, 1944-1945 (Bloomington: Indiana University Press, 1981), 433, 442-444, 459. Weigley commented on the Allied misconception about Hitler's involvement in operations, writing "It is hard to understand why as late as December 1944 any [Allied]) G-2 should have imagined [Field Marshal] Rundstedt rather than Hitler to be in effective command."

4. Liddell Hart, Other Side, 108-110. He writes, "It was designed to profit by the way the Allies had committed their strength...and were unlikely to expect a German counteroffensive at this time, particularly in the Ardennes."

5. Cole, Ardennes, 21-23; Liddell Hart, Other Side, 446, 448-449; Weigley, Eisenhower's Lieutenants, 458; MacDonald, Time for Trumpets, 18-30. Liddell Hart reports that Field Marshal von Manteuffel succinctly summed up Hitler's shortcomings as a "grand tactician" by saying in a postwar interview, "He [Hitler] had a real flair for strategy and tactics, especially for surprise moves, but he lacked a sufficient foundation of technical knowledge to apply it properly. Moreover, he had a tendency to intoxicate himself with figures and quantities."

6. Liddell Hart, Other Side, 108; Cole, Ardennes, 26. Liddell Hart wrote that "Dietrich was an S.S. leader, formerly a rolling stone in various business jobs, who had caught Hitler's fancy by his aggressive spirit. Rundstedt regarded him as responsible for fumbling the crucial part of the offensive."

7. Liddell Hart, Other Side, 446.

8. Cole, Ardennes, 26; MacDonald, Time for Trumpets, 24. Cole explains the German Seventh Army's role in the offensive, "The...plan called for a single powerful thrust on a front about forty miles wide, the breakthrough to be achieved between the Huertgen Forest and Leutzkampen with the Fifth and Sixth Panzer Armees

leading the attack. On the left wing the Seventh Army would not make an immediate advance...but would follow in the track of the Sixth Panzer Armee as a second wave."

9. Liddell Hart, *Other Side*, 7-8, 18, 108, 471. Liddell Hart conducted extensive interviews with the surviving German generals after the war and provides interesting insight into their character as well as their relationships to Hitler. He considered them to be "the best-finished product of their profession—anywhere," but limited by the fact that "they were essentially technicians, interested in their professional job, and with little idea of things outside it." He reports that the Ardennes offensive "was purely Hitler's in respect of aim, timing, and place—though improved by the technical suggestions of Manteuffel." Despite the generals' opposition to Hitler's plan, their sense of duty and loyalty caused them to attempt to carry it out to the fullest. In the end, Liddell Hart thought technical competence and loyalty were not enough, concluding, "But along with [loyalty] often ran a sense of personal interest which undercut their loyalty to their fellows, and their country's best interests, in face of a common threat. The play of individual ambitions and the cleavage of personal interests constituted a fatal weakness in their prolonged struggle to maintain their professional claim in the military field, and to preserve it from outside interference. This struggle went on throughout the twelve years from Hitler's rise to Germany's fall."

10. Frank J. Price, *Troy H. Middleton: A Biography* (Baton Rouge: LSU Press, 1974) 215; Stephen E. Ambrose, *Eisenhower: Volume I, Soldier, General of the Army, President-Elect, 1890-1952* (New York: Simon and Schuster, 1983), 365; Robert E. Merriam, *Dark December* (Chicago: Ziff-Davis, 1947), 75; John Toland, *Battle: The Story of the Bulge* (New York: Random House, 1959), 12.

11. R. Ernest Dupuy, *St. Vith: Lion in the Way—The 106th Infantry Division in World War II* (Washington, DC: Infantry Journal Press, 1949), 72; MacDonald, *Time for Trumpets*, 83-84. MacDonald observed, "The Ardennes was at once the nursery and the old folks' home of the American command. New divisions came there for a battlefield shakedown, old ones to rest after heavy fighting and absorb replacements for their losses." The 4th and 28th Infantry Divisions had each been devastated in the Huertgen Forest fighting the previous month, and the 106th Infantry Division had just arrived at the front a few days earlier. None of the three was at the peak of combat efficiency.

12. MacDonald, *Time for Trumpets*, 84; Cole, *Ardennes*, 650

One of the two tactical combat commands of the new 9th Armored Division was on loan to the V Corps to support its upcoming offensive to capture the Roer River dams. The other was filling a gap in Middleton's front between the 28th and 4th Infantry Divisions. Neither, therefore, was available to Middleton to employ as a powerful, mobile, armored reserve force to counterattack against the German offensive. When V Corps units in the path of the German attack are counted, there were about 83,000 US troops total to defend against the surprise assault.

13. Cole, *Ardennes*, 650; Merriam, *Dark December*, 75; Toland, *Battle*, 12; MacDonald, *Time for Trumpets*, 84. Although Middleton had only 242 medium tanks available, he could supplement these with 182 tank destroyers. More significant, however, were the nearly 400 artillery pieces capable of firing at the German attackers when the battle began.

14. Weigley, *Eisenhower's Lieutenants*, 568, 574; Cole, *Ardennes*, 56, 330-331.

15. Forrest C. Pogue, *The United States Army in World War II. European Theater of Operations: The Supreme Command* (Washington, DC: Office of the Chief of Military History/ GPO, 1954), 396; Weigley, *Eisenhower's Lieutenants*, 568, 574; Cole, *Ardennes*, 56, 330-331.

16. Weigley, *Eisenhower's Lieutenants*, 564-566, 575-579. Eisenhower, according to Weigley, "interpreted the Ardennes as confirming the necessity for his broad-front strategy."

17. Liddell Hart, *The Other Side*, 110; Weigley, *Eisenhower's Lieutenants*, 571-574; MacDonald, *Time for Trumpets*, 618; Cole, *Ardennes*, 673-676. Liddell Hart concluded, "The offensive fell far short of its aims, and when it ended it had fatally impoverished Germany's reserves, leaving her no chance of long-continued defense."

18. John S.D. Eisenhower, *The Bitter Woods* (New York: G.P. Putnam's Sons, 1959); Weigley, *Eisenhower's Lieutenants*; MacDonald, *A Time for Trumpets* and *Company Commander*; Pogue, *The Supreme Command*; Cole, *Ardennes*; Ambrose, *Eisenhower;* David Eisenhower, *Eisenhower at War, 1943-45* (New York: Random House, 1986). These are among the best books written about the Ardennes offensive, the Battle of the Bulge. Anyone wishing to study this battle would do well to consult these first.

19. Kent Roberts Greenfield, Robert R. Palmer, and Bell I. Wiley, *The United States Army in World War II. The Army Ground Forces: The Organization of Ground Combat Troops*

(Washington, DC: Center for Military History/GPO, 1947), 161-226. The Army actually consisted of 90 divisions for a short time, reverting to 89 when the 2nd Cavalry Division was deactivated during the war. The total strength figure includes Army Air Force personnel.

20. Maurice Matloff, "The 90-Division Gamble," *Command Decisions*, ed. Kent Roberts Greenfield (Washington, DC: Office of the Chief of Military History/GPO, 1960), 365-381; Weigley, *Eisenhower's Lieutenants*, 13. Initial estimates of American war planners were that an army of over 200 divisions would be necessary to win the war. General Marshall's "bold, calculated risk" to maintain the ground combat strength at 90 divisions has been described as "wise, courageous, foresighted, and successful." Matloff wrote that, "The decision was a striking illustration of acceptance by Army war leaders of the fact that there were limits to their slice of the American manpower pie. The 90-division troop basis represented their attempt to provide a realistic meeting ground of three fundamentals of modern warfare—strategy, production, and manpower." Matloff credits the manpower burden borne by Russia and other Allies as permitting the United States to maintain a worldwide coalition on such a small troop basis, and concludes that the heavy investment of manpower in an "effective, heavy-fisted, long air arm" helped make the ground gamble successful.

21. Pogue, *Supreme Command*, 540-542.

22. Omar N. Bradley, *A Soldier's Story* (New York: Henry Holt and Company, 1951), 225-226.

23. Pogue, *Supreme Command*, 543. This European Theater casualty total accounted for approximately half of the American losses in World War II—294,000 dead and 671,000 wounded.

24. Greenfield et al., *The US Army*, 2-5.

25. Weigley, *Eisenhower's Lieutenants*, 1-31.

26. Greenfield et al., *The US Army*, 272-278.

27. Russell F. Weigley, *The History of the United States Army* (New York: MacMillan Publishing Company, 1967), 470; Matloff, "90-Division Gamble," 367. Matloff stresses the importance of the United States as the "Arsenal of Democracy" by writing, "The Allies had from the beginning accepted the proposition that the single greatest tangible asset the United States brought to the coalition in World War II was the productive capacity of its industry."

28. Weigley, *History of the US Army*, 461-471.

29. Greenfield et al., *The US Army*, 273.

30. Weigley, *Eisenhower's Lieutenants*, 21-28. The "pooling" concept fits the very nature of the employment of modern fire support, primarily field artillery. Never held in reserve, artillery is meant to be used continually, its fires shifted to targets, in priority, all across the battlefield. Although some artillery units are more or less in continual   support of one maneuver element, its fires remain subject to call when a priority target is engaged.

31. Weigley, *Eisenhower's Lieutenants*, 2, 18-28.

32. Weigley, *History of the US Army*, 470.

33. Ibid., 468-469.

34. Ibid., 470.

35. Ibid., 470. Weigley observed, "The standard triangular infantry division proved a suitable instrument for all theaters in which American ground forces fought."

36. Weigley, *Eisenhower's Lieutenants,* 30.

37. Greenfield et al., *The US Army*, 276-280.

38. John K. Mahon, *History of the Militia and the National Guard* (New York: Macmillan Publishing Company, 1983), 187-188.

39. Greenfield et al., *The US Army*, 274-275.

40. Pogue, *Supreme Command*, 541.

41. Weigley, *History of the US Army*, 464, 468. Weigley wrote, "McNair recognized that the standard division would have to be modified in various theaters to meet various situations, and the theater commanders were the more free to make de facto modifications in the constituents of a division because of the flexibility afforded by pooling the support elements. In practice, the infantry division came to operate usually with a tank battalion and other supporting elements in quasipermanent attachment." McNair said at the time that, "Although the division organically probably will aggregate something like 11,000, you may make it 20,000 if you so desire, simply by adding armored or infantry battalions." The 1st Infantry Division had, by 1 March 1945, 12 company and battalion-sized combat units attached to it on a more or less permanent basis, as opposed to 9 organic formations of battalion and regimental size.

42. Pogue, *Supreme Command*, 541.

43. Weigley, *History of the US Army*, 467-468.

44. Weigley, *Eisenhower's Lieutenants,* 17-19.

45. Martin Blumenson, *Kasserine Pass* (New York: Jove Books, 1983), 303-320; Weigley, *History of the US Army*, 467-468. Although leadership and organization were primary factors in the American disaster at Kasserine Pass (February 1943), the performance of US armored vehicles highlighted the superiority of

the Axis machines and contributed to the defeat.

46.   Weigley, *History of the US Army*, 467-468.

47.   John Ellis, Brute Force: *Allied Strategy and Tactics in the Second World War* (New York: Viking Books, 1990), xviii, 424-26; Weigley, *Eisenhower's Lieutenants*, 24-31.

48.   Ibid.

49.   Ian V. Hogg, *The Encyclopedia of Infantry Weapons of World War II* (New York: Thomas Y. Crowell Co., 1977),38; Weigley, *Eisenhower's Lieutenants*, 26-30.

50.   Ibid.

51.   Hogg, *Infantry Weapons*, 78.

52.   Ian Hogg, *Artillery 1920-1963* (New York: Arco Publishing, 1980), 181-187. An illustration of the great disparity between the American and German antitank weapons is the tremendous difference in armor penetration ability. The best the US weapons could manage was 70mm of armor plate (the 37-mm weapon could only go through 50mm), yet the German weapons could penetrate nearly 200mm (all at ranges from 500 to 1,000 meters).

53.   Weigley, *Eisenhower's Lieutenants*, 20-21.

54.   Hogg, *Artillery*, 19; Weigley, *Eisenhower's Lieutenants*, 20-21. The German 88-mm cannon was a superb weapon, and rightly feared by the Allies. Whether used as a towed antitank gun or mounted as the main gun of a PzKw VI Tiger tank, it was a devastating weapon. However, its fearsome reputation was such that, at times, it produced an irrational fear among Allied troops, who tended to characterize any incoming fire as "88." Troops often terrorized themselves with the fiction that every weapon trained on them was an "88," causing many to panic or proceed overcautiously. Psychologically, it could be intimidating to advancing troops.

55. Christopher R. Gabel, *Seek, Strike and Destroy: U.S. Army Tank Destroyer Doctrine in World War II* (Leavenworth Paper Number 12) (Fort Leavenworth, KS: US Army Command and General Staff College, 1985), 72.

56.   Weigley, *Eisenhower's Lieutenants*, 27-28.

57.   Weigley, *History of the US Army*, 473.

58.   Combat Studies Institute, *Conversations With General J. Lawton Collins* (Fort Leavenworth, KS: US Army Command and General Staff College, 1983), 4-5; Weigley, *Eisenhower's Lieutenants*, 28. General Collins, the outstanding commander of the VII Corps during the campaigns of France and Germany, relates that, "At one time, I massed twenty-two battalions on one target."

59. Weigley, *Eisenhower's Lieutenants*, 28.

60. Weigley, *History of the US Army*, 479.

61. Ibid., 471.

62. Weigley, *Eisenhower's Lieutenants*, 25-26.

63. Ibid.

64. Weigley, *History of the US Army*, 471.

65. Allen H. Mick, ed., *With the 102nd Infantry Division Through Germany* (Nashville: Battery Press, 1980), 147.

66. Hanson Baldwin, *Tiger Jack* (Fort Collins, CO: Old Army Press, 1979), 25-32, 156.

67. 4th Armored Division Combat Interviews. The Lorraine Campaign proved a sharp contrast to the heady days of the "race across France," because bad weather and improved German resistance caused much tougher going.

68. Weigley, *History of the US Army,* 471-472.

69. Weigley, *Eisenhower's Lieutenants,* 26. Weigley relates Bradley's frustration with trying to push the use of "marching fire" among the American troops. Bradley finally resignedly said that, "They seem to need something to shoot at."

70. Mick, *102nd Infantry Division*, 25.

71. Ibid.

72. Weigley, *History of the US Army*, 464-482.

73. Weigley, *Eisenhower's Lieutenants*, 28.

74. Wesley Frank Craven and James Lea Cate, *The Army Air Forces in World War II. Europe: Argument to V-E Day, January 1944 to May 1945* (Washington, DC: Office of Air Force History/GPO, 1983), 228-277.

75. Ibid. Allied air power was so overwhelming by the end of the war, that at least one former German anti-aircraft gunner admitted to the author that his crew often sabotaged their own gun so they could seek safety in a bunker rather than face the aerial onslaught.

76. Galland, *First and Last*, 199-280; Killen, *Luftwaffe*, 264-332.

77. Mick, *102nd Infantry Division*, 66.

78. Morris Janowitz, *The Professional Soldier* (New York: Free Press, 1960), 106; Mahon, *Militia and National Guard*, 186-187; Weigley, History of the US Army, 425-430. Janowitz illustrates the profound effect that World War II had on the American professional Army officer corps when he shows the percentage of US Military Academy graduates in the corps over the years: 1910-79 percent; 1920-86 percent; 1935-81 percent; 1950-48 percent. The world leadership assumed by the United States and the

resulting large peacetime postwar army have fundamentally changed the face of the Army officer corps. Mahon gives the breakout of World War II commissioning sources as follows: 100,000 from the National Guard; 180,000 from the Reserve Officer Training Corps; 100,000 received a direct commission; and 300,000, the largest share, from Officer Candidate Schools.

79. Mahon, *Militia and National Guard*, 186-187.

80. Weigley, *History of the US Army*, 477.

81. Martin Blumenson and James L. Stokesbury, *Masters of the Art of Command* (Boston: Houghton Mifflin, 1975), 4; Weigley, *History of the US Army*, 477. Blumenson and Stokesbury remarked on the timing involved in being in the right place in history, "Ideally, for World War II, a soldier would have graduated from West Point about 1912, had service in France in World War I as a company or battalion officer, taken the right courses and done the appropriate tours during the interwar years, and been a brigadier general or senior colonel in his mid-forties when World War II broke out. With that sequence he could hardly avoid a place in the history books; whether it was a good or a bad place would depend more on personal qualities, but the time sequence itself would be highly desirable."

82. Weigley, *History of the US Army*, 478.

83. Omar N. Bradley and Clay Blair, *A General's Life: An Autobiography of General of the Army Omar N. Bradley* (New York: Simon and Schuster, 1983), 200.

84. Stephen E. Ambrose, *The Supreme Commander: The War Years of General Dwight D. Eisenhower* (Garden City, NY: Doubleday and Company, 1969), 341.

85. Ibid., 175-176.

86. Blumenson and Stokesbury, *Masters of the Art of Command*, 244, 305, 307; Pogue, *Supreme Command*, 34, 42.

87. D.K.R. Crosswell, *The Chief of Staff: The Military Career of General Walter Bedell Smith* (New York: Greenwood Press, 1991), 298-299.

88. Thomas R. Stone, "He Had the Guts to Say No: A Military Biography of General William Hood Simpson," (Ph.D. diss., Rice University, 1974), 2-3.

89. Ibid.

90. Ambrose, *Eisenhower*, 385.

91. Raymond S. McLain, "One of the Greatest: A Study in Leadership," *Military Review* 49 (December 1969): 19.

92. Price, *Middleton*, 268.

93. Weigley, *Eisenhower's Lieutenants*, 2.

94. Weigley, *History of the US Army,* 477-478.

95. Liddell Hart, *Other Side,* 110.

96. Weigley, *Eisenhower's Lieutenants,* 28-30.

97. Ellis, *Brute Force,* 388-392, 426-428.

98. John Toland, *The Last 100 Days* (New York: Random House, 1965).

99. Ibid.

100. Liddell Hart, *Other Side,* 468-469. Manteuffel provides some interesting insight into the "production numbers" that figured so prominently in the postwar analysis of the effectiveness of the Allied bomber offensive. He related that, "When one was discussing a problem with [Hitler], he would repeatedly pick up the telephone, ask to be put through to some departmental chief, and inquire—'How many so and so have we got?' Then he would turn to the man who was arguing with him, quote the number, and say: 'There you are'—as if that settled the problem. He was too ready to accept paper figures, without asking if the numbers stated were available in reality. It was always the same, whatever the subject might be—tanks, aircraft, rifles, shovels.... Even if the numbers had actually been produced, a large part of them were still in the factories, and not with the troops."

101. Ellis, *Brute Force,* 421.

102. Weigley, *Eisenhower's Lieutenants,* 30-31; Ellis, *Brute Force,* 425.

103. Weigley, *History of the US Army,* 479.

104. Ibid.

105. Weigley, *Eisenhower's Lieutenants,* 24.

106. Mick, *102nd Infantry Division,* 51-53.

107. Ibid.

108. Charles B. MacDonald, *The United States Army in World War II. European Theater of Operations. The Siegfried Line* (Washington, DC: Office of the Chief of Military History/GPO, 1963), 617, 621-622.

109. Mick, *102nd Infantry Division,* 40.

110. *Conquer: The Story of the Ninth Army 1944-1945* (Nashville: Battery Press, 1980), 269-330.

111. Martin Blumenson, "Breakout and Pursuit," S.L.A. Marshall Lecture, Fort Leavenworth, Kansas, 13 March 1984.

112. Pogue, *Supreme Command,* 175, 189.

113. Ibid., 192.

114. Martin Blumenson, "The Decision to Take Brest," *Army* 10 (March 1960): 51.

115. William B. Breuer, *Operation Dragoon: The Allied*

Invasion of the South of France (New York: Jove Books, 1988); Pogue, *Supreme Command*, 244.

116. Bernard Law Montgomery, *The Memoirs of Field-Marshall the Viscount Montgomery of Alamein, K.G.* (New York: Signet Books, 1958), 242-281.

117. Ibid., 257-280.

118. W. Denis Whitaker and Shelagh Whitaker, *Rhineland: The Battle to End the War* (New York: St. Martin's Press, 1989), 1-4, 345-348; Conquer, 114-198.

119. Pogue, *Supreme Command*, 302.

120. Charles B. MacDonald, *The Battle of the Huertgen Forest* (New York: Jove Books, 1984), 195-208.

2. Eisenhower and the Supreme Command

Any chance of success for Hitler's Ardennes attack rested firmly on the dictator's assumption that the Allied command would react slowly and deliberately in ordering countermeasures. Indeed, the basic premise for striking at this unexpected time in such an unexpected place was the presumption that the American and British leaders, divided by "nationalistic fears and rivalries,"[1] would haggle for days over the nature of the offensive and how to respond to it. If this went on for as little as 48 hours, Hitler hoped to have his forces across the Meuse River and well on their way to splitting the Allied front, possibly isolating the British forces in the north from the American Army further south. The Nazi leader, however, badly misjudged both the nature of the Allied command structure and the man who led it.

Long before the German attack smashed into the US units in the Ardennes in December 1944, Eisenhower had forged an integrated, effective, totally "Allied" command structure (appendix A) eminently capable of quickly assessing the German attack and reacting appropriately to it. Within hours of the beginning of the assault, Eisenhower and his SHAEF staff had divined the scope of the surprise offensive and had begun to take critical actions necessary to stop its spread and limit its impact on the Allied armies. Sending the first wave of reserves to the threatened region almost immediately, Ike and his SHAEF staff officers continued with a series of critical decisions over the ensuing days that changed the entire nature of the German attack. Eisenhower's prompt actions succeeded in transforming the offensive from a massive breakthrough threatening to split the Allied armies in two, to a localized fight for control of the

Ardennes region.[2] In so doing, he averted a potential strategic disaster for the Allies and created an opportunity to destroy the bulk of Hitler's remaining reserves.

Despite his appropriate actions during this crisis, however, Eisenhower has been criticized for his conduct of the battle as well as for his assumed responsibility for creating the conditions that allowed the enemy the opportunity to launch such an offensive. His critics, both American and British, loudly berated his strategic vision (or lack thereof) for causing the crisis, and second-guessed his decisions impacting on the fight at the tactical level. Field Marshal Sir Alan Brooke, Britain's Chief of the Imperial General Staff, viewed Eisenhower's leadership "with undisguised contempt," charging that Ike's "faulty dispositions and organizations" had caused him to be "thrown off his balance."[3] Even Bradley, Ike's closest friend among the high-ranking commanders, accused the Supreme Commander of having "an acute case of the shakes"[4] during the offensive and characterized one of Ike's biggest decisions as "the worst possible mistake"[5] he could have made.

If Eisenhower's leadership is to be judged, it is necessary to examine the development, characteristics, and influence of Eisenhower's command of the coalition warfare he directed in Europe from 1942 to 1945, and to analyze how his battle leadership influenced the Ardennes offensive. The actions of America's most successful practitioner of coalition war,[6] conducting the American Army's greatest battle, can provide insight into the American style of battle leadership.

IKE'S CAREER

Dwight David Eisenhower's family was of modest means, and the chance for a college education appeared none too promising for the young man.[7] However, a family friend suggested he try for admission to one of the service academies. He passed the competitive exam and, on 14 June 1911, 21-year-old Cadet D.D. Eisenhower joined the Military Academy.[8]

Eisenhower's cadet career was less than brilliant. Robert E. Lee had amazed his classmates in 1829 by receiving no demerits in his 4 years as a cadet; Ike must have astonished his classmates by his ability to collect them by the dozens. Yet he performed adequately in academics and was a star on the gridiron until a knee injury ended his football playing. Cadet Eisenhower was extremely popular with his classmates, well liked for his easy smile and good nature.[9] Ike stood 61st among the 164 members of the Class of 1915 who graduated that June and was commissioned in the Infantry.[10]

Lieutenant Eisenhower's first assignment took him to Fort Sam Houston, TX, for duty with the 19th Infantry Regiment. He missed out on chasing Pancho Villa with General John J. Pershing's Mexican Punitive Expedition in 1916. Instead, he stayed in San Antonio and trained Illinois National Guardsmen.[11] Ike was given several different assignments over the next 2 years, but none got him what he really wanted—overseas combat duty in World War I. In 1918, nearly a year after the United States had declared war on Germany, Captain Eisenhower was assigned to organize and train the 301st Tank Battalion at Camp Meade, MD.[12] He thought at last he had an opportunity to get into the fighting.

During those weeks in the spring of 1918, Eisenhower trained his tank battalion for combat, demonstrating to his superiors a remarkable talent for organization and administration. His ability to organize was so impressive, however, that it caused his commander to pull him out of his unit just as it shipped overseas. In what Ike described as "a black mood," he assumed command of Camp Colt, near Gettysburg, PA, and began to train the Army's Tank Corps.[13] Although he received two more promotions before the Armistice was signed, LTC Eisenhower spent the remainder of the fighting war training tankers. After 11 November 1918, he also had the rather melancholy duty of supervising the demobilization of Camp Colt and the dismantling of the Tank Corps. Above all, he regretted that he had missed battle action. Some years after World War I, Ike met a young officer who had served in France during the war. When the officer complained of the lack of promotions overseas, Ike shot back, "Well, you got overseas—that should be promotion enough!"[14]

Lack of combat experience would continue to embarrass Eisenhower, especially when his British subordinates brought up the subject later during his World War II command. Nevertheless, Ike's wartime service had experiences that would help prepare him to excel as a coalition commander: organizing and training units for war; early appreciation of tanks and the mobility of armored warfare; extensive work with civilians and soldier-civilians; and avoidance of the "Passchendaele" (trench warfare) mentality that characterized the overcautious attitude of some British commanders in World War II. Eisenhower had been better served by his noncombat duty than he suspected.[15]

In July 1920, Eisenhower became a captain once again, as he and his contemporaries reverted to their permanent ranks. However, within a few days, Ike became a major, a rank he would hold for the next 16 years.[16] At about the same time, he took a seemingly innocent action that nearly ended his career. MAJ Eisenhower published an article in the *Infantry Journal* about the role of tanks in future warfare.[17] The article challenged the prevailing mentality by suggesting that the tank was "a weapon that could change completely the strategy and tactics of land warfare."[18] The perceptive and forwardthinking article, however, offended the powerful and influential Chief of Infantry Branch. For straying from the "party line" in his tank article, Ike was summoned before the Chief of Infantry and told that his ideas "were not only wrong, but dangerous and that henceforth [he] would keep them to himself." A chastened Eisenhower wrote that, "Particularly, I was not to publish anything incompatible with solid infantry doctrine. If I did, I would be hauled before a court-martial."[19] This attitude hardly stimulated an atmosphere of enlightened debate or intelligent discussion of strategy and tactics. It was intended, of course, to create just the opposite climate—to produce a lockstep mentality of rigid compliance. Ike complied.

Despite Eisenhower's obedience to higher authority (an obedience that would characterize most of his active service), the incident seemed to trouble his relations with Infantry branch. Throughout the next several years, Ike was continually turned down by his branch for choice assignments (such as the Infantry School) and for further military schooling (primarily the Command and Staff School).[20] Instead, he shuffled from post to post, usually coerced into coaching the unit football team. During this time, General Fox Conner became the younger officer's mentor and guiding influence. The highly regarded Conner had been Pershing's operations officer in the Great War and was, Eisenhower asserted, "the ablest man I ever knew."[21] Conner expanded Ike's intellect by forcing him to read and study military history and by coaching him in command and staff duties. When he thought his pupil was sufficiently prepared, Conner secured Eisenhower a place in the Command and Staff School class of 1925-26, on an adjutant general branch quota. In June 1926, Eisenhower graduated first in his Leavenworth class.[22]

Over the next several years, Eisenhower held a variety of jobs ranging from the American Battle Monuments Commission (a "writing" assignment under General Pershing) to the office of the Assistant Secretary of War (planning the industrial mobilization for a war nobody thought would ever come). Along the way, he completed the War College and met George Marshall.[23]

Marshall, whose impact on the Army in the years leading to World War II is legend, was quietly compiling a list of bright, capable, energetic officers whom he would later use to staff the War Department and rebuild the American military machine. Becoming known to Marshall was sufficient to propel an officer's rapid rise, provided the officer had favorably impressed him.[24] Eisenhower's demonstrated ability to organize, write, administer, and, above all, produce results did indeed favorably impress the future Chief of Staff. In 1930, he met and also impressed another general who would further his career—Douglas MacArthur. Ambrose recounts why both men admired and respected Ike:

> Eisenhower did his work brilliantly. It was always done on time. He loyally supported his chief's decisions. He adjusted himself to his chief's time schedules and to other

whims. He was able to think from the point of view of his
chief, a quality that both MacArthur and Marshall often
singled out for praise. He had an instinctive sense of when
to make a decision himself, when to pass it up to the boss.
MacArthur said of Eisenhower in a fitness report in the
early 1930's, "This is the best officer in the Army. When
the next war comes, he should go right to the top." In
1942 Marshall showed that he agreed with that
assessment by implementing the recommendation.[25]

Eisenhower worked under MacArthur for 7 years, first in
Washington, then for 4 years in the Philippines. Although
much has been made of the difficulties of serving under the
ambitious and egotistical general, Ike learned and benefited
from the experience.[26] While Eisenhower's professional
education profited from observing MacArthur's considerable
intellect in action, he also saw how involvement in partisan
politics could be dangerous for a soldier. Frequent
confrontations with the President, the 1932 smashing of the
Bonus Marchers' camp near the Capitol, and continual
flirting with extremist politics were all examples of the
negative manifestations of MacArthur's flamboyant style.
They reinforced Eisenhower's natural tendency to shun the
political aspects of soldiering whenever possible.[27] Later,
when some of his actions as coalition commander were
criticized as politically naive, Ike would justify them by
claiming that "military necessity" outweighed all political
considerations—as if war and politics could be neatly
separated.[28] It would seem he feared being perceived as
resembling his politically manipulative boss of the 1930s.

Eisenhower learned to work as harmoniously as possible
with an ally whose culture and background were completely
different from his own, forcing him to appreciate the impact
of issues from his opposite number's position, not merely his
own. Working with MacArthur to build an independent
Filipino Army, Eisenhower found the effort frustrating, with
little personal satisfaction.[29] Despite the difficulties of the
job, however, the experience added to his preparation for
allied leadership. The Philippine tour also gave Eisenhower
daily lessons in the value and necessity of compromise. To
succeed, Ike constantly juggled the demands of his egotistical

boss, the Filipino government, an unsympathetic American Army, and his own sense of what was required. Compromises were inevitable and frequent.

This job taught another important lesson: how to accomplish extensive missions with limited resources. There were never enough men, equipment, or especially money to do it right. Eisenhower learned to adjust his aims to the resources available; to be opportunistic and flexible; and to do what was affordable when he couldn't do what seemed necessary.

Finally, despite his aversion to "politics," Ike was required to operate in the political as well as the military arena during this assignment. His extensive duties (and MacArthur's preference to remain majestically aloof) caused Ike to meet, almost daily, with Filipino President Quezon. In fact, Quezon gave him an office adjoining his own in Malacañan Palace to facilitate close coordination and working relations. Eisenhower may have tried later to avoid the political side of military service, but he indulged in the practical application of it during his 4 years in the Philippines.[30] All these lessons helped enhance his leadership.

LTC Eisenhower (he regained his World War I rank in July 1936) escaped from MacArthur and the Philippines in December 1939, shortly after Hitler's panzers and stukas shattered the Polish Army, forcing the start of World War II. Ike was glad to get back to the United States. He sensed that the war would eventually involve America, and he didn't want to miss out this time.[31] For the next 2 years, Eisenhower held several different posts in the expanding American Army. At Fort Lewis, WA, he served with the 15th Infantry Regiment as regimental executive officer and as battalion commander for the 3rd Battalion. Ike worked hard to prepare the unit for combat should America enter the war but reported, "I'm having the time of my life."[32] His reputation as a tireless and efficient organizer who got results continued to grow, and he soon moved up to Chief of Staff of the 3rd Infantry Division, the next higher headquarters.

In March 1941, Eisenhower passed two milestones—he

became the IX Corps Chief of Staff, and he was promoted to full colonel. By June, Eisenhower had become the Third Army Chief of Staff under General Walter Krueger at Fort Sam Houston, TX. According to Ambrose, Kreuger had requested Ike because he wanted an officer "possessing broad vision, progressive ideas, a thorough grasp of the magnitude of the problems involved in handling an army, and lots of initiative and resourcefulness."[33] Significantly, Marshall personally approved the selection of Eisenhower. Ike's rapid rise was about to accelerate.

The Louisiana Maneuvers of 1941 confirmed Eisenhower's superior abilities to Marshall. The Third Army's "victory" in the first large-scale maneuvers for the US Army since World War I were attributed to Ike's tireless work as Krueger's Chief of Staff. In recognition of this, Eisenhower, on Krueger's recommendation, received the single star of a brigadier general in September 1941.[34] More important, BG Eisenhower got the call to report to Marshall for duty on the War Department Staff on 12 December 1941. It was the most important call of his career.[35]

Eisenhower assumed his duties in the War Plans Division on 14 December 1941. This was his first opportunity to work where Marshall could observe him daily, and he made the most of it. By February 1942, Marshall had made Ike the head of War Plans Division. The next month, Eisenhower became the first War Department Chief of Operations, in a general reorganization of the staff.[36] Soon after, on Marshall's recommendation, Eisenhower received his second star. Ambrose relates some reasons why the Marshall-Eisenhower relationship thrived:

> The two men, although ten years apart in age, had much in common. Marshall...had been a football player in college. He was a great fan of Fox Conner and a student of military history. Like Eisenhower, he loved exploring the Civil War battlefields and habitually illustrated his points or strengthened his arguments by drawing on examples from past battles and campaigns. The way he exercised leadership coincided nicely with Eisenhower's temperament. He never yelled, never shouted, almost never lost his temper. He built an atmosphere of friendly

cooperation and teamwork around him without losing the
distinction between the commander and his staff.[37]

Marshall carefully selected his principal subordinates for
their proven ability to exercise certain traits and
characteristics in their work. He sought independent
thinkers with a positive attitude who weren't afraid to make
a decision. He avoided self-promoting careerists who were
content to continually "pass the buck" on every action while
they hogged the limelight. Marshall, whose own equanimity
was frequently mistaken for detached coldness, rejected the
shouter and table-pounder, preferring instead a leader who
commanded respect by force of character. "Eisenhower,"
wrote Ambrose, "was exactly the sort of officer Marshall was
looking for."[38]

Eisenhower completed his apprenticeship for coalition
command under Marshall's able tutelage during the hectic,
early months of American involvement in the war. Ike
especially impressed his chief with his ability to "rise above
national rivalries" and work amicably and closely with their
new British ally. Starting at the Arcadia Conference and
continuing through many US-UK meetings, Ike stood out as
a fair-minded partner.[39]

THE ALLIED COMMANDER IN CHIEF

When Marshall sent Eisenhower to Britain to observe and
report on the massive buildup for the eventual attack on
Nazi Germany, he was taking the first step toward placing
Ike in command of all the Allied forces in the European
Theater of Operations. Ike's uncommonly good judgment,
quick assessment of the situation, and natural ability to win
the friendship and confidence of his British counterparts
convinced Marshall he was the perfect choice to lead the
American effort.

Upon his return from Britain, Eisenhower set to work
drafting the operating directive for the Commander,
European Theater of Operations, United States Army
(ETOUSA). This document spelled out broad goals and
objectives as well as warfighting policy for the senior
American commander in the theater. In it Ike wrote,

"Absolute unity of command should be exercised by the Theater Commander, who should organize, train, and command the American ground, naval and air forces assigned to the theater."[40] Three days after Marshall received the document, he appointed Eisenhower ETOUSA commander to execute it.

Although Marshall probably arrived at the decision to pick Ike independently, he received support for his choice from senior British officials (including Winston Churchill and Lord Louis Mountbatten) and Americans (Air Corps Commander Hap Arnold and General Mark Clark). The British, especially, were "impressed by his dedication to the Alliance."[41]

In July 1942, less than a month after arriving in England, Eisenhower got a third star and promotion to lieutenant general. He continued the buildup of US forces in Britain throughout the next few months, all the while increasing his popularity with Allied leaders.

While it was widely assumed at this early stage of the war that Eisenhower would eventually hand over field command to Marshall, the issue was by no means settled. With responsibilities for the global war causing Marshall to become increasingly tied to his Washington "command post" in the War Department, it became less likely that the Chief of Staff would usurp Ike as overall commander in Europe. When the Allied coalition decided to strike back at Germany in North Africa, thereby deferring the cross-channel invasion until 1944, it effectively settled the coalition field command question in Ike's favor. Eisenhower, the American commander already in the theater overseeing the buildup, was selected to lead Operation TORCH—the Allied invasion of North Africa.[42]

Ike set out immediately to create an integrated, Anglo-American headquarters to coordinate and control TORCH. Principal staff sections were set up with American chiefs and British deputies, or vice-versa. Eisenhower's Allied Force Headquarters (AFHQ) "thus became a balanced collection of British and American officers working closely together to achieve the common aims of the alliance."[43] Ike tolerated no outward manifestations of national jealousy or parochial pettiness. Instead, he worked hard to create "a close-knit organization where differences...were insignificant ones."[44]

Although Marshall and Eisenhower were disappointed that the Allies were taking the offensive in North Africa instead of attacking across the channel, that decision seems a fortunate one. TORCH allowed Ike to learn his trade as a battlefield leader in an environment where his mistakes could not prove fatal to the Alliance or the Allied cause. North Africa became a proving ground for Eisenhower, a laboratory in the conduct of coalition warfare that permitted him to sharpen his skills as an Allied leader in preparation for greater challenges to follow. Forrest Pogue, Supreme Command historian, wrote of Ike's apprenticeship in the Mediterranean:

> The real school for the future commander of Supreme Headquarters Allied Expeditionary Force [SHAEF],...was in the Mediterranean Theater where, as Allied Commander in Chief, he came into contact with most of the political and military problems which were to be found later on a greater scale in the European Theater of Operations. It was at Allied Forces Headquarters [AFHQ] in the Mediterranean that he became familiar with the great burdens of a military leader of a coalition...There, if he had not learned it before, the future SHAEF commander learned that war was not a simple matter of planning and executing tactical operations, but one of balancing many national and international forces against a military objective.[45]

Eisenhower's immediate problem was fighting a coalition war in the Tunisian desert. At a desert chokepoint called Kasserine Pass, he learned a hard lesson about the difficulties of leading allied forces in battle. Ike's teacher this time was Rommel.[46] The conditions leading to the debacle at Kasserine Pass seem obvious in retrospect. The Tunisian front was hundreds of miles from Ike's headquarters in Algiers. He exercised command through a confusing and convoluted system in which no one seemed certain for whom they worked. Supply lines were woefully overextended and intertwined among nationalities and services. The resulting "teeth" that could be supported by this tenuous logistical "tail" mustered insufficient combat power to smash German-Italian resistance. Above all, the commander of US troops, Major General Fredendall, wasn't up to the task.

Fredendall had been Marshall's pick to command the II US Corps in the North African campaign, and he had performed adequately during the landings at Oran and in the limited fighting that followed. Eisenhower, however, didn't know him personally and was unsure of how he'd react in combat against the stiffer German resistance. He soon heard unsettling reports of Fredendall's openly anti-British attitude as well as evidence of a rather bizarre command style.

Fredendall quickly alienated Ike's British overall ground commander, General Kenneth Anderson, and the two men barely spoke—although Anderson was nominally Fredendall's immediate boss. Worse, Fredendall despised and distrusted his own principal subordinate, 1st Armored Division commander Major General Orlando Ward. The American corps commander habitually gave orders directly to Ward's subordinates and continually meddled in details at the division, brigade, and even battalion level. Fredendall also insisted on remaining at his command post far from the front—a heavily fortified bunker chiseled into a remote mountainside. The corps commander seldom left this location and therefore knew little of fast-breaking events at the front.[47] Fredendall made a real disaster seem likely; the battle-wise Rommel made it inevitable.

The German attack smashed into Fredendall's troops on Valentine's Day 1943 and drove them back in disorder. The inexperienced American troops and the incompetent Fredendall made the Battle of Kasserine Pass a disaster for Ike. Fortunately, dissension in the German-Italian high command cost Rommel an opportunity to break the Allied line. Denied the support he needed to achieve a really important breakthrough, Rommel was eventually forced to pull his troops back within the safety of the heavily fortified Mareth Line to await the inevitable Allied assault.

The American tactical defeat was a serious blow to

American prestige and to Eisenhower's reputation. Nevertheless, he retained the confidence of Marshall and Allied political leadership (after all, it was Rommel who eventually withdrew, and final Allied victory in the desert was only weeks away). Ike emerged from the ordeal a better leader for the experience—and with the fourth star of a full general.[48]

In addition to the obvious lessons on supply, organization, and command structure, Ike had learned hard lessons on the value of aggressiveness and team play in his first test as a coalition commander and battle leader. Fredendall's poor performance demonstrated to Eisenhower that friendship must not interfere with the relief of any officer who proved indecisive or a failure.[49] Ike also learned that senior leadership must be aggressively forward during the critical phase of any operation and not wedded to a command post far to the rear. Later, under Ike's command, a perceived lack of aggressiveness or a tendency for a commander to spend too much time in the rear was justification for immediate relief.[50]

The hapless Fredendall also provided Ike with a stark example of the consequences of violating the first rule of coalition warfare—cooperation and team play with one's coalition partners. Fredendall was despised by his British and French counterparts for his outspokenly anti-Allied posture. Ike could not tolerate such an attitude and learned to place a high value on officers (such as the steady Bradley) who earned and maintained the respect of their Allied counterparts.[51] General Eisenhower emerged from the crucible of desert fighting with valuable experience in coalition war, improved skills in battle leadership, and increased confidence in himself.

His newly won self-confidence helped Ike to be more assertive with the British Allies and to make constructive changes in his headquarters' conduct for the remainder of the North African campaign. With the offensive-minded Patton now commanding II Corps in place of Fredendall, and the capable British General Harold Alexander directing the overall ground fighting, the Allies eliminated all Axis forces from the region by mid-May 1943, capturing an astounding

250,000 prisoners in the process.[52]

Eisenhower's next leadership challenge was the Allied invasion and capture of Sicily in July and August 1943. Despite Marshall's (and Ike's) preference for moving forward with Operation OVERLORD (the cross-channel attack into France), the focus of Allied action remained in the Mediterranean, a result of pressure from Churchill and the British service chiefs. This was just as well, because it gave Eisenhower and his American troops another chance to gain combat experience and confidence in their abilities. It also bought more time for the OVERLORD buildup to proceed.

Ike's British and American lieutenants were now some of the best commanders of the war and battle-proven. They included Britons Alexander, Montgomery, Admiral Sir Andrew Cunningham (Navy), and Air Chief Marshal Sir Arthur Tedder and Americans Patton and Bradley.[53] At the successful completion of the Sicilian campaign, Eisenhower had a first-class team that worked well together (although in the privacy of their diaries, some confided a startling degree of personal animosity toward one or more of the others). Clearly, the driving force behind the coalition was Eisenhower.

Historian Pogue wrote that the quality most often stressed about Ike was "the ability to get people of different nationalities and viewpoints to work together," and that "after a year of working with Allied forces in the Mediterranean area, he had demonstrated his knack for making a coalition work."[54] Indeed, when a British politician congratulated him on "his" victory, Ike flashed his famous smile and said, "Ours, you mean, ours."[55] In 1944, Ike brought this reputation for demanding harmony and cooperation to Britain as he prepared to lead the greatest invasion force ever assembled in the cross-channel attack on continental Europe.

President Roosevelt, impressed with Ike's reputation and proven ability to fight a successful coalition war, and professing that he would be "unable to sleep" with Marshall out of the country, had selected Eisenhower as Supreme Commander, Allied Expeditionary Force.[56] Ike's task directive from the Combined Chiefs of Staff read, "You will enter the continent of Europe, and, in conjunction with the other United Nations, undertake operations aimed at the heart of Germany and the destruction of her armed forces."[57] The main campaign of the "great crusade" was about to begin.

THE SUPREME ALLIED COMMANDER

Despite the inevitable complications (among them a chronic shortage of landing craft and, later, unfavorable weather patterns), Eisenhower's invasion force began landing troops in France on 6 June 1944. Establishing and expanding the Normandy lodgment was a logistical undertaking without precedent, designed to create an unassailable base to support the subsequent campaigns across France and Germany.[58] By D-Day plus 13, the Allies had put ashore 630,000 troops, 95,000 vehicles, and 220,000 tons of supplies.[59] Over the next several weeks the beachhead was expanded and secured, and, although German resistance became strong, the Allied Armies broke out of Normandy at the beginning of August. Pogue described why Eisenhower's invasion succeeded:

> The combined Allied command had worked smoothly to bring the full force of naval, air, and ground power to bear on the enemy. The Germans from almost the first blow had been off balance...For this failure there are many explanations. Most striking perhaps was the German lack of the sort of unified command which the Allies had in SHAEF.[60]

It was this unified SHAEF command (appendixes B and C), mainly Eisenhower's personal creation, that led to the continuing Allied successes.

The story of the subsequent successful campaigns across France over the next several months is a familiar one. Montgomery's capture of Caen, Bradley's smashing of the German defensive line at St. Lô, and the unleashing of Patton's dramatic drive to the Seine and beyond are well known. The conduct of the coalition war that produced these successful campaigns, however, and tested Eisenhower's

Competing Allied Strategies
Field Marshal Montgomery's narrow thrust (bottom) and
Supreme Commander Eisenhower's broad front approach (top).

leadership of this "unified command," can be examined for further insight into coalition warfare. Ike had learned through practice and experience how to command the coalition. By necessity operating in the political as well as the military sphere, he would get the chance to apply those lessons in the campaigns of France and Germany.

The first challenge to Ike's coalition leadership (one that would linger through nearly the entire campaign) was the question of an overall ground commander. Field Marshal Montgomery, whose diminutive size concealed one of the war's largest egos, wanted the overall ground command of Allied forces. He held this position, in fact, for the invasion force and only reluctantly gave it up in September when Ike himself incorporated the ground commander duties among the responsibilities of the Supreme Commander. Nevertheless, Montgomery continued to pester him about assuming overall control of the ground war at every opportunity.[61]

Eisenhower resisted Monty's proposal for several reasons. First among these, it appears, was his disapproval of Montgomery's "single thrust" strategy. Monty reasoned that, given about 40 Allied divisions, he could strike rapidly across the northern sector, quickly capture Berlin, and end the war. Ike disagreed, worried about logistics, a long, exposed flank, and the German ability to mass against a single thrust.[62] He preferred to pressure the outnumbered Germans all along their line in a "broad front" strategy, although he assured Montgomery his would be the main attack of the Allied effort.[63]

Ike's wartime Chief of Staff, Lieutenant General Smith, claims his boss's strategy of advancing into Germany along several axes and double enveloping the Ruhr area (Germany's industrial heartland) was the agreed-upon plan well before the invasion. Smith cites Ike's determination to stick by his plan despite pressure from Churchill and others as one of his greatest strengths and an action that should receive more credit for the decisive defeat of the enemy.[64]

Once again, Eisenhower's judgment that it should be an *Allied* victory appears to be foremost. Monty's persistence struck Ike as placing his personal aggrandizement before the best interests of the coalition—probably a great sin to Ike. When Monty returned to this theme after the Ardennes offensive, Ike prepared a "him or me" message to the Combined Chiefs of Staff but never had to send it.[65] Montgomery, who realized that Eisenhower, not he, would be the one to stay, finally shut up, relegating his sniping to his postwar memoirs.

The coalition's junior partner, France, also provided Ike with several challenges to his Allied leadership. The earlier TORCH operation, the liberation of Paris, and numerous incidents related to wounded Gallic pride—all tried the Supreme Commander's patience and tested his skills as a diplomat as well as a commander, but none as much as the Strasbourg affair.

During winter 1944-45, when Eisenhower was diverting as much combat power as possible to the Ardennes, he directed General Devers, the 6th Army Group commander on the Allied south flank,[66] to withdraw to a more defensible line further to the west. Unfortunately, this would mean the evacuation of the recently liberated Alsatian town of Strasbourg.[67] De Gaulle, having established himself as France's new leader, was furious that French soil would be yielded and threatened to remove all French forces from the Allied front lines. He even suggested that the Allied supply lines running through France would no longer be safe. Ike had to give in and let the fiery Frenchman have his way. Once again, however, his motivation was for the best interest of the Alliance. Although he hated to give in to de Gaulle's threats, he swallowed his pride and, according to Churchill, did "the wise and proper thing."[68]

Perhaps the clearest illustration of Eisenhower's successful application of leadership in coalition warfare, however, is his overall direction of the campaign from Normandy to Germany. By taking this larger view of the European fighting, Ike demonstrated his masterful leadership of the Allied forces.[69]

Politically, Eisenhower had to deal with the combined effects of the two different styles of his American and British bosses. Roosevelt gave both Marshall and Eisenhower little political guidance concerning the running of the war. He was not interested in the day-to-day operations of the coalition and provided little information to assist the two soldiers to plan grand strategy. Churchill, on the other hand, was constantly meddling in Ike's business and frequently overloaded the Supreme Commander with both political and military advice. Although such control down to the lowest level was perfectly consistent with the British system, it often appeared to Ike as little more than nagging.[70]

These two conflicting styles caused Eisenhower to demonstrate initiative and assertiveness. In the absence of detailed instructions from his own government, he used initiative to develop politico-military goals for SHAEF, while asserting his independence from Churchill's constant interference. Ike accepted the Prime Minister's advice on many occasions, but he never allowed himself to be bullied by the persuasive British politician. In spite of this (or perhaps because of Ike's attitude), Churchill remained a staunch supporter of Eisenhower throughout the war.[71]

Militarily, Eisenhower showed his skill as a coalition leader throughout the campaigns in France and Germany, and despite postwar criticism of his military strategy from both sides of the Atlantic, he seems to have been right more often than wrong. Indeed, Ike's judgment concerning the Normandy invasion, the pursuit to the Rhine, and the "broad front" strategy and, later, his wise decision not to waste lives in a foolish attempt to beat the Russians to Berlin appear in retrospect to be much keener than his critics'.[72] But perhaps Eisenhower's greatest challenge as the military leader of the Allied coalition was the German Ardennes offensive—the Battle of the Bulge. It was during this greatest of all American battles that Ike's military judgment and sense of strategy were put to their toughest test. Buffeted by pressures and demands from his political and military superiors, and sniped at by his American and British subordinates, Eisenhower needed all the leadership skills he had developed over the preceding 2 years to win this battle.

ATTACK IN THE ARDENNES

When the Ardennes offensive began in the early morning

hours of 16 December 1944, it caught Eisenhower and the SHAEF staff completely by surprise.[73] This does not support later claims of several participants that they foresaw the German attack. Ike realized that he had left the Ardennes region vulnerable to a German counterstroke, but he never considered that such an event would occur. The Allies presumed that the German armies in the west had been thoroughly smashed during the war of maneuver fighting of the previous summer, and their remnants had been steadily worn away through the dreary, bitter fall campaigns of attrition. With the Red armies slowly but relentlessly grinding away at the bulk of the Wehrmacht on the vast eastern front, Germany seemed on the point of collapse. It may have been only half in jest when, in a 15 December letter, Eisenhower refused Montgomery's demand that he pay off on his £5 bet that the war would be over by Christmas, pointing out that he still had 9 days to go.[74]

The thinness of the Allied line in the Ardennes was the inevitable consequence of Eisenhower's chosen strategy for prosecution of the war on the western front and the American gamble that 90 US divisions would suffice to win a global war. Pressing the Germans everywhere in the knowledge that they could not possibly be strong enough all along their line to stop the superior Allied forces, Eisenhower's "broad front" approach was ultimately based on the premise that "more is better"—that is, more tanks, more bullets, more beans, more fuel, and above all, more men.[75] "More men" was Eisenhower's principal worry on 16 December 1944, not the threat of a German attack. He had no fresh US divisions to put into the line to maintain the momentum of the Allied advance, and even the replacement pool for bringing battle-attrited units back up to fighting strength had nearly dried up.[76] By this stage of the war, there could be no thought of Britain providing any more divisions; that war-weary country was having difficulty calling up even modest numbers of fresh troops.[77] Any large number of new men would have to be American—and America had decided to complete the war with the divisions already formed. The war planners' 90-division gamble seemed to be teetering on the verge of failure. The resulting effect on Eisenhower's portion of the World War II global battlefront was his thin front in the Ardennes sector. Weigley correctly analyzed the situation facing Eisenhower:

> Eisenhower's dilemma, when in November and early December he fretted over the Ardennes but perceived no satisfactory solution, points to a flaw in American strategy more fundamental than an excessive emulation of the Lincoln-Grant strategy of the Civil war. It was not that the broad-front strategy was wrong; the more basic trouble was that the Anglo-American alliance had not given Eisenhower enough troops to carry it out safely...There were not enough Anglo-American divisions, or enough replacements for casualties in the existing divisions. Eisenhower could not create a reserve unless he abandoned the broad-front strategy. Far from creating a reserve he could not even rest and refit exhausted units like the 28th and the 4th without risking them in the tissue-thin Ardennes line. More than the misjudgments of the commanders in Europe, the events unfolding in the Ardennes on December 16 indicated that the ninety-division gamble had gone sour. The American army in Europe fought on too narrow a margin of physical superiority for the favored American broad-front strategy to be anything but a risky gamble.[78]

This now-chronic lack of manpower had brought Bradley to Ike's headquarters on 16 December to discuss the problem and plan their strategy for overcoming it. While the two met, received briefings, and prepared to attend the wedding of two members of the SHAEF staff later that day, the lead units of the German attack were crashing into American positions all along the thinly defended Ardennes front. Having begun at 0530 hours that morning, the attack was several hours old before Ike or Bradley received word that something was happening in Troy Middleton's VIII Corps sector. Ike's Intelligence Officer, British Major General Ken Strong, brought the word to Eisenhower and Bradley, announcing that "the Germans had counterattacked in the Ardennes and scored penetrations at five places on the VIII corps front." Strong explained that the attacks had begun early that morning and that the full extent of the attack was still unknown (although he said "the most dangerous penetration seemed to be developing along the V Corps-VIII Corps boundary in the Losheim Gap").[79]

Ike's and Bradley's reactions to Strong's announcement highlight the dramatic differences between the two commanders' battle leadership during the Ardennes crisis and underscore Eisenhower's prompt (and correct) response. Bradley, preferring to regard the German assault as merely a spoiling attack to divert US resources from his own recently begun offensives, thought it could be stopped without difficulty,[80] later writing, "I was not overly concerned."[81] In contrast, Eisenhower seemed to sense immediately that something far bigger had been set in motion. "That's no spoiling attack!" Ike announced.[82]

Eisenhower was the first of all the Allied commanders "to grasp the full import of the attack, the first to be able to readjust his thinking,"[83] and the first to initiate counterstrokes to defeat the unexpected German offensive. After studying operational maps with Bradley and Strong, he directed Bradley to dispatch the 7th and 10th Armored Divisions from their assembly areas in the rear of their respective Ninth and Third Armies to the threatened sector. When Bradley, afraid that Patton would strongly object to losing the 10th Armored, began to demur, Ike "overruled him with a touch of impatience."[84]

The quick decision to rush these two armored units (along with the SHAEF reserve—the 82nd and 101st Airborne Divisions)to the Ardennes was one of Eisenhower's most important decisions of the battle, for it influenced the ultimate outcome of the fighting more than any other single decision taken by a commander on either side.

The doctrinal approach for countering such a breakthrough as the Germans were then attempting in the Ardennes was well known to Eisenhower (and to his subordinate commanders): hold the shoulders of the penetration to prevent the enemy from expanding the base of his salient; restrict the advance of enemy forces by interdicting crucial chokepoints and denying full use of routes of advance; and counterattack along the flanks of the penetration to cut off and destroy the advancing enemy forces. Carrying out this doctrinal approach was another matter altogether.[85]

The most serious problem facing Eisenhower in his attempt to counter the German attack was where to come up with the reserve forces necessary to launch the counterattacks into the flanks of the penetration. Just as the manpower shortage had created the situation that led to the Germans invading the Ardennes, so was it hindering Eisenhower's reaction to counter the assault--SHAEF had no major strategic reserve forces immediately available. Some weeks prior to the launching of the Ardennes attack, Ike had asked his Army Group commanders to begin assembling a reserve force, but this action had not gone much beyond his request to identify units that could be used as such.[86] SHAEF's pitifully inadequate reserve force on 16 December 1944 consisted of the 82nd and 101st Airborne Infantry Divisions, both still resting and refitting after withdrawing from Montgomery's Arnhem-Nijmegen fiasco the past September.

After conferring with Strong, SHAEF Chief of Staff Smith, and his British Deputy Operations Officer, Major General J.F.M. Whiteley, Ike ordered the two airborne divisions (organized under Major General Matt Ridgway as the XVIII Airborne Corps) placed on alert for dispatch to the Ardennes. By the time the units finally got to the threatened area (and after some understandable confusion), the 82nd, along with Ridgway's headquarters, formed up behind St.-Vith, while the 101st found itself at Bastogne—and was soon surrounded there.[87] Eisenhower also told Bradley "to order his army commanders to alert any division they had which was free for employment in the Ardennes area,"[88] for he realized the two armored divisions and the airborne units were not nearly sufficient to stop the German attack, let alone eliminate the rapidly forming salient. Many more were needed.

Eisenhower's quick appreciation of the scope of the German offensive caused him to realize that successfully defeating it would require a complete reorientation of his three army groups from one of Allied offense all along the line to one of defense in all but the Ardennes sector.

SHAEF's focus until the German attack was stopped would have to be on regaining control of the Ardennes. Ike "ordered the cessation of all attacks by the [Allied Expeditionary Force]'and the gathering up of every possible reserve to strike the [Ardennes] penetration in both flanks.'"[89] He directed Bradley and Devers to shift forces so that Devers' 6th Army Group on the Allied southern flank could move its boundary northward to cover a large portion of Patton's sector, freeing the Third Army commander to launch an early counterattack into the salient's southern flank. Ike had the SHAEF staff issue a message for his signature, stating:

> The enemy is making a major thrust...and still has reserves uncommitted...It appears that he will be prepared to employ the whole of his armored reserve to achieve success. My intention is to take immediate action to check the enemy advance, and then to launch a counteroffensive without delay with all forces north of the Moselle.[90]

Issuing this message on 18 December, he supplemented it with instructions that the German line of advance must not be permitted to cross the Meuse River.[91] Major Allied supply dumps were located across the Meuse; if the German offensive reached these critical supplies (especially fuel stocks), the Ardennes attack could explode into a rupture of the entire Allied line.

After sending this message outlining his general, overall strategy on 18 December, Eisenhower summoned his principal American subordinates to a meeting in Verdun on 19 December to issue further orders for countering the German offensive. The meeting was a crucial one; Eisenhower not only outlined his strategy for containing the attack within the Ardennes region, he also set a tone of optimism and opportunism.[92] Ike's personal leadership stabilized the chaotic situation. Ambrose recorded:

> Eisenhower's reaction [to the German Ardennes offensive] was crucial. If he had panicked, shouting orders on the telephone and pulling units from various sectors to throw them piecemeal into the battle, he would have spread panic

all down the line. But he was calm, optimistic, even delighted at this seemingly ominous development... [writing to General Somervell on another subject on 17 December, Ike wrote] "If things go well we should not only stop the thrust but should be able to profit from it."[93]

At the meeting Eisenhower announced, "The present situation is to be regarded as one of opportunity for us and not of disaster. There will be only cheerful faces at this conference table."[94] Patton, realizing Ike was referring to the opportunity to destroy the last major reserve of German forces in the west, presented by their unexpected sally from behind the protection of their Siegfried Line defenses, quickly rejoined, "Hell, let's have the guts to let the sons-of-bitches go all the way to Paris, then we'll really cut 'em off and chew 'em up!"[95]

Lest anyone think the general laughter following Patton's quip indicated approval of his facetious suggestion, Ike said, "George, that's fine. But the enemy must never be allowed to cross the Meuse."[96] The most dramatic part of the discussion came when Patton replied to Eisenhower's query as to how soon the Third Army could launch a counterattack into the south of the German salient. Now at center stage (and no doubt relishing every second of it), Patton announced that his army could attack "on December 22nd with three divisions!"[97] Not realizing that Patton had been quietly preparing for this shift in orientation for several days, the others in the room expressed disbelief. It seemed impossible that Patton's unit could shift 90 degrees from a major offensive to the east to one toward the north in such a short time. To Eisenhower, however, Patton's dramatic announcement seemed to indicate the Army commander was underestimating the actual strength of the German offensive—clearly three divisions would not be sufficient combat power to execute successfully the kind of thrust Ike knew would be necessary to cut off the advancing German formations.[98] After Patton explained that he would follow up his initial 3-division attack with one of three more soon after, Eisenhower approved the plan.[99]

By the end of the day, Eisenhower and the SHAEF staff

had set in motion most of the important elements necessary to isolate the German penetration and ultimately defeat it: the few immediately available reserves had been rapidly dispatched to the threatened area; actions to create more reserves and fling them against the salient had been initiated; and the plan to begin the crucial counterattacks into the flanks of the penetration had been put in motion. Eisenhower's prompt actions on the first 2 days of the offensive were beginning to show positive results, but it was still early in the battle, and German forces continued to gain ground and push westward. Jacques Nobécourt, a Frenchman who wrote a well-balanced, nonpartisan view of Eisenhower's leadership during the Ardennes crisis, summed up the situation facing the Allies on 19 December:

> The decisions he [Ike] had taken on December 16 were beginning to pay off; the flanks of the German salient were holding and resistance was firm at the vital communications points. In the center there was still a gap of 25 miles between the two airborne divisions and the German armor was pouring through it. But already there were signs the offensive was running out of steam.[100]

To complete the isolation of the Ardennes battlefront and prevent the German attack from rupturing the Allied line, Eisenhower realized that firm control needed to be established all along the threatened sector. His northern two armies now separated from Patton's army by the force of the attack, Bradley obstinately refused to relocate his headquarters.[101] One more essential command decision had yet to be made—should the northern half of the bulge remain under Bradley's command? Eisenhower's decision on this question became the most controversial one he made during the battle, but it epitomizes more than any other his firm grasp of the true nature of an *allied* command. Eisenhower shifted command of the Ninth and the rest of the First (all forces north of the Bastogne area) to Montgomery.[102] Despite Ike's close friendship with Bradley and bruised American egos, he knew it was the right thing to do to save the Allied cause. Historian Chester Wilmot, openly pro-British and not noted for being pro-American, wrote, "In all his career as

Supreme Commander there was perhaps no other time when Eisenhower revealed so clearly the greatness of his qualities."[103] The decision was bitterly resented by Bradley, who continued until his death to claim that it was unnecessary.

Given the extent of the German penetration of the American front and Bradley's stubborn refusal to relocate his Luxembourg City command post, Eisenhower felt he had no alternative. David Eisenhower wrote:

> By the night of the nineteenth, a command transfer was inevitable and imminent. After Eisenhower's long, cold drive back to Versailles from Verdun, reports reached SHAEF describing an alarming deterioration in the Ardennes...Word arrived that 10,000 men of the ...106th [Infantry Division at St.-Vith]...had surrendered, the largest battlefield surrender of American troops in the war...By midday the 101st Airborne at Bastogne had been in contact [with numerous German units]...opening the seesaw siege for the city...[and Ike] learned of the near capture of the fuel dumps at Spa, which Bradley had assured him would not be located south of the Meuse.[104]

When Eisenhower's British deputies, Strong and Whiteley, had finally convinced a reluctant Smith of the necessity to alter the command arrangements, the SHAEF Chief of Staff placed the recommendation before the Supreme Commander.[105] Eisenhower immediately approved it and personally phoned Bradley to tell him of his decision. With the SHAEF staff still present, Ike passed the order to his reluctant subordinate, listened to Bradley's protests, then said sharply, "Well, Brad, those are my orders."[106] This short conversation, more than any other action taken by Eisenhower and the SHAEF staff during the battle "discredited the German assumption that nationalistic fears and rivalries would inhibit prompt and effective steps to meet the German challenge."[107] It meant that Hitler's gamble had failed.

Ike next called Montgomery to inform him of the command change and "confirm that he now commanded two American armies."[108] Monty immediately set out in his

typically thorough manner to regroup and reorganize the
northern half of the Ardennes battlefield. A master of
planning and attention to detail, the 21 Army Group
commander had no equal in organizing a "tidy show."
Moving Horrocks' XXX British Corps to blocking positions
along the west bank of the Meuse River, he visited both of
his new American Army headquarters to coordinate
personally the reorganization.[109] What he found at Hodges'
First Army headquarters was disturbing.

It was then 4 days into the battle, and Montgomery was
appalled to find that neither Bradley nor any member of his
staff had visited Hodges' command post to assess the
situation or issue instructions, and the telephone or radio
could not substitute for personal contact during such a
critical time.[110] Hodges seemed to Montgomery to be on the
verge of total collapse, and it took personal intervention by
Eisenhower and Bradley to prevent Hodges' relief.[111]

Despite problems with Hodges and the First Army staff,
Montgomery successfully brought order to the northern
sector of the battlefield and effectively stabilized the
previously fluid situation. Within days of the 20 December
command change (appendix D), the Allies began to stem the
German onslaught and take control of the battle.
Unfortunately, Montgomery proved bitterly disappointing to
Ike in carrying out the crucial counterattacks that
Eisenhower had intended to use to destroy Hitler's last
remaining mobile reserves.

His inability to trap the mass of the German panzer and
grenadier units outside of their Siegfried Line defenses with
well-placed, coordinated counteroffensives on the south and
north flanks was perhaps Eisenhower's greatest failure in
the Ardennes battle. Eisenhower's main intention was to
launch early coordinated and comprehensive counterattacks
of such scope and magnitude that the great bulk of German
forces would not only be defeated, they would be trapped.[112]
Eisenhower adopted this position from the beginning and
clearly laid out his intention at the Verdun meeting of the
senior commanders on 19 December.[113] His annoyance with
Patton's dramatic announcement to launch an attack from
the south of the salient in only 3 days was not directed at

the early timing or premature nature of the assault, but only at its seemingly insufficient strength to accomplish Ike's intention to "bag" the bulk of the German forces. In the end, however, it didn't happen the way Ike and the SHAEF staff envisioned, and the German forces, though defeated, were not annihilated. Although Patton was true to his boast and launched his counteroffensive from the south in a nearly unbelievably short time, there came no corresponding counterattack from the north of the salient. Montgomery wasn't ready.

Despite Bradley's mediocre command performance to this point in the battle, his principal subordinate (indeed, his only subordinate army commander by this time) was fully capable of the task of driving a timely, armored-tipped assault into the southern flank of the German offensive. The battle-proven 4th Armored Division, along with the 26th and 80th Infantry Divisions, jumped off on 21 December from Arlon in an attack toward Bastogne. Three days later, Patton's XII Corps launched a similar attack along the right flank of the earlier one.[114] There was, however, no counteroffensive from Montgomery's command, even as Patton's troops drove steadily into the southern flank of the German offensive. Montgomery felt he had good reason to delay his inevitable counteroffensive: he feared the Germans had uncommitted units with which to continue their offensive (perhaps as many as 30 divisions); he doubted that American units, smashed by the full weight of the German offensive, had the resiliency to shake off their initial shock and counterattack without a complete and methodical reorganization; and he thought that von Manteuffel's Panzer Army could easily contain Patton's southern flank thrust and be prepared to help Dietrich's 6th Panzer Army defeat any Allied counteroffensive on the northern flank.[115] Unwilling to commit troops to what he regarded as a premature counterattack, Montgomery continued his methodically efficient battlefield reorganization. "Sharply critical of Montgomery's overcaution," American commanders like Major General J. Lawton Collins, aggressive commander of the US VII Corps, pulled uneasily against Monty's restraint.[116]

Eisenhower also chaffed at Montgomery's slowness to launch a counterstroke. He could sense the moment slipping away when the two-pronged attack against the German salient would trap the bulk of German forces. Weigley reports that, when an increasingly frustrated Eisenhower heard an oral report that Montgomery was ready to consider a counterattack, he exclaimed, "Praise God from whom all blessings flow!"[117] Unfortunately, Ike's praise was premature; Monty had only agreed to pull Collins' VII Corps out of the line in order to allow it to *prepare* for a counterattack—he still wasn't ready for the real thing.

Weigley suggests that Eisenhower and Montgomery differed fundamentally on the issue of destroying the enemy forces in the Ardennes. Eisenhower was intent on using this unforeseen opportunity to crush the last of the German mobile reserves. Montgomery, it seems to Weigley, remained focused on his own scheme of leading a single Allied thrust to the Ruhr and beyond; defeating the enemy in the Ardennes was secondary to the larger issue of this long-pursued goal. The Ardennes fighting was, it seemed to Montgomery, only a means for achieving his quest of becoming the overall ground commander. Weigley explained:

> Montgomery was not thinking about the Ardennes in terms of an offensive. His whole interest was in eliminating the Ardennes involvement to permit a prompt return to the offensive in the north...Montgomery sought a counterattack, not a counteroffensive; he would pursue a tactical victory and proposed nothing larger... Eisenhower had something more in mind for the Ardennes than a tactical victory....[He] wanted to exploit the opportunity created by the enemy in the Ardennes to destroy the German army west of the Rhine.[118]

Finally, on 3 January 1945, the counteroffensive began in earnest. But instead of being launched to cut off the enemy at the very base of the salient, the Allied attacks struck at the nose and waist of the bulge.[119] The poor road network near the base of the salient, the bitter winter weather, and the skillful German withdrawal (practiced, after all, countless times under similar conditions of weather and superior enemy forces on the vast Russian front) combined to limit significantly the overall "bag" of forces Eisenhower had hoped to achieve. It was not until 7 February that the front line was returned to its original position of 16 December 1944.[120]

The Allied victory in the Ardennes was not as thorough and satisfying as it could have been, nor did it eliminate completely the last of the German mobile reserves in the West. It did, however, drain the Wehrmacht of precious resources of manpower, equipment, and fuel that could have been better used to slow the inevitable Allied offensives to the Rhine and beyond. It also changed the nature of the final Allied offensives against Germany, because it left a German vacuum and an American concentration in the Ardennes-Eifel region, encouraging Eisenhower to let Bradley's 12th Army Group conduct a major drive into central Germany and not simply play out the remainder of the war in limited supporting offensives guarding Montgomery's flank.[121] More than anything else, the Ardennes victory was Eisenhower's victory. Just as he shouldered responsibility for creating the conditions that led to the surprise German attack, so should he receive credit for defeating it.

ANALYSIS OF BATTLE LEADERSHIP

The Battle of the Bulge brought out attributes of leadership in Eisenhower that have often been overlooked by his postwar critics and analysts. Some of his severest detractors, American as well as Allied, were surprised by Ike's decisive command and firm grasp of the mantle of leadership that began at the first moments of the Ardennes fighting. No mere vacillating delegator of authority could have so quickly assessed the scope and magnitude of the German attack, then taken appropriate and immediate actions to defeat it as Eisenhower did. As D. K. R. Crosswell, Smith's biographer wrote, "Opening with portents of disaster, the Battle of the Bulge turned into SHAEF's finest moment."[122] The Allied commander most responsible for that "finest moment" was the Supreme Commander Dwight David Eisenhower.

THE SUCCESSES

Ike's decisive leadership during this battle could not have been as effective as it was, however, were it not for his creation, over the previous months of combat and preparation for combat, of a smoothly functioning, totally integrated Allied headquarters at SHAEF. It was this organization, manned by proven performers and led by Ike, that permitted Eisenhower the flexibility and responsiveness to assess and deal rapidly with the German attack. Despite SHAEF's poor showing during the logistics crisis of the previous summer, when it "proved incapable of responding to rapidly changing conditions,"[123] several more months of combat had significantly improved its responsiveness and effectiveness.

SHAEF was, after all, an evolving organization, created during an ongoing war, with unprecedented operational and strategic responsibilities. The Supreme Command's historian, Forrest Pogue, provides a summary of those headquarters responsibilities:

> In the SHAEF organization one finds the most ambitious effort made in modern times to control the military operations of Allies in the field and deal with political and diplomatic problems bearing on military campaigns. Not only did the Supreme Commander direct the military operations of one British, one Canadian, one French, and five American armies in battle, but he also acted as Theater Commander of more than three million American troops...and was responsible for the planning and executing of civil affairs and military government responsibilities in five liberated countries and Germany. His duties involved acting for the United States and Great Britain on crucial diplomatic issues. Both the Allied governments called on him for recommendations and advice as to the settlement of questions of political, as well as military, import. So great were [Ike's] tasks and so extended [SHAEF's] functions that some historians have asked whether or not such a burden should be imposed on a commander in another war.[124]

By the time the Germans opened their Ardennes

offensive, Ike had created a "truly integrated staff" in which a staff officer could act "for the general Allied good" without regard for the petty national interests of the officer's nation of origin. Pogue asserts that, "in [Ike's] insistence that no one should be able to determine when examining a decision of SHAEF whether it was given by a British or American officer"[125] rested Eisenhower's decisive contribution to Allied victory. In creating this instrument, Ike made it possible for his leadership during the Ardennes crisis to be actually decisive.

That decisiveness was perhaps the predominant characteristic of the Ardennes offensive and had the greatest impact on the outcome of the battle. Ike realized from early reports of the German offensive that it was "no spoiling attack"; this immediate recognition of the scope and strategic implications of the attack caused him to take one of the key actions of the battle—the dispatch of the 7th and 10th Armored Divisions to the threatened area. The timely arrival of these two mobile, powerful units at the two key road junctions of St.-Vith and Bastogne prevented the German attack from swiftly overrunning the towns and allowed the Allies to gain control of the rate of the German advance. Had the decision to dispatch the two units been delayed for even a few hours, it seems unlikely that the crucial road junctions could have been saved from being quickly captured.

It seems clear that if Eisenhower had left the decision to Bradley, Bradley would probably have deferred making it. He erred badly at the beginning of the battle by assuming it was only a limited attack, aimed at disrupting his own offensive to capture the Roer River dams. Ike had to direct him to send the tank divisions to the Ardennes, and in the case of the 10th Armored, he very nearly had to give him a direct order because Bradley, dreading Patton's inevitable rage at having a unit taken from him, tried to demur. Ike's immediate, decisive action here was crucial to the early stopping of the German attack.

Further, Eisenhower's early orders to send the two airborne units to the Ardennes and to completely reorient and reorganize the Allied front from Holland to Switzerland were critical ones whose delay could have helped the Germans reach the Meuse in force. Although the immediate dispatch of all available reserves to the threatened sector was the obvious Allied course of action, it was because of Eisenhower's quick appreciation of the scope of the attack and his decisive, immediate action that total disaster was averted.

An important, often overlooked characteristic of Eisenhower's battle leadership during the Ardennes fighting is the impact of Ike's calm, reasoned, unpanicked response to the crisis. His personal example of steadiness and unflappability affected the entire SHAEF organization as well as his immediate subordinate commanders. His personal leadership was infectious and desperately needed in the early hours of the confusing and overwhelming attack. One need only contrast the positive impact of Ike's personal example with the negative impact of Hodges' panic at First Army headquarters to see the difference. SHAEF reacted superbly to the challenge of the German attack, while First Army headquarters was clearly overwhelmed. Isolated and stunned by the suddenness and power of the offensive, the First Army was very nearly combat ineffective for a time, regaining its bearings only after Montgomery's reorganization. Eisenhower's steady, optimistic personal example set the tone for the leadership climate within his command and created an environment for his commanders to achieve success.

Ike's firm grasp of the overall strategic situation and the quick realization of the significance of the German attack are other important aspects of Eisenhower's battle leadership. His strategic vision was crucial to his rapid response to the assault and was essential in assisting him to determine the correct reactions to take to counter the attack. Indeed, this aspect of his battle leadership is the single prerequisite to all the other demonstrated attributes. Had he not correctly perceived the true nature and scope of the attack, he could not have accurately determined the way to stop it.

That Eisenhower immediately recognized the German offensive for what it was seems assured:

- His statements at the time Strong informed him of the attacks and his subsequent actions confirm that Ike realized immediately that the assault was general and extensive.

- His irritation at and overruling of Bradley's objection to sending the 10th Armored to Bastogne demonstrate that, even at that earliest point in the battle, he correctly perceived the truly serious situation the Allied armies faced.

- His initial dismissal of Patton's dramatic offer on 19 December to attack "in three days with three divisions" shows only that Ike was exasperated with what appeared to be Patton's lack of appreciation of the extensive nature of the German attack, not with the dynamic Army commander's ability to pull off such a maneuver; when Patton promised to quickly follow up the three-division attack with a more robust, corps-sized assault, Ike immediately agreed.

Eisenhower's strategic vision not only recognized the extreme danger his armies then faced, he also clearly saw the unprecedented opportunity presented by the German attack. Throughout the fall Eisenhower had wrestled with the problem of concentrating enough combat power at some place along his extensive front to achieve a significant breakthrough. Indeed, one premise of the "broad front" strategy is that an outnumbered enemy cannot be strong enough everywhere to resist a breakthrough somewhere. The truly significant breakthrough, however, continued to elude him, because nowhere along the Allied line did the German forces seem weak enough to permit such a breach. Even if a breakthrough of the German front could be achieved, the enemy still possessed significant mobile reserves that could be hurled against the flanks of an Allied penetration to limit its success or thwart it completely.

Now, however, the Germans themselves had voluntarily pushed their last significant mobile reserves out from behind the security of the Siegfried Line defenses and into the open.

Moreover, they were creating a salient into the Allied lines and would soon find these last, precious, mobile reserves surrounded on three sides by Allied armies. When the skies cleared, they would also be exposed to punishing air attacks. Such an opportunity seemed almost too good to be true. Eisenhower quickly announced that the theme of the Allied counterattacks would be to trap the German forces in the bulge salient. He wanted no repeats of Argentan-Falaise the previous summer, where thousands of Germans escaped the Allied trap.[126] With Patton already committed to attacking early from the south, Ike needed only to energize Montgomery to launch a coordinated counteroffensive from the north to eliminate the bulk of German mobile reserves remaining on the Western Front.

The discrepancy between Ike's intentions to destroy the German forces in the bulge salient and Montgomery's intentions to merely "see them off" illustrates the fundamental difference in strategic vision between the two commanders on this subject.[127] Although it can (and has) been argued that Monty's "single-thrust" plan to knife quickly through the heart of Germany to Berlin was the correct strategic plan to end the war rapidly, Montgomery's obsession with leading this final campaign obscured his vision of the opportunity presented to the Allies by the German Ardennes offensive. Monty was so preoccupied with gaining approval of his single thrust offensive in the north (and receiving overall command of Allied ground forces) that he treated the Ardennes counteroffensive as a sideshow, to be finished with the least possible effort and expenditure of resources, thereby not detracting from his real priority—the final campaign into Germany. Montgomery's attitude after he assumed command of the northern sector of the Ardennes constantly frustrated Eisenhower's attempts to launch an early, coordinated counteroffensive. When he was finally ready to attack (not until 3 January 1945, 10 days after Patton began his attack in the south),[128] it was too late to trap the mass of German forces. Ike's strategic vision in this case was 20/20, but Monty's myopic view blinded him to the strategic possibilities in the Ardennes.

Ironically, it was Eisenhower's unselfish appointment of

Montgomery as commander of the northern sector of the Ardennes that was the most controversial and most significant manifestation of his overall battle leadership during the Battle of the Bulge. This decision, more than any other action Ike took during the battle (or, indeed during the entire war), proved his greatness as an *allied* commander. It was not only simply the correct course of action for the Supreme Commander to take given the circumstances at that point in the battle, but this transfer of command of the northern sector to Montgomery placed Eisenhower in a category by himself as a genuine "coalition commander." It defined Ike's leadership and revealed the depth of his understanding of the nature of the coalition warfare he was fighting. Nobécourt explains:

> Eisenhower took the decision on his own, merely reporting the matter to the Joint Chiefs of Staff in Washington, without asking for authorisation...The American generals, who considered that they had been betrayed by Eisenhower, failed to take into account the timing of these various steps. They forgot, moreover, that Eisenhower's staff was truly "integrated," and that Whiteley and Strong were merely giving proof that in their view the interests of the Alliance outweighed any national considerations.[129]

Bradley railed against the decision in his memoirs and always insisted the command change was unnecessary. However, his refusal to move his Luxembourg City headquarters to a location better suited to managing and coordinating the defensive phase and subsequent counteroffensive, gave the Supreme Commander no choice. Further, when Bradley admitted to Smith that the command change would make sense "if Monty's were an American command,"[130] he effectively decided the issue in Montgomery's favor.

Forrest Pogue wrote, "Among the many burdens of the SHAEF commander one must list the problem of dealing with some of the field commanders," because of their "misunderstanding...of the nature of the war which was being fought under the Supreme Command."[131] This is exactly the point in the Montgomery-Bradley command change issue. Eisenhower was fighting a true coalition war and made decisions as a coalition commander, not as an American commander of coalition troops. Subsequent arguments on this issue by Ike's critics miss this crucial point, criticizing him solely from an American perspective. These arguments focus completely on what was best for the American commanders involved, or look at the results of the battle only from the American position. By so doing, these critics ignore the first rule of coalition warfare—building and achieving consensus among Allies that will produce a plan "most likely to bring military success"[132] to the Alliance. When Smith briefed Eisenhower on the SHAEF staff recommendation to place Montgomery in command of most of Bradley's forces, the Supreme Commander never hesitated to make the change.

THE FAILURES

Even the best commanders, however, make mistakes in their battle leadership, and Eisenhower is no exception. His leadership during the Ardennes crisis, surely his finest hour as a Supreme Commander, nevertheless must be criticized on at least three major points: his warfighting strategy; his failure to predict the attack; and his inability to close the trap on the bulk of German forces.

WARFIGHTING STRATEGY. Eisenhower's chosen strategy to prosecute the war in France and Germany, called the "broad front" because it featured several major lines of advance all along the Allied line, was not a bad idea. Given the ever-shrinking size of the German manpower pool and the overwhelming superiority of the Allies' industrial production capacity, attacking an inferior enemy everywhere in the (reasonable) expectation that he will break somewhere is a proven war winner.[133] But Eisenhower's plan for prosecuting the war against Germany depended upon a continual superiority in manpower and a constant flow of replacements for the tremendous number of casualties such a strategy produces. He could not attack everywhere and at the same time expect to keep losses to a minimum. The American Army's decision to field only 90 divisions, however, did not provide Eisenhower with the manpower necessary to make the "broad front" strategy work; by fall 1944, the replacement crisis had forced Ike to maintain only a hollow shell defense in the Ardennes. By insisting on a strategy of general assaults all along the Allied line, Eisenhower created the very conditions that made the German Ardennes offensive possible. Because the Combined Chiefs of Staff gave much latitude to the theater commanders in prosecuting their campaigns, the blame is Ike's alone.[134]

FAILURE TO FORESEE. Clearly, Ike and the SHAEF staff were completely surprised by the timing, location, and magnitude of the Ardennes attack. Although Eisenhower and his subordinate commanders were leaving the Ardennes vulnerable to an enemy surprise assault, they never really expected that German forces could mount so powerful and devastating an attack at this stage in the war. The soldiers of Middleton's understrength VIII Corps paid a stiff price in blood for the blunder.[135]

To Eisenhower's great credit, he never attempted to avoid any of the blame for the Ardennes surprise. He accepted all blame for the debacle, saying the fault lay with him and not with his subordinate commanders. Ambrose recorded that:

> Eisenhower accepted the blame for the surprise and he was right to do so, as he failed to read correctly the mind of the enemy. Eisenhower failed to see that Hitler would take desperate chances, and Eisenhower was the man responsible for the weakness of Middleton's [VIII Corps] line in the Ardennes, because he was the one who had insisted on maintaining a general offensive.[136]

Ike confessed his failure to Marshall in a 21 December cable, admitting to the Army Chief of Staff that "all of us, without exception, were astonished" by the offensive.[137] In his postwar memoir, *Crusade in Europe*, Eisenhower categorically removed whatever lingering doubt may have remained about his own responsibility for the surprise and the weakness of the Ardennes defenses by writing:

> The responsibility for maintaining only four divisions on the Ardennes front and for running the risk of a large German penetration in that area was mine. At any

moment from November 1 onward I could have passed to the defensive along the whole front and made our lines absolutely secure from attack while we waited for reinforcements. My basic decision was to continue the offensive to the extreme limit of our ability, and it was this decision that was responsible for the startling successes of the first week of the German December attack...The fighting during the autumn followed the pattern I had personally prescribed. We remained on the offensive and weakened ourselves where necessary to maintain those offensives. This plan gave the German opportunity to launch his attack against a weak portion of our lines. If giving himthat chance is to be condemned by historians, their condemnation should be directed at me alone.[138]

THE OPEN TRAP. Eisenhower's greatest failure during the Battle of the Bulge was, ironically, a consequence of one of his greatest leadership successes—the transfer of command of the northern sector to Montgomery. Ike's inability to energize Montgomery into a timely, coordinated counteroffensive from the north, and thereby maximize Patton's attacks from the south, allowed the Germans to shift their forces within the salient to oppose the Allied counterattacks most effectively. By the time Monty finally got moving, the skillful Germans were in a position to escape successfully.

Despite the early high hopes Eisenhower held for the complete destruction of the German forces within the salient, he had to settle for less than total elimination of Hitler's last mobile reserves in the west. It is clear that Eisenhower intended for Montgomery to attack much earlier than the Field Marshal eventually did, so that the bulk of German forces in the bulge would be trapped. As early as 20 December, Ike sent Monty a cable asking for his "personal appreciation of the situation on the north flank," with intention to "shorten our line and collect a strong reserve for the purpose of destroying the enemy in Belgium."[139] That same day, he sent a message to all three senior commanders (Montgomery, Bradley, and Devers, with information copies to the American, British, and Combined Chiefs of Staff) outlining his intentions regarding the Ardennes situation.

In it, Ike said he intended to take "immediate action to check the enemy's advance and to launch counteroffensives without delay on each side of the enemy salient with all available forces."[140]   For Monty's northern group of armies in particular, he directed that the Field Marshal "launch a counteroffensive against the enemy's salient," requesting the submission of a plan outline "to include strength, direction, and time."[141] It seems impossible that Montgomery did not understand what the Supreme Commander wanted him to do.   Montgomery, the "Master of the Battlefield," would attack in his own time, in his own way.

Part of Eisenhower's problem must undoubtedly be the significant difference between the British and American styles of leadership and command.   Under the British system, subordinate commanders are rarely given the freedom of action that is routine under the American system. While American senior commanders give their subordinate commanders broad, general missions and leave the details of accomplishing those missions to the subordinates, British orders often include the "how" as well as the "what." Surely by this point in the war Eisenhower realized this most basic difference and made allowances for it.   After suffering through Monty's "deliberate" approach in Tunisia and Sicily; at Caen, Argentan-Falaise, and the Scheldt Estuary; and during MARKET-GARDEN (among others), Ike must have known it would require more than just stating his "intentions" to get Monty moving. Yet, even though he had Marshall's unwavering backing and, through him, the backing of the Combined Chiefs of Staff, Eisenhower did not use that leverage until it was too late to make a great difference in the counteroffensive's results.[142]

Eisenhower's refusal to "get tough" with Montgomery until it was too late to influence an early counteroffensive in the north is probably the result of Ike's preferred command style, which was not to bark orders at subordinates and force them to his will.   Although he could make tough decisions when necessary, these tended to be the solitary, agonizing, Supreme Commander decisions, such as pressing on with the Normandy invasion in the teeth of uncertain weather or the decision to remove two-thirds of Bradley's command and give it to an egotistical Briton. Ike preferred to command by reaching general agreement among all the participants, not by fiat.[143] This is probably why he was so successful as a coalition commander, as a successful allied command requires a commander to build consensus carefully, delaying action until all parties are ready to commit. As a coalition commander, Eisenhower was constrained to wait until Montgomery was prepared to take the action Ike wanted. Had he tried to force Monty to do something he was not yet prepared to do, Ike risked jeopardizing the coalition by fomenting "confusion and debate that would...certainly damage the good will and devotion to a common cause"[144] that had so far characterized the Anglo-American coalition. In short, until Montgomery finally backed him completely into a corner and gave him no choice, Eisenhower had to content himself with restating his "intentions" in order to protect the coalition structure he had so carefully built over the previous months.

TRIUMPH OF A COALITION COMMANDER

An assessment today of Eisenhower's battle leadership is quite different from the one some of his postwar critics created. His headquarters, SHAEF, was never a British-dominated, weak organization with the purpose to foil subordinate commanders' quests for decisive action. On the contrary, it seemed a totally integrated, cohesive entity that, by the time of the Ardennes offensive, had evolved on the battlefield into a highly effective organization with wide, unprecedented responsibilities for prosecuting the greatest allied war ever fought. The critics who have asserted otherwise do not understand the demands and requirements of prosecuting coalition warfare. Eisenhower, along with his able Chief of Staff, Smith, and other talented, dedicated subordinate staff officers, was directly responsible for its creation.[145]

Far from being weak and uncertain, from the very beginning of the Battle of the Bulge Eisenhower's battle leadership was characterized by decisiveness and immediate action. He set the example with a calm, optimistic, opportunistic approach to countering the German surprise attack that significantly aided the Allies in putting together a coordinated defense and structuring a massive counteroffensive.

His understanding of the demands of fighting a coalition war places his battle leadership high above that of some of his more highly praised subordinates, especially his diffcult British Army Group Commander, Field Marshal Montgomery.[146] Any comparison of the two commanders' performances in the latter stages of the Ardennes points out, as Weigley has written, "the defects of character that crippled Montgomery as a coalition commander."[147]

Smith's biographer, Crosswell, has provided an excellent wrap-up of Ike's leadership strengths:

> Eisenhower's strength rested not in the traditional realm of strategist or heroic leader but rather in his ability to handle people and avoid divisive problems...Beneath the amiable "Ike" existed the hard-minded operator...He did emerge...as an excellent choice for supreme commander. Indeed, it is difficult to imagine anyone better suited for the role...Eisenhower's virtue as a commander rested in his ability to broker competing national, personal, and strategic sensitivities and susceptibilities. His role as coordinator--more political than military--obliged him to seek compromises rather than provide decisive leadership from above...The one constant in Eisenhower's approach was the effort to preserve Allied harmony...By all accounts he inspired those around him not by force of character but by his simplicity, his commonsense Kansas approach to men and events, and his naturalness and genuine sense of humor...His chief duties involved the preservation of the integrity of the Allied command and the execution of the strategic decisions of the coalition. This required a set of intimate personal skills that gave positive substance to the rhetoric of Allied cooperation and teamwork. These traits Eisenhower possessed in profusion.[148]

Crosswell paints a picture of an outstanding coalition commander, one uniquely suited to exercise Allied command. Eisenhower, when thrust onto the world stage in an unprecedented position, made a complex coalition work effectively. His battle leadership of this coalition during the

Battle of the Bulge is a masterful application of command in a difficult, demanding role. Ike led "the greatest Allied army in history" and won, according to General Marshall, "the greatest victory in the history of warfare." Overcoming "every conceivable difficulty incident to varied national interests and international political problems of unprecedented complications," Eisenhower triumphed.[149] Historian Martin Blumenson, assessing Ike's military prowess, concluded: "America's greatest field commander in World War II, Eisenhower represented more than anyone else the new leadership and the new American role in world history. His achievement was great. His military stature assured."[150]

NOTES

1. David Eisenhower, *Eisenhower: At War, 1943-1945*. (New York: Random House, 1986), 572. David Eisenhower's book about his famous grandfather's military experience as Supreme Allied Commander in Europe is a good one-volume reference on the subject and contains very little obvious bias. When it first appeared, criticism of Eisenhower's war leadership, led mainly by Montgomery's biographer, Nigel Hamilton, was prominently featured in popular publications along with their reviews of the book. Hamilton's pro-Monty bias, however, colors his parochial view of Eisenhower's leadership of the Alliance and lessens the value and impact of his criticism. David Eisenhower's assessment of Ike's wartime leadership is a model of objectivity compared to Hamilton's polemic.

2. Ibid., 574. David Eisenhower explains, "The German plan had banked heavily on speed and maneuver to offset the lack of frontline divisions available and the weight of American air and ground mobility, but ninety-six hours after the attack, it was apparent that what was to have been a quick breakthrough in the Ardennes Forest along prearranged lines to be exploited by armor was evolving into a major battle for control of the Ardennes Forest itself in which the Allied buildup would match the Germans."

3. Arthur Bryant, *Triumph in the West: A History of the War Years Based on the Diaries of Field-Marshal Lord Alan Brooke, Chief of the Imperial General Staff*. (Garden City, NY: Doubleday and Company, 1959), 273. Often Montgomery's co-conspirator in behind-the-scenes political maneuvering against Eisenhower, Brooke resented Ike's command of the Allied Army and probably

jealously coveted the Supreme Command position for himself. Bryant's account is based nearly totally on Brooke's diaries and so reflects the Field Marshal's undisguised contempt for Ike and the Americans.   Brooke used the Ardennes attack to immediately renew his own political offensive to get Monty named overall ground commander.   Once again, his efforts failed (as they would until the end of the war).

4.   Omar N. Bradley, *A Soldier's Story*. (New York: Henry Holt and Company, 1951), 475; D. Eisenhower, *Eisenhower At War*, 570. Bradley and the 12th Army Group staff accused the entire SHAEF organization of having "an acute case of the shakes," not just the Supreme Commander. It seems, however, that Bradley's staff was trying to make SHAEF appear unduly nervous and overly concerned about the 12th Army Group situation after the latter was stung by a curt SHAEF reminder to ensure the enemy captured no intact bridges over the Meuse. Bradley's Chief of Staff complained, "What the devil do they think we're doing, starting back for the beaches?" But SHAEF had discovered that Bradley, despite orders from Ike to the contrary, had allowed large supply dumps to be located in the Ardennes area. SHAEF wanted to make sure there was absolutely no question of its intentions on this critical issue. SHAEF could tolerate no further mistakes from Bradley's army group.

5.   Omar N. Bradley and Clay Blair, *A General's Life: An Autobiography of General of the Army Omar N. Bradley*. (New York: Simon and Schuster, 1983), 368. Finished after Bradley's death, this book spares no criticism of Bradley's contemporaries. It attempts to justify most of Bradley's mistakes by blaming others. Bradley viewed his loss of command of the First and Ninth Armies during the Battle of the Bulge as the worst period of his life, and he never stopped speaking out against it.

6.   Martin Blumenson, *Eisenhower*. (New York: Ballantine Books, 1972), 156-159. This book, written by one of the premiere scholars of American commanders in the European Theater of Operations in World War II, focuses solely on Eisenhower's World War II coalition leadership. Blumenson considers Ike the most successful leader of an Allied coalition in history. The book includes a short biography of Ike's early career and professional development.

7.   Stephen E. Ambrose, *Eisenhower: Volume I, Soldier, General of the Army, President-Elect, 1890-1952*. (New York: Simon and Schuster, 1983), 13, 18. Ambrose is Eisenhower's official biographer and the best source of information on his life

and influence. Ambrose has written several books and articles on Eisenhower's life, career, and impact on the 20th century. He presents Ike's weaknesses along with his strengths, and his works provide a relatively well-balanced picture of Eisenhower's life and influence. Nevertheless, it is clear that Ambrose admires Ike and considers him one of the most important and influential figures of this century. He writes that "only a handful of men--Lenin, Stalin, Hitler, Mao, Churchill, Wilson, Franklin Roosevelt, and perhaps one or two more--had a greater role than [Eisenhower] did in shaping the world of the mid-twentieth century." This chapter relies on Ambrose's books and articles for much of the information on Eisenhower's early life and professional development.

8.   Lawrence Van Gelder, *Ike: A Soldier's Crusade*. (New York: Universal Publishing, 1969), 3-7. Ambrose, *Eisenhower*, 38-43. Eisenhower had made a bargain with his brother Edgar to help put each other through the University of Michigan by alternating years of work and study. Edgar went to school first and, in the meantime, Ike met Midshipman Everett "Swede" Hazlett, a local boy, who convinced him to apply for a "free" education at the Naval Academy. Eisenhower scored second highest on the competitive exam, and the high scorer chose Annapolis, Ike's first choice. He settled for West Point when he discovered that, if he held out another year for Annapolis, he'd be too old.

9.   Ambrose, *Eisenhower*, 43-54. Eisenhower stood a lowly 125th of 164 cadets in his class in "discipline." His demerits were received for such "offenses" as smoking, untidiness, and pulling harmless pranks. He maintained his sense of humor about it all, however, and tried not to take the Academy too seriously. Ike's classmates liked him immensely, and he was genuinely popular.

10.   Van Gelder, *Ike*, 8-10. Ambrose, *Eisenhower*, 43-54. It seems that Eisenhower chose Infantry branch as a result of his bad knee, combined with a relatively low class standing. At his commissioning physical, the Army doctor told him that he could have either Coast Artillery or Infantry, but not Cavalry, since it was considered to be more strenuous than the other branches on his knee. Eisenhower's 1915 USMA class has gone down in West Point lore as "the class the stars fell on," since 59 of its 164 graduates attained general officer rank. These included: Bradley, Stratemeyer, Ryder, McNarney, and Van Fleet.

11.   Ambrose, *Eisenhower*, 56, 60.

12. Van Gelder, *Ike*, 14-18; Ambrose, *Eisenhower*, 60-63. Eisenhower's later difficulties with the leadership of Infantry

branch may have begun during the 1915-18 period when he "pestered the War Department with requests for overseas duty." He even tried for a branch transfer in an effort to get to France.

13. Ambrose, *Eisenhower*, 61. The author points out that, although Eisenhower missed out on an opportunity to get overseas, the Camp Colt Tank Corps assignment was, in reality, a choice one. It involved great responsibility, relatively independent work in a new and exciting type of warfare, promised speedy promotion, and ensured command of thousands of men--all volunteers. Ike was promoted to major in May 1918, and lieutenant colonel that October, only the second member of the class of 1915 to reach that rank.

14. Ibid., 64-65.

15. Ibid., 65-66. Ambrose correctly points out that failing to command soldiers in combat does not necessarily lead to a conclusion that "this fact somehow disqualified him for high command." It certainly helped Ike avoid refighting World War I when he received field command in World War II. Indeed, the best of his chief critic Montgomery's battles, including his famous victory at El Alamein, were more like those of the First World War than those of the Second, and were characterized by an extreme cautiousness, which fit rather uncomfortably in the Blitzkrieg era. The third battle of Ypres (Passchendaele), fought from July to November 1917, cost the British 300,000 casualties for a gain of about 5 miles. It came to epitomize the futile trench warfare mentality of World War I, and the cry, "Passchendaele!" became a rallying-call for the pacifist and peace movements on England's university campuses between the wars. Despite missing out on the combat experience, Eisenhower at least avoided the trauma.

16. Van Gelder, *Ike*, 20; Ambrose, *Eisenhower*, 67.

17. D. K. R. Crosswell, *The Chief of Staff: The Military Career of General Walter Bedell Smith* (New York: Greenwood Press, 1991), 356; Ambrose, *Eisenhower*, 71-72. Eisenhower's article, "A Tank Discussion," appeared in the November 1920 *Infantry Journal*. Patton, whom Eisenhower met and worked with during World War I, published a similar article on "Tanks in Future War" in the May 1920 *Journal*. The articles summarized the two men's conclusions about the importance of the tank in future warfare.

18. Ibid. The official view of the tank was that, since its mission was primarily to assist the infantry in crossing "no man's land," it must not be designed to travel faster than a walking infantryman.

19. Sir Basil Henry Liddell Hart, *The Memoirs of Captain*

Liddell Hart. (London: Cassell and Company, 1965), 64.; General Andre Beaufre, "Liddell Hart and the French Army 1919-1939," *The Theory and Practice of War*, edited by Michael Howard (Bloomington, IN: Indiana University Press, 1965), 139-140; Ambrose, *Eisenhower*, 72. Encouragement to actually "study" the military profession and all of its aspects has not always been forthcoming from the higher levels of leadership of many armies. In Britain, J.F.C. Fuller wrote to Liddell Hart in 1924, "The CIGS [Chief of the Imperial General Staff]...said that no officer on the active list should be allowed to write any military book, as it was detrimental to military discipline!...he had laid it down as a principle that no instructor at the Staff College should be allowed to publish anything." In France in 1935, General Gamelin signed a circular reminding all officers that the High Command alone was qualified to define military doctrine and that officers should refrain on all occasions from advancing any personal views on the question. Eisenhower's experience, while disappointing, is neither surprising nor unique.

20. Van Gelder, *Ike*, 20-21; Ambrose, *Eisenhower*, 73-78; Bradley and Blair, *A General's Life*, 72-73. There can be little doubt that Infantry branch had decided Eisenhower's career was not worth their efforts, and that "choice" assignments should not be wasted on someone with no future. They consistently refused to assign him to career-enhancing positions, and persistently kept him away from the Infantry School--the place Bradley described as the "nursery school for generals" of World War II. Ike was even denied attendance at the Infantry Officer's Advanced Course since, in those days, it was a stepping-stone to the Command and General Staff School.

21. Robert H. Berlin, "Dwight David Eisenhower and the Duties of Generalship," *Military Review* 70 (October 1990): 20; D. Eisenhower, *Eisenhower At War*, 829; Ambrose, *Eisenhower*, 73-79; Berlin, "Duties of Generalship," 20. MG Fox Conner had been Pershing's Operations Officer in World War I and was acknowledged as "the brains of the AEF [American Expeditionary Force]." Patton, who had met Conner in France, introduced him to Eisenhower in 1920. It was chiefly through Conner that Ike later became known to Pershing and Marshall. He became Eisenhower's friend and true mentor, and "saved" the younger officer from a mediocre career of petty assignments. Eisenhower served as Conner's Brigade Executive Officer in the 20th Infantry Brigade in Panama, 1922-24. David Eisenhower writes that Conner "impressed upon Eisenhower the idea of fighting in

cooperation with allies, which he believed the next war would necessitate." Berlin further emphasizes this point by writing, "The man who was reading books about coalition warfare in Panama in 1922 would be organizing and conducting coalition warfare 20 years hence."

22. Mark C. Bender, *Watershed at Leavenworth. Dwight D. Eisenhower and the Command and General Staff College.* (Fort Leavenworth, KS: US Army Command and General Staff College, 1990), 37-41; Ambrose, *Eisenhower*, 79-81. Conner arranged for Eisenhower's appointment to the Command and General Staff School by engineering his assignment to recruiting duty in Colorado with the Adjutant General's branch. Ike spent the first part of 1925 as a recruiter, biding his time while waiting for his orders to Leavenworth. Infantry Branch continued to refuse to further Ike's career in any way, and the Chief of Infantry's Aide-de-camp wrote Eisenhower to warn him, "You will probably fail" the course at Leavenworth.

23. Ambrose, *Eisenhower*, 82-91. The assignment to Washington, DC, to work under General Pershing, who was head of the Battle Monuments Commission, was arranged by Fox Conner. During this assignment, Ike's favorable work became known to then Colonel George C. Marshall. Eisenhower's reward for good service to Pershing was a seat at the Army War College class of 1928. Upon graduation, he served a year in France, revising the Battle Monuments Guidebook he had written for Pershing. Ike returned to Washington, DC, in November 1929, for assignment to the War Department staff. He was responsible for preparing plans for American industrial mobilization in the event of war. Ambrose writes that, given the times, "To most industrialists, Eisenhower's talk about cooperation between America's factories and the War Department in a program of unlimited production for war seemed unreal." A few years later, Ike used his experience in this position to good effect and became a "faculty graduate" of the Army Industrial College.

24. Weigley, *History of the U.S. Army*, 421-423.

25. Ambrose, *Eisenhower*, 93; Weigley, *History of the U.S. Army*, 421-422. MacArthur's claim that Eisenhower "is the best officer in the Army" was high praise, but Marshall had received his own share of such superlatives during his career. In 1916, one of Marshall's commanders even went so far as to write on his efficiency report that he "would prefer to serve *under*" Marshall's command--a remarkable statement, even among the inflated rhetoric found in fitness reports!

26. Douglas MacArthur, *Reminiscences* (New York: McGraw-Hill, 1964), 315; Ambrose, *Eisenhower*, 93-101. MacArthur says little about his association with Eisenhower in his autobiography, but mentions, somewhat condescendingly that, "I have always felt for him something akin to the affection of an older man for a younger brother. His amazingly successful career has filled me with pride and admiration."

27. MacArthur, *Reminiscences*, 94-97; Ambrose, *Eisenhower*, 90-95. The so-called Bonus March was a political event in summer 1932, in which a crowd of unemployed World War I veterans (estimated at about 17,000) marched on Washington, DC, demanding Congress grant them an immediate cash bonus for their wartime service. They established a shanty town camp in Anacostia, near the Capitol, and conducted huge demonstrations. On 28 July 1932, MacArthur, then Army Chief of Staff, was ordered to disperse the marchers. Although he did it with very little damage and few casualties, it was a public relations disaster, making MacArthur and the Army appear to be waging brutal war on the nearly defenseless men. MacArthur called it the "most poignant episode" of his tour as Chief of Staff and complained that he was unfairly treated in the press, which printed "the most extravagant distortions of what had occurred." Typically, MacArthur seems to have been his own worst enemy in this episode, since his strutting, martinet-like performance for the newsreel cameras probably did more than any written account to tarnish his image.

28. Some of these incidents include the Darlan controversy (November 1942); an initial coverup of Patton's slapping incidents (August 1943); debate over who should liberate Paris (August 1944); the Strasbourg incident (January 1945); and the decision to halt at the Elbe River (April 1945). In each of these, Eisenhower claimed that "military necessity" overrode any "political considerations."

29. Ambrose, *Eisenhower*, 101-119. Ambrose writes that "Nothing he [Eisenhower] did there met any of the criteria he himself had set down for a happy life." He goes on to describe some of the frustrations Eisenhower endured: "Eisenhower was more or less miserable. His relations with MacArthur became steadily more difficult. This deterioration was the result of two factors, their respective positions vis-à-vis each other and to the Philippine government, and their temperaments. Eisenhower dealt in details, MacArthur in generalities. Eisenhower worked with Quezon on a daily basis, while MacArthur stayed aloof...Where the

practical Eisenhower saw problems, the visionary MacArthur saw possibilities. To Eisenhower, the Philippine General Staff was beset by rank-consciousness, backbiting, inefficiency, and corruption. To MacArthur, it was composed of loyal, intelligent men who were well on their way to learning how to run an Army."

30. Ibid., 106-107, 109. Eisenhower continually professed to avoid the "political" aspects of military service throughout his career and publicly stated his aversion to "playing politics." However, examination of his Philippine service shows a shrewd compromiser who appreciated the value of an "indirect approach" to problemsolving. If politics can be defined as "the art of compromise," then Eisenhower, despite his protestations, was more adept at its practice than he would like to admit.

31. Ibid., 116-119.

32. Russell F. Weigley, *Eisenhower's Lieutenants: The Campaigns of France and Germany 1944-1945*. (Bloomington, IN: Indiana University Press, 1981), 8-28; Weigley, *History of the U.S. Army*, 421-450; Berlin, "Duties of Generalship," 24; Ambrose, *Eisenhower*, 120. Between 1939 and 1942, the American Army expanded from about 200,000 soldiers to over 5,000,000, was completely reorganized and restructured, and began operations on a global scale. Ike described his excited and positive state of mind about taking part in this unprecedented expansion in a letter to Omar Bradley in July 1940. Eisenhower was popular with his soldiers and made a point of sharing their hardships. He seems to have been an effective and outstanding commander. His personal leadership traits appear to mirror closely those he admired in his subordinates, for he could have been describing himself when he wrote about his comrade, Leonard T. Gerow (according to Berlin) that he was "a good fighter, balanced, calm, excellent planner, always optimistic, selfless, a leader."

33. Blumenson, *Eisenhower*, 16; Ambrose, *Eisenhower*, 127. Eisenhower's series of Chief of Staff positions (3rd Infantry Division, IX Corps, and Third Army) were the result of his superiors' recognition of his exceptional ability as an organizer, planner, and coordinator who got the job done. He was requested, by name, for each of these positions.

34. Richard M. Ketchum, "Warming Up On the Sidelines For World War II," *Smithsonian* 22 (September 1991): 88-103; Christopher R. Gabel, "The 1941 Maneuvers," *Military Review* 71 (August 1991): 88-89; Ambrose, *Eisenhower*, 128-131. The maneuvers run on the eve of World War II were an important proving ground for some of the American Army leaders who would

rise to prominence during the war, such as Eisenhower and Patton. However, as Gabel points out, only 11 of the 42 division, corps, and Army commanders who led in the maneuvers subsequently commanded in combat.

35. Forrest C. Pogue, *The United States Army in World War II. European Theater of Operations: The Supreme Command.* (Washington, DC: Office of the Chief of Military History/GPO, 1954), 33-34; Van Gelder, *Ike*, 24; Blumenson, *Eisenhower*, 16; Ambrose, *Eisenhower*, 131-133. Pogue, the Supreme Command's official historian, relates that Ike's call to the War Plans Division was "in part for his work [Louisiana Maneuvers], but undoubtedly more because of his knowledge of the Philippines," since his position was that of Deputy Chief for the Pacific and Far East.

36. Pogue, *Supreme Command*, 33-34; Ambrose, *Eisenhower*, 133-136. Marshall tested the newly arrived Eisenhower on his first afternoon in town (on Sunday, 14 December 1941), when he called him in and requested that Ike provide him with his assessment of a "general line of action" for the Pacific war. Eisenhower requested "a few hours" to develop his answer and was sent off to work on a reply. At dusk that evening, he presented Marshall with a hand-typed sheet of paper outlining a Pacific strategy. Marshall agreed with Eisenhower's proposed strategy and sent him back to work to implement it. Ambrose characterizes this incident as Marshall's test of Eisenhower's ability to function successfully under the pressures of war. Ike passed the test. Today, Ike's original paper, now in a simple frame, hangs in the Pentagon office of the Army's Director of Strategy, Plans, and Policy.

37. Ambrose, *Eisenhower*, 135-136.

38. Ibid.

39. Ibid., 146-147. Ike's ability to work closely with British officers seemed remarkable to Marshall for, according to Ambrose, "Many American officers found their British opposite numbers to be insufferable not only in their arrogance but their timidity about striking the enemy." Eisenhower, who shared many of these feelings, was able to keep them hidden and confined to his diary. Outwardly, he always projected a spirit of allied cooperation and partnership.

40. Chester Wilmot, *The Struggle for Europe.* (New York: Harper and Brothers, 1952), 116; Ambrose, *Eisenhower*, 152. Wilmot praises Eisenhower's "immediate and continuous loyalty to the concept of unity," and claimed "nobody else revealed Eisenhower's remarkable capacity for integrating the efforts of

different allies and rival services, and for creating harmony between individuals with varied backgrounds and temperaments."

41. Ambrose, *Eisenhower*, 151-152; Pogue, *Supreme Command*, 34. Ambrose points out that the British High Command was not unanimous in its high regard for Eisenhower. Most notably, the Chief of the Imperial General Staff, Field Marshal Alan Brooke, maintained a "deep-seated prejudice against Americans," and "put Eisenhower down as an affable type with no strategic sense or command ability." Brooke, who probably coveted the Supreme Commandership for himself, continued to give Eisenhower only grudging, backhanded compliments in his diary, even after Ike proved extremely successful in the command. For his part, Eisenhower, who thought it was better not to mention someone if nothing good could be said of them, "seldom mentioned Brooke."

42. Maurice Matloff, *The United States Army in World War II. The War Department: Strategic Planning for Coalition Warfare, 1943-1944.* (Washington, DC: Office of the Chief of Military History/US Government Printing Office, 1953), 10-17; Ambrose, *Eisenhower*, 180-181. Although both Eisenhower and Marshall were disappointed that North Africa (TORCH) was chosen over the cross-channel invasion of France (BOLERO-ROUNDUP), both Roosevelt and Churchill were in agreement in the decision-- Roosevelt, because he insisted on getting US troops into combat in 1942; and Churchill, because he considered an early attack on France too risky. There were other practical factors that favored the Mediterranean action, including limited shipping and landing craft, small number of American troops in theater, and the need to free Mediterranean sea lanes.

43. Blumenson, *Eisenhower*, 19; Ambrose, *Eisenhower*, 186-187; Pogue, *Supreme Command*, 42.

44. Dwight D. Eisenhower, "Command in War." Speech, National War College, Fort McNair, Washington, DC, 30 October 1950; Blumenson, *Eisenhower*, 19-20. In his speech on command to the National War College, General of the Army Eisenhower emphasized that, "Allied commands depend on mutual confidence...by development of common understanding of the problems, by approaching these things on the widest possible basis with respect for each other's opinions, and above all, through the development of friendships, this confidence is gained...in Allied Staffs." Epitomizing the "allied unity" attitude at Ike's headquarters is the oft-repeated story that an American could call a British officer an "S.O.B.," provided he didn't refer to him as a *"British* S.O.B."

45. Forrest C. Pogue, "The Supreme Allied Command in Northwest Europe, 1944-45," *Essays in History and International Relations*, edited by Dwight E. Lee and George McReynolds (Worcester, MA: Clark University Press, 1949), 175.

46. Martin Blumenson, *Kasserine Pass* (New York: Jove Books, 1983) 303-320. The Battle of Kasserine Pass (14-22 February 1943) was actually the culmination of a series of actions centering around critical mountain passes in Tunisia.

47. Martin Blumenson and James L. Stokesbury, *Masters of the Art of Command* (Boston: Houghton Mifflin, 1975), 267-286; Ambrose, *Supreme Commander*, 166-184; Blumenson, *Kasserine Pass*, 83-87, 121-123.

48. Ambrose, *Supreme Commander*, 175-178. The fact that Rommel had to withdraw, and since the final victory in North Africa for the Allies seemed inevitable, Eisenhower suffered no permanent damage to his position as Commander in Chief. He turned the reverses to his own troops' advantage by capitalizing on their newfound realization that victory would have to be won the hard way. Ike directed that training would never stop, even for units in the line, and circulated the lessons of this first combat throughout US forces.

49. Ibid., 175-176, 341. Ambrose relates that Eisenhower told Patton upon assuming command of the fired Fredendall's II Corps that "you must not retain for one instant any man in a responsible position where you have become doubtful of his ability to do the job." Ambrose asserts that this attitude of quickly relieving those who can't measure up "was the great lesson of Kasserine Pass."

50. Ambrose, *Supreme Commander*, 168-169, 174.

51. Alfred D. Chandler et al., Editor, *The Papers of Dwight David Eisenhower, The War Years (Volumes I-V)*. (Baltimore: Johns Hopkins Press, 1970), 2:1353; Ambrose, *Supreme Commander*, 167-168. Eisenhower especially respected Bradley for this trait, later writing that he "never caused one moment of worry [and has] the respect of all associates, including the British officers."

52. Blumenson, *Eisenhower*, 48. Blumenson points out that this bag of German prisoners eclipsed even the staggering total the Russians captured at Stalingrad the same month. This undoubtedly helped Roosevelt and Churchill in their political jousting with Stalin.

53. Matloff, *Coalition Warfare*, 68-76, 106-145; Ambrose, *Supreme Commander*, 223-226; Berlin, "Duties of Generalship," 20. Berlin highlights Eisenhower's characteristic concern with Allied

cooperation rather than tactical details by writing, "Throughout these campaigns [Sicily and Italy], Eisenhower was more concerned with furthering cooperation with the British than operational decisions, which he left to the ground commanders."

54. Pogue, *Supreme Command*, 34-35. Pogue makes another perceptive observation of Eisenhower's abilities when he writes, "General Eisenhower's conciliatory attitude was at times misleading. While genial in his approach, he could be extremely stern if the occasion demanded. His temper...was sometimes explosive and his reprimands could be blistering. Those traits were balanced by the gift of enormous patience."

55. Ambrose, *Eisenhower*, 237. The British politician to whom Eisenhower made his "our" victory remark was Harold Macmillan, a future Prime Minister.

56. Dwight D. Eisenhower, *Crusade in Europe*. (Garden City, NY: Doubleday, 1948), 206-208; Ambrose, *Eisenhower*, 271.

57. Pogue, *Supreme Command*, 53-55. The Combined Chiefs of Staff directive, dated 12 February 1944, was an 8-paragraph document that also contained general information on command, logistics, coordination, and relationships with other United Nations forces and Allied governments.

58. Gordon A. Harrison, *The United States Army in World War II. European Theater of Operations: Cross-Channel Attack*. (Washington, DC: Office of the Chief of Military History/GPO, 1951), 269-321; Blumenson, *Eisenhower*, 86-90.

59. Pogue, *Supreme Command*, 175.

60. Ibid.

61. Bernard Law Montgomery, *The Memoirs of Field-Marshal the Viscount Montgomery of Alamein, K.G.* (New York: Signet Books, 1958), 289-299; John Keegan, *Six Armies in Normandy: From D-Day to the Liberation of Paris*. (New York: Penguin Books, 1982), 55-60. Montgomery wrote in his memoirs "It will be manifest to the reader that from 1st September 1944 onwards I was not satisfied that we had a satisfactory organisation for command or operational control." He harped on this point until forced to drop the subject in the spring of 1945. By then, the end of the war was nearly reached, making the question mostly academic.

62. Eisenhower, *Crusade in Europe*, 305. Ike referred to Monty's plan as a "pencil-like thrust" to emphasize its vulnerability.

63. Martin Van Creveld, *Supplying War: Logistics from Wallenstein to Patton*. (New York: Cambridge University Press,

1977), 224-230. Van Creveld calculates that Montgomery's "40 divisions" would, realistically, have been quickly reduced to about 18 when all logistical and operational requirements were considered. He weighs all the many factors in the "Broad Front-Narrow Front" strategy question and concludes, "In the final account, the question as to whether Montgomery's plan presented a real alternative to Eisenhower's strategy must be answered in the negative."

64. Walter Bedell Smith, *Eisenhower's Six Great Decisions (Europe 1944-1945)*. (New York: Longmans, Green and Company, 1956), 158-159.

65. Ambrose, *Eisenhower*, 375.   Francis de Guingand, Montgomery's Chief of Staff, was the one who warned his boss that Ike had prepared a cable. De Guingand pleaded with Eisenhower not to send it until he had talked with Montgomery.   Monty quickly realized the impact of such a message, that neither Brooke nor Churchill would step in to save him and immediately sent Ike a conciliatory note, dropping the ground command question.

66. J.D. Morelock, "General Jacob L. Devers: Commonsense Commander," *Forward Observer*, 3 (December 1988): 10.

67. Weigley, *Eisenhower's Lieutenants*, 552-554. It seems clear that Eisenhower had sadly misjudged the strength of French feelings in this incident, despite the fact that Devers had advised him of the lack of necessity for any withdrawal.   Eisenhower, however, was never close to Devers, and second-guessed him on nearly every point. Devers, who worked daily with the fractious French allies, had an excellent appreciation of all the factors involved and had warned Eisenhower of the consequences of an attempt to withdraw. Ike simply ignored Devers' advice to his own misfortune.

68. Ambrose, *Eisenhower*, 377-378.   Characteristically, Ike complained that he had to give in to the "political" aspects of what should be a straightforward "military" issue.

69. Blumenson, *Eisenhower*, 155-156.   Blumenson calls Eisenhower's "management of the complex establishment that won the war in northwestern Europe" his "superb accomplishment in the Second World War," including, as it did, the full spectrum of military, political, and diplomatic responsibilities.   Blumenson concluded that no one else could have done it as well (including Eisenhower's old boss, MacArthur).

70. Ambrose, *Eisenhower*, 149-154, 216-237; Pogue, *Supreme Command*, 34-37.

71. Churchill remained an unflagging Eisenhower proponent

throughout the war and never failed to support the Supreme Commander's decisions (despite his continual meddling in the military realm). In fact, Churchill was more supportive of the American general than Roosevelt was during the Darlan controversy in the early days of the North African campaign.

72. Blumenson and Stokesbury, *Masters of the Art of Command*, 287-303.

73. Weigley, *Eisenhower's Lieutenants*, 459.

74. Ambrose, *Supreme Commander*, 552; Chandler et al., *Eisenhower Papers*, 4:2350. Ike wrote, "I still have nine days, and while it seems almost certain that you will have an extra five pounds for Christmas, you will not get it until that day."

75. Weigley, *Eisenhower's Lieutenants*, 461-464. Weigley's book is the best reference on this subject, as the inappropriateness of American strategy is one of his book's theses. His major premise, that the American command's inability to reconcile the US Army's dual, competing legacies--mobility and attrition warfare--cites the 90-division gamble as one of his central proofs.

76. US Department of the Army, 12th Army Group, *G-1 Section, 12th Army Group Report of Operations*, 1948, 135-136; Bradley and Blair, *A General's Life*, 354. On the day the German attack began, the 12th Army Group was short 30,000 replacements, nearly 20,000 of them infantrymen. This chronic shortage in units already in the theater was exacerbated by the lack of fresh divisions arriving from the States. There were no more units.

77. Despite the personnel shortages in Great Britain, however, Churchill announced a callup of an additional 250,000 men during the Ardennes crisis. This controversial action threatened to strip some of Britain's critical war industries of their last pool of trained manpower. By the time any of these men could be inducted, trained, and sent to the battlefront, the war would be over.

78. Weigley, *Eisenhower's Lieutenants*, 464.

79. Ibid., 455.

80. Ambrose, *Supreme Command*, 556; Bradley and Blair, *A General's Life*, 351-356. Referring to the entire question of predicting the German attack and assessing its significance, Bradley wrote that he (and others) "were all wrong, of course-- tragically and stupidly wrong."

81. Bradley and Blair, *A General's Life*, 356.

82. Weigley, *Eisenhower's Lieutenants*, 457; Eisenhower, *Crusade in Europe*, 342. Ike wrote that, "I was immediately convinced that this was no local attack; it was not logical for the

enemy to attempt merely a minor offensive in the Ardennes, unless of course it should be a feint to attract our attention while he launched a major effort elsewhere. This possibility was ruled out...other portions of [our] front...were so strong that the Germans could not hope to attack successfully...Moreover, we knew...German troop strength in the Ardennes area had been gradually increasing."

83. Ambrose, *Supreme Commander*, 556.

84. Weigley, *Eisenhower's Lieutenants*, 458; Bradley and Blair, *A General's Life*, 356. Bradley admits that "Ike sensed it [the importance of the attack] before I did," but characterizes the dispatching of the two armored divisions with the words, "urged on by Ike...I made telephone calls...to order the 10th Armored and the 7th Armored" to move. Bradley places the onus on Patton for "demurring," but other accounts support Bradley's reluctance to confront Patton about the 10th Armored move.

85. Peter Paret and Michael Howard (trans.), Karl von Clausewitz, *On War*. (Princeton: University Press, 1976), 119-121; Crosswell, *Chief of Staff*. Crosswell attributes the commonality of the staff and school experiences (especially Leavenworth's Command and Staff School) as ensuring that a common doctrine and response would be understood and applied. Clausewitz cautions, however, that, although everything in war is simple, the simplest things are difficult to accomplish.

86. D. Eisenhower, *Eisenhower At War*, 558; Ambrose, *Supreme Commander*, 555-557.

87. Weigley, *Eisenhower's Lieutenants*, 480-484; Eisenhower, *Eisenhower At War*, 562-565; Eisenhower, *Crusade in Europe*, 344; Ambrose, *Supreme Commander*, 556-558; Bradley and Blair, *A General's Life*, 357. After the defense of Bastogne became iconized as the quintessential American defensive stand during the Battle of the Bulge, everyone who had anything to do with getting the 101st Airborne to the vital crossroads wanted to take the credit for sending it there. In fact, it was only natural that units sent to reinforce the Ardennes should gravitate to the two major road junctions in the area--Bastogne and St.-Vith. Since Bastogne was also the headquarters of MG Middleton's VIII Corps, it required no great amount of military genius or special prescience to determine reinforcing units should be directed there. Somewhat disgusted by the scurry to grab the glory for sending the 101st to Bastogne, Middleton wrote, "One did not have to be a genius to know that St.-Vith and Bastogne were critical points during the Battle of the Bulge." All one had to do, Middleton asserted, was to look at a

map.

88. Ambrose, *Supreme Commander*, 556.

89. Ibid., 557.

90. Chandler et al., *Eisenhower Papers*, 4:2356.

91. D. Eisenhower, *Eisenhower At War*, 567.

92. Weigley, *Eisenhower's Lieutenants*, 499-501; D. Eisenhower, *Eisenhower At War*, 567; Ambrose, *Supreme Commander*, 367.

93. Chandler et al., *Eisenhower Papers*, 4:2355; Ambrose, *Supreme Commander*, 556.

94. Ambrose, *Supreme Commander*, 558.

95. Blumenson, *Patton*, 247; Ambrose, *Supreme Commander*, 558.

96. D. Eisenhower, *Eisenhower At War*, 567. David Eisenhower, writing about his grandfather's wartime leadership, noted: "This set the tone as the group got down to business."

97. Blumenson, *Patton*, 247.

98. Hugh Cole, *The United States Army in World War II. European Theater of Operations: Ardennes, The Battle of the Bulge.* (Washington, DC: Office of the Chief of Military History/GPO, 1965), 486-488; Bradley and Blair, *A General's Life*, 359.

99. Weigley, *Eisenhower's Lieutenants*, 499-501. Weigley explains, "The discrepancy between Patton's and Eisenhower's intentions should also be noted. Eisenhower had asked how soon Patton could attack with six divisions. Patton responded that he could attack within a mere three days with three divisions. Eisenhower doubted that three divisions could strike a hard enough blow and expressed a preference for less speed but greater force: 'I did not want him [Patton] to start until he was in sufficient force so that, once committed, he could continue gradually to crush in the southern flank of the developing salient.'"

100. Nobécourt, *Last Gamble*, 206.

101. Bradley and Blair, *A General's Life*, 357. Bradley insisted the location of his headquarters was not a problem for him, and that he could easily exercise command of his armies in the north. He thought the most important point was to stand fast in his headquarters in Luxembourg City to avoid a panicked response. Yet, with no direct supervision by Bradley or any of his staff forthcoming, panic was very nearly the situation in Hodges' First Army headquarters (which retreated twice during the battle).

102. Ambrose, *Supreme Commander*, 563; Crosswell, *Chief of Staff*, 286; D. Eisenhower, *Eisenhower At War*, 573; Weigley, *Eisenhower's Lieutenants*, 503-506. David Eisenhower points out

that "Eisenhower's timely decision removed all command barriers to containing and defeating the German counteroffensive. In a single stroke he eliminated Bradley's dual mission of containing the Germans in the north and attacking from the south. Montgomery was now able to release Horrock's XXX Corps to man the Meuse between Namur and Dinant, which assured Hodges of British support in Belgium and the British of American support in Holland."

103. Wilmot, *The Struggle for Europe*, 116. Written in the early days of the Cold War, pro-British Australian Chester Wilmot sets out "to explain how the present situation came about; how and why the Western Allies, while gaining military victory, suffered political defeat." In so doing, he fired some of the first salvoes in the postwar transatlantic sniping between the Allied commanders. A Montgomery partisan, he faults American political naivete for the postwar European situation vis-à-vis the Soviet Union. It is, therefore, a significant compliment when he heaps heavy praise on Eisenhower, an American, as an outstanding Allied commander.

104. D. Eisenhower, *Eisenhower At War*, 570.

105. Weigley, *Eisenhower's Lieutenants*, 504-505;   D. Eisenhower, *Eisenhower At War*, 572-573; Ambrose, *Supreme Commander*, 562-563; Crosswell, *Chief of Staff*, 286-287.

106. Ambrose, *Eisenhower*, 368-369; D. Eisenhower, *Eisenhower At War*, 572.

107. D. Eisenhower, *Eisenhower At War*, 572.

108. Ibid.

109. Montgomery, *Memoirs*, 281-289; Cole, *Ardennes*, 411-413. Despite the much-publicized anger of several of the top American commanders (such as Bradley and Patton) at Montgomery's receiving command in the north, many lower level US commanders were delighted to hear the Field Marshal was taking charge of the confusing situation in First Army area. Among the latter were Brigadier General Robert Hasbrouck, commander of the 7th Armored Division, and Brigadier General Bruce C. Clarke, tenaciously defending St.-Vith.

110. Bradley and Blair, *A General's Life*, 357-363. Bradley later insisted "I had been in closest telephone conversation with Hodges and Simpson. As a precaution, we were already laying auxiliary circuits west of the Meuse."

111. Weigley, *Eisenhower's Lieutenants*, 3589; Bradley and Blair, *A General's Life*, 363.

112. D. Eisenhower, *Eisenhower At War*, 572; Weigley, *Eisenhower's Lieutenants*. 500-501.

113. Ambrose, *Eisenhower*, 367; Weigley, *Eisenhower's Lieutenants*, 499-501; D. Eisenhower, *Eisenhower At War*, 568-569.

114. Cole, *Ardennes*, 445-508.

115. D. Eisenhower, *Eisenhower At War*, 578; Weigley, *Eisenhower's Lieutenants*, 546-547.

116. D. Eisenhower, *Eisenhower At War*, 577.

117. Weigley, *Eisenhower's Lieutenants*, 541.

118. Ibid., 544-546.

119. Ibid., 566. Weigley quotes Patton's words at a 1 January 1945 press conference: "If you get a monkey in a jungle hanging by his tail, it is easier to get him by cutting his tail than kicking him in the face."

120. Eisenhower, *Crusade in Europe*, 365; Ambrose, *Supreme Commander*, 576.

121. D. Eisenhower, *Eisenhower At War*, 622; Weigley, *Eisenhower's Lieutenants*, 575-577.

122. Crosswell, *Chief of Staff*, 301.

123. Ibid.

124. Pogue, "Supreme Command," 192.

125. Ibid.

126. Weigley, *Eisenhower's Lieutenants*, 201-209. Bradley's aide, Major Chet Hansen recorded that the 12th Army Group Commander felt that "had he forced the issue [at Falaise] and insisted on the advance of our troops, our bag at Falaise might have been considerably more than it was."

127. Montgomery, *Memoirs*, 285-289; Weigley, *Eisenhower's Lieutenants*, 545.

128. Weigley, *Eisenhower's Lieutenants*, 556-558.

129. Nobécourt, *Last Gamble*, 215.

130. Crosswell, *Chief of Staff*, 286; Weigley, *Eisenhower's Lieutenants*, 504; Ambrose, *Supreme Commander*, 563; Bradley and Blair, *A General's Life*, 363-364.

131. Pogue, "Supreme Command," 188-189.

132. Ibid.

133. Weigley, *Eisenhower's Lieutenants*, 463-464. Weigley points out that despite the (primarily British) criticism that Ike's strategy was only an emulation of the old Lincoln-Grant strategy of the American Civil War, that strategy did, in fact, produce a victory--that is, it worked.

134. Pogue, "Supreme Command," 172-173.

135. Weigley, *Eisenhower's Lieutenants*, 461-463.

136. Ambrose, *Eisenhower*, 365-366.

137. Chandler et al., *Eisenhower Papers*, 4:2368; Ambrose,

Eisenhower, 369.

138. Eisenhower, *Crusade in Europe*, 340-341.

139. Chandler et al., *Eisenhower Papers*, 4:2361.

140. Ibid., 4:2363-2365.

141. Ibid.

142. Weigley, *Eisenhower's Lieutenants*, 544. Pushed to the limit by Monty's badgering for sole command of Allied ground forces during the Ardennes offensive, Ike finally prepared a "him or me" cable to send to the Combined Chiefs. When De Guingand, Monty's capable and popular Chief of Staff read the cable, he convinced Ike not to send it until he'd had a chance to get Montgomery to change his ways. The Field Marshal, finally realizing he'd pushed the genial Supreme Commander past his breaking point, sent a chastened note to Ike asking him to tear up his previous letter and promising to carry out his orders. It saved Monty's job.

143. Crosswell, *Chief of Staff*, 294-301. Crosswell's book is an excellent analysis of the relationship between Eisenhower and his acerbic Chief of Staff Smith. He asserts that, because of the position Ike was in as an Allied commander, he was required to reach compromises, build consensus, and smooth ruffled feathers; but Ike needed someone like Smith to "do the dirty work for him." Crosswell writes, "Since Eisenhower always had 'to be the nice guy.' Smith played the villain." Crosswell points out that, "In achieving his various ends, Eisenhower worked through others, and the individual most responsible for his success was Smith."

144. Weigley, *Eisenhower's Lieutenants*, 543.

145. The overriding requirement for maintaining a successful coalition is building consensus, not self-promotion of one's countrymen at the expense of the Allies.

146. D. Eisenhower, *Eisenhower At War*, 595-609.

147. Weigley, *Eisenhower's Lieutenants*, 565.

148. Crosswell, *Chief of Staff*, 294-296.

149. Pogue, *Supreme Command*, 55; Ambrose, *Eisenhower*, 408. Marshall gave Eisenhower these accolades in a congratulatory message at the end of the war in Europe. Ambrose observes that, "it was the highest possible praise from the best possible source. It had been earned."

150. Blumenson and Stokesbury, *Masters of Command*, 303.

3. Bradley and the 12th Army Group

General Omar N. Bradley is remembered chiefly as the modest, steady, country boy who suddenly rose to fame and glory through the fates and fortunes of World War II. Given the name "the soldier's general" by popular war correspondent Ernie Pyle,[1] his image is that of the quiet but effective commander who made his reputation on sure and efficient performance instead of flashy brilliance. His public persona, popularized by correspondents like Pyle, portrayed a general who inspired great feelings of confidence among the American soldiers he commanded and promoted the opinion that his thorough, no-nonsense approach to the conduct of the great campaigns of the European Theater of Operations would not be based on needlessly expending his soldiers' lives.

Noted as a loyal team player, Bradley stood up for his subordinates when necessary, but he could quickly relieve a corps or division commander if the officer in question was hesitant, weak, or ill disciplined. Bradley's victories were, for the most part, not achieved through brilliant strokes of military genius. Instead, his success seemed generated by his common sense and careful attention to detail that sought to capitalize on firepower and mobility rather than manpower. Bradley was field commander for the largest concentration of American soldiers in history (1,300,000),[2] and his steady leadership is cited as helping to seal ultimate victory.

Yet during the Ardennes crisis, at the moment when such steady and reliable leadership would seem to be needed most, Eisenhower removed the Ninth and most of the First US Armies from Bradley's command. Worse still for Bradley, his successor in command of these units was Field Marshal Montgomery, the egotistical Briton whom he despised. The Battle of the Bulge thus became for Bradley "the darkest of times" of his entire career, and he later reported that, "Never in my life had I been so enraged and so utterly exasperated."[3]

What assessment, then, should history make of Bradley's leadership during this critical time? Patton recorded in his diary that Bradley, as a commander, was a "nothing" who was "insufferably orthodox, predictable, and cautious."[4] Eisenhower, however, went on record to Marshall as saying, "I consider Bradley the greatest battle-line commander I have met in this war."[5] It is worth examining Bradley's demonstrated battle leadership in the Ardennes offensive and assessing its impact on the conduct of the battle.

BRADLEY'S CAREER

Bradley cites his desire for intellectual fulfillment as his father's greatest legacy, along with a deep appreciation for justice, integrity, sobriety and patriotism.[6] To this end, he had a strong desire to complete his education, even through college,[7] and began saving his money to enter the University of Missouri. However, being desperately poor, Bradley applied for admission to the United States Military Academy, because it offered the opportunity for a paid education. After successfully completing the entrance examinations, he entered the Military Academy on 1 August 1911.[8]

Bradley managed to avoid his classmate Eisenhower's penchant for accumulating demerits, so his standing in "discipline" was significantly higher. He shared Ike's love of sports, however, becoming a star on the West Point baseball team. Academically, he was proficient enough to graduate 44 of 164, and although he preferred a commission in Field Artillery or Engineers ("owing to the more rapid promotions"),[9] he settled for his third choice, the Infantry. He assuaged his early disappointment at choice of branch by reflecting that "it is in this branch more than any other that a soldier learns the art of leadership and command and, ultimately, has the best chance of reaching the topmost positions."[10]

Second Lieutenant Bradley's first assignment was the 14th Infantry Regiment in Spokane, WA. He thought it would help him avoid the "rough and disagreeable" duty on the Mexican-American border claiming so many of his classmates (including Eisenhower).[11] Bradley picked the 14th Infantry in the Pacific Northwest because "it was one of the few outfits that had not been skeletonized for Mexican border duty," and he "preferred to begin [his] career in a 'normal garrison' atmosphere."[12] What he found "at the end of a Spokane trolley line" was a typical US Army unit of that era—undermanned, spread out over several isolated posts, and staffed with soldiers considerably less than high caliber.[13]

Bradley's attempt to avoid border duty was unsuccessful, however, as increased problems with Pancho Villa's irregulars caused Bradley's unit to be alerted and moved to Douglas, AZ, in 1916. For the next 18 months, he endured "miserable" conditions amid duties that were "routine and boring" at Douglas and Yuma, AZ.[14] Then in April 1917, the United States declared war on Germany, rescuing the 14th Infantry from interminable border boredom. Bradley accompanied his regiment back to the Pacific Northwest and immediately began maneuvering to get overseas into combat:

> As a professional soldier and a West Pointer, my overwhelming desire at that time was to go to France and prove my mettle in a real war. I immediately perceived that I would not make it there with the 14th Infantry....The 14th was doomed to a fate worse than death—or so I thought at the time: processing an endless stream of recruits. The next sixteen months were, professionally, the most frustrating of my early Army career. I tried every possible scheme I could dream up to get out of the 14th Infantry and into an outfit bound for France. I sincerely believed that if I did not get to France I would be professionally ruined.[15]

Bradley was unsuccessful in leaving the 14th and went with it to Montana in January 1918, to police labor unrest in the copper mines. By that summer, Bradley was promoted to major. His unit was ordered to Camp Dodge, outside Des Moines, IA, to form a cadre for the 19th Infantry Division—a unit scheduled to see combat in France. Bradley rejoiced, exclaiming, "I would have a chance to fight after all!"[16]

His unit went to work training with a vengeance until October 1918, when the global influenza epidemic struck, cramming the camp hospital with sick and dying soldiers and curtailing the extensive training schedule. Coming rapidly on the heels of the epidemic were rumors (soon confirmed) of a German collapse. A bitterly disappointed Bradley wrote, "Once more my hopes of getting into combat evaporated."[17]

When the Armistice was announced, Bradley was heartsick. He was certain that he was now professionally ruined, that he "could only look forward to a career lifetime of dull routine assignments and would be lucky to retire after thirty years as a lieutenant colonel."[18] Instead of continuing to create the most powerful Army in American history, Bradley's task became overseeing its rapid dismantling. He observed that "in a great rush" Camp Dodge (and hundreds of other such camps nationwide) became "a ghost town," as the 3.6 million-man US Army shrank to 150,000 in less than 2 years.[19]

In fact, Bradley did get a chance to see some action when, in July 1919, he received orders to take command of a 1,000-man army unit and lead it to Vladivostok, Siberia. Despite his oft-professed desire to get into combat, he was appalled at the prospects of "another miserable and unhappy assignment." This kind of thankless and confusing combat, helping to police the railways and maintain order in the chaotic situation caused by the Russian civil war (and, presumably, its accompanying lack of promotion potential), was not the kind of action the young major wanted. Because he was then sitting on a court-martial board, he used that as a cover to avoid the assignment, requesting relief on a technicality. The excuse worked. Instead of commanding troops in Siberia, Bradley was assigned to teach ROTC students in South Dakota.[20]

Assignment as a professor of military science and tactics was common for Regular Army officers between World Wars I and II—even multiple tours were frequent. Many of the officers who reached high rank and senior leadership positions in World War II spent several years on college campuses teaching and administering the ROTC program. Bradley's experience, therefore, was somewhat typical with his contemporaries when he reported to South Dakota State College of Agriculture and Mechanical Arts in Brookings in August 1919.[21]

Captain Bradley (he reverted to his permanent rank in 1920) spent only a year in South Dakota, however, because the post-World War I expansion of West Point created an urgent need for instructors to teach plebe (freshman) mathematics. The badly needed reforms instituted by the new superintendent, Douglas MacArthur, included trebling the class size, beginning with the class of 1924. This generated a corresponding need to increase the size of the staff and faculty and created an opportunity for Bradley to return to the Academy.[22] He began a 4-year tour as part of the 37-member department of mathematics in September 1920. Bradley recorded that he was "overjoyed to be back at West Point" and "it was like coming home."[23]

Bradley left West Point in the summer of 1924, shortly after he was promoted to major, a rank he would hold for the next 12 years. He took with him an interest in reading military history and an appreciation for studying the lessons of the past:

> Our four years at West Point had been beneficial to me professionally in several ways. Being on the teaching staff had not only sharpened my wits, it had broadened and matured me considerably. In these years, I began to seriously read--and study--military history and biography, learning a great deal from the mistakes of my predecessors.[24]

MAJ Bradley reported to the Infantry Advanced Officer's Course at Fort Benning, GA, at the end of summer 1924. In those days, the Advanced Courses were also meant to prepare promising officers for assignment to the Command and General Staff School at Fort Leavenworth. Bradley must have impressed the staff at the Infantry School because he finished second in his class of 73; he felt this made his prospects for future attendance at Command and General Staff School and the Army War College very promising.[25] Now, however, he was due for an overseas tour.

Bradley's assignment was to Schofield Barracks, HI. After a brief stint with the 19th Infantry Regiment, Bradley became commanding officer of the 1st Battalion, 27th Infantry Regiment, a job he eagerly sought because it involved troops and field duty. He thoroughly enjoyed his time with the 27th Infantry and wrote, "I look back on those months as the most fulfilling and rewarding of my early career...It is rare that an infantry officer can find an assignment with troops in an area and climate ideal for field training...."[26]

During his final year in Hawaii, however, Bradley drew an assignment as a liaison officer with the Hawaii National Guard, a job he considered a dead end. He was pleased then to be ordered in 1928 to return to the States to attend the Command and General Staff School at Fort Leavenworth-- schooling he was certain would guarantee him "promotion to colonel before retirement."[27] Bradley felt he learned a lot at the school:

> On the whole, I profited from my year at Fort Leavenworth. It was a good intellectual experience, good mental discipline. I was introduced to a new level of war planning and management. Although the teaching methods and solutions to problems left a great deal to be desired, the exposure stimulated my thinking. When the "conventional" solution to a complex military problem is already well known by rote, unconventional—and often better—solutions are more likely to occur.[28]

In 1929, Bradley was offered two assignments as he prepared to leave Fort Leavenworth—as treasurer at West Point, and as instructor at the Infantry School in Fort Benning. Bradley reported that he "chose Benning, the most fortunate decision of my life."[29] At that time, Colonel George Marshall ruled the Infantry School.

As Assistant Commandant of the Infantry School, Marshall personally approved the assignment (and retention) of officers to the faculty. Bradley served his first year there as a member of the Tactics Section and so impressed Marshall that the next year he was chosen to be the Chief of the Weapons Section. Bradley considered Marshall's selection of him to be "the highest possible personal honor." He spent 4 years at Fort Benning, three of them directly under Marshall's influence and observation. Bradley was delighted when Marshall wrote him a letter saying, "I very much hope we will have the opportunity to serve together again; I can think of nothing more satisfactory to me."[30] It would prove highly satisfactory to Bradley, also.

During his final year at the Infantry School, Bradley considered his next assignment carefully. Although he was eligible to request attendance at the Army War College, he was afraid that, as a War College graduate, he might be relegated to serving only in headquarters or staff duties should war ever come again. Bradley wrestled with the decision for weeks before deciding to follow the advice of his close friend, Forrest Harding, to apply for attendance at the War College. Harding pointed out that the school had a good reputation and that its course of instruction (at the highest professional education level the Army offered) would be good preparation for any later assignment, troop or staff. Bradley recorded that he decided to apply because he "had grown professionally with each of the Army schools...attended," and that "it was good background and was beginning to carry weight in the selection of general officers."[31]

Bradley and his 83 classmates began their studies at the Army War College (in Washington, DC, on the site of the current National Defense University) in fall 1933. In his autobiography, describing the course, he seems mildly surprised to find it "more like a graduate seminar or a contemporary think tank" than the Army schools he was familiar with. Bradley notes the absence of pressure (and grades), and remarks that "there was little distinction between students and faculty." He reports that some students refused to take the work seriously and admits there were moments when even he thought he "was wasting...time." Nevertheless, Bradley found the lectures "valuable background later in the European war" and was introduced to strategy on a global scale. Overall, Bradley characterized his time at the War College as "a quiet, uneventful year in the nation's capital."[32]

Bradley remained in an academic environment upon completion of the War College, requesting another tour on the staff and faculty at the Military Academy. This time, responding to a call from Colonel Simon B. Buckner, the Commandant of Cadets, Bradley accepted an assignment in West Point's Tactical Department as a Battalion Tactical

Officer, beginning summer 1934.[33] Because he was "by law" the commander of the cadets for which he was responsible, the duty was considered a "troop assignment"—meaning he would receive another staff job when he left West Point. Fortunately, this staff position, in the War Department, reunited him and Marshall.

When LTC Bradley (promoted in 1936) reported to the War Department staff in Washington during summer 1938,[34] he had spent what would seem today to be an incredibly long time in an academic environment. He had spent such little time in command of troops that any officer serving today who tried to repeat this pattern would very likely be passed over for promotion and not selected for advanced schooling or higher positions, staff or command.   But the interwar American Army, smaller and poorer, seemed to prize intellectual development, appreciating that the "schoolhouse" was an appropriate place to study tactics, strategy, and leadership. Bradley valued his time at Benning and West Point, writing:

> In later years some writers would observe that I had the air of a schoolteacher. Perhaps this was not without good reason. Counting my one year at Brookings in South Dakota, my four years on the Fort Benning School staff and my two four-year tours at West Point, I was in fact officially a teacher for thirteen of my first twenty-three years of commissioned service. I might add that it is not a bad way to learn your profession thoroughly.[35]

Bradley's preparation seemed to serve him well enough, regardless of how he acquired it, in his service on the War Department staff in those months leading up to World War II. Initially assigned to the personnel division of the General Staff, he transferred, at Marshall's request, to the Chief of Staff's office when Marshall became Army Chief of Staff in 1939.[36] Bradley and other officers personally selected by the new Chief of Staff were frantically trying to mobilize and rearm the US Army in attempts to make up for decades of neglect and inadequate funding.

Events in Europe and the Far East created an international situation that drove Marshall and his staff to nearly superhuman efforts in attempts to mobilize. The next 2 years under Marshall became a "trial by fire" for Bradley, and he consistently did excellent work for the Chief of Staff. Marshall came to esteem Bradley's opinions and allowed the younger officer to make decisions and take actions on his own. This delegation of authority to trusted subordinates of proven ability is a pattern Marshall followed throughout the war, and those who seemed best at it, like Eisenhower and Bradley, were elevated to ever higher positions of responsibility. Bradley's opportunity came in February 1941.[37]

Although he had initially accepted an offer to return to West Point as the Commandant of Cadets, Marshall called him in and offered him the position of Commandant of the Infantry School—a brigadier general's position. Bradley, then still a lieutenant colonel, was elated and didn't hesitate accepting the job for a moment. Reporting to Fort Benning on 25 February 1941, Bradley assumed command of the post and the Infantry School, and pinned on the star of a brigadier general ("the first man in my class to make it!" he jubilantly recorded).[38]

Bradley accepted stewardship of Fort Benning "with all its headaches and opportunities"[39] as the Army continued to struggle to mobilize. One problem confronting the Army's leadership significantly affected Bradley's Infantry School: the issue of providing competent and qualified officers to lead the expanding Army. Marshall had realized early in the mobilization that the provisions planned for officering the wartime Army were inadequate. There were only about 15,000 Regular Army officers serving in the interwar Army, and federalized National Guard officers would, at their peak, add only about 100,000. Even with the addition of 180,000 ROTC officers and 100,000 (eventually) commissioned directly from the ranks, there was a significant shortfall. The answer was the Officer Candidate Schools (OCS) program. By war's end, fully 300,000 junior officers for the Army—nearly half the total requirement[40]—had been graduated from OCS.

Despite opposition within the War Department (though not from Marshall, who fully supported OCS), Bradley created the prototype school for officer candidate training at Fort Benning. This Fort Benning "model" was copied by the OCS programs at other Army posts. Bradley was extremely proud of the Infantry OCS program and wrote, "I consider the founding of the Fort Benning OCS my greatest contribution to the mobilization effort."[41]   For that and other accomplishments during the year at Fort Benning, Marshall decided to give Bradley command of a division.

Notified shortly after the Pearl Harbor attack that Marshall had selected him to command the newly forming 82nd Infantry Division, Bradley and his staff began to arrive at Camp Claiborne, LA, in February and March 1942.[42] Along with division command (the first man in his class to get it) came the temporary rank of major general. He assembled a solid group of proven performers as his division staff, including Matthew Ridgway as Assistant Division Commander, and commenced a rigorous training program that drew high praise from the Army's chief trainer, General McNair, Commander of Army Ground Forces.[43]   Bradley's reputation with the 82nd was so outstanding that it won him an assignment requiring the type of tough, demanding leadership he had recently become famous for—command of a unit flat on its face.

Marshall handpicked Bradley to take command of the troubled 28th Infantry Division, a Pennsylvania National Guard outfit that had had three division commanders in 6 months. Marshall felt it necessary to send a strong message to the National Guard that only the highest standards resulting from the toughest training were acceptable in preparing their units for combat.[44] He knew Bradley would demand and receive the maximum effort from the soldiers of the 28th; if he succeeded, Marshall promised him command of an Army corps in combat. The prospect of finally leading troops into combat was the greatest news Bradley could have hoped for and assuaged somewhat his disappointment at having to leave the 82nd.

Bradley whipped the 28th Division into shape with an intensive training program similar to the one he used with the 82nd and fulfilled all of Marshall's expectations. He was delighted, therefore, on his 50th birthday to receive a message from the Chief of Staff announcing his appointment as commander of the X Corps.[45] The very next day, however,

Bradley discovered that his classmate, Eisenhower, had other plans for him.

NORTH AFRICA TO THE ARDENNES

LTG Eisenhower, commanding the Allied forces in North Africa in February 1943, was just then learning some very hard lessons about leadership, cooperation, and coalition warfare. Rommel was inflicting a bloody defeat on the American forces in the southern part of the Tunisian front, at Kasserine Pass, and threatening to split the British and French forces away from the American units. The clumsy command arrangements and inadequate supply network of the Allied forces needed immediate repair, and Ike was soon forced to make changes at the top level of the US command structure.[46] In an effort to take firmer control of the battlefront, to allow him to concentrate on broader strategic and coalition partnership issues, Ike forwarded a list of names to Marshall of officers he would accept to help oversee the tactical side of the fight. Eisenhower placed Bradley's name at the top of the list. Marshall replied quickly, promising that Bradley would remain on detail as long as Eisenhower wanted. "Please dispatch General Omar Bradley by first available air transport," replied Eisenhower.[47]

Shortly after arriving in North Africa, Bradely was sent by Eisenhower to investigate the command climate in Major General Lloyd R. Fredendall's II Corps. Bradley soon confirmed to Ike all the negative reports on Fredendall's leadership failures. Ike then appointed Patton to command the II Corps after the incompetent Fredendall's relief. To help whip the II Corps into shape in preparation for the upcoming final Allied offensive against the Axis forces in Tunisia, Eisenhower sent Bradley as his "liaison officer." In effect, this put Bradley in the position of acting "as Ike's eyes and ears on the Tunisian front, reporting back to him directly." Eisenhower also gave him "authority to make 'suggestive changes' to American commanders at the front"—which caused Patton and others to resent the newcomer as Ike's "spy."[48] Patton, who had already been named as the future Army commander for the Sicily invasion and therefore was concurrently planning for that operation, asked Eisenhower to appoint Bradley as his Deputy Corps Commander (meaning he would work for Patton, not Ike). The upcoming final offensive in Tunisia was critical to regaining lost American prestige and confidence; therefore Ike could hardly deny Patton's request. Bradley became Patton's deputy, with the understanding that, as soon as Patton had reestablished discipline and confidence within the II Corps, Bradley would assume command, freeing Patton for his Sicily responsibilities.

The initial phase of the final Allied offensive in Tunisia began on 19 March 1943, under command of Eisenhower's Deputy Ground Commander, British General Sir Harold Alexander. Despite continued attempts by Alexander (who doubted American combat abilities) to leave US forces out of the main attacks, pressure from Eisenhower, Patton, and Bradley ensured that the II US Corps had a prominent role in the final victory, thereby guaranteeing that it remained an "Allied" victory, not a British one.[49]

On 16 April 1943, while the battle for Tunisia continued, Bradley assumed command of the II Corps, and Patton returned to Morocco to complete the planning for the Sicily invasion. Although Bradley respected Patton's considerable leadership abilities, his own style was completely different. He wrote about his ideas on leadership at his assumption of command:

> My command of II Corps was far less flamboyant than had been Patton's. I administered with a firm but more compassionate hand. I relaxed some of Patton's more drastic edicts, such as one that compelled nurses working in evacuation hospitals to wear heavy, cumbersome steel helmets. I coaxed rather than ordered, and I encouraged my staff and subordinate commanders to solve most problems themselves. It seemed to me that II Corps was soon working smoothly, as a good team should.[50]

Bradley's style of corps command reflected much of the lessons he and Eisenhower had both learned from the North African fighting. Bradley, unlike the now-removed Fredendall, did not try to dictate the details of the tactical conduct of the battle, nor did he bypass his principal subordinates and issue orders directly to his brigades and battalions. Instead, he assigned broad objectives and left the "how-to" questions to his division commanders. Also unlike Fredendall, Bradley did not remain wedded to a fortified command bunker far to the rear but instead regularly visited front-line troops "to show the GIs that their commander was no rear-echelon tent hog."[51]

In this first test of Bradley's abilities as a combat commander, he also demonstrated he was not afraid to trust his own tactical judgment and countermand the orders of his superiors when he was convinced those orders were wrong. He ignored Ike's detailed advice (which he assumed had the force of orders) and deliberately avoided the method and line of attack prescribed by Eisenhower because he was certain it would cause unacceptable casualties. A few days later, he repeated this action when he received "absurd" orders from his British senior, Lieutenant General Kenneth A. N. Anderson.[52] In both instances Bradley was surely correct. Most important, Bradley achieved a significant victory for American arms and, in the process, erased the stain of defeat from the Kasserine Pass debacle—and he did it while demonstrating a spirit of Allied cooperation that helped Ike to repair much of the bad feeling engendered by the Anglophobe Fredendall and to strengthen the coalition. For these reasons, and because Bradley had done "so remarkably well" in his first combat test, Ike explained to Marshall that Bradley and his battle-proven II Corps would lead the American effort in the next major Allied effort—the invasion of Sicily.[53]

Operation HUSKY, the Allied effort to invade and occupy Sicily, was undertaken at the expense of the cross-channel invasion of France. Bradley admits in his autobiography that, although he favored a cross-channel invasion as soon as possible at the time, he later realized it could have been "an unthinkable disaster."[54] The Sicily campaign not only bought time for the buildup of men and materiel for the cross-channel invasion to proceed, it gave commanders like Bradley another valuable opportunity to learn their trade before being tested on the beaches of Normandy.

The fighting in Sicily added to Bradley's growing reputation as a steady, deliberate, and, above all, successful commander. The enemy and terrain on that rugged, primitive island were formidable, and serving under Patton (Seventh Army commander for the operation) was not always easy, but Bradley was blessed with able subordinates.[55]

Bradley's reputation began to become well known to the general public during the Sicilian campaign, chiefly through the writings of the popular war correspondent Ernie Pyle. Bradley's reputation was also growing with Marshall, and this led to his most important combat assignment.[56]

In August 1943, while the II Corps staff began to become involved in the planning for the invasion of Italy, the War Department had finally received agreement among the Allies to proceed with the cross-channel invasion of France. One of Marshall's problems was to determine who would command the principal American fighting force for the invasion and subsequent campaigns in northern Europe. There were several frontrunners for the position, but the most pugnacious and aggressive among them, Patton, had been removed from consideration because of the infamous slapping incidents.[57] The choice seemed to narrow to General Mark Clark, then involved in planning the Italian invasion, and Bradley. Marshall and Eisenhower exchanged several cables discussing the merits of the officers and, in one of these, Ike gave his assessment of Bradley's abilities:

> Next Bradley. There is little I need to tell you about him because he is running absolutely true to form all the time. He has brains, a fine capacity for leadership and a thorough understanding of the requirements of modern battle. He has never caused me a moment of worry. He is perfectly capable of commanding an army. He has the respect of all his associates including all the British officers that have met him. I am very anxious to keep him...as long as we have any major operations to carry out.[58]

On 1 September, Marshall informed Ike of his decision to name Bradley as the commander for the American combat army for the Normandy invasion. His cable read, "Thanks for your generous attitude regarding Bradley. Have him make preparations to leave for England [and] tell him that he will head an Army headquarters and will also probably have to develop an Army Group headquarters...."[59] On 8 September 1943, Bradley left Sicily enroute to England. He had just over 8 months to create the US First Army and prepare it to enter battle on the beaches of France.[60]

Bradley's preparations for D-Day and subsequent invasion activities have been characterized as not overly bold but effective and workmanlike. However, it is interesting to note that he was bold enough to lobby successfully for the inclusion of the major airborne operations, despite British warnings that the risky undertaking could experience casualties of up to 70 percent.[61] Bradley is also credited with advocating (and getting) another American landing area—Utah Beach—to put, as Ike phrased it, "enough wallop in the initial attack."[62] Considering the bloody, near-fiasco that V Corps experienced on Omaha Beach, it seems fortunate that US forces had the additional landing area. Even more important than operational plans, however, was the selection of subordinate corps and division commanders, the choosing of the senior leaders to command the American effort. Marshall gave Eisenhower free rein in the final selection of these important subordinates, but Ike discussed each with Bradley and SHAEF Chief of Staff Bedell Smith. If any of the three disapproved, the man was rejected.[63] Through this process, Bradley exercised great influence on the conduct of the campaigns.

LTG Bradley, as commander of the First US Army, oversaw the D-Day landings on 6 June 1944 from the bridge of the cruiser USS Augusta. While the news from Utah Beach was positive and optimistic, Omaha Beach looked bad. Bradley, feeling helpless on the ship, recorded his thoughts and actions:

> The whole of D-Day was for me a time of grave personal anxiety and frustration. I was stuck on the Augusta. Our communications with the forces assaulting Omaha Beach were thin to nonexistent. From the few radio messages we overheard...I gained the impression that our forces had suffered an irreversible catastrophe. I sent my chief of staff, Bill Kean, and Chet Hanson to the beach for a firsthand look. Their report was more optimistic than I dared hope for. The situation everywhere on the beach was still grave,

but our troops had forced one or two of the draws and were inching inland. Based on their report, I gave up any thought of abandoning Omaha Beach.[64]

By that evening, Bradley had pushed 35,000 US troops ashore on the two beachheads at a cost of about 2,500 casualties (most of these suffered at Omaha Beach). On the First Army's left, the British and Canadians had gotten 75,000 troops ashore, reporting 3,000 as casualties. Bradley moved his command post to Normandy on 10 June, D plus 4.[65]

While the Allied armies continued to build up their forces and supplies in the beachhead area as rapidly as shipping and the changeable weather would allow, German forces rushed to seal off the invasion area. Determined German resistance, the hedgerow terrain, and poor weather combined to slow the Allied advance to a crawl. Throughout the remainder of June and into the first weeks of July, the Allied advance degenerated into a grinding, unimaginative slugfest.[66] Bradley, frustrated at the lack of progress by his forces and alarmed at the high casualty figures, directed his staff to prepare a breakout plan while he continued to badger his subordinate corps and division commanders into pressing their assaults. Numerous regimental and division commanders were relieved of command during this time, including one division commander who was sacked after only 4 days.[67] Bradley, urged on by Eisenhower, was ruthless in relieving any subordinate whom he considered lacking in aggressiveness and fighting spirit. Despite the draconian measures, however, the German opposition and the miserable hedgerow terrain were overcome at last only by the St.-Lô breakout.

Bradley's staff had developed a breakthrough plan, code-named COBRA, that sought to follow up an intensive, saturation bombing of a small section of the German lines by thrusting General J. Lawton Collins' heavily reinforced VII Corps through the breach. The so-called "carpet bombing" involved 2,200 Allied planes that dropped thousands of tons of 200- and 500-lb. bombs on an area only 1 mile wide and 3 miles long near the village of St.-Lô on 25 July 1944. "Lightning Joe" Collins ran his four infantry divisions and two armored divisions through the rubble and over the ground where the opposing German forces had been blown to bits.[68] The resulting breakout was successful beyond its planners' wildest hopes, initiating the "race across France" and the unbelievably rapid destruction of organized German resistance in France. After nearly 7 weeks of bitter hedgerow fighting, Bradley's troops were able to conduct the sweeping maneuver warfare the American Army was uniquely equipped and organized to pursue. One week after the breakout, Bradley was appointed the 12th Army Group commander.[69]

On 1 August 1944, the Third Army became operational in France under command of the rehabilitated George Patton. This caused the contingency for which Bradley's staff had been planning to implement—the activation of the 12th Army Group. Bradley's forces consisted of the First Army on his left flank (now commanded by Lieutenant General Courtney Hodges), with Patton's Third Army on the right. Terrain, circumstances, and Patton's aggressive temperament combined to create a campaign characterized by a rapid, sweeping right wheel by Patton's army, and a slower, steadier sweep on the left by Hodges' forces. Complementing a British-Canadian advance on the Allied far left (Montgomery's 21 Army Group), the American attack rapidly drove across France.[70] Along with the phenomenal success, however, two incidents involving Bradley's battle leadership should be noted.

Bradley's leadership helped cause the failure in August 1944 to rapidly close the Falaise Pocket at Argentan, thereby allowing a large part of the trapped German Army to escape. Although the pocket became a killing ground for thousands of German soldiers as well as a repository for nearly all that army's equipment, thousands more slipped through the gap and joined the defenses at the Westwall. Included in these German escapees were many of the higher level unit staffs, key to rebuilding new units. Although this failure could be blamed as much on Montgomery's caution and slowness as on Bradley, the latter characteristically shouldered the blame. Both commanders were concerned about avoiding friendly casualties when the two Allied Army groups met, and Ike had cautioned about "a calamitous battle between friends."[71]

Therefore, when Patton instructed his subordinate units to drive past the established Army Group boundary to make contact with the lagging Canadians, Bradley ordered him to pull back and wait. Although he later wrote that, "a golden opportunity had been lost," Bradley insisted that the decision "was mine and mine alone."[72] Still a controversial operation, it seems in retrospect that, despite the slowness of the Canadian advance, Patton's instructions to go beyond the boundary and close the gap were sound and could have saved the day—but Bradley overruled him.

In autumn 1944, the great pursuit across France halted along the canals of Holland, through the forbidding Huertgen Forest, and into the mud and misery of Lorraine. Outrunning the ability of the logistical "tail" to maintain a continual flow of fuel, food and ammunition, the fighting "teeth" had to stop.[73] During the run from the Normandy beaches to the German border, Bradley's job had been to constantly push his army and corps commanders to drive their formations ever farther into the German defenses. Generally, the Allied armies were successful far beyond their expectations, but Bradley's bold attempt to jump the Siegfried Line on the run was a disaster. The densely wooded, strongly fortified Huertgen Forest, with its miserable road net, was not an opportune area for a major offensive, yet Bradley pushed Collins' VII Corps into this nightmare because he believed he could crack open the Westwall defenses. Eventually, six divisions were chewed to pieces in the "Passchendaele with tree bursts," and none of them was totally fit for combat in time for the Ardennes offensive several weeks later.[74] Collins later seemed somewhat philosophical about the ordeal, saying that "someone had to cover that sector," and VII Corps got the mission.[75] Critics have chastised Bradley for allowing six divisions to be destroyed in an operation that gained virtually no objectives, but his counterargument is that no other area that could reasonably have been assaulted offered any better opportunity. Coming on the heels of Monty's disaster at Arnhem, it forced the Allies to regroup their forces and rethink their strategy. Meanwhile, the broken units were sent to a quiet sector to refit—the Ardennes.[76]

ATTACK IN THE ARDENNES

When the German attack in the Ardennes began on 16 December 1944, the 12th Army Group's commander was much more concerned with the overall manpower shortage hobbling his armies than he was about the threat of an enemy breakthrough. Bradley later wrote that the "alarming crisis in manpower" totally preoccupied him, and "the possibility of an enemy attack through the Ardennes" seemed remote. Later that day, while Middleton's VIII Corps was reeling backwards from the force of the powerful armored and infantry attacks against the overextended American lines, Bradley was motoring over icy roads to meet with Eisenhower at SHAEF headquarters to discuss the infantry replacement crisis.[77] Even when Ike's intelligence officer interrupted their discussions later in the evening with news of the German attack, Bradley was not alarmed. His own V Corps had recently initiated an attack to seize the critical Roer River dams, so Bradley assumed the German assaults were in reaction to this offensive:

> My initial reaction to these fragmentary and unclear reports was that von Rundstedt had launched a limited spoiling attack through the Ardennes in an effort to force Hodges [First Army] and Patton [Third Army] to slow down or pull back. I was not overly concerned.[78]

Eisenhower, however, sensed the seriousness of the assault almost immediately. The scope of the German offensive seemed to confirm to Ike that the enemy was capitalizing on "the badly stretched condition of our troops" that had bothered him and Bradley for some time.[79] But it was Eisenhower, not Bradley who quickly ordered the dispatch of the 7th and 10th Armored Divisions to help bolster Middleton.[80]

The prompt dispatch of the two armored divisions—the 7th to St.-Vith and the 10th to Bastogne—was one of the most critical decisions the American command took during the entire battle. It is significant that Eisenhower—not Bradley—was the commander who initiated that decision, because it emphasizes the differences in the manner in which the two men conducted the defense in their respective commands. Ike seemed to grasp the developing situation immediately, to reach critical decisions quickly and then to act forcefully to carry out those decisions. Bradley, perhaps indulging in some wishful thinking, was slow to comprehend the extent of his ruptured front, allowed Ike to take the lead in reacting to the attack, and initially seemed more concerned with placating Patton than with stopping the German assault. Writing of the early hours of the Ardennes attack in his autobiography, Bradley admits:

> It gradually became apparent—Ike sensed it before I did—that this was...an all-out offensive by three German armies...Urged on by Ike, who had correctly diagnosed the full extent of the danger, I made telephone calls...to order the 10th Armored and the 7th Armored to turn north and south, to close in on the base of the enemy salient...We had been caught flat-footed.[81]

Bradley later claimed that he feared a German attack through the lightly defended Ardennes and had discussed defensive reactions to such a situation with Middleton. He knew very well that Middleton's VIII Corps was spread much too thinly over the extended Ardennes lines but felt he could not continue offensive action in other sectors of the 12th Army Group (appendix E) if he gave Middleton any more help. Bradley referred to this situation as a "calculated risk" he was willing to take in order to continue the attack in other areas.[82] It seems obvious, however, that Bradley's "calculated risk" was never considered very risky by the 12th Army Group staff or its commander. Bradley never thought the Germans would ever launch a strong offensive in the Ardennes region (or in any region, for that matter). Bradley's "calculated risk" excuse for stripping the Ardennes of the means of conducting a cohesive defense seems hardly credible when all hindsight is removed. It smacks of face-saving—after all, it is more acceptable for an enemy to call one's bluff than to be completely fooled by him. 3If his risk had indeed been as "calculated" as he later claimed, his reactions to the German attack surely would have been quicker, more aggressive, and initiated by the 12th Army Group, not SHAEF. Bradley was completely fooled by the size and location of the German offensive, and he reacted slowly.

It was Eisenhower, albeit now urged on by Bradley, who began the process of sending other reserve forces to the threatened area, but the number of reserve forces available was pitifully small. The XVIII Airborne Corps, consisting of the 82nd and 101st Airborne Divisions, was rapidly dispatched to assembly areas in the Ardennes—the 82nd to Houffalize and the 101st to Bastogne.[83] Their arrivals at the respective towns were timely; they just managed to beat the advancing German forces and secure the important road junctions against capture.[84]

The doctrinal response to the German breakthrough was no secret to the American command—hold the "shoulders," give ground slowly, gather reserves for strong counterattacks to cut off the enemy advances—and SHAEF began immediately to carry it out. Accomplishing this was not easy.[85]

One key factor to successfully conducting this "doctrinal response"[86] was maintaining close and uninterrupted communications between units and commands at all levels. Bradley's battle headquarters, located south of the Ardennes and quite near the front lines at Luxembourg City, was in a terrible position from which to control the overall reaction of 12th Army Group. Yet, when Eisenhower suggested that Bradley relocate his command group to the better-situated Verdun, Bradley balked. To move his headquarters to the rear in reaction to the German assault, "would be a sure sign of weakness—to the Germans, the Luxembourgers, and [his] own troops. A panic would ensue." Bradley told Ike, "I will never move backwards with a headquarters, there's too much prestige at stake."[87] While admirable in its brave attempt to maintain troop morale, this refusal to relocate led directly to a situation Bradley described as "the darkest of times" for his professional career—Montgomery's assumption of command of most of Bradley's 12th Army Group.[88]

The location and momentum of the German attack split the 12th Army Group between St. Vith and Bastogne. To the south, near Bradley's headquarters, was a portion of VIII Corps and all of Patton's Third Army. Remaining north of the

The "Bulge"

bulge was most of Hodges' First Army and all of Simpson's Ninth Army.[89] While Bradley and his staff maintained radio and telephone contact with all their subordinate army headquarters (and, in the case of Middleton's VIII Corps, with corps command posts as well), Bradley was unable to visit these locations physically for crucial face-to-face contact and coordination with his subordinate commanders, nor could he carry out personal reconnaissance of critical portions of the battlefield. Historian Russell Weigley, writing of Ike's command style, noted, "it is essential that a commander should be able to visit his principal subordinates, to feel the atmosphere at their headquarters and hold free and lengthy discussions."[90] Frequent visits to forward units and subordinate commanders had been such a hallmark of Bradely's battle leadership up to this point that it is nearly inconceivable that he proposed to Ike that he command the toughest battle to be faced in the war solely by telephone and radio. Given Ike's experience in combat to date, it seems even less likely that Eisenhower would agree to such a command and control arrangement.

Eisenhower, perhaps thinking back to the disastrous battle at Kasserine Pass in Tunisia in February 1943 and remembering the hapless Fredendall's failure to leave his command post and visit any unit, was not comforted by Bradley's insistence that he could adequately control his units in the north by radio and telephone. Ike, setting aside all issues of "national pride" as Supreme Commander, placed Montgomery in command of all US forces north of the St.-Vith/Bastogne split on 20 December.[91] Bradley raged at the decision in his memoirs:

> Giving Monty operational control of my First and Ninth armies was the worst possible mistake Ike could have made. Owing to Monty's caution and conservatism, it practically assured that we would fail to cut off the German salient with a bold thrust from the north. The enemy would escape in force as it had escaped from the Falaise Gap. We were going to lose a golden opportunity to destroy the German war machine...[92]

Bradley's concern with the failure to completely cut off the

German forces in the bulge appears to be more hindsight than foresight. At the time Ike split his command, Bradley was still trying to find a way to stop the German attack, not cut it off. Indeed, his outrage seems more the result of hurt pride than of missed tactical opportunities in future operations, as he did concede that he would not object if 21 Army Group were commanded by an American.[93] The shift in command left Bradley and most of the 12th Army Group staff sitting on the sidelines while Monty's 21 Army Group and Patton's Third Army executed the maneuver portions of the battle to stop the Germans and eliminate the salient. To facilitate Patton's drive against the southern edge of the bulge, even the remnants of Middleton's VIII Corps, Bradley's only remaining First Army unit, were attached to Patton. Not the kind of subordinate who easily tolerates his superior looking over his shoulder, Patton and the Third Army staff accomplished the complicated shift of direction of the Army's attack and the difficult relief of Bastogne without much assistance from 12th Army Group.[94]

The celebrated 90-degree turn of Patton's Third Army to attack into the southern half of the bulge was suggested by Patton, not Bradley. Although Patton was initially skeptical of the power and extent of the German attack, once he focused on the size of the panzer and panzer-grenadier formations sweeping through the Ardennes, he realized it was a major offensive.[95] After rebuffing Bradley's early attempts to prepare to shift some Third Army units northward to help VIII Corps, Patton had devised his own counterattack plan by 18 December, presenting it to Eisenhower and the assembled commanders at Verdun the following day. Bradley, according to Weigley, "remained uncommonly impatient and irritable" at the conference, and allowed his aggressive subordinate, Patton, to do much of the talking for the Army Group.[96] Certainly it was Patton who took the lead in presenting his counterattack plan, and Bradley, apparently, was content to let him carry the ball by himself. Patton's "masterful design, masterfully executed" was a Patton-Third Army staff creation, with little credit owed to Bradley and his 12th Army Group staff.[97]

Despite the 20 December shift in Army Group boundaries,

Bradley "kept in close touch with Simpson and Hodges by telephone" throughout the remainder of the Ardennes fighting,[98] letting them know he intended to return them to 12th Army Group command as soon as Eisenhower would agree. What he learned from Simpson and Hodges depressed and alarmed him. Monty's "stagnating conservatism"[99] was postponing a counterthrust from the north side of the salient, jeopardizing the Allies' ability to trap the bulk of the German forces. Bradley, observing Patton's successful attack into Bastogne, saw no corresponding thrust from the north:

> Monty's penchant for tedious planning, the massive buildup and the "set-piece" battle were only too well known...it seemed to me that he talked like a man who had lost touch with reality. Every scrap of intelligence we had available...indicated beyond doubt that...Hitler's last great, ill-advised gamble had failed...Now was the time to hit back. Not three months from now.[100]

Bradley's protests were in vain. Montgomery failed to launch a timely counterstroke; the bulge was pushed back, not cut off.

This counteroffensive to eliminate the German forces within the Ardennes salient proved to be a highly frustrating undertaking for Bradley and the 12th Army Group. With Montgomery commanding all forces in the north (and the bulk of the forces engaged in eliminating the salient), Bradley had little control over the timing of the ultimate linkup of the northern and southern pinchers. Nevertheless, it was Bradley who persistently proposed to Eisenhower the necessity to begin the counteroffensive immediately in order to trap as many enemy forces as possible.[101] Patton, hardly needing much coaxing from his Army Group commander, kicked off his half of the attack to cut off the salient on 30 December, just 4 days after relieving Bastogne. But Monty, fearing a renewed German attack, postponed his assault until 3 January 1945. This late start, combined with terrible weather and the poor road network, delayed the final linkup of Bradley's and Montgomery's converging columns until 16 January. The result resembled the Falaise Gap of the previous summer; again, thousands of German troops, this time with much of their equipment, managed to escape. Reorganized and reconstituted into new formations, they joined the defenses at the boundary of Germany and along the Rhine.[102]

Montgomery's tardiness in launching the counterstroke from the north of the bulge[103] only succeeded in angering and frustrating Ike,[104] confirming his original position that he could never support Montgomery as his deputy for ground operations.[105] The result greatly benefitted Bradley, however, because Ike returned the First Army to his operational control the day following the linkup, 17 January 1945.[106]

Although the great majority of the fighting had proved to be a trying and frustrating time for Bradley personally, the battlefield performance of units that had been 12th Army Group formations had, at times, been magnificent. Middleton's delaying actions with his shattered VIII Corps saved Bastogne and the southern shoulder. The 7th Armored's defense of St.-Vith and the stand of the First Army units on the northern shoulder effectively choked to death the German main attack. And Patton's rapid counterstroke into the southern flank of the salient to relieve Bastogne was masterful. True, each of these portions of the Battle of the Bulge was fought primarily as individual actions by the commanders on the scene, with little assistance from 12th Army Group, but they all had learned their trade while serving under Bradley.

ANALYSIS OF BATTLE LEADERSHIP

The commander who emerges from an examination of Bradley's leadership in the Ardennes fighting and the battles of France and Germany is a much more complex individual than the shy, farmer-boy image the Bradley legend perpetuates. There is abundant evidence that much of the image is supported in fact—particularly his genuine concern for the lives and well-being of the common soldier—but other aspects of Bradley's exercise of command rest rather uncomfortably alongside the more benign image: he was a patient and supportive commander, yet ruthlessly relieved subordinates in the Normandy fighting; he was nearly always a "loyal team player," but could be jealous and petty when dealing with his co-equal Army Group commanders,

Montgomery and Jake Devers; he exercised bold, aggressive leadership as in the OVERLORD landings, the St.-Lô breakout, and the drive across France, yet was overcautious and unimaginative in his timid control of the Brittany campaign and the closing of the Falaise gap; he firmly backed Ike as a supporter of the Anglo-American alliance, but he reacted to Montgomery's expanded command of US troops during the Ardennes crisis with resentment, hurt pride, and pique; and he could display a calm, steadying command presence who recovered quickly in the heat of battle, but during the Battle of the Bulge he completely misjudged the strength and location of the attack, displayed little initiative in moving troops to the threatened area, and reacted slowly in devising efforts to stop the German drive.

Any accurate overall assessment of the influence of Bradley's battle leadership on the Ardennes fighting and the campaigns of France and Germany must lie somewhere between Eisenhower's judgment that he was the war's "greatest battle-line commander" and Patton's condemnation that Bradley was an "insufferably orthodox...nothing."[107] A closer look at the battle leadership he demonstrated is necessary before an overall assessment can be made.

Bradley's greatest strength as a leader of large formations of citizen-soldiers was his ability to motivate and inspire the common soldier with confidence in the top-level leadership of the American Army. The tag line "soldier's general" seems entirely appropriate for this commander who really did care deeply about the lives and welfare of the soldiers in his charge, evident from the very beginning of his introduction to combat in North Africa. He continued to retain the trust and confidence of the common soldier even when he was promoted to First Army, then 12th Army Group command. He continually visited units at or near the front lines during a battle, several times narrowly missing being wounded by bombs or shells.[108]

Bradley took pains to ensure that his troops didn't think he was wedded to his command post during a battle. He made sure his subordinate division commanders did the same, going so far as to relieve one division commander during the hard fighting in the hedgerows of Normandy when he and

Eisenhower found both the division commander and his assistant at their command post at the same time during an operation; one of them, Bradley felt, should have been at the front visiting the troops and getting a personal feel for the flow of battle.[109] Bradley regularly visited his subordinate commanders, even during the rapid sweep across France in the summer of 1944, refusing to let distance or difficult terrain keep him away.

It is curious, then, and out of character when he seems to break from this pattern during the Ardennes fighting. Although his tactical headquarters location in Luxembourg City (designed to facilitate his control of Patton's upcoming offensive) was isolated by the terrain and the German breakthrough, he never seemed to even try to overcome these difficulties to visit his hard-pressed commanders. When Montgomery visited the visibly shaken and nervous Hodges at First Army headquarters on 20 December, he noted incredulously that "neither Army Commander (Hodges and Ninth Army's Simpson) had seen Bradley or any senior member of his staff since the battle began, and they had no directive on which to work."[110] Although historian Weigley points out that Bradley had kept in telephone contact with all his subordinate headquarters throughout the battle, the telephone and radio cannot substitute for personal contact and on-scene observation of actual conditions.[111]

Had Bradley visited Hodges' headquarters during the first few days of battle, demonstrating to Eisenhower that he could effectively maintain personal control of all his units despite the German breakthrough, Ike would probably not have deemed it necessary to give Monty command of the northern half of the bulge. (Eisenhower and his chief of staff, Smith, had reacted extremely negatively to the Monty suggestion when it was first made in the early part of the battle, yielding only when Bradley declined to move his headquarters).[112] Bradley's excuse—that he could not move his headquarters to the rear during the battle without panicking the troops and the locals—seems to miss the point. The real issue seems to be not so much the location of his headquarters but where he himself chose to be during the battle.

As the fighting wore on and the Allied countermaneuvers

began to develop, Bradley and the 12th Army Group staff seemed to become more and more superfluous in their headquarters at the southern half of the salient. The only major troop formation Bradley controlled at that point, Patton's Third Army, was attacking northward into the German flanks with little assistance required from Bradley and his staff. A few days prior, however, Hodges and his Army staff could have greatly benefitted from Bradley's calm leadership and sound tactical advice.[113] In fact, Hodges kept insisting that Gerow, V Corps commander, continue his recently launched offensive throughout 16 December and into 17 December—an incredibly poor appreciation of the true tactical situation that could have proven disastrous for the defense of the crucial northern shoulder on Elsenborn ridge if Gerow had complied.[114] By disregarding one of his own basic tenets of battle leadership—regular personal visits to frontline units and commanders—Bradley not only jeopardized the cohesion of his defense of the Ardennes area but probably precipitated the shift in command that so enraged him.

Another of Bradley's battle leadership characteristics, however, did not desert him during the Ardennes fighting and proved to assist greatly the defense of the threatened areas as well as facilitate the counterattack. That characteristic was his ability to allow his subordinate commanders—the leaders actually on the scene and closest to the fighting—to control the flow of battle without interference from Bradley's headquarters. When supported by talented, aggressive division, corps and Army commanders, Bradley's technique of "holding the reins loosely" proved extremely successful. Middleton, Eddy, and Truscott, as division commanders in Sicily, Collins of the VII Corps in Normandy, and, of course, Patton in the sweep across France, all succeeded by being firmly backed (but not interfered with) by Bradley's headquarters.[115]

As 12th Army Group commander, in the drive through France to the German border, Bradley's genius lay in pushing his Army commanders forward and providing them with the materiel and moral support they required to keep up their offensives. With Patton driving the Third Army, and corps commanders such as Collins leading the way for Hodges' First Army, Bradley's principal task was to issue broad, mission orders, then turn his commanders loose.[116] It usually worked well.

There were two critical instances in the Ardennes fighting in which Bradley could have interfered but did not, choosing to allow the on-scene commanders to fight the battle as they wished. The first of these was Middleton's defense of the approaches to Bastogne, including the VIII Corps commander's masterful use of his pitifully small armored, infantry, and engineer reserves. Middleton maintained telephone contact with Bradley and the 12th Army Group headquarters throughout the critical phases of the German assault, and he discussed his countermeasures personally with Bradley.[117] In every case, Middleton received approval and support of his (sometimes unorthodox) measures from the Army Group commander. This strengthened Middleton's control of the battle, especially when he found it necessary to issue controversial orders to commanders not normally part of his corps (such as Colonel William B. Roberts of the 10th Armored Division, for example, when his combat command was rushed from Third Army to help defend Bastogne on 17 December).[118] Bradley allowed Middleton to conduct his own fight, but underwrote his actions.

The other Ardennes example of Bradley successfully letting a skilled subordinate run his own show was Patton's brilliantly conceived and masterfully executed shift northwards and counterattack to relieve Bastogne. Although it can be argued successfully that it should have been Bradley and his 12th Army Group staff who devised and ordered the counterattack, nevertheless, once it was set in motion, Bradley was wise to let Patton conduct the action at his own rapid pace. Even though Bradley and his staff became superfluous during Patton's countermaneuvers, having little to do with controlling the details, this situation was largely the result of Eisenhower's decision to shift command of the US Armies to Montgomery. Had the shift in command not occurred, Bradley would undoubtedly have had his hands full managing the counteroffensives and coordinating the maneuvers of his three armies. To Bradley's credit, he did not compound his error by attempting to manage the details personally of Patton's attack; the Third Army commander needed scant pushing and little oversight in this operation. In the case of Middleton and Patton, then, Bradley significantly assisted their overall defense and countermeasures by remaining consistent with this characteristic of his battle leadership.

One strength of Bradley's leadership during the campaigns of the Mediterranean and of France—his commitment as an Allied "team player" who firmly supported Ike as SHAEF's commander—was absent throughout much of the Ardennes battle. Bradley deeply resented the decision to give Monty command of his northern armies, despite his own admission during the battle that the logic behind Ike's decision was apparent—that is, he agreed with the necessity of rearranging the command setup.

The arguments Bradley uses to justify his opposition to Montgomery's assumption of command of the US Armies seem especially disingenuous, because they center around Bradley's supposed fear of Monty's unnecessary delay in launching a counteroffensive.[119] If, as Bradley claims, he held these misgivings at the time the change in command was made, then his failure to take action to firmly establish his own personal control and contact with his two armies in the north appears even more damning. Indeed, Bradley himself was not pushing Hodges or Simpson to organize a counteroffensive at the time Monty assumed command, and it was Patton, not Bradley, who initiated the thrust into the southern part of the bulge. His arguments seem to be the result of damaged pride more than of any genuine fears held before the change.

In addition, Bradley's criticisms seem even more petty because he fails to acknowledge the positive aspects of Montgomery's timely assumption of command in the north. Lacking Bradley's presence in the north (or any of his 12th Army Group staff, for that matter), Hodges, Simpson, and their subordinate commanders fighting desperately to stop the German drive welcomed Montgomery's arrival (along with his liaison officers and other 21 Army Group staff). Brigadier General Bruce C. Clarke, who, along with the remainder of the 7th Armored Division, was conducting a magnificent defense of St.-Vith with no help or guidance from any higher headquarters, reflected that he was elated when the Field Marshal arrived on 20 December. Clarke and his division commander, Brigadier General Bob Hasbrouck, reported that Montgomery raised their own self-confidence and had a positive effect on the morale of their battle-weary troops.[120]

Although Monty has been criticized for emphasizing a "tidy show" too much over a rapid counterattack, it cannot be denied that he brought needed order and discipline to a confused and chaotic situation. By 18 December, Hodges' First Army headquarters was in a shambles, his staff having abandoned their command post in Spa in such a panic that Hasbrouck's staff, trying to find anyone from First Army who could give them information about the battle, discovered the deserted command post with secret documents and classified operational maps left scattered about.[121] Monty's presence (and that of his British armored units, which now guarded the previously undefended Meuse River bridges) helped to remedy this panicky situation by steadying the shaken Hodges and freeing his staff to concentrate on the conduct of their defense. On the other hand, by allowing his personal pride to overcome his previously well demonstrated ability to act unselfishly as an Allied team member, Bradley had a negative impact on the northern defenses and the Ardennes outcome.

Bradley could show boldness and initiative in his battle leadership—and sometimes not. During the planning for the Normandy invasion, he was a leading advocate of a major airborne operation to precede the landings. This risky undertaking was opposed by many in the Allied camp, but Bradley's firm support of it convinced Eisenhower to let it proceed.[122] His willingness in July and August of 1944 to let Patton's Third Army race off across the French countryside, trailing a long, exposed right flank was also risky, but it helped the Allied armies get hundreds of kilometers and several weeks ahead of the pre-invasion schedule.[123] And later in the war, when the 9th Armored Division presented him with the ultimate prize—an intact bridge across the Rhine at Remagen—Bradley did not hesitate to exploit it.[124]

These stunning successes were sometimes counterbalanced by failures to capitalize on the possibilities they presented. After the Normandy breakout, Bradley seemed content to follow blindly the pre-invasion plan to capture the Brittany ports, despite some of his more perceptive subordinates' urging to the contrary. He allowed his armored strength to be diverted to the west, into Brittany, instead of driving quickly east to the main enemy forces.[125] This conventional approach to the campaign delayed Patton's offensive. Later, after supporting the bold plan to swing Patton's army northward to trap the German Army in the Falaise Pocket, Bradley suddenly became more orthodox in his exercise of command and prevented Patton from closing the gap in a timely manner. This allowed a great number of the enemy to escape from the trap that Allied initiative had created.[126] In the Ardennes, initiative and boldness seemed to desert him completely.

A weak argument can be constructed that Bradley's boldness was a factor leading to the early success of the German Ardennes attack, for it was partly because of his decision to hold the Ardennes with a thin line of wornout or green divisions (his so-called "calculated risk" to permit offensive action inother areas) that allowed the enemy to crack American defenses. However, this theory presumes that Bradley's "calculated risk" explanation for the thinness of the Ardennes sector holds up to scrutiny—but it doesn't.[127] Bradley never really thought there was any chance the Germans would launch a mobile counteroffensive, and he certainly didn't think any German counterattack would strike the Ardennes. This time boldness was not a factor.

Once the German attack began, Bradley's battle leadership displayed none of the initiative shown in Normandy or across France. He allowed Eisenhower to take the lead in reacting to the German attack and was slow in getting his own headquarters into the fight. His principal subordinate, Patton, devised the bold counterstroke delivered by the Third Army, with Bradley seemingly content to let events sweep him along.[128] Although he was correct in letting his talented subordinate execute the southern drive without interference from 12th Army Group, a bolder Bradley would have played a greater guiding role in its creation. If he had taken the initiative to visit Hodges, he surely could have assisted the overwhelmed First Army commander in sorting out a proper defense and would likely have avoided the galling command change. Despite Bradley's postwar harping on Montgomery's slowness to begin a counterattack in the north, it appears that Bradley's own lack of action was a big contributor to the reverses. Had he displayed the same aggressiveness and risk-taking shown during OVERLORD and the battles in France, Bradley would have had a good chance of trapping the bulk of German forces in the salient. Instead, his leadership during the Battle of the Bulge did not live up to its potential.

As a final insight into Bradley's demonstrated battle leadership during the Ardennes fighting, it may be instructive to delve briefly into his personal character, to examine the image of the simple farmer boy suddenly raised to fame and glory by fate and circumstance. Not surprisingly, much of this image appears to be more perception than reality. Bradley's simple beginnings notwithstanding, he emerges as a much more complex individual than the Bradley legend perpetuates. If his autobiography is accurate (some would argue it is more Clay Blair than Omar Bradley), Bradley was concerned with rank and prestige from his earliest days in the service. He describes his failure to get to France in World War I in terms of reduced promotion possibilities in future years[129] and actually turned down a combat command in Siberia because it offered no chance for advancement.[130]

He selected unit assignments for the sought-after positions they offered and accepted schooling if it promised chances of future promotions.[131] Bradley exults when he receives a plum assignment and is positively ecstatic when Marshall offers him command of the Infantry School in 1941 because it comes with a brigadier general's star.

Bradley's resentment of Montgomery's assumption of command during the Ardennes seems to be that of a man who has been personally humiliated, not that of an Allied commander who thinks Ike has made an error that will damage the coalition. Further, Bradley may have feared this command move placed his upcoming four-star rank in jeopardy.[132] Whatever his actual motivation, it is evident in his own and other witnesses' writings that the reassignment of his First and Ninth Armies to Montgomery was personally devastating to him. The unconcealed bitterness in his autobiography bespeaks a man watching his career being destroyed, and when he writes in response to Ike's decision that "I prayed for the souls of the dead American GI's,"[133] the overdramatic imagery seems to lack sincerity.

Perhaps the inconsistencies in Bradley's leadership that arose in the Ardennes fighting can, at least in part, be explained by his personal character—his shock and disappointment at having the bulk of his command given to a man whom he despised, because of an attack he never imagined would be launched.

Thus there is evidence that the Bradley reality doesn't quite fit the Bradley legend, but, like most stories, Bradley's legend contains kernels of truth. Historian Russell Weigley points out, "Bradley's Lincolnesque, homespun kindliness readily inspired devotion" among his staff and throughout the great mass of American citizen-soldiers in the European Theater.[134] Bradley actually was "unassuming and softspoken" and seems to have genuinely cared about the lives and welfare of his soldiers, all 1,300,000 of them.[135] They believed this and responded with raised morale and improved self-confidence. And because the Battle of the Bulge was in many ways a soldier's fight of small units refusing to quit, then the morale and confidence inspired by the Bradley image throughout the earlier campaigns in the Mediterranean and in France can be said to have affected positively and significantly the battle's outcome by laying the groundwork for his soldiers' ultimate success.

DARKEST OF TIMES

Historian Forrest Pogue said, "You never get it absolutely right. History is always escaping us."[136] And so it must be with any attempt to gain an exact assessment of the "true" impact of Bradley's leadership in the Battle of the Bulge. Although it appears from an analysis of his actions and decisions during the battle that the overall impact of his leadership was not positive, such an assessment must be seen within the context of the entire war in the European Theater in order to gain a proper perspective. Much of his battle leadership in the Ardennes was inconsistent with his earlier conduct and seems uncharacteristic of his overall command. Damning Bradley's leadership during one battle of the war (great though this battle was) overshadows his significant accomplishments, both prewar and during the war as Eisenhower's principal American lieutenant.

Despite the various criticisms leveled against Bradley's actions, decisions, and abilities during the Ardennes and other campaigns of World War II, it is nevertheless true that his careful, cautious, and steady approach to the management and direction of nearly one and a half million American soldiers was a key contributing factor to organizing the final Allied victory.[137] His most important accomplishment was his often-demonstrated ability to provide a calm and steady hand at the helm while continually pushing his army commanders forward. Bradley was, for the most part, a team player who usually supported Eisenhower and Allied leadership. He backed his army commanders and supported their plans with a minimum of interference. Bradley understood and empathized with the common soldier and his cautious approach made it possible to preserve their lives by replacing manpower with firepower and mobility.

After his campaigns in North Africa and Sicily, he seldom was involved in the frontline management of the fighting of his forward units, but his influence was felt throughout the Army Group. Despite Bradley's lackluster and disappointing performance in the Ardennes—truly his darkest of times—any assessment of his overall battle leadership will inevitably fall closer to Eisenhower's judgment of his skill as a battle-line commander than to Patton's condemnation as an "orthodox...nothing."[138] Thus, Bradley retained the Supreme Commander's confidence to the end of the war, and Ike was inspired to send this assessment of him to Marshall:

> [Bradley] has never once held back in attempting any maneuver, no matter how bold in conception and never has he paused to regroup when there was opportunity lying on his front. His handling of his Army Commanders has been superb and his energy, common sense, tactical skill and complete loyalty have made him a great lieutenant on whom I can always rely with the greatest confidence.[139]

NOTES

1. Omar N. Bradley and Clay Blair, *A General's Life: An Autobiography of General of the Army Omar N. Bradley* (New York: Simon and Schuster, 1983), 159, 200. This book, completed 2 years after General Bradley died, caused some controversy because of Blair's insistence that it was an autobiography. He purportedly explained the fact that he, not Bradley, had written much of the book by saying that, because he and Bradley had worked so closely together on preparing the book, he had come to think like Bradley, thereby justifying his completion of the book as a posthumous autobiography. Despite the difficulty in determining exactly what part of the book is Bradley and what part is Blair, it nevertheless seems to provide an excellent insight into the inner workings of the American Army in Europe in World War II. Concerning the Ernie Pyle story, Bradley writes: "Pyle caught up with me in Nicosia (Sicily, August 1943). I was still very leery of publicity, but my aide Chet Hansen convinced me I should cooperate. Pyle was a little leery, too. Up to now, he had written exclusively about GI's and he was not comfortable with the brass. He stuck with me like a shadow for three days. Then he wrote a six-part series (about 5,000 words) that was widely published in the States. The series hardly made me a household name, but it was my first extensive national publicity. Even with all his creative gifts, Pyle had a difficult time making me 'colorful.'"

2. US Department of the Army, Headquarters Department of the Army, *General Orders Number 11*, 27 April 1981. This document is the official announcement of General Bradley's death. It contains an abbreviated official military biography.

3. Russell F. Weigley, *Eisenhower's Lieutenants: The Campaigns of France and Germany 1944-1945* (Bloomington: Indiana University Press, 1981), 503-505; Bradley and Blair, *A General's Life*, 368, 370. Bradley went on to write of this incident, "It required every fiber of my strength to restrain myself from an insulting outburst."

4. Martin Blumenson, *Patton: The Man Behind the Legend 1885-1945* (New York: Berkley Books, 1985), 228, 306; Martin Blumenson, *The Patton Papers II* (Boston: Houghton-Mifflin, 1974). Blumenson explains, "Patton made caustic remarks privately about his contemporaries, Eisenhower, Bradley, Clark, Bedell Smith, Montgomery. No one, according to Patton, was as good as he. They were all mediocre or tired or clerks or unimaginative or afraid or cautious or just plain old dumb."

5. Alfred D. Chandler et al., eds., *The Papers of Dwight David*

Eisenhower, The War Years (Baltimore: Johns Hopkins Press, 1970), 4:2375. This accolation was contained in a cable Eisenhower sent to Marshall on 30 March 1945, primarily concerning Bradley's actions in commanding 12th Army Group during its "spectacular successes" in the final campaign through Germany. However, it was intended to compliment Bradley's overall performance throughout his tenure as Army Group commander and, perhaps, draw some publicity upon Bradley's accomplishment (and away from Patton who was, by this time in the war, monopolizing the press coverage).

6. Bradley and Blair, *A General's Life*, 17-23. This account relies heavily upon Bradley's autobiography for information about his early life and career. When possible, information has been verified in other sources; however, Bradley (or Blair) must be taken at their word for the most part.

7. Ibid., 17-23.

8. Forrest C. Pogue, "General of the Army Omar N. Bradley." *The War Lords: Military Commanders of the Twentieth Century*, ed. Field Marshal Sir Michael Carver (Boston: Little, Brown and Company, 1976), 538; Bradley and Blair, *A General's Life*, 25-29. Pogue notes that, even early on, Bradley's image was better suited to a schoolteacher's than a soldier's, and writes, "He taught briefly before going to the Military Academy, exhibiting early the ability to teach. His modest bearing and gentle manner suggested less the fiery soldier than the sympathetic mentor eager to instruct the men entrusted to his care."

9. *The Howitzer* (West Point: The United States Military Academy, 1915); Bradley and Blair, *A General's Life*, 30-35. Bradley's entry in *The Howitzer*, the West Point yearbook (written by his classmate and friend Eisenhower), seems prophetic when it says, "[Bradley's] most promising characteristic is 'getting there,' and if he keeps up the clip he's started, some of us will some day be bragging to our grandchildren that, 'Sure, General Bradley was a classmate of mine.'"

10. Bradley and Blair, *A General's Life*, 35. Bradley related that engineers and field artillery were sought-after commissions because the army then promoted officers by branch (instead of at large) and promotions in these two branches occurred quicker. When that policy was changed in 1916, all officers were placed on an equal footing, and Bradley felt better about his promotion opportunities in the Infantry branch.

11. Ibid., 36. Eisenhower described Mexican border duty: "This service was disagreeable. Usually, it separated a man from his family. Living conditions were rough. Anything was better to

most officers than the border."

12. Ibid.

13. Ibid., 37. Bradley's first garrison, Fort George Wright, was located 3 miles outside the town of Spokane. His company was severely understrength, mustering no more than 70 men. Fort Wright was the garrison for the 14th Infantry Regiment's 3rd Battalion. The 2nd Battalion was in Seattle, and the 1st Battalion was on detached duty in Alaska.

14. Ibid., 41-43.

15. Ibid., 44-45.

16. Bradley and Blair, *A General's Life*, 45-46. Camp Dodge, located only a few miles outside Des Moines, in the farm suburb of Grimes, IA, serves today as the headquarters for the Iowa Army National Guard. A training camp in both World Wars, it has changed very little from Bradley's day.

17. Ibid., 46.

18. Ibid.

19. Russell F. Weigley, *History of the United States Army* (New York: Macmillan Publishing Company, 1967), 396; Bradley and Blair, *A General's Life*, 46. Weigley laments, "The laws authorizing the wartime army entitled nearly all who served in it to prompt discharge, and the soldiers returned to the United States and to their homes in a rush that dwarfed the Civil War demobilization: 2,608,218 enlisted men and 128,436 officers received discharges by June 30, 1919. By January 1, 1920, only 130,000, mainly the Regular Army, stood under arms..."

20. James L. Stokesbury, *A Short History of World War I* (New York: William Morrow and Company, 1981), 259, 313; Bradley and Blair, *A General's Life*, 47-48. The Allied intervention in Russia, primarily near Archangel in North Russia and Vladivostok in Siberia, eventually involved 15 anti-Soviet nations. Without achieving much, save long-lasting distrust and hard feelings from the Soviets, it ended "after some ineffectual interference."

21. Weigley, *History of the U.S. Army*, 399-414; Bradley and Blair, *A General's Life*, 47-48. Some of Bradley's contemporaries who served in lengthy ROTC assignments included Troy H. Middleton, John S. Wood, Bruce C. Clarke, and James A. Van Fleet.

22. Douglas MacArthur, *Reminiscences* (New York: McGraw-Hill, 1964), 77-83; Bradley and Blair, *A General's Life*, 49. MacArthur, as USMA Superintendent 1919-22, instituted many sweeping changes at the Military Academy and brought the floundering school into the 20th century. Among his reforms were increased class size, improved and emphasized academics,

abolishment of much of the hazing of underclassmen, strengthened honor code, increased cadet participation in athletics, and a return to a 4-year course (after a wartime hiatus that saw accelerated classes).

23. Bradley and Blair, *A General's Life*, 50.

24. Ibid., 53-54.

25. Ambrose, *Eisenhower*, 72, 74, 78-79; Bradley and Blair, *A General's Life*, 54-56. Bradley finished second in his Infantry Advanced Course class at Fort Benning, just behind Leonard T. "Gee" Gerow (later V Corps, then 15th Army commander in 1944-45). Gerow was Ike's study-mate at Leavenworth during the Command and Staff School, 1925-26. Gerow graduated second in his class—behind Eisenhower.

26. Bradley and Blair, *A General's Life*, 57-59.

27. Ibid., 59. Of the National Guard assignment, Bradley wrote: "In effect, I became liaison officer between the U.S. Army and the Hawaiian National Guard, responsible for training standards and a wide variety of administrative duties, none of them overly taxing or challenging. Duty called; I responded, but not happily."

28. Bradley and Blair, *A General's Life*, 61.

29. Ibid., 62. There can be little doubt that Bradley's fortuitous association with Marshall here at the Infantry School marks the real beginning of his rise to prominence in the Army. Marshall was immediately impressed with the younger officer and added Bradley's name near the top of his list of promising officers to help him mold the World War II army.

30. Pogue, "General Bradley," 539; Bradley and Blair, *A General's Life*, 63-73. According to Pogue, Marshall said Bradley was "conspicuous for his ability to handle people and his ability to do things carefully and simply."

31. Bradley and Blair, *A General's Life*, 71. In fact, Bradley's friend and fellow faculty member at the Infantry School, Joe Stilwell, advised him not to go, saying, "Brad, why would you go to a school and prepare yourself for a job you don't want?" Bradley also remembered Marshall's example from World War I, where Marshall's excellent reputation as a staff officer had kept him in Pershing's headquarters and out of a combat troop command throughout that war.

32. Ambrose, *Eisenhower*, 85; Bradley and Blair, *A General's Life*, 74-75. Ambrose described the War College of this era: "The college, in theory, was the capstone of an officer's postgraduate education. Its mission was to prepare men for high command. In

practice, it was a reward rather than a challenge, a relaxing year [students were neither examined nor ranked], spent mainly listening to lectures on world affairs by government officials and army generals. The idea was to broaden the outlook of officers tapped for future high command; the reality was more a pleasant sabbatical."

33. Bradley and Blair, *A General's Life*, 75-77. As a "Tac Officer" working for the Commandant of Cadets, Bradley assumed responsibility for the discipline, character development, physical fitness, and military instruction of the cadets in his charge. Pure academic subjects, such as the mathematics he had taught during his previous tour at West Point, remained the responsibility of the Dean of the Academic Board and the professors. This tour as a "Tac" allowed Bradley to experience the other elements of the transformation of young cadets into officers, and he enjoyed it immensely.

34. *General Orders Number 11*, 1.

35. Bradley and Blair, *A General's Life*, 79.

36. *General Orders Number 11*, 1; Bradley and Blair, *A General's Life*, 80-81.

37. Ibid., 83-92.

38. Ibid., 94. With this promotion to Brigadier General (skipping the rank of Colonel completely), Bradley jumped ahead of his (until now) faster-moving classmate, Eisenhower. Ike would catch, then pass him, however, in the next 18 months.

39. Ibid., 95.

40. John K. Mahon, *History of the Militia and the National Guard* (New York: Macmillan, 1983), 186-187; Robert R. Palmer, et al., *The United States Army in World War II: The Army Ground Forces. The Procurement and Training of Ground Combat Troops* (Washington, DC: Office of the Chief of Military History/GPO, 1948), 91-92.

41. Bradley and Blair, *A General's Life*, 97. It should be noted that at least two other major training projects were occurring at Fort Benning during Bradley's tenure—the formation of the first US airborne combat units, and the 2nd Armored Division. Although Bradley became an ardent supporter of both types of unit, there is no evidence he was instrumental in their development or fielding. Nevertheless, as commandant of the school, he must have kept abreast of new developments in both formations, a fact which would benefit his battle leadership in the Mediterranean and northern Europe.

42. *General Orders Number 11*, 1.

43. Palmer, et al., *Army Ground Forces*, 489-493; Bradley and Blair, *A General's Life*, 102-105.

44. James W. Bradin, "28th Infantry Division: The Forgotten Pennsylvanians," *Army*, 37 (August 1987): 62-67; Bradley and Blair, *A General's Life*, 108-109. Bradley complained, "The 28th National Guard Division, to which Marshall had consigned me in June 1942, was plagued with all the faults of most Guard divisions. It was based at Camp Livingston, ten miles north of Alexandria, Louisiana, only thirty-eight miles from our own camp, part of Oscar Griswold's IV Corps, to which the 82nd Division was assigned. Griswold and I had often discussed its problems in private."

45. Bradley and Blair, *A General's Life*, 112. The cable, received at noon on 12 February 1943, read: "It is only fitting that your birthday should precede by only a few days your transfer to command a corps which comes as a long-delayed acknowledgment of your splendid record with the 28th Division. Congratulations and Best Wishes. Marshall."

46. Martin Blumenson, *Kasserine Pass* (New York: Jove Books, 1983), 1-7; Martin Blumenson and James L. Stokesbury, *Masters of the Art of Command* (New York: Da Capo, 1975), 263-286.

47. Stephen E. Ambrose, *The Supreme Commander: The War Years of General of the Army Dwight D. Eisenhower* (Garden City, NY: Doubleday and Company, 1970), 174-176, 185; Blumenson, *Kasserine Pass*, 307; Bradley and Blair, *A General's Life*, 131; Chandler, et al., *Eisenhower Papers*, 2:816. In an 11 February 1943 cable to Marshall, Eisenhower listed, in this order, the following general officers (major generals) who would be acceptable to act as his "eyes and ears": John H. Hester (CG, 43rd Infantry Division); Terrell (CG, 90th Infantry Division); Bradley; Rapp Brush (CG, 40th Armored Division); "Pinky" Bull (Head of Replacement and School Command, Army Ground Forces); Charles H. Gerhardt (CG, 91st Infantry Division); Matthew B. Ridgway (CG, 82nd Airborne Division); Paul L. Ransom (CG, 98th Infantry Division); Charles H. Corlett (upcoming CG, 7th Infantry Division); John B. Wogan (CG, 14th Armored Division); and William G. Livesay (35th Infantry Division, then CG, 91st Infantry Division). Interestingly, Ike also listed a retired officer, recently recalled to active duty on the War Department Manpower Board, Lorenzo D. Gasser. Eisenhower specified that the job required "brains, tact and imagination more than it does thorough acquaintanceship with the theater, so that any man of ability could begin to operate efficiently after a week of indoctrination." Marshall wired back that Bradley was immediately available. Ike quickly accepted.

48. Blumenson, *Patton*, 182; Bradley and Blair, *A General's Life*, 133. Bradley described his duties: "When I concluded my indoctrination at Ike's headquarters and received my formal orders, I was not overjoyed at my assignment. I was not only to act as Ike's eyes and ears on the Tunisian front, reporting back to him directly, I also had authority to make 'suggestive changes' (as Ike put it) to American commanders at the front. Inevitably, I would be regarded as an odious spy for Ike, carrying tales outside the chain of command. Any suggested corrections from a rank newcomer from an exalted rear-echelon headquarters would be bitterly resented and probably ignored or laughed at behind my back. I decided my best policy was to keep a very low profile, eyes and ears open, mouth shut."

49. Maurice Matloff, *United States Army in World War II: The War Department. Strategic Planning for Coalition Warfare 1943-1944* (Washington, DC: Office of the Chief of Military History/GPO, 1959), 50-51; Ambrose, *Eisenhower*, 236-237; Bradley and Blair, *A General's Life*, 153-159.

50. Bradley and Blair, *A General's Life*, 151, 155. Bradley claims that, even in this early point in Ike's exercise of coalition command, he tended to favor the British too much. he wrote, "If I were to continue to serve as one of [Eisenhower's] battlefield lieutenants, it was clear that I must be much, much firmer in advancing American interests and strategy."

51. Ibid., 156. Bradley records that he was nearly killed three times while visiting forward units at the Tunisian front.

52. Ambrose, *Eisenhower*, 234; Bradley and Blair, *A General's Life*, 154-157. During the final Allied offensive in Tunisia (April-May 1943), Bradley's II U.S. Corps was technically under command of British General K.A.N. Anderson, commander of the First British Army, and British General Sir Harold Alexander, Eisenhower's Deputy Ground Commander. Bradley indicates in his autobiography that he had little respect for Anderson's abilities as a commander, and thought "he was in over his head as an army commander." Bradley had more respect for Alexander, but found his lack of faith in the American soldier's fighting abilities as a cause of friction (in Tunisia as well as later in Sicily).

53. Chandler, et al., *Eisenhower Papers*, 2:998. By this time, Ike had recommended Bradley for his third star and promotion to Lieutenant General.

54. Bradley and Blair, *A General's Life*, 159.

55. Frank J. Price, *Troy H. Middleton: A Biography* (Baton Rouge: LSU Press, 1974), 137, 140-141; Ambrose, *Eisenhower*, 222.

Bradley and Blair, *A General's Life*, 169-172.

56.   Ibid., 200.

57.   Blumenson, *Patton*, 207-215; Bradley and Blair, *A General's Life*, 201-202; Ambrose, *Eisenhower*, 250-252, 274-275. There were two "slapping" incidents, occurring a week apart during early and mid-August 1943. Both soldiers were suffering from combat fatigue, but drew Patton's wrath since they showed no outward manifestations or obvious wounds. Bradley soon learned of the second incident: "After leaving the hospital, Patton came to my CP. He mentioned that he had had to slap a malingering soldier, but the remark was so casual and vague it didn't fully register on me. Two days later I had good reason to recall his remark. Bill Kean [Bradley's Chief of Staff] handed me an explosive official letter to the II Corps from the hospital commander reporting in damning detail the entire incident. I was horrified. Even for George Patton it was excessive conduct. I realized that if word of this incident got out, we might lose Patton's talents forever. I ordered Kean to lock the letter in my safe and say nothing whatsoever about it. Not aware of the first slapping incident, I naively hoped the matter would be forgotten or go away." Bradley's inaction in this famous incident is disappointing for one who has a reputation as a "soldier's general." His excuse for covering up the incident seems weak. Apparently, he never even confronted Patton with the official report he received, let alone alert Eisenhower to a potentially disastrous situation. Not only did Bradley's coverup let down the soldier victimized by Patton, it placed Eisenhower in an extremely embarrassing position a short time later when the story, inevitably, got out. If these actions had occurred in today's Army, it is highly likely that Bradley would have also been relieved of command.

58.   Chandler, et al., *Eisenhower Papers*, 2:1205.

59.   Omar N. Bradley, *A Soldier's Story* (New York: Henry Holt and Company, 1951), 8; Chandler, et al., *Eisenhower Papers*, 2:1209-1214. In his first book, published shortly after the end of the war, Bradley described his feelings at being told by Ike on 1 September 1943 that he would have a major command in OVERLORD: "A bare five months before, I had been given command of a corps; now it was to be an Army. After 28 years of snail's-pace, peacetime promotions, I was now finding it difficult to keep stars in stock. As a result of the Tunisian campaign I had become the only U.S. corps commander with battle experience against the Germans. And in Sicily I had cut my teeth on a large-scale amphibious assault. Both assignments were invaluable experience of me for the invasion of Europe."

60.   Bradley and Blair, *A General's Life*, 208.

61. Gordon A. Harrison, *United States Army in World War II: The European Theater of Operations. Cross-Channel Attack* (Washington, DC: Office of the Chief of Military History, 1951), 183-187; John Keegan, *Six Armies in Normandy: From D-Day to the Liberation of Paris* (New York: Penguin Books, 1983), 21-67; Bradley, *A Soldier's Story*, 233-236; Bradley and Blair, *A General's Life*, 226-227. Bradley reports that British Air Marshal Leigh-Mallory, the most vocal opponent of large-scale airborne landings, estimated that paratroopers would take casualties of up to 50 percent, glider troops up to 70 percent. According to Bradley, Ike had to make the final decision, and "after hearing all the pros and cons, ruled in [Bradley's] favor."

62. Bradley and Blair, *A General's Life*, 226.

63. Ambrose, *Supreme Commander*, 597.

64. Bradley and Blair, *A General's Life*, 251.

65. Ibid., 252, 259.

66. Martin Blumenson, *United States Army in World War II: European Theater of Operations. Breakout and Pursuit* (Washington, DC: Office of the Chief of Military History/GPO, 1961), 36-47. Blumenson summed up the situation facing Bradley and his American troops: "...the situation of the U.S. First Army just before it began its July offensive [was] an attack pointed through a flooded pastoral region of ten thousand little fields enclosed by hedgerows. Through this region, made for ambush, where the German defenders had dug into the hedgerow banks and erected strong defense, the Americans were to fight from field to field, from hedgerow to hedgerow, measuring the progress of their advance in yards. Over it all a steady rain was to pour, and the odors of the Normandy soil were to mingle with the smell of decaying flesh and become part of the war."

67. Harold J. Meyer, *Hanging Sam: A Military Biography of General Samuel T. Williams, From Pancho Villa to Vietnam* (Denton TX: University of North Texas Press, 1990), 72-73; Blumenson, *Breakout and Pursuit*, 36-47. Brigadier General Jay W. MacKelvie led the 90th Infantry Division in just 4 days of combat (10-14 June 1944) before being relieved for cause. He was replaced by Major General Eugene Landrum, who was also relieved a short time later.

68. Blumenson, *Breakout and Pursuit*, 198-304.

69. *General Orders Number 11*, 1; Bradley, *A Soldier's Story*, 358; Bradley and Blair, *A General's Life*, 283, 321. Montgomery remained Ike's Ground Commander (and technically Bradley's immediate superior) until 1 September 1944, when Eisenhower took formal command of all ground forces. Bradley and Montgomery

then became co-equal army group commanders.

70. Weigley, *Eisenhower's Lieutenants*, 175-286.

71. Ambrose, *Eisenhower*, 331-334; Bradley and Blair, *A General's Life*, 299.

72. Bradley, *A Soldier's Story*, 375-377; Bradley and Blair, *A General's Life*, 293-297.

73. Martin Van Creveld, *Supplying War: Logistics From Wallenstein to Patton* (New York: Cambridge University Press, 1977), 224-230; Weigley, *Eisenhower's Lieutenants*, 268-277; Blumenson, *Breakout and Pursuit*, 655-656.

74. Charles B. MacDonald, *The Battle of the Huertgen Forest* (New York: Jove Books, 1984), 2-4. The phrase "Passchendaele with tree bursts" is attributed by MacDonald to Ernest Hemingway. Passchendaele refers to the bloody World War I battle in Flanders (Third Battle of Ypres, July to November 1917) which cost the British 300,000 casualties for a gain of about 5 miles.

75. Combat Studies Institute, *Conversations With General J. Lawton Collins* (Fort Leavenworth, KS: U.S. Army Command and General Staff College, 1983), 9-10. Collins comment that "someone had to cover that sector" begs the question of why an all-out US offensive was thrown into the Huertgen. It was only later that First Army awoke to the key objective of the Roer River dams in the Huertgen area, so it seems likely that Collins' offensive was launched because poorly prepared staff officers and commanders thought the Siegfried Line could be easily breached in this area.

76. MacDonald, *Battle of the Huertgen Forest*, 195-205.

77. U.S. Department of the Army, 12th Army Group, *G-1 Section, 12th Army Group Report of Operations*, 1948, 135-136; Bradley and Blair, *A General's Life*, 354. Bradley signed a memorandum to Eisenhower dated 15 December 1944, the day prior to the Ardennes attack, which complained that 12th Army Group had a total understrength of 19,069 infantrymen (17,581 riflemen) out of a total understrength of 30,327. The situation showed no signs of improving and appeared to Bradley to have reached a crisis stage. (The war planners' "90 Division Gamble" very nearly failed.)

78. Bradley and Blair, *A General's Life*, 355-356.

79. Weigley, *Eisenhower's Lieutenants*, 458.

80. Bradley and Blair, *A General's Life*, 356; Ambrose, *Eisenhower*, 365; Weigley, *Eisenhower's Lieutenants*, 458. Ambrose, referring to the decision to send the two armored divisions to the Ardennes, reports that Ike said, "'I think you had better send Middleton some help,' he told Bradley. Studying the operations map with Strong [Ike's G-2], Eisenhower noted that the 7th Armored

Division was out of the line in First Army sector, and that the 10th Armored Division, a part of Third Army, was currently uncommitted. He told Bradley to send the two divisions to Middleton, in the Ardennes. Bradley hesitated; he knew that both Hodges and Patton would be upset at losing the divisions, Patton especially, as the 10th Armored was one of his favorites. With a touch of impatience, Eisenhower overruled Bradley, and orders went out that night, sending the 10th to the southern flank of the penetration, while the 7th occupied a road junction named St. Vith, on the northern flank."

81. Bradley and Blair, *A General's Life*, 356.

82. Price, *Middleton*, 214; Bradley and Blair, *A General's Life*, 354.

83. Hugh M. Cole, *The United States Army in World War II: European Theater of Operations. Ardennes: Battle of the Bulge* (Washington, DC: Office of the Chief of Military History/GPO, 1965), 305-306.

84. Ibid., 269, 289.

85. Weigley, *Eisenhower's Lieutenants*, 465-490.

86. Ibid., p. 465.

87. Bradley and Blair, *A General's Life*, 357.

88. Ibid., 368.

89. Cole, *Ardennes*, 411.

90. Weigley, *Eisenhower's Lieutenants*, 503.

91. Ambrose, *Eisenhower*, 368. Ambrose reports that Ike had a stormy conversation with Bradley when he notified him of the command change on the morning of 20 December: "He called Bradley on the telephone to inform him. By now, Bradley was set against any such change. Strong [Ike's G-2] could hear him shouting at Eisenhower, 'By God, Ike, I cannot be responsible to the American people if you do this. I resign.' Eisenhower flushed with shock and anger, drew a deep breath, then said, 'Brad, I—not you—am responsible to the American people. Your resignation therefore means absolutely nothing.' There was a pause, then another protest from Bradley, but this time without any threats. Eisenhower declared, 'Well, Brad, those are my orders.' He then turned the conversation to Patton's counterattack, which he declared he wanted mounted in the greatest possible strength."

92. Bradley and Blair, *A General's Life*, 368.

93. Ibid., 364.

94. Blumenson, *Patton*, 246-250; Weigley, *Eisenhower's Lieutenants*, 498-501; Cole, *Ardennes*, 331-334.

95. Blumenson, *Patton*, 246-247; Bradley and Blair, *A General's*

Life, 358; Weigley, *Eisenhower's Lieutenants*, 498. Weigley, quoting Ladislas Farago, one of Patton's biographers, writes that even prior to the German attack, Patton had surmised that there was something brewing across the front from Middleton's VIII Corps: "Patton sniffed danger. '...the First Army is making a terrible mistake,' he confided to his diary on November 25, 'in leaving the VIII Corps static, as it is highly probable the Germans are building up east of them.' By December 12, Patton's hunch about an enemy assault against VIII Corps was strong enough that he instructed General Gay, his chief of staff, and Colonel Halley G. Maddox, his G-3, to study 'what the Third Army would do if called upon to counterattack through...a breakthrough' in VIII Corps front." He had his staff prepare contingency counterattack plans for three axes, one of which turned out to be the Bastogne "corridor." Patton was prepared, therefore, when Bradley asked him on the morning of 18 December what he could bring to bear against the bulge.

96. Weigley, *Eisenhower's Lieutenants*, 499.

97. Blumenson, *Patton Papers II*, 599-600; Blumenson, *Patton*, 252; Weigley, *Eisenhower's Lieutenants*, 500. Weigley, while admiring Patton's "masterfully executed" plan, notes perceptively, "the operation should also be kept in appropriate perspective; it was not a unique stroke of genius. Other competent military commanders have accomplished similarly rapid disengagements, turns of direction, and recommitments. Patton, rather immodestly, bragged to his wife, "The relief of Bastogne...is the most brilliant operation we have thus far performed and is in my opinion the outstanding achievement of this war." At a press conference on New Year's Day 1945, he praised his troops' "marvelous feat," claiming, "I know of no equal to it in military history." Like the 101st Airborne Division's defense of Bastogne, Patton's maneuver has become a miliary icon, whose brilliance is accepted on faith. Anyone having the temerity to challenge either of these actions (or to write critically of them) is branded a heretic and dismissed out of hand.

98. Bradley and Blair, *A General's Life*, 369.

99. Ibid., 371.

100. Ibid., 370.

101. Weigley, *Eisenhower's Lieutenants*, 540-541; Bradley and Blair, *A General's Life*, 371-373.

102. Martin Van Creveld, *Fighting Power: German and U.S. Army Performance 1939-1945* (Westport, Connecticut: Greenwood Press, 1982), 65-66; Bradley and Blair, *A General's Life*, 385. Bradley wrote: "Our forces met at Houffalize on January 16, cutting the German salient at the waist, exactly one month after von

Rundstedt launched the Bulge offensive. But we were too late to trap the mass of Germans. They had withdrawn toward the Westwall, maneuvering skillfully under difficult circumstances." Throughout the campaigns of France and Germany, the German Army demonstrated a remarkable ability to reconstitute forces that continued to fight effectively right up to the end of the war.

103. Montgomery, *Memoirs*, 28.

104. Weigley, *Eisenhower's Lieutenants*, 540-547.

105. Ibid., 545.

106. Bradley and Blair, *A General's Life*, 387.

107. Chandler, et al., *Eisenhower Papers*, 4:2375; Blumenson, *Patton* 228, 306; Blumenson, *Patton Papers II*.

108. Bradley and Blair, *A General's Life*, 156.

109. Meyer, *Hanging Sam*, 88-89; Bradley and Blair, *A General's Life*, 269. The relieved officer was Major General Eugene Landrum, 90th Infantry Division. Meyer quotes Bradley's war diary: "Everytime I went to see [Landrum], he was in his command post, which was usually in the basement of some building. He never got outside of it."

110. Bernard L. Montgomery, *The Memoirs of Field Marshal the Viscount Montgomery of Alamein, K.G.* (New York: Signet Books, 1958), 283.

111. Weigley, *Eisenhower's Lieutenants*, 505.

112. Ibid., 501-504.

113. Bradley and Blair, *A General's Life*, 358. In his autobiography Bradley tries to justify his failure to visit Hodges: "I intended to fly to Spa that day [18 December 1944] to see Hodges and brief him on the change in strategy. But Hodges' First Army had been hit by the full weight of the Sixth Panzer Armee. Gerow's V Corps, as well as Middleton's VIII Corps, was under severe attack. Hodges himself was in the process of retreating, moving his headquarters rearward from Spa to Chaudfontaine, outside Liège. It became clear in several telephone conversations with Hodges and Bill Kean [First Army Chief of Staff] that part of the First Army was in a bad way...Hodges was in no shape to mount a counterattack. It would take all of his planning and resources merely to hold the northern shoulder." Far from providing Bradley a good excuse for not visiting Hodges, these reasons seem to demand even greater energy on Bradley's part to get his calm, steadying presence to Hodges' side as quickly as possible.

114. Weigley, *Eisenhower's Lieutenants*, 465; Cole, *Ardennes*, 53-54.

115. Bradley and Blair, *A General's Life*, 155-156; Pogue,

"General Bradley," 547-548, 551-553.

116. Pogue, "General Bradley,": 551.

117. Price, *Middleton*, 214, 223, 226; Cole, *Ardennes*, 331.

118. U.S. Department of the Army, 4th Armored Division, *Armor at Bastogne*, Armored School, Student Research Paper, May 1949, 181. Roberts was extremely upset when Middleton ordered him to break up his armored combat command into small tank-infantry task forces. He complied, however, with Middleton's unorthodox use of armor. It helped save Bastogne for the 101st Airborne's arrival.

119. Bradley and Blair, *A General's Life*, 364-365.

120. Bruce C. Clarke, interview, 10 November 1987; Robert W. Hasbrouck to Bruce C. Clarke, undated (probably circa 1983-84). Hasbrouck goes so far as to say that Montgomery "saved the 7th Armored Division."

121. Hasbrouck to Clarke, undated. General Hasbrouck wrote, "I am sure you remember how First Army HQ fled from Spa leaving food cooking on the stoves, officers' Xmas presents from home on their beds and, worst of all, top secret maps still on the walls...First Army HQ never contacted us with their new location and I had to send an officer to find them. He did and they knew nothing about us. That's when Montgomery got into the picture. He was at First Army HQ when my officer arrived. A liaison officer from Montgomery arrived in my HQ within 24 hrs. His report to Montgomery is what saved us...."

122. Harrison, *Cross-Channel Attack*, 183-187; Keegan, *Six Armies in Normandy*, 21-67; Bradley and Blair, *A General's Life*, 226-227.

123. Bradley and Blair, *A General's Life*, 295.

124. Weigley, *Eisenhower's Lieutenants*, 626-633.

125. Blumenson, *Breakout and Pursuit*, 655-656.

126. Bradley and Blair, *A General's Life*, 302-305. In retrospect, Bradley referred to his action as "imprudent" and a "mistake."

127. Weigley, *Eisenhower's Lieutenants*, 460-463. Weigley remarks, "Bradley did not imagine a [German] stroke so unorthodox as a beaten enemy's rising up for an armored counteroffensive through some of the worst tank country on the Western front."

128. Ibid., 491-501.

129. Bradley and Blair, *A General's Life*, 46.

130. Ibid., 47.

131. Bradley and Blair, *A General's Life*, 60, 71.

132. Chandler, et al., *Eisenhower Papers*, 4:2237. The issue of Bradley's promotion to 4-star rank had initially been raised prior to

the Ardennes attack, but Eisenhower prodded Marshall about it during the reduction of the Ardennes salient, cabling the Army Chief of Staff, "I hope that...you will consider [Bradley] at once for four star promotion. I think it would have a fine general effect."

133. Bradley and Blair, *A General's Life*, 368.

134. Weigley, *Eisenhower's Lieutenants*, 171.

135. Ibid.

136. Forrest C. Pogue, "Over the Beaches: D-Day," S.L.A Marshall Lecture, Fort Leavenworth, KS, 17 January 1984.

137. Pogue, "General Bradley," 551-553.

138. Blumenson, *Patton*, 228, 306.

139. Chandler, et al., *Eisenhower Papers*, 4:2375.

4. Simpson and the Ninth Army

The fighting power of General Omar Bradley's 12th Army Group was contained in the three American field armies deployed along the Army Group front (appendix E). Stretching nearly 200 miles, from Holland in the north, through Belgium and Luxembourg, then south to the Lorraine region of France, the long, twisting battleline was manned by nearly a million soldiers.[1] The three armies in which these soldiers served reflected, in many ways, the characters and personalities of their three, very different commanders.

The First Army, the senior formation of the three, a "temperamental" unit that had "trudged across Europe with a grim intensity" through the summer and fall of 1944, was commanded by Lieutenant General Courtney H. Hodges.[2] Commissioned from the ranks in the pre-World War I Army, Hodges was a battlefield hero of that war and a crony of Marshall from their Fort Benning Infantry School days. Described by Bradley as his "idea of the quintessential 'Georgia gentleman'" who was a "faultless...military technician,"[3] Hodges has also been described, less flatteringly, as "the model of a rumpled, unassertive, small-town banker," who allowed much of the day-to-day running of First Army to be conducted by his Chief of Staff, the "prickly" Major General William B. Kean, Jr. Under Kean's direction, First Army headquarters became "critical, unforgiving, and resentful of all authority but its own."[4]

The Third Army was commanded by the most famous of Bradley's subordinates—Lieutenant General George S. Patton, Jr. "Fiercely ambitious" and hungry for publicity, Patton created the Third Army in his own image.[5] Historian Russell Weigley described Patton's product: "At its headquarters...Third Army was a cavalry army, with

153

movement and pursuit the passions not only of the commanding general but of the whole army command."[6] Surrounding himself with like-minded cavalrymen, Patton created a "noisy and bumptious,"[7] free-wheeling army that had "advanced further and faster than any Army in the history of the war" the previous summer.[8] Unlike First Army, there was no question in anyone's mind as to who commanded Third Army—Patton's dynamic personality and flamboyant command style left no doubt. And also unlike First Army, it was Patton, not his Third Army staff, who controlled the unit's day-to-day operations and gave it its unique personality.

The Ninth Army, the junior formation of Bradley's three armies, also reflected the personality of its commander—Lieutenant General William H. Simpson. A tall Texan with an ever-present smile, Simpson guided the Ninth Army from its inception and training through the campaigns of France and Germany. A West Point classmate of his more famous friend, Patton, the modest Simpson created an organization Bradley admitted "was in some respects superior to any in my command."[9] Ably assisted by his outstanding Chief of Staff, Brigadier General James E. Moore, Simpson skillfully applied the techniques, principles, and procedures he had been taught over the years at the Army's schools to build a unit that was a model of efficiency, organization, and staff administration. Simpson, described by Bradley as "big, bald and enthusiastic," earned for himself and his Ninth Army a reputation for dependability and disciplined duty performance that spread to the highest echelons of the Allied command.[10] Eisenhower paid Simpson a high compliment by reflecting, "If Simpson ever made a mistake as an Army Commander, it never came to my attention."[11] Ninth Army's smooth execution of even the most difficult assignments earned Bradley's praise that the "Ninth remained uncommonly normal."[12]

Each of Bradley's three armies and their much different commanders were deeply involved in the Ardennes offensive, and each army reacted to the German attack in a manner consistent with its unique character and personality. One of them, Hodges' First Army, bore the full brunt of the initial enemy assault and was sent reeling by the force of the offensive. The other two—Patton's Third and Simpson's Ninth—were called upon to implement the US Army's doctrinal response for countering such a massive attack. This chapter examines the leadership of these commanders, with a greater emphasis on the "uncommonly normal" battle leadership of General Simpson.

SIMPSON'S CAREER

Born 19 May 1888 and raised in the north-central Texas town of Weatherford,[13] in the shadow of Fort Worth, William Hood Simpson developed a respect for the frontier values of hard work, determination, and a cheerful calmness in the face of adversity. Despite what would soon painfully emerge as extremely poor academic preparation, Simpson received an appointment to the United States Military Academy at West Point in 1905.[14] He entered the Academy that summer, joining the other members of the Class of 1909, including a "turn-back" from the Class of 1908—George S. Patton, Jr. Patton and another member of the Class of 1908, Courtney H. Hodges, had failed mathematics during Plebe (freshman) year. Patton had been allowed to re-enter West Point with Simpson's class; Hodges, however, was not allowed to re-enter and he enlisted in the Regular Army as a private.

Simpson became a popular, well liked member of the class and was noted for his good nature if not for his scholarship.[15] The 1909 *Howitzer* (class yearbook) describes him as "Cheerful Charlie," and the entry includes this description of his usual demeanor: "The slow cracking of that aboriginal visage terminates in a beaming countenance of good will that no glumness can withstand."[16] This outstanding trait would serve him well in later years and would be remarked upon by virtually all who worked for him.

After 4 years at West Point, during which his poor secondary educational background put him constantly in danger of failing,[17] Simpson graduated 101 out of 103. Commissioned a second lieutenant of Infantry, he was assigned to the 6th Infantry Regiment at Fort Lincoln, ND, following his graduation leave.[18]

In January 1910, Simpson accompanied his regiment to

the Philippines where he saw some combat in the bloody, nasty, and confused fighting against the Moro insurgents.[19] He served with the 6th Infantry on Mindanao until posted back to the States in 1912. After spending 2 years at the Presidio, San Francisco, the 6th Infantry moved to El Paso, TX.[20] In 1916 Simpson and his regiment, like many US Army units scattered over the West in small, isolated posts, were dispatched to the Mexican-American border to deal with Pancho Villa's irregulars and the troubles caused by the turmoil of the Mexican revolution. From his base in El Paso, Simpson participated in General Pershing's Mexican Punitive Expedition into the Mexican interior, winning a promotion to first lieutenant on 1 July 1916.[21] Like his classmate Patton, Simpson saw some action in Mexico, as he had on Mindanao.

When the United States entered World War I, Simpson was still serving in El Paso. By spring 1917, however, he had been assigned as aide-de-camp to Major General George Bell, Jr., the El Paso Military District commander.[22] This fortunate assignment proved to be Simpson's ticket to France—and combat duty.

Unlike Eisenhower and Bradley, Simpson managed to get overseas and into the fighting when his boss, Bell, assumed command of the 33rd Infantry Division at Camp Logan, TX, in July 1917.[23] Nicknamed the "Prairie Division," the 33rd Infantry Division was an Illinois National Guard outfit training at Camp Logan, filling its ranks with draftees and "enlisted"[24] men prior to shipping out for France. While the unit trained and prepared for its movement overseas, CPT Simpson (promoted May 1917) accompanied his division commander on a tour of the British, French, and American Armies in France.[25] This observation tour assisted him in his duties as commander of the 33rd Division's School of Arms from December 1917 to April 1918. Simpson escorted the division to Brest, France, in April 1918, and soon after attended the Army General Staff School of the American Expeditionary Forces at Langres, France.[26]

Major Simpson (promoted June 1918) gained invaluable experience during his unit's 7 months of combat, especially after assuming duties as the Division Operations Officer in August 1918. He added immeasurably to his knowledge of high-level staff procedures by serving as the division's Chief of Staff from the Armistice in November 1918 until he returned to the States in June 1919.[27] After serving the final months of overseas service as a temporary lieutenant colonel (promoted November 1918), Simpson reverted to his permanent rank of captain on 20 June 1920. However, the following day Simpson was promoted a permanent major, where he would stay for the next 14 years.[28]

Simpson's experiences between the wars are similar to those of most of his contemporaries and include a combination of staff, command, instructor, and student assignments. Immediately upon his return to the States in June 1919, Simpson served as the chief of staff of the 6th Infantry Division in Camp Grant, IL.[29] This was the period of rapid disintegration of the large, wartime American Army, and divisions like Simpson's melted quickly away in the pacifistic, antimilitary environment of the times. By the time Simpson was assigned to the Office of the Chief of Infantry in Washington, D.C., the Army barely numbered 150,000. Despite the Army's pitiful size, the chiefs of the branches wielded considerable power and prestige. Simpson's assignment to the Chief of Infantry's office, therefore, was a significant and positive step in his career.[30]

After 2 years as an assistant executive officer in the Infantry Chief's Training Section, Simpson was rewarded with attendance at the Advanced Course at the Infantry School in Fort Benning, GA.[31] In those days, this course was a 9-month preparation for promising infantry officers for future attendance at the Command and Staff School at Fort Leavenworth, KS. An attendee at the following year's Infantry Officers Advanced Course, Omar Bradley, described the Georgia post:

Fort Benning—the Infantry School—was then a mere six years old...[it] soon grew far beyond musketry training. It evolved into the "home" of the U.S. infantry, a broad-gauge school dedicated to the task of producing the best-trained infantry leaders in the world. In 1922, Congress decreed Benning a "fort," and...two years later, a massive construction program was under way...The reservation itself was enormous—some 97.000 acres. about half that in valuable yellow pine, the rest open and suitable for military maneuvers.[32]

Simpson did well enough during his attendance at the Infantry Advanced Course to secure for himself a place at the following year's class at the Command and Staff School at Leavenworth; he reported for this year-long assignment in July 1924.[33] His class was only the second 1-year course since the consolidation of Leavenworth's School of the Line and General Staff School the previous year.[34] Mark Bender describes the "Leavenworth doctrine" of warfighting in Simpson's era:

> To avoid trench warfare, school doctrine directed strong and aggressive offensive action to envelop or penetrate enemy defensive positions. Follow-on pursuit required units to push both friendly and enemy troops to the limit to deny the enemy time to reorganize. Mobility and finesse were keys to the offense, rather than concentrated brute force, which required a greater investment of men and materiel. Surprise was also advantageous, because the attacker was able to choose the time and place of attack. While a commander in the defense could choose ground and buy time, doctrine considered the defense as a temporary expedient until the offense could be resumed. Furthermore, extended periods of defense forfeited freedom of maneuver and had a negative impact on troop morale.[35]

Learning this common doctrine was important to Simpson and his contemporaries, for it provided them all with a shared base of understanding and a "common language of war."[36] This common doctrine proved its worth in the campaigns of France and Germany in 1944-45 and was especially critical in assisting the American commanders to react to halt the German Ardennes offensive. The Army school system, epitomized in courses such as the Command and Staff School Simpson attended that year, was crucial to forging the battle leadership of the American commanders of World War II.

Following graduation, Simpson finally returned to troop duty and was assigned as the battalion commander of the 3rd Battalion, 12th Infantry Regiment, reporting to that unit in

June 1925.[37] Simpson's battalion was then stationed at Fort Meade, MD, located in the sleepy, rural Maryland countryside between Baltimore and Washington, D.C. Six weeks after he assumed command, however, Simpson moved his battalion to Fort Washington, MD. A smaller post with fewer "tenant" units, Major Simpson assumed the additional duty of Post Commander when he arrived. He held this position for 2 years, then received orders sending him back to school again—this time to the Army War College.[38]

MAJ Simpson arrived at the Army War College in Washington, D.C., in August 1927. Along with him reported his new War College classmate, Major Dwight D. Eisenhower.[39] Although most officers would serve in later "academic environments," such as teaching positions at West Point or in ROTC, the War College was usually the last time these officers would be students.[40] Eisenhower's biographer, Stephen Ambrose, described the course Ike and Simpson attended that year as "a pleasant sabbatical."[41]

After graduation from the War College in June 1928, Simpson was assigned to the War Department General Staff.[42] His position was in the military intelligence division of the general staff in that division's Latin American section. The following year, in the summer of 1929, Simpson became the executive officer of the military intelligence division, a position held until he was reassigned in June 1932.[43]

Like his contemporaries in the small, inter-war officer corps, Simpson drew an assignment as a professor of military science and tactics in a civilian university's ROTC unit. Also like his contemporaries, his tour was lengthy; he spent the next 4 years at Pomona College in Claremont, CA. At the conclusion of his ROTC duty, LTC Simpson (promoted October 1934) remained in an academic environment.[44]

Simpson returned to the Army War College in Washington, D.C., in August 1936, this time as an instructor on the school faculty. A year later, Simpson became the director of the military intelligence division of the War College faculty, capitalizing, no doubt, on his several years' service in military intelligence on the War Department General Staff. While serving in this position, he became Colonel Simpson, pinning on his eagles 1 September 1938.[45] During his 4-year tour at the War College, the Army began its long road back to preparedness, as the war in Europe erupted, then threatened to involve other nations—including the isolationist United States. George Marshall and other men of vision started to rebuild America's military forces and rectify the nearly two decades of shameful neglect.

Simpson benefitted from the increasing size of the American Army when he was selected to command the 9th Infantry Regiment at Fort Sam Houston, TX, in June 1940. Less than 4 months later, he became a brigadier general and with the promotion came an increase in responsibility. Simpson was transferred to Camp Wolters, TX, to assume command of the Infantry Replacement Training Center.[46] By April 1941, training camps and division posts across the country were beginning to swell with draftees and volunteers as the prewar buildup got into full swing. Simpson must have continued to demonstrate outstanding performance of duty in his several assignments because in October 1941 he received one of the highest compliments a soldier can get—the two stars of a major general and command of a division.

Simpson assumed command of the 35th Infantry Division, then forming up for its initial training at Camp Robinson, AR, in October 1941.[47] Continuing to build his fine reputation as an outstanding trainer of troops, Simpson began a rapid succession of training commands. From October 1941 until September 1943, he commanded the 35th Division in Arkansas and California, then the 30th Infantry Division at Fort Jackson, SC, and finally the XII Corps, also at Fort Jackson. Each of these units was, for him, a training command—someone else would take them into combat.[48] Simpson, however, wanted to capitalize on his combat experience from the Philippines, Mexico, and World War I France. In October 1943, he began a command tour that would eventually lead him into combat, taking charge of the Fourth Army—later to be redesignated the Ninth Army.

TRAINING COMMAND TO COMBAT COMMAND

In October 1943, upon assuming command of the Fourth Army, Simpson received his third star and promotion to lieutenant general.[49] Simpson's association with the unit he would lead into combat actually began at San Jose, CA, when he received command of the Fourth Army as another training outfit. But, unlike his previous three commands, Fourth Army headquarters was formed at double normal strength to permit the subsequent activation of a combat army. Simpson's Fourth Army was to be deployed to the European Theater in spring 1944, then used in combat as a follow-on unit to the cross-channel invasion forces.[50] Simpson couldn't have been happier—but there remained one hurdle.

Even though Simpson had formed, trained, and activated this Army, it was by no means a foregone conclusion that he would lead it into combat. As late as March 1944, Eisenhower, preferring seasoned combat leaders to promote to Army command, wrote to Marshall:

> ...on the subject of providing us with battle experienced commanders. To take up first the question of next Army headquarters, I much prefer Simpson to Fredendall. I think it is possible that our coming operations [cross-channel attack and subsequent campaign in France] will bring to light some corps commander whose promotion to Army command might become obviously desirable. I am thinking of such prospects as Collins [VII Corps], Middleton [VIII Corps], and Corlett [XIX Corps].[51]

Nevertheless, Marshall continued to support Simpson's presence at the head of the next combat army. The Chief of Staff did so not just because Simpson had proven himself to be an extremely capable commander, but also, apparently, "to assure generals who trained large formations in the states...that they did not face dead ends, that they were not altogether excluded from leading their armies into combat."[52] In addition to fulfilling his long-time personal ambition to lead a unit into combat, Simpson would be an encouragement to a whole class of officers. Eisenhower, admitting that the time available effectively precluded waiting for corps commanders to prove their mettle in the upcoming campaigns, bowed to Marshall's wishes. It seems fortunate that he did, for as Weigley noted, "In his army's first test in combat, Simpson began repaying Marshall's trust."[53]

The smartest thing Simpson did while preparing his unit

for combat service was to select Brigadier General James E. Moore to be his Army's Chief of Staff. The relationship between the two men proved to be the key to influencing and directing the performance of the entire organization. Simpson and Moore had worked together in several units in the past and had a comfortable and effective working relationship. Simpson's biographer, Thomas R. Stone, described Moore as "an intelligent, thorough, dedicated and loyal staff officer [who] well complemented Simpson."[54] In return, Simpson "was careful to enhance Moore's position" by passing his guidance and questions through the Chief of Staff, and having him "sit in on his discussions with the staff officers" and commanders.[55] Stone says:

> ...they understood, trusted and admired each other. Moore usually could anticipate Simpson's reactions while Simpson gave Moore a great deal of latitude. Often while Simpson was in the field, Moore would issue orders in the Commander's name, then tell Simpson later. So closely did the two work together that in many instances it is impossible to sort out actions taken or ideas conceived.[56]

Simpson and Moore initiated the difficult process of structuring an effective organization through which to focus and direct the efforts of their army by establishing the tone and tenor of the unit early in its history. They built their team well, and, while an attempt was made to nominate officers from the Army at large, Simpson had Moore do much of the actual selecting as Moore knew the Army's younger officers. With very few changes, these officers served in their original Army headquarters positions throughout the European campaigns. Mostly infantrymen, the men who made up the Army organizational structure began focusing their group effort toward the goal of preparing the Army for combat operations in fall 1943 while still a part of the Fourth Army's expanded staff.[57]

After organizing the staff, Simpson and Moore proceeded to train it to function in a manner designed to produce the best results in combat.[58] They rejected any trick ideas or those that promised to be only temporarily effective, preferring sound, proven procedures that gave a positive answer to the question, "Would it work effectively in combat?"[59] Simpson established the training of his staff as an early top priority task, and both he and Moore "made it a practice to monitor closely the training" of the staff sections.[60] During stateside preparations for overseas deployment, the army staff participated in highly beneficial map exercises lasting more than a month. This allowed for a number of problems in staff functioning to be identified and addressed. Such intensive training could not, however, identify or cover all the practical aspects of each staff section's broad scope of responsibility.[61]

Upon arriving in England in May 1944, a number of other problems were identified. Solutions were found by closely studying the manner in which other headquarters had approached problems, through reading their directives and procedures and sending staff officers on temporary duty with deployed armies to obtain practical experience.[62] This prompted the practice of sending observers from Simpson's staff across the channel to France (after D-Day) to gain firsthand experience in the way the deployed armies' headquarters were dealing with battlefield procedures. These observers, upon returning to headquarters in England, conducted night schools to teach the new procedures to other staff members.[63]

These visits to the already-deployed Army headquarters served also to emphasize to Simpson some fundamental differences in the three armies. First Army, probably reflecting its Chief of Staff Kean's suspicion and resentment of outsiders, would allow only Simpson and his chief of staff to visit his headquarters and staff sections. On the other hand, Simpson's West Point classmate, Patton, allowed anyone from Simpson's staff to visit his army—all were welcome at Third Army headquarters.[64]

Training of the staff did not end when the now-redesignated Ninth Army[65] moved to France and began combat operations in September 1944. The staff continued to reappraise and adjust working methods during the unit's initial combat operations, and later, any break in the action was seized upon by Simpson or Moore to refocus the organization on the ultimate goal by refining and aligning procedures.[66]

After staging and training in England for nearly 3 months, Simpson's Ninth Army headquarters moved to France on 27 August 1944[67] and entered combat on 5 September 1944. Units under Ninth Army command were the 2nd, 8th, 29th infantry divisions besieging Brest, and the 83rd Infantry Division and the 6th Armored Division guarding a long, exposed flank.[68] The Ninth Army assumed army command responsibilities for combat operations currently under way in the Brittany peninsula, which included Middleton's VIII Corps assault on the fortified port city of Brest.[69] After a bloody siege, VIII Corps successfully captured Brest on 18 September, but was rewarded with only a smashed, unusable, rubble-strewn shell of a town. The German defenders had rendered the port useless for months to come. The fall of the fortress, however, ended the Army's combat operations in Brittany, and a shifting of units to the Allied front in Belgium began shortly thereafter.[70]

Although the Brittany campaign became controversial later because of the amount of precious resources expended, there occurred two incidents involving Simpson that shed light on his leadership and character. The first was his unflagging personal support to Middleton while the VIII Corps commander was deeply involved in the frustrating, unglamorous task of reducing the fortress at Brest. Although Eisenhower, Bradley, and others became impatient with the drawnout siege, and pestered Simpson and Middleton to hurry and complete it, the Ninth Army commander was steadfast in his support of his harried subordinate. Simpson protected Middleton from harassment from higher command as much as he could and went so far as to assume personal control of the 83rd Infantry Division and 6th Armored Division to allow VIII Corps (his only corps headquarters) to concentrate fully on the siege.[71] The other incident occurring during the Brittany campaign serves to demonstrate the difference between Simpson and his classmate, Patton. Simpson demonstrated his loyalty to subordinates and his nonpublicity seeking nature by refusing to personally accept the surrender of some 20,000 German soldiers—an event that promised extensive news coverage. Stone wrote:

Simpson could have taken [the German] surrender personally, but he had chosen to miss the ceremony, for he felt that as representatives of the 83rd Division had made contact with the Germans and had handled the entire operation, Macon [83rd Division commander] was entitled to the limelight. Such an action would not make the Army commander's name a household word, but it would help earn the loyalty of his subordinates. Thus, Simpson attended to Brest, while the newsreel cameras whirred at the Beaugency Bridge.[72]

It seems highly improbable that Patton, given the same circumstances, would have taken Simpson's actions. Indeed, on occasion, Patton took just the opposite action, grabbing the limelight and publicity from his subordinates. A short time later, when Brest finally fell, Simpson repeated the gesture, allowing Middleton to accept the German surrender.

With the conclusion of the Brittany campaign, the Ninth Army began to move eastward to take up positions along the Allied front. On 2 October 1944, Ninth Army headquarters opened for business in a former teacher's college in Arlon, Belgium.[73] Located in the quiet Ardennes sector of the front, Ninth Army's portion of the line was eventually to be the site of the great German offensive two months later. The Ninth Army sector was manned by the 2nd, 8th, and 83rd Infantry Divisions and was generally the same area later held by Middleton's VIII Corps in December.[74] But Simpson's stay in the Ardennes proved to be short lived.

In less than 2 weeks, the 12th Army Group commander, Bradley, ordered the Ninth Army headquarters to pack up once more, this time moving to the far left flank of the American line—to Maastricht, Holland. Bradley, anticipating Eisenhower's eventual shifting of a US Army to the control of Field Marshal Montgomery's British 21 Army Group, reasoned that the relatively green Ninth Army could more easily be spared than the veteran First. Bradley also perceived that Simpson's easy-going temperament made him a better choice to serve under the egotistical Montgomery. Certainly Simpson was a better choice than Hodges to survive service under the Field Marshal--and there could be no thought of Patton ever submitting to Montgomery's command.

Bradley wrote that "Simpson and his staff had not yet been subjected to Monty's megalomania and were, on the whole, more diplomatic and adaptable."[75]

Before Simpson and the Ninth Army staff moved north, however, another incident occurred that demonstrated the commander's genuine concern for the well-being of his troops, even those who would soon transfer to another command. As Simpson prepared to shift his headquarters north, just prior to the approach of the wet, miserable fall and winter weather, he personally "directed the initiation of a massive supply effort designed to issue winter clothing" to the 83rd Infantry Division.[76] Even though he would soon leave this division behind to be looked after by another army, Simpson felt a responsibility to the men who had served him well. This kind of loyalty was appreciated by the men in the foxholes.

By the time the November offensive began on the 16th, Ninth Army was in position as Bradley's left flank unit. It consisted of two corps, the XIII and XIX, comprising the 29th, 30th, 84th and 102nd Infantry Divisions, and the 2nd Armored Division.[77] This first major offensive for Simpson and the Ninth Army turned into an ineffective, plodding slog through the mud and misery of western Germany. The 102nd Infantry Division's official history describes the terrible conditions:

> During an average year, rain falls...15 days in November, but in 1944 precipitation was recorded for 28 days. This excessive rain and almost constant cloudiness frequently grounded our air forces. Overcast skies likewise reduced the small amount of evaporation that normally occurs, so that fields became bogs, foxholes turned into wells, trenches into stagnant canals. Vehicles were often roadbound. Unimproved thoroughfares quickly disintegrated. Artillery observation was reduced to short ranges; and infantrymen, directed to guide on various landmarks could not locate them in the mist and fog. Weapons were clogged and jammed with mud in spite of all precautions and always the troops were wet, miserable and cold.[78]

The weather was not the only enemy during this drive to close up on the Roer River. The German soldier, for the first

time defending his Fatherland, took every advantage of
observation and field of fire that the open and cultivated
countryside offered, fortifying each small town and village
with trenches, mines, and anti-tank ditches.[79] By the time the
Roer was reached at the end of November, Ninth Army was
ready for a rest and a chance to recuperate before the assault
crossings of the river were undertaken.

Ninth Army's role in the November offensive, which
involved each of Bradley's three armies, has never received
much recognition, being overlooked in favor of Hodges' bloody
fiasco in the Huertgen Forest, or Patton's problems on
Bradley's right flank. But the Ninth's fighting in this first
real incursion into Germany was just as significant. Harold
Leinbaugh and John Campbell, fighting with the 84th
Infantry Division, described the terrible but typical combat
during Operation CLIPPER, their regiment's attack to seize
the high ground east of the Rhineland city of Geilenkirchen in
the final 2 weeks of November 1944:

> The three rifle platoons [of K Company, 333rd Infantry
> Regiment] had been thoroughly clobbered trying to advance
> beyond the chateau. The concentration of German firepower
> was absolutely overwhelming with its violence, surprise and
> intensity. Artillery fire, 88s and 75s from hidden tanks, and
> 120 mortars with apparently limitless supplies of
> ammunition hit us. Machine-gun fire whipping in from
> pillboxes across the Würm seemed almost an afterthought.
> The noise, the shock, the sensation of total helplessness and
> bewilderment, the loss of control, the sudden loss of every
> familiar assumption—nothing in civilian life or training
> offered an experience remotely comparable. The barrage
> went on and on. The company had lost the initiative and
> taken several quick casualties. Men scooped slit trenches in
> the mud; others grabbed cover wherever they could find it.
> Our new-boy illusions of the past two days dissolved in a
> moment.[80]

The horror of this kind of grinding combat continued into the
first 2 weeks of December as Simpson's troops attempted to
close up on the Roer River. Initially it was envisioned that
this offensive would possibly drive on to capture the

important city of Cologne and reach the Rhine. This optimism
vanished in the mud and mire along the banks of the Roer
River. Weigley's assessment of the Ninth's first combat
performance stated, "Like Hodges' First Army, Simpson's
Ninth had achieved nothing resembling a breakthrough."[81]
But he also observed that "in its first major campaign, Ninth
Army had advanced more rapidly" than First Army, "produced
no major mistakes," and began to claim Bradley's affections as
"the army he could count on."[82]

ATTACK IN THE ARDENNES

Bradley's decision in October to move Ninth Army to his left
flank had put Hodges, not Simpson, directly in the path of the
German offensive. While the Ninth Army was still rebuilding
units and recuperating from its November offensive in the
Rhineland, the First Army (appendix F) had already begun
another corps-sized attack, launching Gerow's V Corps on 13
December to seize the vital Roer River dams.[83] Further to the
south, on Bradley's right flank, Patton's Third Army was
nearly ready to launch its own offensive to close up on the
Rhine. In the early morning hours of 16 December 1944,
however, the carefully made plans of all three American Army
commanders were radically altered by the three German
Armies crashing into the Ardennes.

The main German attack, "Sepp" Dietrich's 6th Panzer
Army, was carefully planned to hit Hodges' lines at their
weakest point—just along the V Corps-VIII Corps boundary.[84]
Lightly defended by scattered units of the 14th Cavalry
Group, the point of attack was the so-called "Losheim Gap,"
the classic invasion route through the Ardennes region.
Although termed a "gap," the 9,000-yard-wide corridor
defended by the cavalry group was heavily wooded and only
slightly less rugged than the surrounding Ardennes.[85] Just as
Rommel's panzer division had done in the blitzkrieg of 1940
over this same ground, Dietrich's tanks and grenadiers
overran their lightly armed opposition, driving west toward
the Meuse River.[86]

To the north of the Losheim Gap, in the V Corps sector, is
an area of high ground known as the Elsenborn Ridge. The
desperate but successful defense here anchored the bulge's

northern shoulder.[87] Units from Dietrich's attacking forces hit the US 99th Infantry Division, forcing it back onto the Elsenborn Ridge and, ironically, placing the unit in positions better suited to halting the German attack. The 99th, like its southern neighbor in the VIII Corps sector, the 106th Infantry Division, was inexperienced and new to combat. But unlike the unfortunate 106th, the 99th did not allow itself to be surrounded and broken by the German assault. Instead, it joined with the veteran 2nd Infantry Division in executing one of the key defensive stands of the battle.[88] This important stand, however, owed little to the battle leadership of Hodges and the First Army staff.

Hodges and his staff were slow to recognize the German offensive for what it was, wasting precious time before responding to it. Concerned primarily with Gerow's V Corps offensive, launched 3 days before the German assault began, First Army refused to believe early reports of the size of the enemy attack. Historian Charles B. MacDonald, an infantry company commander during the fighting on Elsenborn Ridge, wrote of Hodges' reaction to the attack:

> Full realization of what was happening in the Ardennes had been slow to come at headquarters of Courtney Hodges' First Army, located in the Hotel Britannique in the once fashionable watering place of Spa, the same hotel from which Hindenburg and Ludendorff had directed the German armies in World War I. Because the opening artillery bombardment had knocked out most telephone lines to forward units, and because not all units resorted promptly to their radios, reports from some sectors were slow to come. Emanating mainly from the northernmost divisions, the first reports seemed to indicate only a local spoiling attack designed to upset the 2d Division's drive on the Roer dams.[89]

Hodges persisted in his mistaken belief that this was only a limited attack throughout the first day of the German offensive. Gerow, whose V Corps was discovering that its attack toward the dams had been pre-empted by the massive German assault, tried unsuccessfully to convince Hodges and his staff to call off the V Corps attack. Hodges, however, told Gerow that he "did not intend to dance to the Germans' tune"

and ordered the attack on the dams to continue.[90] Receiving
no orders to the contrary from Bradley's headquarters until
late afternoon, Hodges insisted that Gerow continue to attack.
Fortunately for the American defense of the Ardennes, Gerow
and the 2nd Infantry Division's commander, Major General
Walter Robertson, disobeyed First Army's orders.[91]

Gerow, described by Weigley as "the epitome of the
meticulous, painstaking staff officer,"[92] had had no combat
experience prior to assuming command of V Corps for the
Normandy invasion. Considered by some to be a risk when
Ike placed him in command of V Corps, Gerow had proven
himself to be a steady, tireless, competent combat leader who
"possessed an admirable feeling for the ebb, the flow, the
portents of battle."[93] Gerow, along with Eisenhower, was one
of the first of the American commanders to realize the
German attack was a full-blown offensive, not a local
counterattack. Yet, he could not convince Hodges (or Kean,
the "gray eminence" at First Army)[94] that any attempt to
continue his offensive was not only futile, it was dangerous.
Continuing to drive east was only putting V Corps' neck
further into the German noose, risking the loss of the whole
corps. Hodges still stubbornly refused to recognize the true
situation, so Gerow took responsibility upon his own
shoulders and ordered Robertson to stop the attack. He
ordered the 2nd Division's reserve regiment to move to back
up the hard-pressed 99th Division, holding precariously to
positions around the Elsenborn Ridge. At the same time
Gerow took another action that would have just as important
an effect on the successful defense of the critical high
ground—he directed all available artillery units to the
threatened area.[95]

V Corps and, later, First Army artillery units, were critical
to solidifying the American defense of the Elsenborn Ridge
and holding the northern shoulder of the bulge. In the Army's
official history of the battle, historian Hugh Cole assessed the
overall impact of the artillery units in the north:

> At Monschau [near the eastern end of the ridge] the
> artillery stopped the attack cold, effectively narrowing the
> German assault front. In the 99th Division sector the

division artillery held its ground until the close of the 17th when the V Corps artillery groupment at Elsenborn took over the fight with such a weight of metal that one infantry battalion was covered by a defensive barrage of 11,500 rounds during the night of 17 December...The Americans fired about 1,255,000 artillery rounds during [the battle] and by 23 December had brought a total of 4,155 artillery pieces into action.[96]

This concentration of American artillery battalions on and behind the Elsenborn Ridge was not only crucial to holding the valuable terrain against the German onslaught, it was also instrumental in applying the Army doctrine for slowing and stopping the overall enemy offensive—restricting the attacker's mobility. Because the impenetrability of the Ardennes is largely due to its limited road network, denying the enemy unrestricted use of the roads by maintaining nearly continuous artillery fire on them was critical to implementing this doctrine. The massed artillery units positioned along the ridge maintained a torrent of shellfire on the 6th Panzer Army's advance, effectively choking it.[97]

By mid-morning of 17 December, the second day of the attack, Hodges had finally begun to realize the full extent of the German offensive. He permitted Gerow to withdraw Robertson's forward regiments from their attack positions (Gerow had stopped the attack on his own initiative but had not yet moved the entire division) and sent them to join their reserve regiment and the 99th on the Elsenborn Ridge. Soon other reserves were rushed to back up the 2nd and 99th Divisions, and the high ground was saved.[98]

Meanwhile, Hodges' other threatened corps, Middleton's VIII, was in serious trouble just to Gerow's south. Like Gerow, Middleton suspected early on that the attack all along his thinly defended front was more than a local spoiling attack. By 1000 hours on 16 December, elements of 16 different German divisions had been identified among the attackers, and the 14th Cavalry Group was disintegrating in the face of Dietrich's main attack.[99] Yet Hodges and First Army headquarters were as slow to come to Middleton's aid as they had been to listen to Gerow. Exacerbating Hodges' problem with VIII Corps was the nature of the

German assault.

The attack of the 6th Panzer Army, striking nearly directly along the V Corps-VIII Corps boundary, was effectively splitting Hodges' First Army in two. From the Losheim Gap/St.-Vith area southward (the sector containing the bulk of Middleton's command), the area was being isolated from First Army control. This left Middleton on his own. Rallying his broken units and making the most effective use of his pitifully small reserve forces, the VIII Corps commander began to conduct a skillful and successful defense, holding the key road centers until outside help arrived.[100]

Neither Hodges nor his Army Group commander, Bradley, was responsible for sending the much-needed help to Middleton. First Army's contribution to the VIII Corps defense was to allow Middleton the use of several First Army combat engineer battalions in his makeshift delaying actions along the corps front, but these units were already working in the VIII Corps sector when the battle began, and it was Middleton, not Hodges, who initiated their use. First Army merely acquiesced to Middleton's appropriation of these valuable assets.[101] Additionally, First Army had no role at all in dispatching the units that became Middleton's greatest saviors in rescuing his defensive line—the 7th and 10th Armored Divisions.

More than anything else, it was Eisenhower's nearly instant appreciation of the scope of the German offensive that started the two armored divisions on the road to the Ardennes. Rejecting Brandley's conclusion that it was merely a spoiling attack, Ike directed the 12th Army Group commander to "send Middleton some help."[102] Bradley reluctantly did so at Eisenhower's direction, not "urging."[103] Bradley made two calls to get the two divisions moving on the roads to the Ardennes: one to his Army Group chief of staff, Major General Leven C. Allen, and one to mollify a skeptical Patton.[104] Bradley also called Hodges at First Army and issued orders for him "to stand by to move other available divisions to reinforce the armor."[105] Hodges was still adamant that Gerow continue his futile attack to capture the dams. Perhaps it was Bradley's phone call that alerted him to the gravity of the situation, for by the next morning, 17

December, he permitted Gerow to forget the Roer dams and concentrate his forces on the defense of the Elsenborn Ridge.[106] Bradley's phone call to Patton, on the other hand, seems to have been a more difficult one. The 12th Army Group commander described the call in his autobiography:

> Patton scoffed [at the order to move 10th Armored Division]; he thought [as I had at first] that it was merely a spoiling attack and that Middleton could handle it. I was compelled to give Patton a direct, unequivocal order to get the 10th Armored moving. He did so reluctantly, logging: "Bradley admitted my logic but took counsel of his fears and ordered...the move. I wish he were less timid."[107]

Patton had been reluctant to give up his 10th Armored Division at first, but, once committed, he threw his Third Army staff into the fight with seemingly limitless energy. Patton had suspected a German offensive for the past several weeks, going so far as to order his staff to prepare a counterattack plan for Third Army along three possible axes of advance into a supposed southern flank of an enemy salient in the Ardennes.[108] By the time Patton met with Bradley on 18 December, his staff had already begun the "masterful feat" of disengaging from Third Army's own offensive, swinging a large part of the army a full 90-degrees, and preparing to attack toward Bastogne.[109] Although initially just as reluctant as Hodges to terminate his army's ongoing offensive, Patton and the Third Army staff proved much quicker at recognizing the need for action and much more adaptable at generating and applying combat power in stopping the enemy. Chester Wilmot, an ardent Montgomery supporter and therefore no fan of Patton, nevertheless praised the Third Army commander by writing: "There was no holding back on his part now [after 18 December]. He was not losing divisions; he was being given a new chance to fight and there was nothing he liked better."[110] Wilmot goes on to claim that Patton had no "equal on the Allied side in the rapid deployment of troops."[111] A keen observer of what was taking place at that time at Ninth Army headquarters to the north of the bulge might take issue with Wilmot's claim.

Whereas Bradley had been forced to order Patton to send

the 10th Armored to the Ardennes, no such order was necessary in Simpson's case. Bradley's chief of staff, Allen, had notified Simpson of the need of the 7th Armored in VIII Corps' sector, and the steady, reliable Simpson had the unit on the road in record time.[112] The Ninth Army G-3 After Action Report for the first day of the German assault reads:

> On 16 December 1944 a major German attack began in the First U.S. Army zone in Luxembourg and Belgium...Ninth U.S. Army immediately began to regroup its forces in order to release elements for movement to the south to aid First U.S. Army in holding the German advance. The 7th Armored Division was alerted on 16 December at 1745A hours to move south as soon as possible. An advance party departed at 1930A hours to report to the Commanding General of the VIII Corps...On 17 December both the 7th Armored Division and the 30th Infantry Division were attached to First U.S. Army and started movement to the First U.S. Army area.[113]

Simpson's unselfish and competent battle leadership was shown continually throughout the European campaign, but no instance demonstrates those qualities of his command ability more clearly than the Ninth Army's response to the Ardennes offensive. During this critical time, Simpson was quick to appreciate that a team effort was desperately needed to turn back the German assault and, as John S.D. Eisenhower noted in his book, *The Bitter Woods,* "it was unnecessary to make personal explanations to...General Simpson" as were necessary for Patton.[114] Simpson and Moore began immediately to refocus their army's actions on applying the unit's considerable combat power to stopping, then countering, the German offensive. First priority was to get the 7th Armored Division to the VIII Corps sector.

As soon as Ninth Army headquarters received the call from the 12th Army Group to dispatch the armored division, the unit was placed on alert. Hasbrouck, the 7th's commander, called the commander of his Combat Command B, Brigadier General Bruce C. Clarke, and ordered him to report to Middleton at the VIII Corps command post in Bastogne, explaining that his unit would be sent to follow as soon as road clearance was obtained. Clarke, who was just then about to depart for a much-needed weekend pass to Paris, immediately began the long drive south to find Middleton.[115]

Sent by Middleton to St.-Vith to rescue the crumbling situation at that key crossroad, Clarke's combat command arrived the afternoon of 17 December—literally with no time to spare, as the Germans closed in on the outskirts of St.-Vith.[116] Ninth Army's prompt reaction (delayed only by First Army staff's inability to get the proper road clearances in a timely manner)[117] saved the vital crossroads. Clarke's inspired defense of the town and surrounding area over the next week was, according to Weigley, "the battle...that bought the time required by Allied generalship to recapture control of the [overall] battle."[118] If Simpson's only contribution to the Battle of the Bulge had been getting the 7th Armored to St.-Vith in time to save it, he well deserved a place in the history books. As it was, Simpson and the Ninth Army contributed much more.

Simpson and Moore's early realization of the scope of the German offensive was similar to Eisenhower's. On their own initiative, they began to reconfigure the Ninth Army's defensive posture in order to send more badly needed combat units to the Ardennes. Shortly after receiving the call from 12th Army Group to send the 7th Armored south, Simpson personally called Hodges at First Army and offered to send him the 30th Infantry Division and the 2nd Armored Division as well.[119] Major General Raymond McLain, commander of XIXth Corps in Ninth Army recalled:

> Big-hearted Simpson voluntarily offered Hodges [one of my divisions] to cover the critical situation developing at Spa [First Army headquarters], and I soon received an order to send the 30th Infantry Division through Spa to meet the oncoming Germans and to prevent the latter from swinging around toward Aachen.[120]

Within the first 6 days of the battle, Simpson had sent five full divisions to Hodges' assistance—two on the very first day, the third a day later. By the end of the 10th day of the

German attack, seven Ninth Army divisions were in combat against the enemy.[121]   Facilitating this, as Cole noted, was Simpson's unselfish spirit of cooperation and team play: "In many cases, the transfer of units would be accomplished in simple fashion by telephone calls and simultaneous agreement between the higher commanders concerned."[122]

Before the end of December, there were 4 infantry divisions and 3 armored divisions as well as 28 nondivisional combat units from Ninth Army fighting in the First Army sector against the German main attack.   This prodigious effort compares more than favorably with the better known and much-heralded contribution by Patton's Third Army.[123]

In addition to sending the majority of the Ninth Army's combat power to the Ardennes region, Simpson and Moore reorganized and regrouped the remaining units in order to provide a viable defense along their long front. Shifting the army boundary southward to encompass the former sector of the First Army's VII Corps, Simpson now had an extended front of over 40 miles to defend.[124]   In his characteristically well-organized and thoughtful manner, Simpson had his Ninth Army staff methodically "turn its thoughts from an impending drive across the Cologne plain and devote its energies to...cope with this threatening surprise move:"[125]

In a Letter of Instruction dated December 19, the Army had set forth detailed directives for the organization of the ground and defined defensive lines to be prepared by the corps. Priority for work on various defensive positions was laid down and coordination between adjacent units provided. An engineer annex supplemented the general instructions with specific details in regard to mines, wire, and demolitions. Overlays showing the locations of vital highway and railroad structures were issued to corps, and priorities were established for the destruction of the installations if this should become necessary. In addition, the Army developed counterattack plans which included the use of the 5th Armored Division, which would be made available...if needed, and various British units whose operational control would be exercised from time to time during the ensuing month.[126]

Ninth Army reaction to the surprise German offensive does seem "uncommonly normal" when compared to the near-panic at First Army headquarters and a command level "beset by conflicting pressures" at Third Army.[127] Simpson's remarkable ability to cause his army to react in what seems to be an ordinary manner in such an extraordinary situation is a great compliment to his battle leadership. His personal reaction to Eisenhower's decision on 20 December to place the Ninth Army and most of the First Army under Field Marshal Montgomery's command compliments Simpson's character and sense of duty as well.

Most American senior commanders below the Supreme Commander deeply resented Eisenhower's decision to give the egotistical British field marshal command of all Bradley's forces on the northern half of the salient. Bradley was outraged, writing later that it "was the worst possible mistake Ike could have made."[128] Patton, who probably despised Montgomery more than any other American general, suspected the move was due to "the machinations of the Prime Minister [Churchill]," and wrote disgustedly in his diary, "Eisenhower is unwilling or unable to command Montgomery."[129] Hodges, visibly shaken by the German attack and appearing to lack confidence, barely escaped being relieved of command by Montgomery after the latter visited First Army headquarters the day he assumed command. He kept his job only through Ike's and Bradley's intercession.[130] Simpson, however, was nearly alone among the senior American commanders in complying with Eisenhower's instructions to "respond cheerfully and efficiently to every instruction [Montgomery] gives."[131] Weigley records that, during the battle, Simpson sent the following message to Ike:

> I and my Army are operating smoothly and cheerfully under the command of the Field Marshal. The most cordial relations and a very high spirit of cooperation have been established between him and myself personally and between our respective Staffs. You can depend on me to respond cheerfully, promptly and as efficiently as I possibly can to every instruction he gives...The Field Marshal paid me a visit and at his request I took him to the headquarters of my XIX Corps where I had all of my Corps and Division

Commanders assembled to meet him. After all had been
introduced to him, he made us a splendid talk on the
present situation.[132]

Simpson's professional and straightforward attitude toward
Montgomery and his willing obedience to the field marshal's
commands stand out in stark contrast to his contemporaries'
undisguised loathing and antipathy. Appreciative of this
attitude, Ike later wrote a personal message to Simpson,
thanking him for his outstanding leadership, noting "I have
been particularly gratified to note that your relationships
with our British friends, including your seniors...have been
based on mutual respect and friendly cooperation."[133]
Eisenhower, dismayed that Bradley's "12th Army Group was
getting as difficult to work with as [Monty's] 21 Army
Group,"[134] must have welcomed Simpson's refreshing attitude
and been delighted to find a kindred soul.

After the German offensive had run its course and the
three American armies had stopped the westward movement
of the panzers and grenadiers, the campaign to reduce the
bulge and return the front to its original position began. Both
First and Third Army headquarters were heavily involved in
this phase of the Ardennes battle; Ninth Army staff, however,
had little impact on the counter-offensive. Although the
majority of Ninth Army combat units continued to fight on in
the First Army area, they remained under Hodges'
operational command until the battle ended. Simpson and his
Ninth Army staff spent the remainder of the Ardennes battle
protecting their wide front against any possible German
threat to their area and also preparing detailed plans for their
upcoming offensive—the Rhineland Campaign, to begin in
February.[135]

First Army, under Montgomery's 21 Army Group, and
Third Army, under Bradley's 12th, executed the Allied
counteroffensive to reduce the German salient. Hodges, kept
under tight rein by Monty, chafed under the field marshal's
heavy hand until returned to Bradley on 17 January. Patton,
now Bradley's only subordinate, fought his usual aggressive
and successful battle.[136]

ANALYSIS OF BATTLE LEADERSHIP

Bradley's characterizations of his three army commanders, written later after years of reflection, seem extraordinarily appropriate descriptions of their three, very different approaches to battle leadership.[137] The Ardennes offensive served, like a magnifying glass, to enlarge these commanders' differences and point out exactly how their differing leadership approaches affected each of their armies and the outcome of the battle. The strengths and shortcomings of each man stand out, in many ways, as strengths and shortcomings of the overall American leadership in the European campaigns.

THE FIRST ARMY

LTG Hodges was overwhelmed by the German offensive that cut his First Army in two during the early days of the attack. The impact of the attack striking his forward units produced something akin to a physical shock to him personally, and his command reaction reflected it. Weigley reports that, when Montgomery visited First Army headquarters on 20 December, the field marshal "soon judged that under the strain of the battle Hodges was on his way to becoming one of the 'cardiaques' who used to frequent the spas now inhabited by the First Army," hinting to Eisenhower that Hodges might have to be relieved of command.[138] That Hodges continued in command of First Army is undoubtedly because of the intercession of both Bradley and Eisenhower.[139]

Bradley felt protective of the man who had taken over from him as First Army commander and was more inclined to excuse his shortcomings—especially now that Montgomery's assumption of command in the north implied criticism of all American senior leadership:

> One important factor in determining [SHAEF's] position [to give Monty command in the north], I believe, was a sudden temporary loss of confidence in Courtney Hodges. Hodges had been under immense pressure for four days [by 20 December] and he was exhausted. He was not a man like Patton, who naturally radiated unbounded confidence and dogged determination. In fact, even in the most optimistic

circumstances he had an air of caution. Now, as I knew,
Hodges was sounding more and more depressed at a time
when we needed Pattonesque bravado.[140]

Others involved in the desperate fighting in the First
Army's area were not as sympathetic with Hodges' lack of
strong leadership and firm control of the battle. Hasbrouck,
commander of the 7th Armored Division, fighting fiercely to
keep control of the vital St.-Vith area, became disgusted with
First Army's lack of support (or even knowledge) of his hard-
pressed unit. Years later, he wrote that "Hodges was a poor
excuse for an Army Commander. He was too old and too
frail."[141] Hasbrouck went on to write contemptuously of "how
First Army HQ fled from Spa, leaving... top secret maps still
on the walls," and how finally, in desperation, he "had to send
an officer to find them."[142]   It must be concluded that
Hasbrouck and Clarke's masterful mobile defense of St.-Vith
and the surrounding area was brought off successfully despite
Hodges and his First Army staff, not because of them.

Further, the outstanding defenses created by V Corps on
the Elsenborn Ridge and VIII Corps in front of St.-Vith and
Bastogne were the direct result of the efforts of the local
commanders and not those of Hodges and the First Army. In
the case of Gerow's V Corps, Hodges' stubborn insistence that
the attack toward the Roer River dams be maintained all
through that critical first day of the German offensive
seriously threatened the defense of the northern shoulder and
nearly doomed Gerow's entire corps to being cut off and
destroyed. It is true that the lack of reports from frontline
units restricted the amount of information relayed to Hodges
and the First Army staff; nevertheless, the commander on the
ground, Gerow, had attempted to set them straight most of
the day. That the army commander and his staff refused to
believe Gerow's reports is an indication of how little faith and
trust Hodges' staff had in the judgment of their subordinate
commanders. Hodges' justification for his insistence on
continuing the V Corps attack—"He did not intend to dance
to the German's tune"[143]—sounds more like an excuse for his
headquarters' well-known penchant for being "resentful of all
authority but its own."[144]

Part of the confusion and lack of appreciation in Hodges' headquarters may be due to the absence of guidance or direction from Bradley's 12th Army Group. Out of his headquarters for nearly the whole day on 16 December, Bradley, too, was still unconvinced of the scope of the attack when he called Hodges later that day.[145] It is difficult to determine exactly what kind of signals Bradley gave Hodges in these conversations. Over the next several days Bradley did not see fit to visit Hodges' headquarters at all (although he contacted him by telephone several times during that period).[146] Wilmot records that Montgomery was justifiably amazed to note on 20 December that "Hodges had been left without clear direction. Since the German offensive began, [Hodges] had seen neither Bradley nor any senior member of Bradley's staff," receiving "only the briefest orders, many of which were out of date by the time they reached [First Army]."[147]

But there were other headquarters, at army, corps, division, and lower, who needed no detailed guidance from their higher commanders to instruct them on what to do during this critical, confusing time. First Army was Bradley's senior Army headquarters and, therefore, his most experienced, yet their reaction to the initial German assault was poor. Perhaps too used to having things their own way, the First Army commander and his staff were unable to adapt quickly to the changing conditions on the battlefield. Even later, after the initial shock of the enemy attack had passed, Hodges seemed to persist in an inappropriate response to countering the German drive.

Perhaps echoing Bradley's earlier refusal to move his exposed headquarters to the rear, Hodges demanded that no First Army unit be allowed to withdraw from positions already held.[148] Despite Montgomery's suggestions that he withdraw from some of the more exposed positions, Hodges refused to order a retreat. While holding fast was exactly the correct action for the units on the Elsenborn Ridge, it was suicidal a few days later for the 7th Armored Division's combat units who were trying to escape the German trap at St.-Vith. Having conducted a brilliant mobile defense of St.-Vith and the surrounding area for nearly a week, Clarke's combat command was now ready to withdraw to safety behind the Salm River. First Army (and XVIII Airborne Corps commander Major General Matthew B. Ridgway) thought that Clarke should stay put and conduct a static defense like the defenders of Bastogne, an action sure to cause the armored unit's destruction.[149] Fortunately for Clarke, Montgomery stepped in this time and overruled Hodges and Ridgway. Clarke's division commander, Hasbrouck, later wrote that "Montgomery...saved us from Ridgway's crazy idea."[150]

First Army's successes during the battle seem more the result of the initiative of other units rather than its own. Gerow began the crucial massing of units on the Elsenborn Ridge, not Hodges. Without prompting from Hodges, Middleton requested the use of the First Army combat engineer units already in his area to flesh out his meager reserves. It was Middleton again who asked for the return from V Corps of Brigadier General Bill Hoge's Combat Command B, 9th Armored Division, which he used to bolster the defense near St.-Vith; First Army merely acquiesced.[151] Eisenhower initiated the timely dispatch of the 7th Armored Division to the VIII Corps area before First Army even acknowledged that it was needed. And it was Simpson who called Hodges to begin the process of sending the bulk of Ninth Army's combat power to the First Army area. Weigley assessed First Army as having "a competent staff [that] needed a cool...and dominant commander."[152] Clearly Hodges was not that man.

THE THIRD ARMY

The battle leadership of the Third Army fares much better compared with the First Army—hardly surprising given the obvious abilities of its famous commander. Lieutenant General George S. Patton, Jr., was in his favorite element during the desperate, fluid, mobile warfare in the Ardennes. With his army situated well out of the path of the German attack, Patton accepted the "cavalry to the rescue" mission seemingly tailormade for his Third Army—"a cavalry army, with movement and pursuit [its] passions."[153] Initially disappointed that his own offensive had to be cancelled, Patton warmed to the task when he realized he could now

Photo courtesy US Army

M4A3 "Sherman" tank, the principal armored fighting vehicle of World War II. Although often out-classed by some of the later German panzers, American assembly lines produced about 50,000 of these sturdy tanks during the war, a number the Germans could never hope to achieve.

Photo courtesy of US Army

M2A1 105-mm howitzer, the ubiquitous US artillery piece of World War II and a key element in a fire control system that made American artillery the most feared killer on the battlefield.

Photo courtesy US Army

M7 self-propelled 105-mm howitzer. Integrating firepower and mobility, the M7 consisted of a 105-mm howitzer mounted on a modified M4 tank chassis. LTC Roy Clay's 275th Armored Field Artillery Battalion used these weapons to good effect during the fighting around St.-Vith.

A 155-mm howitzer, manned by African-American soldiers. The critical manpower shortage, exacerbated by the huge Ardennes casualty lists, led Eisenhower to issue a circular calling for infantry volunteers "without regard to color or race." Unexpectedly large numbers of African-Americans volunteered—almost 5,000 in the first month—which helped to reshape attitudes toward the Army's policy of racially segregated units.

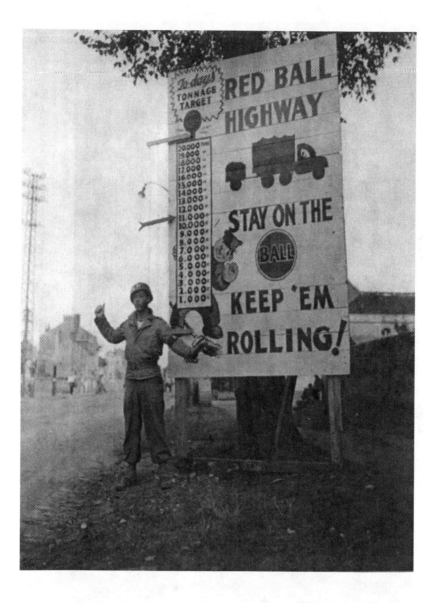

The "Red Ball Highway" was the US response to keeping the rapidly advancing Allied armies sufficiently supplied with the "sinews of war" as ever-lengthening lines of communication put increasing strains on the over-burdened logistics system. Truck convoys rolled over this highway day and night, moving supplies from the beachheads to the fighting front.

Captured German combat photo shows advance elements of the 6th SS Panzer Army at an Ardennes crossroads between Malmedy and St-Vith. 17 December 1944.

Photo courtesy National Archives

In a posed propaganda photo taken a few kilometers from St.-Vith early in the battle, an SS trooper gestures to comrades to move forward past abandoned and burning US jeeps and half-tracks (probably from the 14th Cavalry Group).

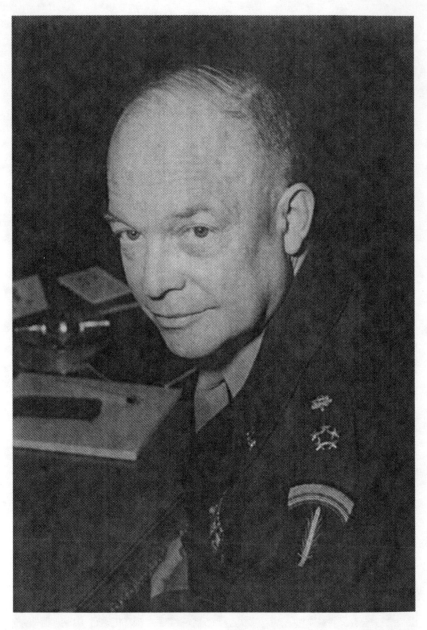

General of the Army Dwight D. Eisenhower, Supreme Allied
Commander, wearing the 5-star insignia of a General of the Army
and the unit patch of the Supreme Headquarters Allied
Expeditionary Force (SHAEF). The photo was taken shortly after
the conclusion of the Battle of the Bulge.

Photo courtesy National Archives

Supreme Command, Allied Expeditionary Force meets for the first
time in London on 1 February 1944. Seated, left to right: Air Chief
Marshal Sir Arthur Tedder; General Eisenhower; and General Sir
Bernard Montgomery. Standing, left to right: Lieutenant General
Omar N. Bradley; Admiral Sir Bertram Ramsey; Air Chief Marshal
Sir Trafford Leigh-Mallory; and Lieutenant General Walter Bedell
Smith.

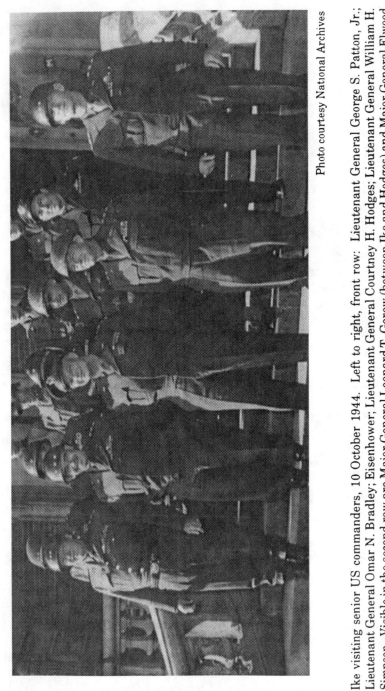

Ike visiting senior US commanders, 10 October 1944. Left to right, front row: Lieutenant General George S. Patton, Jr.; Lieutenant General Omar N. Bradley; Eisenhower; Lieutenant General Courtney H. Hodges; Lieutenant General William H. Simpson. Visible in the second row are Major General Leonard T. Gerow (between Ike and Hodges) and Major General Elwood R. Quesada (between Hodges and Simpson).

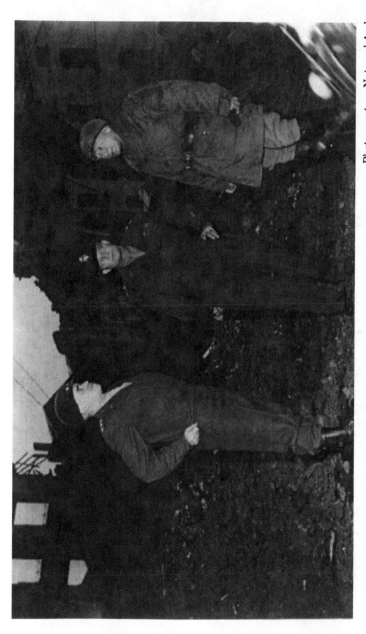

Eisenhower meeting with Bradley (left) and Patton in the ruins of Bastogne, Belgium, after the siege had been lifted by Patton's 4th Armored Division.

Lieutenant General Courtney H. Hodges, First Army commander during the Battle of the Bulge.

Lieutenant General William H. Simpson, Ninth Army commander during the Battle of the Bulge.

Photo courtesy National Archives

Major General Troy H. Middleton, VIII Corps commander.

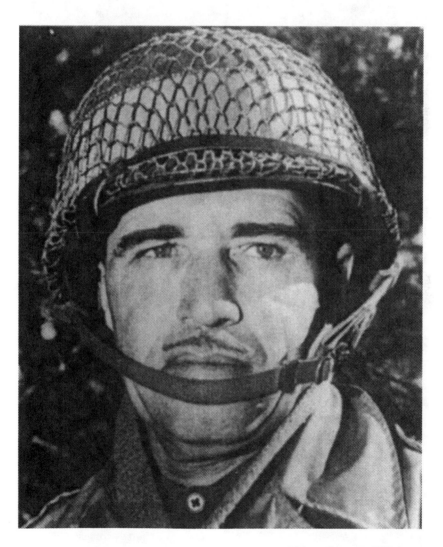

Photo courtesy US Army

Major General Alan W. Jones, 106th Infantry Division commander.

Photo courtesy US Army

Brigadier General Bruce C. Clarke, Commander, Combat Command B. 7th Armored Division.

Senior Allied commanders Field Marshal Sir Alan Brooke, Chief of the Imperial General Staff (left), Eisenhower, and 21 Army Group commander Montgomery near the end of the war. 12th Army Group commander Bradley is on the right.

Photo courtesy National Archives

Ike and Middleton share a light moment during a visit by Eisenhower to the VIII Corps area in the "quiet" Ardennes sector, 9 November 1944. A little over a month later, the smiling stopped.

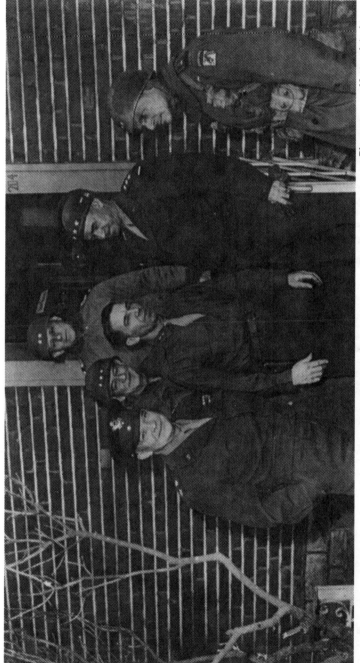

Eisenhower and Bradley (second from right) visit Lieutenant General Hodges (second from left) and some of Hodges' subordinate commanders following the Battle of the Bulge. Rear, Major General Clarence R. Huebner, V Corps; center, Major General Edwin P. Parker, Jr., 78th Infantry Division; and left, Major General Matthew B. Ridgway, XVIII Airborne Corps.

Generals of the Ardennes. Some of the US senior leaders who fought at the Battle of the Bulge join Eisenhower shortly after the end of the war in Europe. Left to right, front row: Simpson; Patton; General Carl A. Spaatz, US Army Air Forces Europe; Eisenhower; Bradley; Hodges; and Lieutenant General Leonard T. Gerow, Fifteenth Army. Second row: Brigadier General Ralph F. Stearley, IX Tactical Air Command; Lieutenant General Hoyt S. Vandenberg, 9th Air Force; Lieutenant General Walter Bedell Smith, SHAEF Chief of Staff; Major General Otto P. Weyland, XIX Tactical Air Command; and Brigadier General Richard E. Nugent, XXIX Tactical Air Command.

play the hero once again, driving his tanks to the relief of the "gallant defenders" of besieged Bastogne. He could hardly have written a better script for himself.

Third Army's rapid, 90-degree shift from its offensive facing east, to an attack into the southern flank of the German salient reflected both the strengths and weaknesses of an army built around Patton's personality. Weigley examined Third Army's staff and concluded:

> Any weakness in Patton's staff lay less in individuals than in organization. It was occasional bursts of individual exertion and ability that had to compensate for the lack of a consistently effective organization, which failed to manage the day-to-day activities of the Third Army with the consistency of staff supervision in the First or Ninth Army. This absence of constant, detailed, untiring staff work at Third Army headquarters was at the same time a corollary of the personalized command that Patton exerted over his army in contrast to Hodges or Simpson. It was not Patton's design that his army should be directed by anonymous staff officers...The Third Army was commanded by George S. Patton, Jr., in person or through his Household Cavalry.[154]

The dynamic Patton could slash through the "staff inertia" normally found in large organizations, quickly imposing his will. If this overpersonalized control of the Third Army was a shortcoming in some situations, it seems a definite strength in permitting the army to react rapidly to the German attack. Assisting in this procedure was Patton's prescient planning for just such a situation.

Admirers of the Third Army's rapid reaction to the German attack usually fail to appreciate the amount of prior planning Patton conducted in the days leading up to the decision to launch the Bastogne counterattack. Suspecting that the Germans were preparing an attack in the Ardennes region, Patton had already devised a counterplan to strike into the flank of such an attack. As early as November Patton became worried about the "static" VIII Corps front on his army's left flank, with its "newly arrived" or "tired units."[155] When Patton was briefed the week before the offensive began that "the Germans were possibly...concentrating forces opposite Middleton," Blumenson records "he set his staff to plan to 'be in position to meet whatever happens.'"[156] Third Army staff preparations "included surveying the roads and bridges" along likely counterattack routes the army might use.[157] When Bradley alerted him to the need to help rescue First Army, therefore, much of the staff work had been initiated.

Patton's proposal to "attack within a mere three days with three divisions,"[158] however, seems somewhat of a miscalculation of the actual scope of the German attack. As Eisenhower realized from the moment Patton made the dramatic offer at the meeting in Verdun on 19 December, three divisions would not be sufficient combat power to smash through the enemy's southern flank. As it turned out, "Patton's initial fast-moving narrow thrust...misfired."[159] Although one of 4th Armored Division's tank-infantry-artillery task forces actually entered Bastogne unopposed on 20 December, it was rapidly withdrawn back to the division's lines to avoid "a piecemeal commitment of [the] division."[160] Even so, Patton's initial three divisions were not powerful enough to force their way through to Bastogne. It required six divisions from Third Army's III and XII Corps, plus the remnants of Middleton's VIII Corps to finally lift the siege on 26 December.[161]

Weigley writes that although "the Third Army turn to Bastogne was effectively enough administered by the Third Army staff,"[162] the inherent weakness of Patton's style of battle leadership—his overpowering dominance of his staff—actually delayed the relief of the town. "Patton tried to do too much and thereby crowded his strategic and tactical vision with too many details," Weigley concluded.[163] By establishing himself as indispensable, Patton created his army's great strength as well as its principal weakness. While he could order (and get) sudden, rapid shifts in his army's focus, doing too much by himself could hamstring his staff's efforts. One of Patton's contemporaries observed that "Patton can get more good work out of a bunch of mediocre staff officers than anyone I ever saw,"[164] But this is more a critique of one of the principal drawbacks of Patton's style of battle leadership than it is a criticism of his staff. Although forced to work constantly in the shadow of "the Great Man," the Third Army staff "had individual members capable of rising to a demanding occasion,"[165] who, when allowed to do their jobs without undue interference from their army commander, produced excellent results.

THE NINTH ARMY

Lieutenant General William H. Simpson seemed to blend all the favorable qualities of a sympathetic, inspiring leader whose Ninth Army staff operated as an extension of his own thoughts and will. The "uncommonly normal" functioning of Simpson's staff seems to be a textbook example of the procedures and techniques taught in the American Army's service schools. The healthy relationship between Simpson and the highly competent Moore produced a responsive, smoothly operating headquarters that seemed a model of staff organization and administration.[166]

Far from being disrupted and disoriented by the German attack (as the First Army was), the Ninth Army quickly adapted to the changing nature of the battlefield in order to bring the maximum possible amount of the army's combat power to bear on the enemy offensive. And while it was primarily the force of Patton's personality that got Third Army quickly oriented on the Ardennes, Simpson's success in rapidly getting his divisions into combat in the First Army area seems more the result of his army's coolly efficient organization. When most other American commanders were wasting time worrying about their reputations when Montgomery assumed command in the north, Simpson was cooperating cheerfully with the British commander.

Of the three army commanders, Simpson seems to have been closest to Eisenhower in his appreciation of the scope of the German offensive. Hodges, certainly, was completely in the dark during the initial part of the German attack, only recognizing the danger after Bradley (on Ike's direction) alerted him. Although Patton correctly surmised that some kind of German attack was in the offing in the VIII Corps area, and planned accordingly, he seemed to misjudge the massive extent of the attack. His hurry-up counterattack of three divisions towards Bastogne was shown to be not nearly powerful enough to force a corridor and keep it open. Simpson, on the other hand, must have quickly realized the huge scope of the offensive, as his subsequent actions are those of a commander who knows that all his combat power will be necessary to stop it.[167]

That Ninth Army's seven divisions and 28 nondivisional combat units were instrumental in stopping, then defeating the German offensive is obvious in retrospect. The stand of Ninth Army's 7th Armored Division at St.-Vith is, by itself, reason enough to heap praise on Simpson's units. It is also significant that Simpson surmised the necessity of sending his units south before Hodges even asked for them. It was Simpson, on his own initiative, who called Hodges and offered his units; and the Ninth Army commander, unlike the "headstrong" Third Army commander, needed no personal appeal from Bradley to get his armored division moving to Hodges' aid. Once Eisenhower directed the 7th Armored be sent to help Middleton, Simpson began action on his own to speed his other combat units to the threatened area. And, despite Patton's prior planning and admirably rapid shift of focus, Simpson actually got more Ninth Army units into combat than did the Third Army—and faster as well.[168]

It is primarily Simpson's personal nature that has prevented recognition of his army's significant achievements in the Battle of the Bulge (and Ninth Army's outstanding performance throughout the remainder of the war). Selfless and steady, Simpson placed teamwork and mission accomplishment above publicity and personal recognition. Had he sought the limelight, like the better known Patton, or had he been more colorful, it seems highly probable that Ninth Army's significant accomplishments would have been more widely reported. As it was, by the time Simpson and the Ninth Army became operational in Europe and began to achieve significant successes, there seemed to be only one army commander and only one army to stir the war correspondents' imagination and generate headlines—George Patton and his Third Army. Simpson, who seemed actively to avoid publicity, remained in the background, identified in reporters' dispatches as "the Ninth Army commander" and rarely by name. This contrasts to the reporters' habit of virtually always referring to Patton's unit as "Patton's Third Army."[169]   To Simpson, such personal recognition was unnecessary.

Simpson's ability to get his combat power into action during the Ardennes offensive while simultaneously shifting his army boundary and establishing a cohesive defense of a longer, thinner front must be credited to the superior performance of the Ninth Army staff—clearly the best organized, most effective staff of any army in the theater. The amazement with which the Ninth Army's consistently normal operation, even in times of crisis, was observed is eloquent testimony of its pre-eminence. The command climate in Ninth Army headquarters created by Simpson and Moore established the kind of staff organization and functioning that produced these outstanding results.

In contrast, First Army was, at heart, "an unhappy headquarters."[170] Weigley wrote that "the prickly General Hodges presided over a staff headed by the prickly General Kean, and over an army so accustomed to being first in priority...that First Army headquarters treated primacy as a natural right."[171] Such a command climate creates a staff attitude hardly suited to rapidly adapting to reverses like the German attack in the Ardennes, but it does help explain Hodges' reluctance to believe Gerow's sound advice to stop the Roer dams attack. Third Army, incapable of maintaining a "consistently effective organization,"[172] could manage to produce brilliant feats in the short run, such as the dramatic 90-degree shift, but it was hobbled by Patton's personalized, heavy-handed control over the long run. Neither the First nor Third Army could match the day-to-day efficiency and effectiveness of the Ninth Army. Their operations during the Ardennes offensive clearly bring this out.   Simpson's operations officer credits his army commander for why the Ninth Army staff worked so well:

> General Simpson's genius lay in his characteristic manner, his command presence, his ability to listen, his unfailing use of his staff to check things out before making decisions, and his way of making all hands feel that they were important to him and to the Army...I have never known a commander

to make better use of his staff than General Simpson.[173]

Ninth Army's success in all its operations, including the Battle of the Bulge, is directly attributable to Simpson's ability to form, train, and direct his team toward its well-defined goal.

The battle leadership displayed by Patton, and, most notably, Simpson reflected many of the strengths that seem common to the best American combat leadership during the European campaign:

- A calm steadfastness under pressure.
- A nearly instinctive appreciation of the situation and what it required.
- An aggressive spirit that demanded offensive action.
- An understanding of the importance of tactical mobility.
- An ability to focus overwhelming firepower on a threat.
- A sound education in a common doctrine of warfare that allowed the rapid coordination of the combat power of several commands.

The reaction of the army commanders contained all of these to greater or lesser degrees. Their combined application of the "doctrinal response" required by the massive German attack in the Ardennes effectively doomed the enemy offensive within days of its commencement. Certainly the nearly instantaneous responsiveness of Patton and Simpson in rushing reinforcements to the First Army area was decisive to the outcome of the battle, condemning the Germans to failure even as they continued to gain ground.

There were also shortcomings in the battle leadership, particularly prevalent in the First Army's reactions:

- A failure to predict the timing and location of the massive assault.
- A stubborn resistance to alter existing plans when confronted with a changing battlefield situation.
- A slow appreciation of the scope of the enemy offensive; an attitude that prohibited any tactical withdrawal, even when warranted.

- A dangerous anti-Montgomery jealousy that put "American" interests above "Allied" ones.

THE "UNCOMMONLY NORMAL" NINTH ARMY

When measured against all these strengths and shortcomings, it is clear that Simpson's "uncommonly normal" Ninth Army fares best. It could be argued that, because the First Army had to bear the brunt of the attack, it only follows that their reaction would naturally be more confused and less orderly. Yet, this seems to ignore the truly outstanding reactions of some of their subordinate units, such as V and VIII Corps, who actually bore the full impact of the offensive. These subordinate units would seem to have an even greater claim on such an excuse, but their actions don't require one.

The great difference seems to come back to the battle leadership of the army commanders. Simpson's showed an abundance of leadership strengths, Hodges' did not. The First Army's reaction to the crisis was characterized by many of the shortcomings pointed out, while Ninth Army's showed few of these weaknesses. Simpson and his Chief of Staff Moore created a command climate in their organization that greatly facilitated their army's outstanding response to the demands of the Ardennes offensive. Hodges and his Chief of Staff Kean had, by the time of the Battle of the Bulge, produced a command climate in First Army within which a real battlefield disaster was highly likely. Patton, whose headquarters showed both strengths and shortcomings during the battle, had created a Third Army staff so dependent on his own persona that it is difficult to separate the two. Still, Third Army demonstrated more strengths than shortcomings, clearly outperforming First Army, and Patton's abilities purely as a battle leader are legend.

As an army commander, however, Simpson demonstrated battle leadership during the Battle of the Bulge difficult to top. His mixture of commonsense command style with a textbook staff organization produced a smoothly functioning headquarters, remarkable for its efficiency and consistency. Perhaps the best summation of Simpson's leadership was made by Major General Alvan C. Gillem, Jr., who commanded the XIII Corps, Ninth Army, when he wrote:

We see leadership best reflected, for example, when firmness is substituted for harshness, understanding for intolerance, humanness for bigotry, and when pride replaces egotism. General Simpson's every action exemplified the best of these traits of character. His integrity inspired a high degree of loyalty. His conduct on all occasions was scrupulous, and his associates of all ranks found him to be patient, impartial, courageous, sympathetic, and confident. They also found him equally loyal to seniors and juniors alike. He was an able, respected commander for whom all were willing to give their best endeavors.[174]

Possibly the only fault which can, in retrospect, be attributed to Simpson is that he never allowed himself to garner the publicity due him and his unit. If better known, his outstanding battle leadership could have provided later generations of Army officers a better example than Patton's often bizarre personal leadership style.[175]

NOTES

1. US Department of Army, 12th Army Group, *G-1 Section, 12th Army Group Report of Operations*, 1948, 81-83. Forrest C. Pogue, *The United States Army in World War II: European Theater of Operations. The Supreme Command* (Washington, D.C.: Office of the Chief of Military History, 1954), Map IV. Strengths of the three armies as of 2400 hours on 15 December 1944 were: First Army—341,569; Third Army—257,518; Ninth Army—188,285. Shortages (mostly combat infantrymen) for all of 12th Army Group on that day totaled 32,000.

2. Omar N. Bradley, *A Soldier's Story* (New York: Henry Holt and Company, 1951), 225-226, 422. Bradley used these adjectives to characterize Hodges' command in his first autobiography, written shortly after the war: "Without the flair of Patton's Third Army and the breeziness of Simpson's Ninth, First Army trudged across Europe with a serious and grim intensity."

3. Omar N. Bradley and Clay Blair, *A General's Life: An Autobiography of General of the Army Omar N. Bradley* (New York: Simon and Schuster, 1983), 94-95. Bradely writes of Hodges: "For countless years [prior to relieving Hodges as Commandant of the Infantry school at Fort Benning in 1941] Hodges had been to me an august figure like Marshall and a man I admired almost equally...he was on a par with George Patton [as an army commander], but

owing to his modesty and low profile, has been all but forgotten."
Hodges, born 5 January 1887 in Perry, GA, had entered West Point
with the class of 1908, but flunked out in mathematics his first year
there. He enlisted in the Army and received a commission from the
ranks in 1909. On the battlefield in France in World War I, Hodges
won a Distinguished Service Cross, a Silver Star, and a Bronze Star
for bravery. He rose to temporary lieutenant colonel and
commanded a battalion in combat for several months. A crack shot,
Hodges was on the Army rifle team in national rifle matches for
many years. He served on the Infantry Board at Fort Benning while
Marshall was there at the Infantry School. Upon handing over
duties as Commandant of the Infantry School to Bradley in 1941,
Hodges became the Chief of Infantry in Washington, D.C.

4. Russell F. Weigley, *Eisenhower's Lieutenants: The
Campaigns of France and Germany 1944-1945* (Bloomington:
Indiana University Press, 1981), 84-85.

5. Bradley and Blair, *A General's Life*, 98-99; Weigley,
Eisenhower's Lieutenants, 170-171, 177. Weigley notes the
deteriorating good feelings between Patton and his Army Group
commander, Bradley, by July 1944: "Close friends in North Africa,
Bradley and Patton since Sicily had come more and more to regard
each other warily under an outward show of continued camaraderie.
Bradley feared the activation of Patton's army as the inauguration
of a generalship reckless to the point of utter irresponsibility.
Patton in turn disdained Bradley's generalship as "unsufferably
orthodox, predictable, and cautious...Bradley's...devoted
followers...developed a strong dislike of the bombastic, egotistical
'gorgeous George' with his tailored green jackets, bright buttons,
fancy leather belt and boots, and initialed pistols...When George
came visiting at Bradley's headquarters, the staff made no effort to
be more than lukewarm, and when possible...'quickly turned him to
a movie' to be rid of him." Patton, on the other hand, looked down
on Bradley with the cavalryman's disdain for the footsoldier,
writing, "I am also nauseated by the fact that Hodges and Bradley
state that all human virtue depends on knowing infantry tactics."

6. Weigley, *Eisenhower's Lieutenants*, 180-181.

7. Bradley, *A Soldier's Story*, 422; Weigley, *Eisenhower's
Lieutenants*, 180.

8. Martin Blumenson, *Patton: The Man Behind the Myth 1885-
1945* (New York: Berkley Books, 1987), 233; Weigley, *Eisenhower's
Lieutenants*, 238.

9. Bradley and Blair, *A General's Life*, 395. Bradley wrote: "[Ike
and I] were immensely impressed with Simpson and his staff and

the planning they had done. Simpson's Chief of Staff, James E. Moore, was one of the least known yet ablest officers in the ETO...Moore 'minded the store' while Simpson toured his corps and division headquarters. Owing to Moore's intelligence and talent for administration, Ninth Army's staff, although least experienced in battle, was in some respects superior to any in my command. Moreover, both Simpson and Moore get along remarkably well with Monty and the British staffs...".

10. Ibid.

11. Dwight D. Eisenhower, *Crusade in Europe* (New York: Doubleday and Company, 1948), 376. Ike recorded a short assessment of Simpson's abilities as well: "Alert, intelligent, and professionally capable, he was the type of leader that American soldiers deserve."

12. Bradley, *A Soldier's Story*, 422.

13. Thomas R. Stone, "He Had the Guts to Say No: A Military Biography of General William Hood Simpson" (Ph.D. diss., Rice University, 1974), 3; T.M. Dunleavy, ed., "Lieutenant General William H. Simpson," *Generals of the Army and the Air Force* 2 (June 1954):19-21. Much of the information in this chapter on the life, career, and impact of General Simpson is based on Colonel Stone's excellent dissertation, as well as the two articles he has written about him (including his award-winning article in *Military Review*). Col. Stone's works are the primary start points for anyone wishing to study the life of this outstanding soldier. The "Simpson" listing in *Generals of the Army* contains much factual data concerning his career, including promotions, assignments, awards, and decorations.

14. *Generals of the Army*, 19; Stone, "Simpson," 3.

15. Weigley, *Eisenhower's Lieutenants*, 84; Blumenson, *Patton*, 52-52; Bradley and Blair, *A General's Life*, 95, 340-341; Stone, "Simpson," 3.

16. *The Howitzer* (West Point: The United States Military Academy, 1909), 77.

17. Ibid.

18. *Generals of the Army*, 19; Stone, "Simpson," 3. Often, when discussing the merits of famous West Point graduates, much is made of their relative class rankings at graduation, the presumption being that a high class standing ensures a brilliant career (and vice-versa). In fact, one can find successful and outstanding military leaders who represent the top, middle, and bottom of their respective classes at the Military Academy. For example, while MacArthur and Lee were at the top of their classes, Eisenhower and

Bradley were closer to the middle. Patton actually flunked out of the class of 1908, requiring an extra year to graduate. Grant was an indifferent student, excelling only in horsemanship. Additionally, it can be considered something of a feat merely to graduate from an institution in which fully one-third of each entering class fail to complete the 4 years (and that is one-third of a carefully screened, highly competitive group). Therefore, it appears that no special significance should be attached to Simpson's place at the bottom of his class. His outstanding military career certainly makes his class ranking irrelevant. Further, because he lacked a high school diploma when he entered West Point, the simple fact that he managed to graduate at all seems remarkable.

19. Stone, "Simpson," 3.

20. *Generals of the Army*, 19.

21. Bradley and Blair, *A General's Life*, 340; *Generals of the Army*, 19.

22. Stone, "Simpson," 3; *Generals of the Army*, 19; Bradley and Blair, *A General's Life*, 340.

23. Stephen E. Ambrose, *Eisenhower: Volume One, Soldier, General of the Army, President-Elect 1890-1952* (New York: Simon and Schuster, 1983), 64-65; Bradley and Blair, *A General's Life*, 44-45; Stone, "Simpson," 3; *Generals of the Army*, 19. Eisenhower and Bradley complained so much about missing out on overseas combat duty during World War I that Simpson's good luck in getting to France and into action seems even more fortuitous. Ike and Bradley feared their careers were ruined; they must have assumed, therefore, that the "lucky ones" like Simpson had had their future careers made.

24. Private Louis Hummel to Kathryn Hoffert, 4 March 1918. It is interesting to note that, at least in some parts of the World War I Army, the terms "draftee" and "enlisted man" were not synonymous. In this letter, written by a recently drafted Iowa soldier training at Camp Cody, NM, to his sister in Colfax, IA, the term "enlisted men" is used to distinguish those who had volunteered from those like himself who had been drafted. Later, of course, the term has been applied to any soldier who is not a commissioned or warrant officer.

25. *Generals of the Army*, 19.

26. Center for Military History, *American Armies and Battlefields in Europe* (Washington, DC: GPO, 1992) (reprint of 1938 edition prepared by the American Battle Monuments Commision), 515-518; Stone, "Simpson," 3; *Generals of the Army*, 19. The "Prairie Division" [33rd Infantry Division, Illinois National Guard] trained

at Camp Logan, TX, and sailed for France in May 1918. It served with the Australians in the Amiens sector and had units at Verdun and at the Meuse-Argonne. The 33rd spent 27 days in active sectors, capturing 3,987 prisoners—a record for a National Guard Division—and advanced 36 kilometers. The price was 989 dead Americans and over 6,000 wounded.

27. *Generals of the Army*, 19; Stone, "Simpson," 3.

28. *Generals of the Army*, 19-20.

29. Ibid. Camp Grant, located west of Chicago, served as one of the demobilization centers for the rapidly disappearing army.

30. Stone, "Simpson," 3; Ambrose, *Eisenhower*, 72. Considering the problems Eisenhower's career suffered after his run-in with the powerful chief of infantry at about this same time, Simpson's future must have been brighter after successful service in the chief's own office.

31. *Generals of the Army*, 19; Stone, "Simpson," 3.

32. Bradley and Blair, *A General's Life*, 54. Bradley writes that it was customary for two groups of officers to begin classes at the Infantry School each fall—an Advanced Course (senior captains, majors and lieutenant colonels), and a lower level Company Officers' Course. About 70 officers were in the senior class. As a major, Simpson, of course, was in the Advanced Course.

33. Stone, "Simpson," 3; *Generals of the Army*, 19.

34. Mark C. Bender, *Watershed at Leavenworth: Dwight D. Eisenhower and the Command and General Staff College* (Fort Leavenworth, KS: US Army Command and General Staff College, 1990), 28-34. Prior to the reorganization of the Command and General Staff School in 1923, officers first attended the year-long School of the Line, which focused on "military operations up to division level." A second year, focusing on the corps and army level, was the General Staff School course. Since the second year's General Staff School was reserved for only the top 40 to 60 percent of graduates of the School of the Line, "competition became quite keen for admission to the second year course"—a competition not always seen as healthy. The school Commandant at the time of the consolidation, Brigadier General Robert H. Allen, noted: "The consolidation into one class will do away with the disappointment which heretofore existed in the minds of those who had not made the General Staff class." Bender records, however, that the real "purpose of the consolidation was to accommodate a large group of over a thousand officers who had entered service during World War I and who had no schooling in general staff or higher command duties. In order to consolidate the two courses into a single course

(now renamed the Command and General Staff School), some of the instruction in the separate arms was transferred to the various branch schools. Subjects pertaining to army and theater levels of operation were transferred to the Army War College." Although the school, for a time, returned to 2-year courses in 1928, Simpson's class was one of the standard 1-year courses.

35. Ibid., 34-35. According to Bender, "The major subjects emphasized the tactics and techniques of the various branches, including their individual capabilities and their potency when incorporated with other branches. The command, staff, and logistics subject area required officers to compare administrative and field orders, to develop the details of moving a division by truck and rail, and to determine the logistics of supply during attack, pursuit, and defense. Perhaps the most important course, Tactical Principles and Decisions, took up the full spectrum of tactical considerations and principles and was reinforced by the students' application in staff rides, map maneuvers, and problem solving."

36. Ibid., 3, 31-35. Bender notes: "The mission of the new Command and General Staff School was to provide instruction on (1) the combined use of all arms in the division and in the army corps; (2) the proper functions of commanders of divisions and of army corps; and (3) the proper functions of general staff officers of divisions and of army corps." During Simpson's attendance, "the bulk of the...curriculum consisted of three main subjects: tactics and techniques; tactical principles; and command, staff, and logistics. Other subjects taught included history, training, leadership, military organization, combat order, field engineering, military intelligence, strategy, and legal principles."

37. *Generals of the Army*, 19; Stone, "Simpson," 3.

38. Stone, "Simpson," 3; *Generals of the Army*, 19.

39. Ambrose, *Eisenhower*, 85; Stone, "Simpson," 3; *Generals of the Army*, 19.

40. Bradley and Blair, *A General's Life*, 74. Bradley writes, "There was very little pressure. We were not graded on our work; there was no class standing to be achieved, no one of importance to impress."

41. Ambrose, *Eisenhower*, 85.

42. Stone, "Simpson," 3.

43. *Generals of the Army*, 19-20; Stone, "Simpson," 3.

44. *Generals of the Army*, 20.

45. Ibid.

46. Stone, "Simpson," 3-4.

47. *Generals of the Army*, 19-20.

48. Robert R. Palmer, et al., *The United States Army in World War II: The Army Ground Forces. The Procurement and Training of Ground Combat Troops* (Washington, D.C.: Office of the Chief of Military History, 1948), 102; *Generals of the Army*, 20. While commanding general of XII Corps, Simpson made an observation tour of the North African Theater of Operations. He was fortunate to be allowed to do so, since the powerful, influential commander of Army Ground Forces, General Lesley J. McNair, felt that a commander's place during training was always with his unit. Palmer wrote: "By supervising the training of his unit...a commander trained himself for his role in combat. General McNair insisted that the principle of keeping officers with troops applied to generals as well as to others...as a rule General McNair frowned upon higher commanders taking trips which diverted them from their essential duties. The opening of operations in North Africa gave training commanders an inviting opportunity to make tours of observation [but]...when General Marshall asked whether it might be wise for division commanders, halfway through their training periods, to see some combat operations in North Africa, General McNair replied that division commanders were needed with their divisions; he suggested that a few corps commanders go instead." Simpson was one of only four corps commanders allowed to tour North Africa.

49. *Generals of the Army*, 19.

50. *Conquer: The Story of the Ninth Army 1944-1945* (Nashville: Battery Press, 1980), 15-17; Stone, "Simpson," 4. *Conquer* is the "official" history of the Ninth Army, written shortly after the war by the Ninth Army staff under the direction of its chief of staff, BG Moore. It is an excellent operational history of the unit, well organized, straight-forward, and lacking the usual "how great we were" flavor of the typical postwar unit histories.

51. Alfred D. Chandler, et al., ed., *The Papers of Dwight D. Eisenhower, The War Years (Volumes I-V)* (Baltimore: Johns Hopkins Press, 1970), 3:1795. There was no question that Eisenhower preferred Simpson to Fredendall, since Ike had fired the former II Corps commander the previous year for Fredendall's terrible leadership performance at the American defeat at Kasserine Pass. Marshall, however, who had gotten the relieved Fredendall promoted to lieutenant general with command of a training army in the States (Second US Army), continued to try to get Ike to take him back in a combat command capacity. Eisenhower would have none of it. Ike would prefer one of his combat-seasoned corps commanders as his next army commander, but realized that

circumstances made that impractical.

52. Weigley, *Eisenhower's Lieutenants*, 431. Weigley points out that Marshall's use of Simpson as an example to the other training commanders who were conscientiously building combat units in the States, was, in principle, "similar to the elevation of General [Raymond] McLain with his National Guard background to a corps" command (XIX) later in the war. Both would serve as examples to their different classes of officer.

53. Ibid.

54. Thomas R. Stone, "General William Hood Simpson: Unsung Commander of US Ninth Army," *Parameters* ll (February 1980): 46.

55. Ibid.

56. Ibid.

57. Charles B. MacDonald, *The United States Army in World War II: European Theater of Operations. The Siegfried Line* (Washington, D.C.: Office of the Chief of Military History, 1963), 379-380; *Conquer*, 15.

58. US Department of the Army, *Army Service Forces Report No. 169, Command and Staff Procedures*, 31 July 1945; US Department of the Army, *Ninth United States Army Administrative Instructions*, 30 November 1944; Stone, "Unsung Commander," p.44. The agreed upon staff procedures of the general staff sections were basically those as taught in the Army's service schools. Unlike those of the First and Third Armies, the special staff sections did not function under any general staff section, although they coordinated closely. Furthermore, unlike First and Third Armies, Simpson's deputy chief of staff did not directly supervise any of the special staff sections, whose heads reported directly to the chief of staff. A review of Simpson's Administrative Instructions confirms the "normalcy" of the Army's organizational arrangements, showing a standard G1/G4 standing operating procedures. Stone notes that "headquarters functions were conducted according to well established principles...and the lessons learned at Leavenworth were followed in practice."

59. *Conquer*, 16.

60. Stone, "Simpson," 27-28.

61. *Conquer*, 17.

62. Ibid., 37. Ninth Army's relatively late introduction to combat allowed Simpson's staff the opportunity to reap the benefits of the early mistakes of First and Third Armies. Before it deployed to combat in France, First and Third Army permitted some staff visits by Ninth Army officers.

63. Stone, "Simpson," 28.

64. Ibid., 13-14.

65. *Conquer*, 17-18; Stone, "Simpson," 1-2. A new Ninth Army patch was adopted after the change in designation. The new patch was a white heraldic rosette placed on a red nonagon. Based on its Fourth Army heritage, this new patch strongly resembles the Fourth Army's old one—a white clover on a red diamond background.

66. US Department of the Army, *Ninth United States Army After Action Report, January 1945*, 3; Stone, "Simpson," 87.

67. *Conquer*, 366.

68. Martin Blumenson, "The Decision to Take Brest," *Army* 10 (March 1960): 44-47; *Conquer*, 47, 366-367. Instead of a quick siege of 6 days as the high command expected, Middleton's VIII Corps was tied up for a month and had 10,000 casualties. In addition to attacking the port city, Ninth Army units had to guard an exposed flank of some 250 miles, receive and process all incoming personnel replacements of the theater (regardless of ultimate unit of assignment), and provide trucks, personnel, and "housekeeping detachments" to run the famed "Red Ball Highway." This simultaneous accomplishment of these important, but very diverse tasks, was a truly monumental endeavor for the brand-new Ninth Army.

69. *Conquer*, 47-48.

70. Blumenson, "Brest," 47; *Conquer*, p. 366.

71. Martin Blumenson, *The United States Army in World War II. European Theater of Operations. Breakout and Pursuit* (Washington, D.C.: Office of the Chief of Military History, 1961), 637, 644; *Conquer* 38-39.

72. Stone, "Simpson," 81.

73. *Conquer*, 55, 366.

74. Ibid., 54.

75. Bradley and Blair, *A General's Life*, 340; Stone, "Simpson," 103. Bradley wrote: "In preparation for [the November] offensive, I shifted Simpson's Ninth Army from the southern Belgium-Luxembourg area to the area north of Aachen formerly held by Hodges' XIX Corps. This, in effect, inserted the Ninth Army between Monty's forces and Hodges' forces. I did this for two principal reasons. First, I felt there was a good likelihood that at some future date Monty would again attempt to incorporate a U.S. army into his command. The U.S. First Army staffers—those mule-headed, swaggering veterans of North Africa and Sicily—were so bitterly anti-Monty that I feared they might mutiny if they were

again compelled to serve under him. Simpson and his staff had not yet been subjected to Monty's megalomania and were, on the whole, more diplomatic and adaptable. Secondly, the Ninth Army was far less experienced than the First Army. If I were again forced to lend Monty an army, I preferred to give him my green troops rather than trusted lieutenants such as Collins, Gerow...Middleton and others."

76. Stone, "Simpson," 101.

77. *Conquer*, 72, 366-367.

78. Allen H. Mick, ed., *With the 102nd Infantry Division Through Germany* (Nashville: Battery Press, 1980), 41. Another "official" unit history written shortly after the end of the war, this one is truly impressive in its ability to capture the flavor and feel of the battlefield, and the common soldiers' reactions to it.

79. Mick, *102nd Division*, 40.

80. Harold P. Leinbaugh and John D. Campbell, *The Men of Company K: The Autobiography of a World War II Rifle Company* (New York: Bantam Books, 1987), 16, 39. This book, co-authored by two former commanders of Company K, 333rd Infantry Regiment, is one of the best, most realistic accounts of combat to be written about the European Theater. It follows the unit from its callup and training, through combat, to the end of the war.

81. Weigley, *Eisenhower's Lieutenants*, 430-431. Weigley writes: "In twenty-three days of campaigning, the [Ninth] army had advanced only nine to twenty kilometers. It had lost 1,133 killed, 6,864 wounded and 2,059 missing. How many German casualties the Ninth Army had inflicted was and is unknown, though the bag of prisoners was 8,321, and the army buried 1,264 enemy dead."

82. Ibid., 431.

83. Combat Studies Institute, *Conversations With General J. Lawton Collins* (Fort Leavenworth, KS: US Army Command and General Staff Collage, 1983), 10; Weigley, *Eisenhower's Lieutenants*, 320-321, 434, 603. Weigley describes the importance of the Roer River dams: "Just ahead [of the advance of the 12th Army Group] lay the Schwammenauel and a series of other dams on the Roer River and its tributaries, which if opportunely ruptured by the Germans could flood [the armies'] invasion path and effectively close it for several weeks...The Roer dams were soon [fall 1944] to cast their shadows over almost every movement of [the American armies]"; Years after the war, General J. Lawton Collins, wartime commander of First Army's VII Corps, explained why the dams were initially overlooked: "They [intelligence people] didn't [see the dams as an important objective] and they didn't recognize the threat they posed. We all knew there were some dams. We had not studied that

particular part of the zone. They came as a surprise to most of the intelligence people in the army. There were two or three of them [dams]. It was sometime before First Army realized their capacity to flood the southern [sic; actually northern] part of the army zone of action. That was an intelligence failure, a real combat intelligence failure, on the part of the top intelligence people." As it happened, by the time the dams were finally captured by First Army troops (February 1945), the enemy had sabotaged the discharge valves, delaying Simpson's assault crossings of the Roer for about 2 weeks.

84. Hugh M. Cole, *The United States Army in World War II: European Theater of Operations. The Ardennes. Battle of the Bulge* (Washington, D.C.: Office of the Chief of Military History, 1965), 22, 75-92.

85. Ibid., 78, 80.

86. Charles B. MacDonald, *A Time For Trumpets: The Untold Story of the Battle of the Bulge* (New York: Bantam Books, 1985), 101-123; Cole, *Ardennes*, 80-95.

87. Cole, *Ardennes*, 39-47, 110.

88. Charles B. MacDonald, *The Mighty Endeavor: The American War in Europe* (New York: Quill, William Morrow, 1986), 400-403. MacDonald, a participant in this phase of the battle, writes: "In a brutal four-day fight [2nd and 99th Infantry Divisions] had jammed the north shoulder of what would become known as the 'bulge.' They had denied the vital road network in the north. Together with the 99th, the 2nd Division had incurred heavy casualties—probably a total of six thousand...Yet in the process the two units had dealt heavy losses to three German divisions and...'knocked a part of Hitler's personal operations plan into a cocked hat.'"

89. Ibid., 427.

90. John S. D. Eisenhower, *The Bitter Woods* (New York: G.P. Putnam's Sons, 1969), 221; Weigley, *Eisenhower's Lieutenants*, 465, 471; MacDonald, *A Time for Trumpets*, 188.

91. MacDonald, *Mighty Endeavor*, 427; Weigley, *Eisenhower's Lieutenants*, 471; Cole, *Ardennes*, 103-104.

92. Weigley, *Eisenhower's Lieutenants*, 471.

93. Ambrose, *Eisenhower*, 144; Weigley, *Eisenhower's Lieutenants*, 471. Leonard "Gee" Gerow had been Eisenhower's study-mate during their year at the Command and General Staff School at Fort Leavenworth. Gerow was also an Honor Graduate of their class (top 10 percent). In early 1942, Gerow had initially been Eisenhower's boss as the head of the War Plans Division on the

Army staff, but Ike replaced him in that position in February 1942, when Gerow left to take command of a division.

94. Weigley, *Eisenhower's Lieutenants*, 471, 520; MacDonald, *Mighty Endeavor*, 427.

95. Cole, *Ardennes*, 102, 109-110, 656-660.

96. Ibid., 659.

97. Weigley, *Eisenhower's Lieutenants*, 473; Cole, *Ardennes*, 656-660.

98. Eisenhower, *Bitter Woods*, 220-222; MacDonald, *A Time for Trumpets*, 188-189. In fairness to Hodges and Kean, it should be noted that, on the afternoon of 16 December and during the night of 16-17 December, First Army headquarters approved the movement, or alert of movement, of several units to the threatened sector. One of these was BG Hoge's Combat Command B, 9th Armored Division, on loan from VIII Corps to Gerow's V Corps. This unit, released back to Middleton at his request, significantly assisted in the defense of the area surrounding St.-Vith. Other units alerted for movement included the 1st Infantry Division and a combat command of the 3rd Armored Division. But MacDonald notes that, despite these actions, "When Gee Gerow telephoned [late on 16 December] to ask authority to call off the 2d Division's attack for the Roer River dams, Hodges said no. If the Germans were trying to divert that attack, why give them what they were after."

99. Frank J. Price, *Troy H. Middleton: A Biography* (Baton Rouge: LSU Press, 1974), 215.

100. Weigley, *Eisenhower's Lieutenants*, 480; Cole, *Ardennes*, 311.

101. MacDonald, *A Time for Trumpets*, 188-1889; Weigley, *Eisenhower's Lieutenants*, 486; Cole, *Ardennes*, 157-158.

102. Weigley, *Eisenhower's Lieutenants*, 458.

103. Bradley and Blair, *A General's Life*, 356; Weigley, *Eisenhower's Lieutenants*, 458.

104. Bradley and Blair, *A General's Life*, 356-357.

105. Ibid., 356.

106. Robert H. Berlin, "United States Army World War II Corps Commanders: A Composite Biography," *Journal of Military History* 53 (April 1989): 166; Eisenhower, *Bitter Woods*, 221; Cole, *Ardennes*, 103-104; Weigley, *Eisenhower's Lieutenants*, 491, 493, 562, 668, 678. Gerow weathered the incident successfully and, in January 1945, was promoted to command the newly formed Fifteenth Army. This unit was intended to relieve the other armies of mopping-up and occupation duties west of the Rhine. Gerow continued to retain Ike's confidence and was highly rated by the

Supreme Commander (Ike placed him 8th overall on a list of general officers in the European Theater of Operations near the close of the war).

107. Bradley and Blair, *A General's Life*, 356.

108. Blumenson, *Patton*, 245-247; Weigley, *Eisenhower's Lieutenants*, 497-500. Weigley observed that, "Patton's military intuition was as acute as any in the American army. He was so intent on attacking that it made him nervous not only to stand idle himself, but to observe idleness in any friendly troops on his flank...Thus, during the weeks when Middleton's VIII Corps on his left flank had not done these things, Patton sniffed danger."

109. Weigley, *Eisenhower's Lieutenants*, 500-501; Blumenson, *Patton*, 250-253.

110. Chester Wilmot, *The Struggle for Europe* (New York: Harper and Brothers, 1952), 588-589. An Australian journalist, Wilmot spent much time at Montgomery's headquarters during the war. His obvious admiration for the field marshal is nearly unbounded and lacks objectivity.

111. Ibid.

112. Eisenhower, *Bitter Woods*, 215; Bradley and Blair, *A General's Life*, 356; Weigley, *Eisenhower's Lieutenants*, 458.

113. US Department of the Army, *Ninth United States Army G-3 After Action Report, 16-31 December 1944*, 1; *Conquer*, 115-118.

114. Eisenhower, *Bitter Woods*, 215.

115. Bruce C. Clarke, interview 10 November 1987, tape recording; US Department of the Army, U.S. Armor School, *The Battle of St.-Vith, Belgium, 17-23 December 1944*, 1949, 4.

116. Clarke interview; *Battle of St.-Vith*, 6-9.

117. Cole, *Ardennes*, 274-275. The issue of road clearances, seemingly a rather mundane subject, is actually directly related to the arrival time of 7th Armored Division combat elements at St.-Vith. It is a crucial issue, since it has a direct impact on the information Middleton provided to MG Alan Jones, commander of the 106th Infantry Division at St.-Vith, on the night of 16-17 December 1944. Acting on convoy information provided by the First Army staff, Middleton told Jones that a combat command of 7th Armored Division would "arrive at 0700 hours" on 17 December. Based on this information, Jones anticipated an early counterattack by this armored unit to try to save his surrounded troops. But that estimated arrival time was only for the initial convoy elements of the unit to *begin* showing up at St.-Vith; the "closure time" (that is, the estimated time when all elements of the unit would be at their destination) was no earlier than 1900 hours. Whether First Army

staff or Middleton (or Jones) caused the confusion in transmitting these arrival times is unknown. However, given their subsequent actions, it seems more than likely that the problem lay at First Army headquarters. Directly related to this problem was the inability of First Army staff to obtain timely road clearances for the 7th Armored to begin the journey south. The earliest that combat elements of the unit could begin was 0330 hours on 17 December, even though the unit itself had been alerted to move the previous afternoon. This (as well as the fact that it took First Army nearly as long to get road clearance for Bill Hoge's combat command of the 9th Armored—a unit even closer to St.-Vith) seems to support the charge that First Army simply didn't think the threat was very serious. Had they promptly discerned the real nature of the attack, it seems they must have gotten these critical clearances earlier.

118. Weigley, *Eisenhower's Lieutenants*, 490.

119. *Conquer*, 117; Cole, *Ardennes*, 333.

120. Raymond S. McLain, "One of the Greatest: A Study in Leadership," *Military Review* 44 (December 1969): 26. McLain commanded the XIX Corps under Simpson during the majority of the unit's time in combat and was the only National Guard officer to command a corps in WWII.

121. *Ninth Army After Action Report*, 2-3.

122. Cole, *Ardennes*, 333.

123. *Ninth Army After Action Report*, 2-3; Weigley, *Eisenhower's Lieutenants*, 520-521.

124. *Conquer*, 116.

125. Ibid., 117.

126. Ibid., 119.

127. Weigley, *Eisenhower's Lieutenants*, 520-521.

128. Bradley and Blair, *A General's Life*, 368.

129. Blumenson, *Patton*, 251-251; Bradley and Blair, *A General's Life*, 364.

130. Weigley, *Eisenhower's Lieutenants*, 493, 505; Bradley and Blair, *A General's Life*, 367. Bradley records that, hearing of Montgomery's dissatisfaction with Hodges, Ike wrote Monty, saying "I know you realize that Hodges is the quiet, reticent type and does not appear as aggressive as he really is. Unless he becomes exhausted he will always wage a good fight." Bradley lobbied vigorously to keep Hodges in command.

131. Chandler, et al., *Eisenhower Papers*, 4:2369. Ike sent identical messages to Hodges and Simpson on 22 December 1944. They read, in part: "Now that you have been placed under the Field Marshal's operational command I know that you will respond

cheerfully and efficiently to every instruction he gives. The slogan is 'Chins Up.' Please make sure that all your subordinate commanders exert the maximum of leadership and example in sustaining morale and convincing every man that he is in better condition than the enemy. Good luck and let us seek real victory." Ike also sent a message to Monty the same day explaining his directives to Hodges and Simpson.

132. Weigley, *Eisenhower's Lieutenants*, 615. The conspicuous use of "cheerfully" is obviously in response to Ike's use of it.

133. Chandler, et al., *Eisenhower Papers*, 4:2545. Ike's reference to "British seniors" can only mean Montgomery.

134. Ambrose, *Eisenhower*, 380.

135. *Conquer*, 115-160.

136. Weigley, *Eisenhower's Lieutenants*, 520-521; Bradley and Blair, *A General's Life*, 367-368.

137. Bradley, *A Soldier's Story*, 225-226, 422.

138. Weigley, *Eisenhower's Lieutenants*, 505.

139. Bradley and Blair, *A General's Life*, 367.

140. Ibid.

141. Robert W. Hasbrouck to Bruce C. Clarke, undated (probably circa 1983-1984).

142. Ibid.

143. Weigley, *Eisenhower's Lieutenants*, 465.

144. Ibid., 84.

145. Bradley and Blair, *A General's Life*, 354-356; Weigley, *Eisenhower's Lieutenants*, 457-458; MacDonald, *Mighty Endeavor*, 427.

146. Weigley, *Eisenhower's Lieutenants*, 505.

147. Wilmot, *Struggle for Europe*, 592. Another factor that would make it difficult for Montgomery to understand the lack of direction Hodges had received was the different degrees of control of subordinates in the British and American command systems. While it was common in the British system for higher commanders to be very specific in their instructions to subordinate commanders, dictating the "how" as well as the "what" in most cases, the American system was quite different. Americans were taught to give only broad mission statements to subordinates, allowing the subordinate commander nearly a free hand in determining the "how" of the mission. As a result, many American commanders were reluctant to intervene in a subordinate's conduct of a battle, even if he appeared to be doing badly. Senior British commanders, such as Montgomery, felt no such compunctions, intervening when they felt it necessary.

148. Jacques Nobécourt, *Hitler's Last Gamble: The Battle of the Bulge* (New York: Schocken Books, 1967), 218-219. To Montgomery's suggestion, Hodges replied, "No. American troops will not withdraw."

149. Clarke, interview.

150. Hasbrouck to Clarke.

151. Cole, *Ardennes*, 330-331.

152. Weigley, *Eisenhower's Lieutenants*, 84.

153. Ibid., 180-181.

154. Ibid., 519-520.

155. Blumenson, *Patton*, p. 245.

156. Ibid.

157. Ibid., 246.

158. Weigley, *Eisenhower's Lieutenants*, 501.

159. Ibid., 521.

160. Ibid., 520. The 4th Armored Division task force that entered Bastogne on 20 December was desperately needed by the hard-pressed defenders. Task Force Ezell consisted of a company each of tanks, infantry and artillery—a significant addition to the defenders' forces. But the 4th Armored's commander, MG Hugh Gaffey, fearful lest his unit be used piecemeal (as other units were—and to good effect) withdrew the unit later in the day. The question seems to remain that, if Task Force Ezell could drive unopposed into Bastogne that day, why couldn't Gaffey have pushed the rest of the unit in behind it? Granted, the 4th Armored's main body was strung out to the south, struggling along icy roads, but a better explanation may lie in the fact that the 4th Armored's brilliant commander, MG John S. Wood, was no longer at the head of what had become, during the previous summer's lightning warfare, "Patton's Best."

161. Cole, *Ardennes*, 515-555.

162. Weigley, *Eisenhower's Lieutenants*, 520-521.

163. Ibid.

164. Ibid., 519.

165. Ibid., 520.

166. Stone, "Unsung Commander," 49-50.

167. *Conquer*, 115-119; Eisenhower, *Bitter Woods*, 215.

168. Eugene Garrett, interview, November 1987, tape recording; Weigley, *Eisenhower's Lieutenants*, 520-521; *Conquer*, 115-119; *Ninth Army After Action Report*, 1-2. One of Simpson's units, hurrying south to help the defenders of St.-Vith, paid the ultimate price in the battle, and made the town of Malmédy nearly as famous as Bastogne. Battery B, 285th Field Artillery

Observation Battalion, was part of the 7th Armored Division Artillery convoy speeding south towards St.-Vith on 17 December when, soon after it had passed the town of Malmédy just north of the St.-Vith area, it ran into the lead combat elements of SS Lieutenant Colonel Joachim Peiper's armored battle group (Kampfgruppe). Intercepting the American convoy at Baugnez Crossroads, on the outskirts of Malmédy, Peiper's powerful armored unit soon overpowered the poorly armed Americans, capturing about 100 men, most of Battery B. Marching the helpless captives into a nearby field, the SS men opened fire, mowing them down with machine gun and small arms fire. Passing SS units continued to fire into the mounds of wounded and dead Americans for the remainder of the day. At darkness, the dozen or so captives who had feigned death, bolted for the woods or the presumed safety of a nearby cafe. The men who reached the woods eventually worked their way back to Malmédy, rejoining the American units there. The ones who tried to hide in the cafe, however, were murdered when the Germans set fire to the building, shooting the men as they ran out. It is estimated that Peiper's men murdered at least 400 people (including defenseless Belgian men, women and children) along their route of advance during the battle. At the Nuremburg Trials, Peiper and many of his men were convicted and sentenced to death, but through the efforts of some American sympathizers, all were eventually released. Peiper was apparently murdered in his home in France 30 years after the atrocities his unit committed took place.

169. Chandler, et al., *Eisenhower Papers*, 4:2564-2565. Ike cabled Marshall on 30 March 1945, attempting to enlist Marshall's aid in helping publicize the exploits of Bradley and the army commanders (other than Patton). Ike felt the others' achievements had been overlooked in favor of the flashy Patton. Chandler noted, however, "Eisenhower was fighting a hopeless cause, at least insofar as the *New York Times* was concerned. Every European headline...prominently mentioned Patton by name; Hodges', Simpson's and Patch's (7th Army) forces were identified only by number."

170. Weigley, *Eisenhower's Lieutenants*, 384.

171. Ibid.

172. Ibid., 520.

173. Stone, "Unsung Commander," 47.

174. Alvan C. Gillem, Jr., "William H. Simpson," *Leadership at Higher Levels of Command as Viewed by Senior and Experienced Combat Commanders*, Edmund B. Sebree, ed. (Monterey: USALRU,

1961), 26.

175. The finest combat exploits of Simpson's Ninth Army came after the close of the Battle of the Bulge. Operation GRENADE, the Roer river crossings, took place in February-March 1945, and the Rhineland Campaign followed on its heels. The Ninth Army performed magnificently during these battles, earning praise from American as well as British commands. Simpson's army participated in Montgomery's set-piece crossings of the northern Rhine near Wesel, and, once across the Rhine, the Ninth raced across Germany. Simpson was returned to American control on 3 April 1945, then was the first Allied commander to reach the Elbe. Simpson pushed a bridgehead across the Elbe at Magdeburg and was prepared to fling his army at Berlin when ordered to stop by Eisenhower. General Simpson retired from active service for reasons of health shortly after the end of the war and was promoted to four-star rank on the retired list in 1954. General Simpson died in 1980 at age 92.

5. *Middleton and the VIII Corps*

$\mathbf{T}$he man whose command was most directly affected by the 16 German divisions crashing through the Ardennes was sound asleep in his headquarters at Bastogne when the barrage began on 16 December.[1] Major General Troy Houston Middleton, a 55-year-old infantryman, had commanded the VIII Corps since its introduction into the Normandy fighting on 12 June 1944. He had an Army-wide reputation as an excellent tactician and as a tough, experienced fighter whose demeanor in desperate combat was described as "cool as an icicle."[2] Eisenhower had personally selected him to lead VIII Corps in combat. Once the US Army's youngest regimental commander, Middleton inspired George Marshall to describe him as "...the outstanding infantry regimental commander on the battlefield in France" during World War I.[3]

Although outwardly he reminded observers of a fatherly, bespectacled college professor, the VIII Corps commander possessed a steely resolve and stubborn tenacity of purpose that allowed him to relieve overly excitable or unsuccessful subordinates without hesitation. Middleton used all the tactical knowledge, sound judgment, and shrewd sense of his troops' capabilities he could muster to retain a semblance of control over his shattered corps during the Battle of the Bulge—but it was primarily the calm leadership he displayed in the eye of this manmade hurricane that will stand as his greatest achievement.[4]

MIDDLETON'S CAREER

Troy Middleton was born on 12 October 1889 in Copiah County, MS, the middle of nine children. After a childhood in this rural section of the country, Middleton finished his

229

formal education at Mississippi A & M, graduating in 1909. Just missing out on an appointment to West Point, he enlisted as a private in the 29th Infantry Regiment in March 1910.[5]

During his nearly 3 years as an enlisted man, Middleton gained much valuable practical experience as well as an insight into the common soldier's perceptions and attitudes. He successfully completed a commissioning exam while stationed at Fort Leavenworth, KS, in 1912 and was commissioned a second lieutenant of infantry in 1913. Posted shortly thereafter to the Mexican border, Middleton saw service in Texas until the United States entered the First World War.

Middleton accompanied the 4th Infantry Division to France in spring 1918 and was promoted to major in June. He took a battalion into the line, ready for combat in July. Middleton led his battalion throughout the intense combat at St. Mihiel and Meuse-Argonne, learning his job as he went. His coolness under fire and obviously quick grasp of the elements necessary for success in this style of infantry combat led to his rapid promotions to lieutenant colonel and then colonel by October. He assumed command of the 39th Infantry Regiment on the battlefield on 11 October 1918, becoming the youngest regimental commander in the US Army. His regiment continued to score resounding successes until the Armistice halted its advances on 11 November. After a brief tour of occupation duty, Middleton returned to the United States in early 1919.[6]

In the rapid demobilization at the conclusion of the war, Middleton reverted to his peacetime rank of captain and assumed duties as an instructor at the Infantry School in Fort Benning in July 1919. After several years as an instructor during which he further enhanced his reputation as a tactician, Middleton was selected to attend the Command and General Staff School in 1923, where he became an Honor Graduate. He remained at Fort Leavenworth on the staff school faculty from 1924 to 1928. Many of the men who would lead the US Army to victory in World War II, including Eisenhower, were taught by Middleton during his tenure as an instructor.[7] Following this tour as a teacher, he became a student once more, attending the Army War College in 1928-29. After brief service in the 29th Infantry Regiment at Fort Benning, Middleton was selected as Commandant of Cadets for the ROTC program at Louisiana State University (LSU) in 1930. He remained there for the next 6 years. Promoted to lieutenant colonel near the end of his stay at LSU, he was sent to the Philippines as an inspector general in 1936. It was while serving in the Philippines that Middleton wrestled with the decision to remain in the service or to retire and accept a lucrative position with LSU. While trying to decide, he sought the advice of Eisenhower, also serving in the islands. Ike urged him not to resign. He argued that a future war was unavoidable and that with Middleton's record from the First World War, he was certain to receive high command, maybe even a division. Despite Eisenhower's advice, Middleton retired and accepted the position at LSU.[8]

Ike was right of course. Middleton enjoyed the comfortable academic life, but when war engulfed the United States, he wrote Marshall to volunteer for active duty. The Chief of Staff quickly accepted the offer, promoted Middleton to brigadier general, and assigned him as assistant division commander of the 45th Infantry Division, then training at Fort Devens, MA, in 1942. Later that year Middleton was appointed division commander of the Oklahoma-Texas National Guard outfit and prepared to lead the 45th into its first combat in the invasion of Sicily.[9]

Bradley, Middleton's superior for this invasion, didn't know him personally but had heard of his reputation "...which was very, very good."[10] The 45th's initial combat performance completely validated Bradley's confidence in its commander, performing well throughout the Sicilian campaign. Middleton led his division into Italy and continued his outstanding performance until November 1943, when he was forced to give up command of the 45th to enter a hospital at Naples because of a chronic and painful knee injury. Eventually this recurring ailment forced his evacuation to Walter Reed Hospital in Washington, D.C. The condition was serious enough that it nearly led to Middleton's permanent stateside assignment, but his combat

reputation was so outstanding that Ike asked for him for
corps command during the Normandy invasion.

Proven combat leaders were still in acutely short supply
in the American Army, and continued British skepticism of
the competence of senior US commanders forced Ike to insist
that only those who had demonstrated combat excellence
would get OVERLORD commands. As D-Day approached,
Middleton prepared his corps to enter the fighting war. He
would go back into combat "despite the gimpy knee."[11]

NORMANDY TO THE ARDENNES

The VIII Corps' initiation to combat at D plus 6 days was a
bloody, frustrating struggle through the hedgerows of
Normandy's Cotentin Peninsula. Middleton's progress was
kept at a crawl more by the marshy, unyielding terrain than
the determined German defenders. Advances were measured
in hundreds of yards, causing observers to characterize the
fighting as a "...dismal failure."[12] In spite of Middleton's
almost ruthless relief of several subordinate commanders, his
corps made little real progress. This rather inauspicious
beginning was soon followed by resounding success, however,
when Bradley's COBRA operation finally blasted a hole in
the German defenses. The operation's carpet-bombing
devastated the area surrounding St.-Lô, but it allowed J.
Lawton Collins' VII Corps to break through the crust of
German resistance. Free at last from the restrictive confines
of the beachhead area, Middleton's VIII Corps swept rapidly
forward as the right flank unit of the US front. Throughout
the remainder of July and August, Middleton's attack gained
momentum. Led by the 4th and 6th Armored Divisions, VIII
Corps units were advancing farther and faster than anyone
had thought possible. The corps' bag of German prisoners
nearly overwhelmed their capacity to guard them, and the
two armored divisions were slashing forward at an
unprecedented rate.[13]

At the beginning of August, in compliance with
OVERLORD plans to logistically expand the Normandy
lodgment area, VIII Corps units turned westward into the
Brittany Peninsula and headed for the port cities of Lorient
and Brest. This decision to route an entire corps of 50,000

troops away from battle against the principal German forces to the east and send them in the opposite direction has been surrounded with controversy and second-guessing. Nevertheless, VIII Corps' spearheads, the 4th and 6th Armored Divisions, drove rapidly into the Brittany Peninsula, besieging the two major port cities of Brest and Lorient. By this time, Middleton's corps was assigned to Patton's Third Army, eager to roll against the main German strength; soon, however, the VIII Corps lost its premier armored division, Wood's 4th, to the drive across France. Back in Brittany, Middleton moved his infantry divisions up to begin the assault upon the fortress city of Brest.[14]

Securing Brest was difficult, and the costly, frustrating siege warfare took nearly a month and 10,000 American casualties. The result of this "knockdown, dragout, slugging contest over a secondary objective" was the capture of a devastated port, now useless as a supply base, and resulted in the debatable allegation that Brest's capture had a serious negative effect on the pursuit across France.[15] At any rate, Middleton's battered corps was withdrawn from the Brittany Peninsula in September and eventually moved to a quiet sector of the Allied front in order to refit, recuperate and recover its full combat abilities. During October, the VIII Corps was moved into positions in the dark forests and twisting narrow roads of the Ardennes.

VIII CORPS IN THE ARDENNES

For Middleton and the VIII Corps, the Ardennes remained a quiet sector through November and into December as the fighting war swirled around it on both sides. In this haven for played-out, exhausted units or troops fresh from the States, by 16 December the VIII Corps (appendix G) had four divisions to secure an 85-mile "long, desolate front."[16] This is three times the frontage a corps was doctrinally expected to defend, but it was a logical and expected result of Ike's "broad front" strategy. The units assigned to Middleton's command at this time were a mixed bag of understrength veteran units and untried recent arrivals.[17]

His two experienced infantry divisions, the 4th and the 28th, had been nearly destroyed in the nightmarish debacle in the Huertgen Forest (October-November 1944). The 28th Infantry Division, which began the war as a Pennsylvania National Guard outfit, was especially roughly handled at the battle of Schmidt and other phases of the Huertgen attacks. Afterwards, its grim-humored GIs referred to the unit as "the bloody bucket," finding that epithet a macabre but apt description of its red, keystone-shaped shoulder patch.[18] Despite its battered, understrength condition, the division had two exceptional leaders in key positions who were to prove invaluable during the upcoming fight. Major General Norman 'Dutch' Cota, the 28th's commander, had been in tough combat since he landed on Omaha Beach with the 29th Infantry Division on D-Day. In command of the 28th since August, he was unlikely to panic easily. The other leader was Colonel Hurley Fuller, commander of the 110th Infantry Regiment, which occupied a critical position in the 28th's overextended line. An irascible, argumentative, pugnacious World War I vet, Fuller would prove to have just the right temperament for the upcoming struggle.

Middleton's other veteran unit was the 4th Infantry Division, under Major General Raymond O. Barton. Also a battered survivor of the Huertgen, the 4th had lost over 6,000 troops to the Germans and the weather in the forest fighting. Two weeks after being relieved by the 83rd Infantry Division, it was far from full strength. It was, however, on the far right of Middleton's thin corps front, not in the path of the main German panzer assault. Nevertheless, in its depleted state it would find itself hard pressed by the infantry forces of the German Seventh Army.[19]

Arguably, in the worst position of all of Middleton's units was the brand-new 106th Infantry Division. It had never seen combat and had been "in the line" only 4 days before the German assault began. The "Golden Lions" of the 106th had taken over the northern portion of the VIII Corps line from the veteran 2nd Infantry Division, now part of the V Corps assault to capture belatedly the Roer River dams. The 106th relieved the 2nd foxhole by foxhole, constrained to occupy every fighting position the 2nd had held.

Although the 106th's commander, Major General Alan W.

Jones, felt that some of these positions, especially those on the Schnee Eifel plateau, were too exposed to offer a proper defense, he was not allowed to change any dispositions.[20] The Schnee Eifel positions were actually part of the Siegfried Line, and any withdrawal from those hard-won bunkers would not play well on the home front. Adding to Jones' difficulties was his unit's proximity to the Losheim Gap, the "classic" invasion route through the Ardennes. Not only was this a primary armored avenue of approach, it was defended by the weak 14th Cavalry Group, a unit more suited to screening than defending against a determined panzer attack. To top it off, the V Corps-VIII Corps boundary ran through the northern portion of the gap. Because unit boundaries are particularly vulnerable to enemy assault, it was doubly unfortunate for the 106th and the VIII Corps to be saddled with these dispositions.[21]

Middleton had one additional unit with which to defend his impossibly wide front, one combat command of the 9th Armored Division (the other was detached to V Corps to assist in its offensive). Middleton used his armored combat command to plug a gaping hole in his defensive line, inserting it between the 28th and the 4th. The third portion of the 9th, Combat Command R, was in reserve near Marnach (although not primarily a "maneuver unit" like Combat Commands A and B, it could be used in a pinch).[22] Middleton's only other potential reserves were four corps engineer combat battalions.

Total troops available to Middleton and the VIII Corps on the early morning of 16 December 1944 were 68,822, or about one soldier for every 2 meters of defended front—hardly a formidable force. As the Ardennes attack eventually gained strength, the Germans were able to achieve an eight to one advantage in infantry, and a four to one advantage in tanks against the VIII Corps front.[23] Bad weather became a German ally, grounding the Allied air forces and neutralizing the strong Allied air arm.

THE INITIAL GERMAN ASSAULT

The full force of the German attack fell on the veteran 28th Division in the center and the untried 106th Division in the north of the VIII Corps sector. Not surprisingly, the Germans were once again using the Losheim Gap as a main axis of attack. Over the course of the next few days, both infantry divisions were destroyed as effective fighting forces, and Middleton was compelled to use every asset at his command to try to slow the German advance.

The disruption caused by the overwhelming attack made the maintenance of a cohesive defense impossible. As the panzer and panzer grenadier spearheads slashed farther to the west, Middleton found it increasingly difficult to exercise control over his northernmost units from his command post in Bastogne. Ultimately, he lost effective control of those units, because he had his hands full trying to react to the attacks on his units immediately in front of Bastogne. As the 28th Division continued to disintegrate under relentless German pressure, Middleton exercised personal command and control over the disposition of each precious unit, ordering individual tank-infantry-engineer teams to threatened sectors to parry each German thrust.[24]

When the guard awakened Middleton in his headquarters van that early morning of 16 December, the corps commander could hear the German barrage rumbling in the eastern distance. Although not particularly alarmed at first, a steady stream of reports flooded into the VIII Corps headquarters throughout that morning, and by 1000 hours elements of 16 German divisions had been identified among the attackers. Clearly, this was no demonstration or spoiling attack to relieve the pressure of V Corps' offensive. This was a major German offensive slamming into the weakest sector of the entire Allied line.[25]

Middleton's ability to rapidly grasp the implications of the German attack allowed him to focus the efforts of the corps staff quickly to make maximum effective use of his corps' battered units. The problem was obvious: how to regain control of the battle to a sufficient degree to stabilize the front long enough for reserves (from outside the corps area) to counterattack into the flanks of the assault. Solving the problem was another matter. By the evening of the first day of the attack, the VIII Corps no longer had a "front" in the strict military sense. Instead, it consisted of a large number of individual units or parts of units, in varying stages of disintegration, some clinging to important road junctions or strongpoints, some fleeing westward.[26]

While Middleton and his staff certainly realized the immensity of the attack by this time, it appears unlikely that they as yet were aware of the precarious position of most of their units. For example, the corps commander thought that he had made clear to the 106th's commander, Alan Jones, that his two exposed regiments on the Schnee Eifel should be withdrawn to more defensible terrain. Instead, Jones thought Middleton wanted his two units to stand fast and await relief by an armored counterattack. The result was the largest single surrender of US troops in the European Theater, as the 8,000 men of the 422nd and 423rd Infantry Regiments were turned over to the enemy by their commanders on 19 December.[27] The loss of two-thirds of the combat power of his only full strength division was a serious, and nearly fatal, blow to Middleton's defense.

By the evening of the first day's attack, VIII Corps was in an extremely bad situation along the major portion of its "front." In the north, the main German attack had shattered the weak 14th Cavalry Group, and panzer grenadiers were about to encircle the two ill-fated 106th Division regiments. The 28th Division in the center was clinging to strongpoints and road junctions, but giving ground slowly and inexorably. In the south the news was slightly better. The 4th Infantry, along with the combat command of the 9th Armored, was having an easier time against the infantry attacks of the German Seventh Army.[28] How Middleton and his corps staff reacted from this point through the end of the battle bears careful examination.

COMMAND REACTION AT VIII CORPS HEADQUARTERS

"One did not have to be a genius to know that St.-Vith and Bastogne were critical points during the Battle of the Bulge." So wrote Middleton in 1967 in his assessment of command reaction during the battle. All one had to do, he pointed out, was look at the map.[29] Or even without a map, all you had to do was watch the advancing German spearheads, and they would show you these same critical points. Those "geniuses" who crawled out of the woodwork after the battle wanting to claim credit for picking Bastogne and St.-Vith as critical hubs of the fighting were far behind Middleton and the VIII Corps staff in realizing the obvious.[30]

Middleton appreciated from the beginning that he would have to hold the two critical communications centers if he were to slow the German advance. To carry out any workable delay, Middleton was forced to use tactics not always consistent with doctrine. His frontage was too extended and too pierced to use a conventional defense, so he counted on his subordinate unit commanders to make the best use of the restrictive terrain and their meager resources to establish "islands of defense [to make] the Germans pay a disproportionate price for their moves against [the VIII Corps]."[31] Units had to react piecemeal, and Middleton began almost immediately to grab any unit he could find to "plug the yawning gap in [his] front."[32] Historian Hugh Cole, writing in the Army's official history, eloquently described this effort:

> The story of the units that were retained under tactical control and employed directly by General Middleton in the attempt to form some defense in depth in the VIII Corps center has been partially recorded....The effect that these units had in retarding the German advances, a course of action evolving extemporaneously, must be considered along with the role played by the uncoordinated front-line formations in the haphazard sequence of delaying actions...With the very limited forces at his disposal...the VIII Corps commander found it physically impossible to erect any of the standard defenses taught in the higher Army schools or prescribed in the field service regulations. The best he could do to defend the extended front was to deploy his troops as a screen retaining local reserves for local counterattacks at potentially dangerous points.... Under the circumstances there could be no thought of an elastic defense with strong formations echeloned in any depth...[He had to] attempt to plug a few of the gaps in the
>
> forward line, slow the enemy columns on a few main roads, and strengthen by human means two or three of the natural physical barriers deep in the corps rear area.[33]

Beginning to sort some order out of the mass confusion, Middleton and his staff dispatched units to critical portions of the line, reacted to enemy advances as best they could, and continued to try to stay current with the extremely fluid situation. Almost immediately, the direction of the main German attack combined with the poor road network began to sever Middleton from his northernmost unit.

The most important decision Middleton made to influence the fighting in the north and the resulting defense of St.-Vith was his dispatch of Brigadier General Bruce C. Clarke to the 106th Division's command post in the early morning hours of 17 December. Clarke had sped on ahead of his Combat Command B, 7th Armored Division, to locate the VIII Corps headquarters and determine where Middleton wanted his armored force to enter the battle. The VIII Corps commander calmly told Clarke that, "Alan Jones is having some trouble at St.-Vith—grab something to eat and a little sleep and go to him...if he needs help give it to him."[34] So began the 7th Armored Division's epic defense of the crucial northern crossroads.

The other major input Middleton made to the 106th's defense was not as helpful, for it contributed to the disastrous surrender of the two regiments on the Schnee Eifel. Middleton's command style was such that he deferred decisions, whenever possible, to the subordinate commander "on the spot." He believed, usually correctly, that the commander on the ground had the best overall picture of the tactical situation at his location and was therefore the best judge of action most appropriate for the moment.[35] At St.-Vith on 17 December, however, Jones and his unit were totally inexperienced and had been in the line only 4 days prior to the German assault. In this situation, it would appear reasonable to expect a combat experienced corps commander with an Army-wide reputation as a premiere tactician to provide stronger guidance to the less experienced subordinate. Instead, Middleton let Jones make the final decision regarding the two regiments, with terrible results.[36]

Other factors also contributed to the debacle, including Jones' much too sanguine reporting of the situation in a controversial phone conversation with Middleton late on the

16th (and again on the 17th), as well as a completely unreasonable expectation of the arrival time of the bulk of Combat Command B at St.-Vith. To further muddle an already confusing situation, the switchboard operator during the phonecall on the 16th mistakenly unplugged the connection for a few critical moments, thus allowing each commander to believe the other had concurred in exactly the opposite course of action each assumed. This entire episode could be cited as a textbook example of Clausewitz' "friction" or "fog of war," and remains today a highly controversial incident.[37]

Beyond these two critical episodes, Middleton exercised little impact over the outcome of the fighting at St.-Vith. Indeed, he lost even the nominal control he had over his northern units on 20 December, when Eisenhower divided command responsibility for the bulge, placing the St.-Vith units under command of Ridgway's XVIII Airborne Corps.

Events therefore rapidly evolved to cause VIII Corps' defensive efforts to be concentrated on the 28th Division's sector immediately in front of Bastogne. As Cole related, this inaugurated "the period of 'piecemeal reaction'...when Middleton's VIII Corps was trying to plug the yawning gaps in its front with rifle platoons of engineers and mechanics, and before an American riposte could be made in force."[38] Colonel Hurley Fuller's 110th Infantry Regiment, spread out along the wide, empty frontage of "Skyline Drive," got the worst of it in the 28th's sector. As Fuller's overwhelmingly outnumbered units slowly yielded ground, Middleton tried to organize the best defense he could given his meager reserves.

While Fuller's front collapsed, the VIII Corps commander grabbed his only armored reserve, Combat Command R, 9th Armored, and sent mobile teams to critical road junctions east of Bastogne. The fate of Task Force Rose, one of these teams, is illustrative of the desperate nature of the fighting and the paucity of reserves available to VIII Corps. It also shows Middleton's personal involvement in the fighting details.[39]

Middleton ordered Colonel Joseph H. Gilbreth, commander of Combat Command R, 9th Armored, to dispatch two task forces to two critical road junctions on the eastern approaches to Bastogne after the corps commander received word of the German success against the 110th Infantry at Clervaux. Middleton personally selected positions guarding crossroads commanding approaches to the main paved road from St.-Vith to Bastogne. Captain L. K. Rose of Combat Command R had a company of tanks and one of infantry, bolstered by an armored engineer platoon to try to defend the northernmost of the two road junctions.[40]

Task Force Rose got the order to move out for the crossroads village of Lullange at 2140 hours on the 17th, just 10 minutes after the corps found out that German columns had cleared Clervaux and were heading for the same road junction. Gilbreth was told to establish the roadblocks "without delay," as the enemy was crossing the Clerf River only 5 miles away. Indeed, enemy fire was already falling around Lullange. Rose and his force were in position on the hills commanding the approaches to the junction shortly after midnight.

By midmorning on the 18th, German reconnaissance elements, backed up by two panzer battalions, began to appear along the road in front of Rose. The task force, aided by the fires of the 73rd Armored Field Artillery Battalion, kept the enemy at bay throughout the morning and into the early afternoon, but by 1400 hours Rose was in trouble. His infantry company swept away by the panzers, Rose's tanks were hemmed in on three sides and about to be surrounded. If Task Force Rose was to extricate itself, it would have to move immediately. The decision was Middleton's. Cole relates that, at 1405 hours, VIII Corps received the following message from Combat Command R's Gilbreth:

> TF Rose...is as good as surrounded...have counted 16 German tanks there...TF is being hit from 3 sides. Recommend that they fight their way out. They could use 2 platoons of A/52d Armd Inf Bn...everything else is committed...Did not commit any of the TDs, will wait until the over-all plan is known. Plan to push TF Rose toward the other road block. If the decision is to stay, some units will be sent there to help them out.[41]

Not only could Middleton not allow Rose to withdraw, but

he couldn't even permit Gilbreth to attempt to reinforce the doomed task force. He knew that any force sent to assist Rose would itself be overwhelmed by the overpowering numbers of panzers and grenadiers swarming down the St.-Vith-Bastogne road. The corps commander needed every tank and rifle to establish new roadblocks at other critical locations all along the disintegrating front. The armored infantrymen Gilbreth proposed to send to Rose's aid were the last infantry reserves in Gilbreth's command. Committing them in a hopeless cause was out of the question. At 1430 hours, word was received at Combat Command R headquarters that Task Force Rose had been overrun.[42]

This scenario was repeated many times during the critical hours that Middleton tried to slow the advancing Germans while his senior commanders at SHAEF, Army Group, and Army rushed to assemble reserves from outside VIII Corps. The fact that the corps commander himself was personally ordering and approving the dispositions of company and battalion task forces emphasizes the gravity of the overall situation. But, more importantly, the sum of all these actions clearly demonstrates Middleton's personal command in this critical situation and establishes, irrefutably, his impact on the course of the battle.

As Gilbreth's painfully inadequate forces were slowing, if not stopping the Germans who had broken through the 110th Infantry, fresh troops were arriving in Bastogne to help Middleton. On 16 December, Eisenhower had directed Bradley to rush two armored divisions from the First Army's flanking units to the threatened area. The 7th Armored Division moved from reserve positions in the Ninth Army area and was assembled at and behind the St.-Vith roadblock. Now, late on 18 December, the leading combat command of the 10th Armored Division began to reach Bastogne. Rushing north from Patton's Third Army, Colonel William Roberts' Combat Command B was arriving just in time to allow Middleton to continue to delay the enemy advance.[43]

Almost immediately upon arrival at Middleton's headquarters in Bastogne, however, Roberts and the VIII Corps commander clashed. The issue was the "proper"—and most effective—employment of Roberts' combat command to stop the Germans. Roberts naturally wanted to fight his force as a single unit. Armored warfare doctrine, seemingly proven in the unprecedented dash across France the previous summer, called for the weight and shock power of the tank-infantry-artillery team to be maximized by the combat commands operating as a single combined arms team unit. Middleton, on the other hand, wanted Roberts to break his command into small company teams and battalion-sized task forces scattered across the VIII Corps front at critical locations as the ill-fated Task Force Rose had done. The very idea was anathema to the true tanker.[44]

Middleton, the former Staff College teacher and tactics instructor knew very well the proper doctrine stipulated by "the book" for employment of armor, and he completely understood Roberts' objections. However, he also appreciated much better than the newly arrived Roberts the utter hopelessness of attempting any "conventional" defense or "textbook" deployments in the nightmarish situation his battered corps occupied. Middleton later recalled:

> I went against the book and broke up our armor into task forces. When Bill Roberts came up to Bastogne on December 18 with his combat command, I asked him how much strength he had. Then I told him to break up his fine outfit into three task forces. Bill didn't like it at all. He told me, "Troy, that's no way to use armor." And I told him that I knew it as well as he did. But we weren't fighting any textbook war there. Without some armor to back up our roadblocks, we couldn't have stopped anything.[45]

Luckily for the defense of Bastogne, the corps commander won the argument. Roberts' assets proved to be key to both buying time to allow the 101st Airborne Division to reach Bastogne and later assisting the paratroopers in holding the town. Without the defense of the key road junctions (as well as the 28th Infantry Division's gallant but piecemeal fighting further east), Bastogne would have fallen long before the 101st Airborne moved up to occupy it. It is highly unlikely that the 101st could have fought its way into the town against the German forces then rushing toward it.

The last "major" reserve force Middleton had to help slow the attackers was also a source of controversy after the battle. These were the engineer units assigned to VIII Corps or working in the corps area when the offensive began. Middleton had four engineer combat battalions under his command, and an additional Engineer Group of three engineer combat battalions from First Army was in direct support in his corps area.[46] Although engineer troops are trained to accomplish the mission of "fighting as infantry" when necessary, this is not the most effective use of these trained technicians; the situation in VIII Corps was one of those necessary times, however.

The first to be put into the fight was the 168th Engineer Combat Battalion. Middleton gave this unit to Jones at St.-Vith on the 16th in an attempt to stabilize the rapidly deteriorating situation in the north. The next day, he sent the 44th, another of his engineer combat battalions, east to back up the crumbling 28th Division sector, and a third engineer unit, the 159th, was given to Barton's 4th Division and headed south. By late afternoon on the 17th, of his corps units he had only the 35th Engineer Combat Battalion uncommitted.[47] The 35th, along with one of the First Army engineer battalions, was also soon committed, as it became part of the defensive line established east of Bastogne. This line, extending from Foy to Neffe, was suggested to Middleton by his corps engineer officer and served as a virtual "last ditch" infantry barrier to hold Bastogne long enough for the arriving paratroopers to get into position. These units did the job along with Roberts' tankers from the 10th Armored and Cota's infantrymen in the 28th. Delayed long enough by numerous small unit actions, German forces were unable to enter Bastogne before the 101st Airborne Division arrived in strength on the night of 18-19 December.[48]

Many of Middleton's remaining engineers were used in more traditional engineer roles, such as demolition, minefield emplacement, and obstacle construction as VIII Corps attempted to establish a corps barrier line. The "VIII Corps Barrier Line." if the scattered collection of obstacles built (and also defended) by Middleton's engineers can be called that, extended from the general vicinity of Houffalize in the north to south of Bastogne. It was neither a barrier nor a true "line" but consisted mainly of isolated positions at road junctions, river crossings, and other critical points in the path of the German drive. Middleton tried to lay down the barrier line across the front of the advancing German columns, but the speed of the enemy advance forced the efforts to be concentrated more along the edges of the penetrations. Nevertheless, the combined effect of the engineer effort contributed considerably to the German delay and frustrated many of the enemy's efforts to seize crucial bridges and road junctions quickly.[49] The ongoing argument, however, continues to focus on the most effective use of engineer forces to delay a rapidly advancing enemy. Cole sums up the question well in his official history of the battle:

> Students of the retrograde action fought by the VIII Corps between 16 and 22 December will wish to examine the question as to the most profitable use of engineer troops who formed the backbone of the rear area defense in such circumstances. The "magnificent job" which General Middleton later ascribed to the engineers credits the engineers in their role as infantry. The VIII Corps engineer and the various engineer group commanders at that time and later believed the engineer battalions and companies could have done more to impede the German advance if they had been denied the eastern firing line and employed in a tactically unified second line of defense in the western part of the corps area. For this latter purpose General Middleton would have had some 3,300 engineers in addition to those organic in the divisions. But it is questionable whether the 7th Armored Division would have had time to establish itself at St.-Vith, not to speak of the 101st Airborne Division at Bastogne, without the intervention of the engineer battalions.[50]

Assault on Bastogne

While Middleton and his beleaguered staff were fighting the piecemeal delaying actions to buy some precious time, forces were assembling at Bastogne which would ultimately prevent its capture. The first reinforcements to arrive at Bastogne were the elements of Roberts' Combat Command B of the 10th Armored. These were now engaged at numerous critical locations, helping Middleton keep the Germans out of the town. The next units to arrive which would play an important role in the city's defense consisted of several artillery battalions (or parts thereof). Most of these units were withdrawing from the fighting to the east after supporting the 28th Division's futile efforts to stop the enemy advances.

The artillery units would be especially useful to the 101st in its defense of Bastogne, because the airborne troopers' organic artillery consisted of only three battalions of short-ranged light artillery and one battalion of 105-mm howitzers. Brigadier General Anthony C. McAuliffe, the 101st's acting commander and himself an artilleryman, eventually had several additional artillery battalions and collections of guns to help support his lightly armed paratroopers. These included the 155-mm guns of the 755th Armored Field Artillery Battalion, sent from outside the sector, and the 969th Field Artillery Battalion, which straggled in after firing for the 28th Division. They joined Roberts' 420th Armored Field Artillery Battalion of the 10th Armored and parts of other units such as the 58th and 73rd Armored Field Artillery Battalions who fought their way rearward from the east.[51]

The last significant group to join the Bastogne defense were the survivors from the 28th Division and other units who had fought the battle to the east. There is no way to determine the number of soldiers who thus complemented the 101st's defense of the city, but in this desperate fight, every man counted. These tankers, gunners, infantrymen, and others added significantly to the 12,000 or so officers and men of the 101st at Bastogne, and they played an important, if unheralded, role in the defense.[52]

While this force assembled in Bastogne, Middleton began moving his VIII Corps headquarters to safer ground to the southwest. Although Middleton himself remained in Bastogne for 2 more days to complete the coordination for the city's defense, on 18 December the bulk of the corps headquarters moved 18 miles southwest to the town of Neufchateau, out of the path of the main German attack.[53]

As he drove away from the soon-to-be-surrounded city, however, Middleton left behind a further point of controversy. Much like the situation at St.-Vith, Middleton had neglected to establish firmly and unquestionably a command structure for the conglomeration of units defending Bastogne. Instead, he had merely requested that the two senior officers, McAuliffe and Roberts, "cooperate" in the conduct of the battle. Such an ambiguous command setup in a confusing fight, involving as it did multiple units from several different parent commands, was unacceptable. Middleton belatedly realized this and appointed McAuliffe (who was anyway the senior officer present) as overall commander in Bastogne.[54]

Middleton's departure from Bastogne by no means ended his participation in the Battle of the Bulge. Instead, under Patton's Third Army after Ike's splitting of command responsibility, Middleton and the VIII Corps continued to be instrumental in ultimately defeating the German attack. He helped supervise the relief of Bastogne by the 4th Armored Division on 26 December and, with his newly reorganized VIII Corps, led one of the initial counteroffensives to throw back the Germans to their original jumping-off positions.

Middleton's counteroffensive in the south of the bulge began as early as 30 December, but its effectiveness was crippled by the ever-cautious Montgomery delaying any offensive action in the north until later in January. Middleton later blamed Montgomery's tardiness for seriously reducing the potential capture of German prisoners and allowing much German equipment to be withdrawn.[55]

Middleton and the VIII Corps finished out the war in the Third Army, winning well-earned respect from this famous army's blustering commander. Near the end, Patton wrote a personal note to Middleton, saying, "None of us will ever forget the stark valor with which you and your Corps contested every foot of ground during von Rundstedt's attack.

Your decision to hold Bastogne was a stroke of genius."[56]
This last praise came from the same man who had earlier
ranted at Middleton for allowing the 101st Airborne to
become surrounded.   Apparently, cooler reflection on
Middleton's commandership caused the famous but volatile
Patton a greater appreciation of the opportunities presented
by the unprecedented situation in the soon-to-be-famous city.

ANALYSIS OF BATTLE LEADERSHIP

An attempt to assess the impact of an individual's actions
upon a nearly 50-year-old event is difficult, but especially so
when the event in question has become surrounded by
legend, and aspects of the battle, such as the 101st
Airborne's defense of Bastogne, have become military icons.
Over the years, the legend has become the reality. And
legend, although inspiring, has little substance with which
to instruct later generations of soldiers who may benefit from
the experiences of those who led the fighting. The task is to
demystify the event by examining the actions of the
commanders and then attempt to draw some conclusions
from the demonstrated battle leadership. In the case of
Middleton, we must determine the characteristics of his
battle leadership and how they affected the conduct of the
Ardennes fighting.[57]

Middleton's most outstanding characteristic, remarked
upon time and again by those observing his leadership in
battle, was his overpowering calmness. His ability to remain
cool and collected while the absolute worst was happening
was probably the single most important aspect affecting his
conduct of the defense.[58] Indeed, Middleton's great asset
during the entire war was his unflappable calmness in
adversity.   He singled out this trait in a postwar
questionnaire on senior leadership, advising would-be
commanders, "Be calm.   Guard against becoming
excited....Calmness is one of the greatest virtues. Every
officer I relieved during the war could be classed among the
excitable and jittery. The good Lord gave every person his
share of common sense, the commander who does not use
this valuable commodity is doomed."[59]

Middleton displayed this trait consistently during his

combat command, but in no instance was it better demonstrated or more critically needed than during the dark days of the Battle of the Bulge. Even amidst the most difficult and crucial phases of the fighting, Middleton remained "completely calm and in command of himself."[60] While rallying his shattered units and confidently directing their desperate delaying actions, Middleton was outwardly "calm and optimistic."[61] This steadying influence was exactly what was needed in this unprecedented situation, and in what was probably Middleton's finest hour it was his greatest contribution as a battle leader.

This superb attribute was not always viewed positively by his superiors, however. During the difficult fighting in Normandy on the Cotentin Peninsula, Eisenhower would have preferred a more outwardly enthusiastic, aggressive reaction from Middleton, and wrote, "Middleton does not display the enthusiasm in his leadership that do the others." Ike admitted, however, that "he is tactically sound and a very fine, straightforward workman."[62] Despite misgivings concerning his enthusiasm, Eisenhower retained confidence in Middleton's steady, undramatic ability to command his corps skillfully and accomplish the mission.

This unflappability and apparent lack of aggressiveness may also be what caused Matt Ridgway, the XVIII Airborne Corps commander, to relate on 19 December that he assessed the VIII Corps headquarters to be completely unaware of the total situation.[63] There is little doubt that the VIII Corps staff was exercising no real control of the events occurring around St.-Vith (nor in the 4th Infantry Division sector, for that matter), but Middleton and his staff had as complete a picture as any higher headquarters did of the fluid situation at the time.[64] Middleton's undramatic demeanor and lack of stormy aggressiveness could have been interpreted by the flashy paratrooper as being out of touch with events. Ridgway's concern is understandable, however, as his mission was to bring the defense of the northern area, including St.-Vith, under command of his corps, and he was rushing to sort some order out of a totally confusing situation. But he would have to get the information he needed to establish his defense from the on-scene commanders at St.-Vith--Hasbrouck, Clarke, and Jones—not from Middleton.

The importance of Middleton's calm and steadying influence on the VIII Corps defense in the Ardennes cannot be overemphasized, because it formed the bedrock upon which the critical decisions affecting the conduct of the battle rested. Middleton's refusal to panic provided the VIII Corps staff with an outstanding personal example as well as giving them unyielding support to initiate the best defense possible in a completely confusing and fluid environment. The defense permitted by the units available to the VIII Corps commander was characterized by immediate and disciplined responses to each of the German threats as they developed. A calm and steady appraisal of each of these threats, coupled with a realistic utilization of the meager reserves, was crucial to the piecemeal delaying tactics that Middleton was forced by circumstances to employ. He had to coolly evaluate each impassioned request from his hard-pressed subordinates before allowing any of his tiny reserve to be committed.[65] Middleton may have wished desperately to send reinforcements to save Captain Rose and his outgunned task force, but he had to resist that temptation. It was not in his nature to play the blustering showman in this critical situation, nor would it necessarily have proven effective. What proved useful was his calm, measured, and workmanlike response in this fight.[66]

Middleton's steadying calmness provided the atmosphere for another of the demonstrated leadership characteristics he employed to good effect in the fighting—his flexibility. Middleton's ability to adapt his defense to the nature of the German assault was a critical factor in the VIII Corps' efforts to slow the advance in its sector. Mixed with large measures of initiative and innovation, plus a generous dose of moral courage, Middleton's adaptability proved essential to the overall defense.

It may be argued that the inherent weakness of the VIII Corps initial dispositions, coupled with the overwhelming nature of the German assault, necessitated the type of defense eventually used, but this reasoning ignores the tactical choices available to the corps commander. For example, Middleton was under no order or obligation to hold Bastogne, and as mentioned earlier, Patton initially chided Middleton for allowing the 101st Airborne to become surrounded in the key city. Further, Middleton's decision to fight for time by delaying with small task forces at each critical road junction seemed to orthodox tankers to fly directly in the face of the proper doctrine of the time. Armored warfare doctrine demanded concentrating the maximum available tank and mechanized forces for a decisive counterattack against the enemy's vulnerable point, thus Roberts of the 10th Armored resisted when Middleton told him to break up his combat command into smaller task forces and scatter them across the landscape. Middleton realized, however, that the unprecedented situation demanded that he adapt any textbook tactics to the realities of the situation. If the enemy could not be delayed immediately, then Bastogne would be lost and the VIII Corps front quickly overrun.[67]

Even prior to the German attack, Middleton had used his adaptability to maximize the defensive potential of his available troops. Hurley Fuller of the 110th Infantry received Middleton's permission to abandon any attempt to hold an uninterrupted line along his impossibly wide sector. Instead, he planned to delay any enemy assault by clinging as long as possible to each of the critical road junctions his widely scattered units garrisoned. When put to the test, Fuller's plan worked, justifying his corps commander's approval. In fact, this became Middleton's strategy as well.[68]

A final example of Middleton adapting tactics to resources must be the controversial employment of the engineer combat battalions. Middleton has been criticized for his initial use of these engineer battalions to fight as infantry. As Cole has pointed out, however, it is doubtful if either the 7th Armored or the 101st Airborne could have gotten into their respective defensive positions without the time bought by the engineers. To argue that they could have gained more time by being employed purely in an engineer role demonstrates a lack of understanding of the desperate tactical situation facing VIII Corps at the time and a poor appreciation of Middleton's flexibility.[69]

Fortunately, Middleton displayed an outstanding ability to adapt his tactics to the actual threat. As he told his biographer years later, "If the method you're using doesn't work, try something else. The fellow who wrote the book couldn't think of everything." Although Middleton didn't write the book, he spent several years teaching it at the Command and General Staff School and the Infantry School. His refusal to follow blindly what he termed the "Leavenworth solution" was a triumph of his good common sense coupled with a keen appreciation of what was necessary at the time.[70]

To be fair, Middleton's battle leadership did not always feature the flexibility it demonstrated in the Ardennes fighting. During the hedgerow combat in the early phases of VIII Corps' European campaign, for example, Middleton's units were uninspired and unimaginative. Persisting in an attempt to force well-prepared positions using orthodox tactics, despite heavy casualties, the corps failed to achieve its objectives. Middleton's principal effort at a solution was to relieve several of his subordinate division and regimental commanders, including one who was in command for only 4 days.[71] Nothing worked, however, until the massive COBRA carpet-bombings blasted a gap in the German defenses.

The Normandy breakout provided another instance in which Middleton's adaptability and flexibility didn't seem to measure up to his Ardennes performance. Freed from the confines of the Cotentin Peninsula and the frustrating hedgerow fighting, the VIII Corps' two fine armored divisions, Wood's 4th and Grow's 6th, raced through the crumbling German resistance and ranged far ahead of the remainder of the corps. Although Middleton was perfectly content to use oral orders and other informal techniques to control his units, he was definitely uncomfortable when the speed and distance of his advancing units took them out of radio and telephone contact for relatively long periods.[72] This problem was particularly acute during the race across the Brittany Peninsula. The two armored commanders "regarded themselves as belonging to the Patton school of thought" and they and "their units became infected with an enthusiasm and self-confidence...perfectly suited to exploitation but proved...a headache to those who sought to retain a semblance of control."[73] Middleton was gravely concerned about his ability to manage these units effectively as they became more and more independent of his corps command. The situation was never satisfactorily controlled by VIII Corps and improved only when the armored units reached the limits of their advance at the shores of the peninsula. Middleton's battle leadership never adapted an effective means of managing the activities of these rapidly moving units.

The seeming disconnect between Middleton's outstanding ability to adapt his tactics during the Ardennes fighting and his failure of flexibility in Normandy and Brittany could perhaps be answered by the differing types of combat involved. In Normandy and Brittany he was attacking, seeking to find his opponent's weakness and exploit it. In the Ardennes, Middleton was reacting to the overwhelming enemy assault. The Germans held the initiative, and Middleton, like an overmatched boxer, was counterpunching for all he was worth. It may be, simply, that the infantryman in Middleton was more capable of defending against an armored assault than he was of conducting and controlling such a mechanized attack. After all, the defense he ultimately employed was primarily infantry oriented, using tanks as support for infantry-engineer roadblocks. He rejected (and rightfully so it would seem, given the situation in the Ardennes) any bold and overambitious use of larger armored formations when those units were available. It can never be determined whether Middleton's outstanding adaptability during the Battle of the Bulge was inspirational or circumstantial in origin, but it is indisputable that it was exceptionally effective.[74]

In addition to calmness and flexibility, Middleton's battle leadership exhibited other positive characteristics that had an important, albeit lesser, effect on the battle: his talents as a tactician and organization of his staff. Middleton's technical competence as a tactician, and the common background and understanding this allowed him to have with his superiors who, like himself, were all infantrymen, was important because it permitted all the primary senior commanders involved in countering the German attack to work quickly toward a common end with roughly the same strategy.[75]

Bradley asserted postwar that he and Middleton had discussed and agreed upon a plan for defeating just such an attack in the Ardennes as the Germans launched, but this seems a demonstration of hindsight. Nevertheless they both must have realized beforehand that holding the "shoulders" of the penetration and restricting the flow of enemy forces at crucial chokepoints while awaiting counterattack by outside reserves was the proper doctrinal response.[76] The problem, however, was not figuring out what Middleton was supposed to do—it was how to come up with the necessary forces with which to counterattack into the flanks of the German thrust. It was Middleton's predictability at the operational level that provided the advantage.[77]

Middleton's organizational leadership and management of his staff directed his corps to institute and employ management techniques and procedures that emphasized standard and well-established practice. This permitted an uncomplicated and simple approach to fighting the corps for Middleton's staff members.[78] Having a simple and streamlined system for conducting operations is a definite advantage in a confusing and rapidly moving situation like the Ardennes fighting. Middleton was right when he wrote after the war, "Avoid complicated maneuvers. To expect results from large numbers of men the operations must be kept simple."[79] Such ideas seem to show perfect understanding of Clausewitz' observation that "in war everything is simple; but the simplest things are difficult to accomplish."[80]

Certainly there were also negative aspects associated with Middleton's battle leadership. The most glaring example of the leadership failings exhibited by the VIII Corps commander was his incredible reluctance to appoint an overall commander in several situations that desperately required one. Notably at St.-Vith and again at Bastogne, he refused or delayed placing one officer in overall command, weakly requesting the men on the spot to "cooperate" with each other.[81] Such a failure could have created a fatal

confusion through lack of unity of command, especially at
St.-Vith. If Bruce C. Clarke had been less willing to assume
responsibility for the crumbling defense of St.-Vith, or had
Alan Jones been more willing to cling to control of a
situation that had already overwhelmed him, a disaster
could have resulted. As it turned out, and with no thanks to
Middleton, command unity devolved upon Clarke and later,
Hasbrouck, his division commander.

In fairness to Middleton on this issue, there were some
mitigating circumstances present. Hasbrouck's and Clarke's
unit, the 7th Armored Division, belonged to Simpson's Ninth
Army and were outside Middleton's normal chain of
command. Additionally, both tankers received only vague
orders about what was going on in the VIII Corps sector and
what their ultimate mission was to be.[82] Formal operations
orders and detailed plans were out of the question in this
situation, and probably would have been out of date within
hours of their issue anyway. Further complicating matters
was a seniority problem among the three generals. Jones, a
major general and the ranking officer, had the smallest and
weakest unit, while Hasbrouck, although commanding a full-
strength armored division, had not yet been promoted and
was still a brigadier general. While there was no question
that Hasbrouck outranked Clarke, his direct subordinate,
before Hasbrouck arrived on the scene, Jones had voluntarily
turned over command of all troops in the St.-Vith area to the
junior brigadier, Clarke.[83] As if that wasn't confusing
enough, the 9th Armored Division Combat Command B
commander, Bill Hoge, also a brigadier general, arrived in
the St.-Vith area and joined the defense. Despite all the
confusing factors present at St.-Vith (or, precisely because of
the confusion), Middleton should have quickly appointed an
overall commander, assuming responsibility as the ranking
officer in the overall area whose headquarters was charged
with coordinating the entire defense. Instead, he merely
asked the several commanders to "carry the ball" for
him—hardly what could be characterized as definitive
guidance.[84] If he felt he lacked the authority to place
Simpson's subordinates under command of one of his own
unit commanders, he could have phoned Bradley. (He spoke

to his Army Group commander several times during this period, which shows that communications was not a factor.)[85] It is highly doubtful that Bradley would have said no, as he sent the 7th Armored to Middleton in the first place. At any rate, the genial and cooperative Simpson was no stubborn Patton, and the Ninth Army commander would not have fought the command arrangement.[86]

Middleton never did establish command unity at St.-Vith. When responsibility for the defense of St.-Vith transferred to XVIII Airborne Corps on 20 December, the issue was still undecided and had to wait for Ridgway to sort it out. When John S. D. Eisenhower wrote that, "Middleton's preference for cooperation rather than unity of command caused less confusion than might be imagined," he was not complimenting Middleton.[87]

Nearly the same situation was repeated at Bastogne, although this time temporarily. Middleton spoke to Tony McAuliffe, acting commander of the 101st Airborne, and Roberts of the 10th Armored and "asked the men to cooperate, with neither in charge."[88] In this instance, both units involved came from outside Middleton's corps, but at least there was no seniority question, McAuliffe was the only one with stars on his collar. This time, however, Middleton corrected his mistake in a short time. He called Roberts in and told him McAuliffe was in sole command. There is evidence that Middleton took this action after receiving advice to do so from the 28th Infantry Division's commander, Norm Cota, who with his division staff had just passed through Bastogne after being run out of Wiltz by the advancing Germans. When Cota observed the confusion and lack of overall direction in the town, he called Middleton and made the suggestion.[89] Whatever the motivation, Middleton's establishment of command unity in Bastogne was propitious and necessary. Nevertheless, he rightfully deserves criticism for failing to appoint an overall commander sooner at both critical locations. It was a major flaw in his battle leadership in the Ardennes.

Although Middleton's failure to establish unity of command quickly at critical locations had the greatest potential for disaster during the battle, the one failing that actually resulted in a serious setback took a slightly different form. Alan Jones and the 106th Infantry Division were new to VIII Corps and the Ardennes and had never seen combat. In addition to the unit's inexperience, it suffered from being in a weak location and occupying exposed positions. Yet Middleton apparently failed to provide Jones or his staff with anything close to proper guidance or advice the critical situation would seem to demand. Instead, it appears that the battlewise, veteran corps commander allowed his completely inexperienced subordinate to flounder on his own mistakes. As a consequence, the two regiments in the Schnee Eifel positions were lost, the largest single surrender of American troops in the European theater.[90]

Middleton's defense seems to be anchored on his belief that the commander actually on the ground was the best judge of the situation and therefore should make the final decision. He wrote that he felt the senior commander should not unduly interfere with the subordinate's attempts to carry out a mission, and he "followed the principle that once you have assigned a task to a person leave him alone. If he needs advice he will come to you...there is no need for constant interference."[91] While this belief is laudable in general, Jones' specific situation in the Ardennes warranted more direction from Middleton than he received. During the inevitable postmortems on the disaster, Middleton allowed Jones to shoulder the blame for the surrender, while excusing his own actions with the magnanimous pronouncement that "although Jones made the wrong decision, he made it in good faith, based on information then available to him."[92] That may sound fine and high principled, but it lets Middleton off too easily, especially considering the fact that Middleton had expressed grave concern about the exposed positions on the Schnee Eifel long before the German attack began. According to one source, "Several times General Middleton requested permission to withdraw from this penetration of the German defensive positions [the exposed area] to straighten out his line along more tenable positions...."[93] Because Middleton knew the vulnerability of Jones' dispositions well prior to the attack, he should have insisted clearly and unambiguously that

Jones withdraw the two regiments, instead of leaving the ultimate decision to the less knowledgeable division commander.

After the battle, Middleton rather forcefully expressed his opinion that, had the veteran 2nd Infantry Division still occupied the northern flank instead of the untried 106th, "they'd never have broken through!"[94] This is revealing, as it shows Middleton admitting that the 106th was far from up to the standards needed to stop the Germans. Knowing this then, he had a duty to exert more control over the green 106th and its inexperienced commander. Ultimately, the primary responsibility for failing to ensure the regiments were swiftly withdrawn to more defensible terrain was Middleton's, not Jones'.

"MIDDLETON DID IT MAGNIFICENTLY"

Assessment of Middleton's battle leadership shows that the successes outweigh the failures. Above all, his calm and steady guidance of the VIII Corps in an almost hopelessly confusing situation was exactly what was needed to maintain the best possible defense under the circumstances. Members of his staff, subordinate commanders, and outside observers all noted this important influence and remarked upon it in later years. It seems that they would all agree with Middleton's aide, who wrote, "I never knew a man who had such equanimity under stress and who had the ability to master all the details with such apparent ease...everyone had complete confidence in his ability."[95]

Although his failures of command had potentially serious consequences, they did not affect the ultimate outcome to the same degree as his successes. The surrender of the 106th's two regiments, although a disaster for the nearly 8,000 soldiers involved, was counterbalanced by Middleton's dispatch of the 7th Armored Division to St.-Vith. Likewise, his failure to establish command unity quickly at St.-Vith and Bastogne was mitigated by the initiative and cooperation of excellent subordinates. Finally, Middleton's flexibility in adapting his tactics to the nature of the German threat created just the right defense needed to delay the attackers for the maximum amount of time possible.

Middleton's battle leadership was an important element in the American victory in the Ardennes. Although the 101st Airborne's defense of Bastogne has emerged as the popular image of this greatest of all American battles, without Middleton's steady leadership there would have been no siege of that famous city. Indeed, much more can be learned about command in combat by analyzing Middleton's battle leadership than by focusing totally on the defense of Bastogne. One of Middleton's subordinates, who himself became a highly respected corps commander in World War II combat, has written as good a bottom line on Middleton in the Ardennes as can be recorded: "His objective, with his crippled corps, was to slow down the German armies. Middleton did it magnificently, and has never been given adequate credit for his great performance."[96]

NOTES

1. Frank J. Price, *Troy H. Middleton: A Biography* (Baton Rouge: LSU Press, 1974), 215. Price had been a student of Middleton's at LSU and worked extensively with him on the preparation of this biography, the only major work on Middleton's life and career. A large portion of the book deals with Middleton's experiences during the Ardennes offensive of December 1944 to February 1945. While the book provides many outstanding examples of Middleton's character and personality, it appears that Price may have too readily accepted some of Middleton's reminiscences of events of 30 years previous without independent verification.

2. Services Cinema Corporation, prod. *The Ardennes Offensive, 1944* (London: United Kingdom Ministry of Defence, 1979). General (Ret) Julian Ewell, a battalion commander in the 101st Airborne Division at Bastogne, gives this graphic description of Middleton's composure in an on-camera interview in this film prepared for the British Army. He went on to say that the VIII Corps staff appeared "physically beaten" and "psychologically spent," but that Middleton, in addition to his calmness, appeared to be in complete control of the situation exerting a steadying influence. A discussion of Eisenhower's selection of Middleton for command of the VIII Corps is presented in Stephen E. Ambrose, *Eisenhower: Volume I, Soldier, General of the Army, President-Elect, 1890-1952* (New York: Simon and Schuster, 1983), 296.

3. On the eve of the US entry into World War II, Middleton, in retirement at LSU, petitioned the War Department to return to active duty. Army Chief of Staff General George C. Marshall wrote across the top of the file copy of Middleton's request, "This man was the outstanding infantry regimental commander on the battlefield in France." Price, *Middleton*, 135.

4. Hugh M. Cole, *The United States Army in World War II. European Theater of Operations. The Ardennes: The Battle of the Bulge* (Washington, DC: GPO, 1965), 55.   Russell F. Weigley, *Eisenhower's Lieutenants: The Campaigns of France and Germany 1944-1945* (Bloomington: Indiana University Press, 1981), 157-158. Price, *Middleton*, 206-207, relates that, "When he was faced with the necessity of relieving a commander, Middleton did not hesitate."

5. Price, *Middleton*, 4-141. The details of Middleton's life and early years of service are adequately covered in Price's biography which serves as the primary reference for this section.

6. Middleton was promoted to lieutenant colonel on 17 September 1918, and to colonel on 14 October 1918, 3 days after assuming command of the 39th Infantry Regiment. At the time of his promotion to colonel, he was the youngest officer in the US Army to hold that rank, having passed his 29th birthday 2 days earlier, Price, *Middleton*, 67-68.

7. US Department of the Army, *Annual Reports of the Commandant, the General Service Schools, 1923-1928* (Fort Leavenworth, KS). Officers attending during Middleton's tenure as an instructor who later attained higher command in ETO were: Devers, Patch, Simpson, Haislip, and Hodges (1924-25); Eisenhower, Gerow, Millikin, Terry Allen, Collins, and Walton Walker (1925-26); Kenny (1926-27); and Brereton (1927-28). Price, *Middleton*, 89-91, makes much of Middleton's tenure as an instructor, claiming, "Through the four classes Middleton taught from 1924-1928 came almost all the men who were to command divisions in Europe in World War II. At one time in World War II, every corps commander in Europe had been a student under Middleton at the Command and General Staff School." Price's claim may be somewhat exaggerated. Inspection of the General Staff School records shows that, while this was true very early in the campaigns following D-Day, as the number of corps rose, the number of corps commanders who attended the Staff School during Middleton's tenure dropped.   However, of the officers who completed Staff School while Middleton was there, a large number were highly placed leaders.

8. Ambrose, *Eisenhower*, 114; Price, *Middleton*, 113-122. Middleton had formed a close association with LSU during his service there as an ROTC instructor and Commandant of Cadets. When the lucrative offer came to join the staff of the university as a civilian, he had completed 27 years of active duty and his outlook for further promotion and advancement in the Army was not promising. At the time of his retirement, his promotion to full colonel, a rank he had previously held in 1918, appeared to be several years away. Nevertheless, Eisenhower apparently held Middleton's retirement against him, at one point late in the war recommending that Marshall not promote Middleton to permanent Regular Army two-star rank. Ambrose writes that Eisenhower growled, "He left us when the going was tough." In fairness to Eisenhower, it was obvious that Middleton would return to retirement at the close of the war. Since promotion is not a reward for "services rendered" but a recognition of *potential* value to the service, Eisenhower wanted to promote those officers who would lead the post-war army.

9. Price, *Middleton*, 137, 140-141. Marshall thought very highly of Middleton's abilities and quickly accepted his offer to return to active duty. He remained a Middleton supporter throughout the war despite Eisenhower's occasional slights.

10. Omar N. Bradley and Clay Blair, *A General's Life: An Autobiography of General of the Army Omar N. Bradley* (New York: Simon and Schuster, 1983), 171; Price, *Middleton*, 143-147.

11. Weigley, *Eisenhower's Lieutenants*, 121-122; Price, *Middleton*, 170-171. However, one D-Day corps commander, Major General Leonard T. Gerow, an Eisenhower intimate and long-time friend, did not have the extensive combat experience of Middleton or Collins. Throughout his combat service in World War II, Middleton was plagued by an arthritic knee which prevented him from being in top physical condition at all times. Hospitalized in November 1943, he was forced to give up command of the 45th Division in Italy and seek treatment at Walter Reed Hospital. It was during this treatment that Eisenhower selected him, despite his physical disability, to lead a corps in Europe. Ambrose, *Eisenhower*, 296, repeats the following anecdote about Middleton's selection: "For the first follow-on corps, Eisenhower picked...Middleton, but only after an exchange of views with Marshall. An objection had been raised to Middleton on physical grounds, which--according to Bradley--led Marshall to remark, 'I would rather have a man with arthritis in the knee than one with arthritis in the head.' Eisenhower's version was different: he

recalled that he had asked Marshall for Middleton but Marshall replied, 'Fine. I agree with you in his values. But he's in Walter Reed Hospital with his knees.' To which Eisenhower replied, 'I don't give a damn about his knees; I want his head and his heart and I'll take him into battle on a litter if we have to.'"

12. John S. D. Eisenhower, *The Bitter Woods* (New York: G.P. Putnam's Sons, 1969), 39.

13. Martin Blumenson, *The United States Army in World War II. European Theater of Operations. Breakout and Pursuit* (Washington, DC: GPO, 1961) is the best reference for the costly Normandy campaign and the subsequent race across France; Weigley, *Eisenhower's Lieutenants*, 174.

14. Martin Blumenson, "The Decision to Take Brest," *Army*, 10 (March 1960): 44, contains a good explanation of why a significant share of the Allied forces turned westward, away from the main German force; Blumenson, *Breakout and Pursuit*, 367; Weigley, *Eisenhower's Lieutenants*, 179-180.

15. Robert W. Grow, "Mobility Unused," *Military Review*, 32 (February 1953): 22-24. Grow, commander of the 6th Armored Division, bitterly attacked Middleton and other Allied commanders for what he felt was a tragically missed opportunity to swiftly capture the fortress city of Brest, and thereby free his division for the fight against the large German formations to the east. Grow termed the whole operation "totally without value." Blumenson, "Decision to Take Brest," 46; Blumenson, *Breakout and Pursuit*, 635-636. Expected by the higher command echelons to take 6 days and to be completed by 1 September, Brest's capture on 19 September came after 27 days of grueling, bloody fighting; Middleton's headquarters documented the effort as well as "lessons learned" in US Department of the Army, *VIII Corps, Attack of a Fortified Zone*, 9 October 1944.

16. Bradley and Blair, *A General's Life*, 352-353; Price, *Middleton*, 211-215.

17. US Department of the Army, *VIII Corps After Action Report, June to December 1944*, records that VIII Corps assumed responsibility for the Ardennes sector at noon on 4 October 1944. When VIII Corps initially occupied the Ardennes sector, the front was manned by only the 2nd and 8th Infantry Divisions. Later (11 October 1944), the 83rd Infantry Division joined the other two, and then the new 9th Armored Division arrived on 20 October. When units began to be badly chewed up in the disastrous Huertgen Forest offensive, VIII Corps' divisions were used to replace them, with the shattered units taking their place in the Ardennes. By 16

December 1944, the VIII Corps consisted of the 4th, 28th, and 106th Infantry Divisions and most of the 9th Armored. Price, *Middleton*, 210-212; Bradley and Blair, *A General's Life*, 352-353; and Cole, *Ardennes*, 56.

18. Charles B. MacDonald, *The Battle of the Huertgen Forest* (New York: Jove, 1984) 120. James W. Bradin, "28th Infantry Division: The Forgotten Pennsylvanians," *Army*, 37 (August 1987): 62-67. In this article, Bradin gives an alternate story of how the 28th got its "Bloody Bucket" nickname. In Bradin's version, enemy soldiers first began referring to the unit as "Blutig Eimer"; US soldiers adopted the English translation later.

19. MacDonald, *Huertgen Forest*, 180; Eisenhower, *Bitter Woods*, 205.

20. US Department of the Army, *VIII Corps Letter of Instruction, 7 December 1944* which directed the handover reads, in part, "b. Relieve 2d Inf Div, in place, on or about 11 December 44. c. Responsibility for defense of 2d Inf Div Z, protection N (L) flank of VIII Corps and maintenance of contact with V Corps will pass to CG, 106th Inf Div at a time to be mutually agreed upon by CG's concerned. CG 106th Inf Div will notify this headquarters when change of responsibility has been accomplished."; Price, *Middleton*, 211; Weigley, *Eisenhower's Lieutenants*, 448; Robert E. Merriam, *Dark December* (Chicago: Ziff-Davis, 1947), 79. R. Ernest Dupuy, *St.-Vith: Lion in the Way—The 106th Infantry Division in World War II* (Washington, DC: Infantry Journal Press, 1949); Charles Whiting, *Death of a Division* (New York: Stein and Day, 1981).

21. *VIII Corps After Action Report*, 145, describes the "Siegfried Line" positions as follows: "In the two areas of the Siegfried Line in which V Corps had made penetrations, the construction and arrangement of the fortifications...consisted [first] of dragon's teeth arranged in rows and usually six rows deep. In a few cases, a concrete wall 31 in high and 21 in thick was built in front of the dragon's teeth. Roadways through these tank barriers were blocked by heavy steel gates, concrete plates or removable I beams. The dragon's teeth were not continuous...in...places no artificial barrier was present, as the rugged country and thick forest were sufficient to bar the progress of tanks. Behind the tank barriers were the main defenses, consisting of a double row of concrete forts. These varied in size and design, but could be classified into three general categories; viz., machine gun forts, anti-tank forts and command posts. The forts contained from 3 to 6 rooms and accommodated from 12 to 25 men. The embrasures

were small and were covered with 4 in armor plate. They permitted a limited field of fire, usually to the flanks. The entrances to the forts were protected by steel doors and these were covered by the fire from an adjacent fort. No tunnels nor connecting trenches between forts were found, but the forts were connected by power and communications cables. Apparently the Germans did not improve or maintain the installations...after the fall of France. Four years of natural growth of trees and brush obstructed many of the fields of fire and the anti-tank pillboxes, designed to accommodate the 37mm weapon, had never been modified to house the modern...calibers. Nevertheless, the system of fortifications still furnished an excellent defensive line on which to place the mobile elements of defense."; Price, *Middleton*, 211; Cole, *Ardennes*, 55.

22. Cole, *Ardennes*, 55; Weigley, *Eisenhower's Lieutenants*, 480; General Bruce C. Clarke explained to the author that, although the combat command armored division was formed on a triumvirate of tank, infantry, and artillery battalions, only Combat Command A and Combat Command B were intended to be regularly used as maneuver units. Combat Command R was used essentially to control movement of the reserve and seldom used for combat. This became a source of confusion and friction between senior infantry and armor commanders from time to time when the senior infantry commander assumed all three combat commands were equally capable of operating as maneuver units, Bruce C. Clarke, interview, by author, tape recording, McLean, Virginia, April 1985. See also US Department of the Army, *4th Armored Division Tactics and Administration, Armored Division*, War Department Observer's Board Draft Report, June 1945, 1-2.

23. Cole, *Ardennes*, 56; Weigley, *Eisenhower's Lieutenants*, 480, 574; Ambrose, *Eisenhower*, 365. On the first day of the German assault, 16 divisions struck the four division equivalents in the VIII Corps zone. Eventually, as the attack proceeded, 24 German divisions were involved. Cole, *Ardennes*, 650, has documented the balance sheet (including the V Corps units also struck) and writes, "On the morning of 16 December the American forces in the path of the German counteroffensive comprised four and two-third divisions with an effective strength of about 83,000 men [includes V Corps' 99th Infantry Division]. The heavy weapons then available numbered 242 Sherman tanks, 182 tank destroyers, and 394 pieces of corps and divisional artillery. The troops and weapons were deployed on a meandering front of 104 miles. The enemy assault divisions poised to the east had

concentrated behind some ninety miles of front manned by Army
Group B, and during the night of 15 December over 200,000
combat troops gathered in the forward assembly area, about three
miles in depth. The German attack...was made on an assault front
of sixty miles and included 5 armored divisions, 12 2/3 infantry
divisions, and about 500 medium tanks, the whole supported by
the fires of 1,900 guns and werfers [rocket launchers]."

24. Cole, *Ardennes*, 310-311; Weigley, *Eisenhower's
Lieutenants*, 480; Ambrose, *Eisenhower*, 366-367. The progress of
the German main attack in the northern area rapidly cut off
Middleton's northernmost units--106th Infantry Division and 14th
Cavalry Group--from the remainder of VIII Corps. Although
Middleton maintained communications with the defenders of St.-
Vith, the fighting was controlled by the commanders on the ground
at that location. The 7th Armored Division, the unit providing the
bulk of the defenders for St.-Vith beginning 17 December, received
only eight messages from VIII Corps headquarters during the days
prior to Eisenhower's reorganization of the command lines. Of
these messages, one was simply a retransmission of a "hold at all
costs" order previously issued by Middleton (and of only historical
interest by the time it was received), one was Middleton's
exhortation to VIII Corps troops to "take apart" the enemy's "final
and desperate" attack, two were unit boundary confirmations, two
established supply procedures, and one was a false report that the
Germans had captured Malmedy. Most of the messages appear to
be of little practical use to the St.-Vith defenders, US Department
of the Army, *7th Armored Division After Action Report*, 84-85.

25. Price, *Middleton*, 215.

26. Jacques Nobecourt, *Hitler's Last Gamble* (New York:
Schocken Books, 1967), 146-147; Cole, *Ardennes*, p 306; Bradley
and Blair, *A General's Life*, 354. Bradley claims to have "discussed
the possibility [of a German Ardennes attack] in detail with
Middleton and...made plans to defend against it. If the Germans
hit his sector Middleton was to make a fighting withdrawal--all the
way back to the Meuse River if necessary...he would slow the
enemy as much as possible, and I would order reserve armored
divisions...and other units to close pincers at the base of the
German salient and cut him off." Bradley even identifies the 7th
and 10th Armored Divisions as specific units he had planned to
use, although these units weren't even selected until Eisenhower
picked them and directed Bradley to send them to VIII Corps'
assistance on 16 December. Also making Bradley's postwar
assertions suspect is his claim that, on 8 November he "toured part

of the long, desolate front and inspected several of [Middleton's] divisions, including the...badly mangled 28th, which had been assigned to VIII Corps for rest and rebuilding." The 28th didn't even arrive in the Ardennes until 29 November (Cole, *Ardennes*, 179). It's possible that Bradley is confusing this inspection of the Ardennes with an actual meeting he attended with Eisenhower, Hodges, and Gerow at Cota's 28th Division headquarters in the Huertgen Forest on 8 November (MacDonald, *Huertgen Forest*, 119).

27. John Toland, *Battle: The Story of the Bulge* (New York: Random House, 1959), 53; Cole, *Ardennes*, 170, 274-275, 331; Merriam, *Dark December*, 111-112, 150; Dupuy, *Lion in the Way*, 23; Price, *Middleton*, 216; Weigley, *Eisenhower's Lieutenants*, 451.

28. Cole, *Ardennes*, 240-245.

29. Franklin Institute, *Art and Requirements of Command, Volume 2, Generalship Study* (Philadelphia: Systems Science Department of the Franklin Institute, 1967), "Middleton Questionnaire," 15. The question that elicited Middleton's observation of the obviousness of the criticality of St.-Vith and Bastogne concerned command followup and monitoring of execution. It asked respondents how to be at the critical place at the critical time.

30. US Department of the Army, *4th Armored Division, Armor at Bastogne*, May 1949, 6.

31. Price, *Middleton*, 269.

32. Cole, *Ardennes*, 513.

33. Ibid., 311.

34. Bruce C. Clarke, "The Battle for St.-Vith: Armor in the Defense and Delay," *Armor* 83 (November-December 1974): 40. Clarke found Middleton reading in his headquarters van at 0400 hours, 17 December, and received the simple instructions from the VIII Corps commander; Clarke, interview.

35. Franklin Institute, *Generalship Study*, 10; Weigley, *Eisenhower's Lieutenants*, 451, writes that, "Jones later telephoned Middleton, suggested that the Schnee Eifel would have to be abandoned, and predictably found the Corps commander passing the buck back to him as the man on the spot."

36. Merriam, *Dark December*, 111-112; Dupuy, *Lion in the Way*, 23; Weigley, *Eisenhower's Lieutenants*, 448; Whiting, *Death of a Division*, 26-32.

37. Another manifestation of Jones' inexperience was his reluctance to order a "retreat" that, if proven premature, would not reflect positively on his unit or himself, Whiting, *Death of a*

Division, 52. The foulup at the switchboard, which helped result in the misunderstanding on the 16 December call, was not generally known until 1986 when the switchboard operator, a military government soldier helping out at the switchboard that night, began circulating letters about the incident to some surviving participants. The individual's motivation in waiting over 40 years to publicize his role in the incident is not completely known, but the thrust of the communications appeared to be an attempt to place the majority of blame on General Clarke and the "late" arrival of Combat Command B, 7th Armored, Bruce C. Clarke and J.C. Triplett, interview by author, Carlisle Barracks, PA, February 1986. The announced arrival time of the 7th Armored Division at St.-Vith (0700 hours, 17 December) was an unreasonably early expectation. The unit had to road march from Holland on icy roads, clogged with fleeting units, across the path of the German offensive. Cole, *Ardennes*, 275, provides one source of the confusion. Apparently, First Army headquarters had notified Middleton on the evening of 16 December that "the west column [of 7th Armored] would arrive at 0700 and close at 1900 on the 17th...It was on this estimate that...their plans for a counterattack [were based]." Weigley, *Eisenhower's Lieutenants*, p.451, states that "Anyone believing this [arrival time] was not looking carefully at his maps." Dupuy, *Lion in the Way*, 23-24; Price, *Middleton*, 216; Whiting, *Death of a Division*, 51-53.

38. Cole, *Ardennes*, 513.

39. Ibid., 224-226.

40. Price, *Middleton*, 224.

41. Cole, *Ardennes*, 294-295.

42. Ibid., 296, relates that, "The early winter night gave the Americans a chance. Captain Rose broke out cross-country with five tanks and his assault gun platoon, rolling fast without lights through little villages toward Houffalize, near which the detachment was ambushed. A few vehicles and crews broke free and reached Bastogne."

43. Weigley, *Eisenhower's Lieutenants*, 458.

44. Eisenhower, *Bitter Woods*, 308; *Armor at Bastogne*, 181, severely criticized Middleton's decision which caused, "Portions of CC'B', 10th Armored [to be] drawn into separate isolated actions instead of being employed decisively as a unit."

45. Price, *Middleton*, 270.

46. Cole, *Ardennes*, 311, reports that the 1128th Engineer Group, a First Army unit of three engineer combat battalions, was working in the VIII Corps sector in direct support of the "normal

operations" of the corps. These, along with the four VIII Corps engineer combat battalions, gave Middleton an additional seven "infantry" units with which to continue his delaying tactics.

47. Ibid., 312-313.

48. Weigley, *Eisenhower's Lieutenants*, 480; Nobecourt, *Last Gamble*, 171; Price, *Middleton*, 228; Cole, *Ardennes*, 450.

49. Cole, *Ardennes*, Chapter XIV, provides an excellent and detailed account of the engineers and other VIII Corps troops who created, manned and fought the "Barrier Line" battle.

50. Ibid., 329. Cole goes on to point out, however, that "the story of the Ardennes barrier line does make clear that the use of engineers in their capacity as trained technicians often paid greater dividends than their use as infantry, and that a squad equipped with sufficient TNT could, in the right spot, do more to slow the enemy advance than a company armed with rifles and machine guns." This assessment is certainly a correct one, provided the engineers had time to prepare properly the defensive positions--exactly the point in question.

51. Ralph M. Mitchell, *The 101st Airborne Division's Defense of Bastogne* (Fort Leavenworth, KS: Combat Studies Institute, 1986), 8-10; Weigley, *Eisenhower's Lieutenants*, 484; Cole, *Ardennes*, 460; Eisenhower, *Bitter Woods*, 321.

52. Robert H. Phillips, *To Save Bastogne* (New York: Stein and Day, 1983), is a fine overall account of the fighting by small units of the 28th Infantry Division to buy time for reinforcements, such as the 101st Airborne, to occupy Bastogne. Phillips correctly points out, "Overshadowed by accounts of the 101st Airborne Division's gallant defense of Bastogne in December 1944, the story of the desperate delaying actions east of Bastogne which bought time for the occupation and defense of that city by American troops has so far been a closed book to most of the world." Phillips, 11; Cole, *Ardennes*, 307-308, 323; Price, *Middleton*, 269.

53. Mitchell, *The 101st Airborne*, 8-10; Weigley, *Eisenhower's Lieutenants*, 484; Cole, *Ardennes*, 460; Eisenhower, *Bitter Woods*, 321.

54. Eisenhower, *Bitter Woods*, 311, 320; Merriam, *Dark December*, 177; Cole, *Ardennes*, 309; Nobecourt, *Last Gamble*, 230.

55. Franklin Institute, *Generalship Study*, 24-25. Middleton answers a question concerning what "inadequate techniques" of command were used during the Battle of the Bulge by writing, "Failure of Allied troops on the north side of the Bulge to launch an earlier counter attack. To me this was one of the great mistakes of the war." Cole, *Ardennes*, Chapter XXIV; Price,

Middleton, 264-273.

56. Chester Wilmot, *The Struggle for Europe* (New York: Harper and Brothers, 1952), 583; Price, *Middleton*, 292-293.

57. LTC Boyd M. Harris, Leadership and Ethics Committee, Department of Command, US Army Command and General Staff College, Fort Leavenworth, Kansas, interview with author, 9 Sept 1983.

58. Virtually every visitor to VIII Corps headquarters during this time made it a point to remark upon Middleton's calm outward appearance and coolness under pressure. These included Ridgway, Clarke, McAuliffe, and Ewell; "The Ardennes Offensive"; Eisenhower, *Bitter Woods*, 244, 311; Cole, *Ardennes*, 55; Nobecourt, *Last Gamble*, 168, attributed this characteristic to self-control, when he wrote that "General Middleton was...expert at concealing any fears he may have had...."

59. Franklin Institute, *Generalship Study*, 18-19, 26.

60. Eisenhower, *Bitter Woods*, 311, quotes Ewell who elaborates on his earlier personal assessment of Middleton's nature under fire.

61. Ibid., 244. These are Ridgway's words describing Middleton's demeanor.

62. Alfred D. Chandler, Jr., et al., eds., *The Papers of Dwight David Eisenhower, The War Years* (Baltimore: Johns Hopkins Press, 1970) 3:1971.

63. Matthew B. Ridgway, *Soldier: The Memoirs of Matthew B. Ridgway (As Told to Harold H. Martin)* (New York: Harper and Brothers, 1956); Price, *Middleton*, 228.

64. Price, *Middleton*, 228, relates that the Germans helped VIII Corps gain a better understanding of the overall situation when, on 16 December, "American troops had captured a young German officer carrying complete plans for the lightning stroke at the VIII Corps area." Middleton rapidly forwarded the captured documents up through the chain of command.

65. Cole, *Ardennes*, 311-312, 513.

66. Franklin Institute, *Generalship Study*, 26. Middleton wrote that there was "no place for the showman in command of others,...the bluffer would not last long in command of troops."

67. *Armor at Bastogne*, 19; Price, *Middleton*, 230; Eisenhower, *Bitter Woods*, 308. It was only after Middleton explained the advantages of continuing to physically occupy the crucial transportation center that Patton later referred to Middleton's action as "a stroke of genius."

68. Price. *Middleton*. 217-218; Eisenhower. *Bitter Woods*, 205;

Weigley, *Eisenhower's Lieutenants*, 454.

    69. Cole, *Ardennes*, 310.

    70. Price, *Middleton*, 85, 270.

    71. Harold J. Meyer, *Hanging Sam: A Military Biography of General Samuel T. Williams* (Denton, TX: University of North Texas Press, 1990), 59-100, presents the story of one of Middleton's "victims" in the reliefs for cause during the post-invasion, hedgerow fighting. General Williams, at the time of his relief, was the assistant division commander of the 90th Infantry Division until 16 July 1944. Williams, who was also reduced from brigadier general to colonel at the time of his relief, felt strongly that he had been unfairly treated by Middleton, who "barely knew him." Williams may be right, but from Middleton's perspective, it seems a reasonable action given the 90th's poor record of combat achievement up to that time. In addition to the fact that Williams' division commander at the time, Major General Eugene Landrum, had formally requested that Middleton relieve Williams, the fiery assistant was the only "common denominator" remaining in the division's hierarchy (he had already seen three division commanders reassigned or relieved). It doesn't seem unreasonable that the senior remaining officer who had any personal responsibility for the unit's pre-combat training (and, at least by implication, for the unit's poor performance in combat up to that time) should be removed, too. At any rate, Williams had engaged in loud, public remonstrances with both Landrum and his predecessor, MacKelvie, on more than one occasion. It seems no great mystery, then, that Landrum sought his relief. Landrum, of course, was also relieved of command of the division at about the same time. To Williams' credit, he served on, regained his lost rank, and retired as a Lieutenant General in 1960. Eisenhower, *Bitter Woods*, 39; Blumenson, *Breakout and Pursuit*, 63.

    72. Blumenson, *Breakout and Pursuit*, 350-351.

    73. Ibid.

    74. Weigley, *Eisenhower's Lieutenants*, 480; Cole, *Ardennes*, 311.

    75. With the obvious exception of Patton (cavalry, armor), as well as the not-so-obvious exception of General Jacob L. Devers (field artillery), commander of the 6th Army Group, all of the men in senior command under Eisenhower were infantrymen. This can undoubtedly be traced directly to Marshall and the "Ft. Benning connection." Sometimes it caused resentment, when an outstanding officer who was not an infantryman perceived himself as being "passed over" in favor of someone wearing crossed rifles

on his collar. For example, this may explain some of the problems that the 4th Armored Division's outstanding commander, Major General John S. Wood (field artillery), began experiencing when command of the XII Corps was given to Major General Manton S. Eddy (infantry). Bruce C. Clarke, serving under Wood's command in the 4th Armored at the time, related that Wood thought the corps command was rightfully his, and subsequently resented Eddy's appointment. Whiting, *Death of a Division*, 56, records a conversation between (then Colonel) Bruce C. Clarke and Patton in which the Third Army commander says, "Hell, Clarke, if you had been an infantryman instead of an engineer and had served at Fort Benning you would be a major-general by now." Whether this attitude was widespread or not is difficult to determine, but at least the common background of the senior commanders facilitated operations during the Ardennes campaign.

76. Raymond S. McLain, "One of the Greatest: A Study in Leadership," *Military Review*, 49 (December 1969): 24; Bradley, *Soldier's Story*, 453-454; Bradley and Blair, *A General's Life*, 354.

77. Dwight D. Eisenhower, *Crusade in Europe* (Garden City: Doubleday and Company, 1948), 347-350; Weigley, *Eisenhower's Lieutenants*, Chapter 26; Cole, *Ardennes*, 56, 305-306.

78. Price, *Middleton*, 178.

79. Franklin Institute, *Generalship Study*, 2-5.

80. Peter Paret and Michael Howard (trans.), Karl von Clausewitz *On War* (Princeton: University Press, 1976), 119-121. This translation continues with, "Countless minor incidents--the kind you can never really foresee--combine to lower the general level of performance, so that one always falls short of the intended goal...The military machine...is basically very simple and very easy to manage. But we should bear in mind that none of its components is of one piece: each part is composed of individuals, every one of whom retains his potential of friction."

81. Eisenhower, *Bitter Woods*, 235, 286; Dupuy, *Lion in the Way*, 160-161.

82. Clarke, "Battle for St.-Vith", 40; Clarke, interview; Whiting, *Death of a Division*, 65, 76.

83. Clarke, interview. Whenever the subject of command at St.-Vith was raised after the war, Clarke always maintained that, at all times during the fighting, he remained under command of Hasbrouck, his parent division commander. He insists that he was never under Jones' command at any time prior to Hasbrouck's actual arrival in the area. Clarke's position was that, since Combat Command B, 7th Armored, never formally received orders

placing it under Jones' 106th Infantry, he answered to Hasbrouck regardless of Jones' rank. Since Jones was clearly overwhelmed by the events and turned over command to Clarke on 17 December, the point seems moot.

84. Eisenhower, *Bitter Woods*, 286.

85. Price, *Middleton*, 223, 226; Bradley and Blair, *A General's Life*, 363.

86. It should be noted that his Third Army was newly engaged in an offensive while Simpson's Ninth Army had not yet begun its Rhineland campaign. This fact was strongly emphasized in a letter to the author from historian Hugh M. Cole, 4 September 1990.

87. Eisenhower, *Bitter Woods*, 235.

88. Ibid., 311.

89. Ibid., 320.

90. Cole, *Ardennes*, 136, 170; Dupuy, *Lion in the Way*, 18, 160-161; Merriam, *Dark December*, 150; Whiting, *Death of a Division*, 26-32.

91. Franklin Institute, *Generalship Study*, 10.

92. Weigley, *Eisenhower's Lieutenants*, 451; Dupuy, *Lion in the Way*, 23; Merriam, *Dark December*, 111-112, 150; Price, *Middleton*, 216.

93. Merriam, *Dark December*, 74. Apparently, Middleton even went so far as to withdraw some of his most exposed units without authority, and blew up about 25 pillboxes on his own initiative. It's clear, therefore, that he was extremely concerned about the vulnerability of the Schnee Eifel positions.

94. Price, *Middleton*, 268. Middleton's remarks were, "It sometimes gives me the creeps when some of our latter day tacticians ask why Middleton didn't hold the Germans at the Our River. If the Germans had launched their attack against the divisions originally on that line, they'd never have broken through."

95. Price, *Middleton*, 176.

96. McLain, "One of the Greatest," 25. General McLain served under Middleton as commander of the 90th Infantry Division in the last stages of the Cotentin fighting. After his successful handling of this troubled division, he was promoted to command of a corps in Simpson's Ninth Army. McLain finished the war as the highest ranking National Guard officer in Europe. General Middleton returned to retirement after the war and became, eventually, President Emeritus of LSU. He spent the remaining years of his life at the university (Price, *Middleton*).

6. The Defense of St.-Vith

If there is one lamentable figure among the senior American commanders in the Battle of the Bulge, it must be Major General Alan W. Jones of the ill-fated 106th Infantry Division. His unit was destroyed as a cohesive fighting force so rapidly and so decisively that, at the darkest moment during the defense of St.-Vith, he remarked to Brigadier General Bruce C. Clarke, who had just arrived with his reinforcing armored command, "I've lost a division quicker than any division commander in the U.S. Army."[1] Indeed, when his two surrounded regiments on the Schnee Eifel capitulated to the Germans after fighting only 4 days, they represented the largest single surrender of American troops in the European Theater of Operations.[2] Such a disaster for American arms in such a key portion of the Ardennes could have been fatal to the entire US effort had it not been for one of the heroes of this same battle—Brigadier General Bruce C. Clarke of the 7th Armored Division.

JONES' CAREER

THE BEGINNINGS

At age 22, Alan Walter Jones was commissioned a second lieutenant of infantry after graduating from the University of Washington. This was in 1917, the first summer of the Great War for the United States and the beginning of the buildup of our tiny, constabulary Army into a major fighting force.[3]

Appointed at Fort Leavenworth, KS, as a member of the 43rd Infantry Regiment, Jones joined the regiment in Camp Douglas, UT, in October 1917. Although anxious to see combat overseas, Jones shared the fate of Eisenhower and

Bradley and remained in training in the United States throughout the war. Unlike Middleton, who won fame and rapid promotion on the battlefield in France, 1LT Jones served in more mundane places such as Camp Pike, AR, and Pensacola, FL, winning only a modest promotion to temporary captain in summer 1918. Even that rank was lost a year later when, like all officers in the rapidly demobilizing American army, Jones reverted to his permanent rank, first lieutenant, in October 1919.

As quickly as it had grown, the powerful American Army stood down, becoming once again a small, professional force performing mostly policing duties in widely scattered locations such as the Philippine Islands, a Pacific outpost and remnant of the "Big Stick" days of the beginning of the century.[4] By the early 1920s, CPT Jones was in Manila with the 45th Infantry Regiment. For the 15,000 or so officers who made up the Regular Army in those years between the world wars, service in the Philippines was a pleasant posting. Families routinely accompanied Army officers serving in the islands, and cheap native labor promised many amenities otherwise hard to afford on a captain's meager salary.[5]

Jones' next assignment was a fortunate one, for it took him to the Infantry School at Fort Benning during the years when George C. Marshall reigned as Assistant Commandant. Marshall kept a close eye on all officers passing through the school, personally selecting or approving all officers who served on the school faculty. The future Army Chief of Staff made notes to himself about those officers who impressed him and would later call on these men to fill the important command and staff positions during the war.[6] Jones' rapid rise after American entry into World War II seems likely to have been at least partly the result of favorably impressing Marshall during those years. If so, Jones was in good company, joining the likes of Bradley, "Vinegar Joe" Stilwell, J. Lawton Collins, Matthew Ridgway, and Smith.

Apparently, Jones had impressed others as well, for his next assignment was to attend the Field Artillery Officers' Advanced Course at the Field Artillery School at Fort Sill, OK. This early version of cross-fertilization within branches of the Army was usually restricted to above-average performers who showed promise. Jones' selection also indicated that he scored higher than his infantry officer contemporaries in mathematics, otherwise he would not have been allowed to attend.[7]

Jones' next tour of duty was with the 12th Infantry Regiment at Fort Washington, MD, in 1931. Just over a year later, he was reassigned in the Washington, DC, area to the Office of the Chief of Infantry, an influential and important assignment for MAJ Jones. Favorably impressing one's branch chief was not only a ticket to higher schooling (e.g., Command and Staff School and Army War College), but also an avenue to a choice command or staff assignment.[8] It is hardly surprising, then, that Jones' next assignment was as a student at the Command and Staff School at Fort Leavenworth, KS, in the Class of 1936.

After graduation from the Staff School, Jones returned to Washington, joining the 7th Infantry Regiment at Vancouver Barracks in summer 1936, before returning to Washington, D.C., to attend the Army War College the following summer. After Jones completed the War College in the summer of 1938, he was reassigned to the 19th Infantry Regiment in Schofield Barracks, HI. Duty in Hawaii was another choice assignment in the prewar army. Jones spent nearly 3 years there, advancing to lieutenant colonel on 1 July 1940.[9] By this time the war in Europe was nearly a year old, and the French Army—the largest army in Western Europe—had been humiliated by Germany in 6 weeks of "lightning war." Marshall and others of foresight were frantically trying to rebuild the pathetically small American army into some kind of credible fighting force before it was too late.[10]

As part of his efforts to restructure and revitalize the American army, Marshall was gathering around him in the War Department and the Army Staff those young, competent, and capable officers he had identified in the years between the wars. Jones was among those summoned to Washington, D.C., to report for duty in the Office of the Assistant Chief of Staff, G-3, in 1941. On Christmas Eve of that year, just over 2 weeks after the United States had officially entered the war, Jones pinned on the eagles of a full colonel.[11]

By April 1942, COL Jones had transferred from the Army Staff to General Lesley J. McNair's Army Ground Forces Command, located in Washington, D.C. Next to Marshall, McNair had the greatest impact on the creation of the American Army that fought World War II. The "triangular" division organization, standardization of like units, "pooling" of assets (such as artillery), and nearly complete motorization of army units were all McNair innovations.[12] Jones was fortunate to serve under McNair at a time of such change and must have learned many valuable lessons from the association. It must be assumed that McNair was also suitably impressed with Jones' performance, because Jones gained the single star of a brigadier general barely 6 months after his promotion to colonel.[13]

Jones could now reflect on his quarter-century of Army service with justifiable pride in achieving the top levels of his chosen profession. He had much in common with other soon-to-be famous infantrymen like Eisenhower and Bradley. They had all missed out on combat in World War I but shared similar schooling and career assignments, such as duty in the Philippines and Army Staff G-3 (Eisenhower) and Fort Benning's Infantry School and Hawaii (Bradley).

His preparation to meet the challenges he would face on the battlefield, so much like that of his near-contemporaries, would seem in retrospect to suggest that he, like them, would succeed in the test of battle.[14] But the cruel circumstances of combat following hard on the heels of stateside decimation of his division for replacements would single out Jones for disaster.

THE 106TH DIVISION

General Jones continued to progress in rank and responsibility through the next few months in the rapidly expanding Army. He was appointed Assistant Division Commander of the 90th Infantry Division and was clearly being trained and groomed (and evaluated) for higher command. He held the assistant position until January 1943, when he was entrusted with the post that all his contemporaries strove to achieve--command of a combat division. Jones took command of the 106th Infantry Division at Fort Jackson, SC, in January, and on 16 March 1943 received his promotion to major general.[15]

Units comprising the 106th Division began arriving at Ft. Jackson, SC, on 29 November 1942, and it was formally activated on 15 March 1943. Its components came from all the various branches to Fort Jackson to complete a rigorous and comprehensive training program that would take the better part of 2 years. General Jones led the unit and trained it hard to prepare for combat in Europe. In the unit's history, *St.-Vith: Lion in the Way*, Colonel R. Ernest Dupuy explained the purpose of the training:

> The theory was that each of these new divisions would begin and end as homogeneous groups--recruits brought in around a hard core, called a cadre, gathered from already trained units. The training, laid down by Army Ground Forces, would be progressive from the beginning, balanced and coordinated, to the end that when each division moved to the battle front it would be a team. Its officers and men would know one another, would know their business. The only thing lacking would be that first thirty minutes of combat....[16]

After nearly 2 years of diligent training (including participating in the Second Army maneuvers in Tennessee in early 1944), the 106th Infantry Division became a reasonably well-trained outfit of 708 officers, 42 warrant officers, and 12,523 enlisted men.[17] The division had demonstrated it could operate effectively as a combat team, and small-unit leaders among the soldiers had been identified and placed in key positions. The unit was nearly ready to enter combat. Jones must have been confident of his unit's ability to perform its job on the battlefield with the team he had trained. In April 1944, however, after the unit had completed the Second Army maneuvers and moved to Camp Atterbury, IN, it was picked apart.

Thousands of Jones' men were reassigned out of the division, primarily because of mounting casualty lists in the European fighting. The manpower crisis was also, indirectly, a result of such things as the huge Army Service Forces structure, the decision to limit the number of ground combat divisions (vice the air effort, for example), and the suspicion of planners that the war was winding down.[18] In April, 3,100 enlisted men were ordered out of the 106th and shipped overseas. By August 1944, a total of 7,247 had been shipped out. To make matters worse, most of the infantrymen taken from Jones were the aggressive, capable small unit leaders occupying key positions—the very men a trained unit can least afford to lose and still maintain combat efficiency.[19]

Regardless of how well trained a unit is, it cannot lose over 60 percent of its best and brightest and retain a high level of combat efficiency. By the time the 106th moved to Massachusetts and its port of embarkation in October 1944, it had regained its full number strength by transfers from the Army Air Forces, Specialized Training Program, Army Service Forces, and other noninfantry fields, but the division could in no way quickly make up for the staggering loss of trained, key infantrymen. Nevertheless, the war would not wait on the 106th to retrain itself, so the division shipped out for the European Theater in mid-October. General Jones collected his rebuilt division in England at the end of October, and he and the division staff began to oversee the unit's drawing of equipment in preparation for the impending movement to combat.[20]

Drawing equipment was about all the 106th had time to do before beginning its shift to the combat zone on 1 and 2 December 1944. Winter conditions on the English Channel were unpleasant and made worse by having to endure several shipboard days either crossing or waiting on storm-tossed troopships around the Channel ports before disembarking. Once they finally landed, troops still had to contend with the bone-jarring trip to the front in Belgium in wet, freezing weather. Dupuy describes the miserable conditions:

> Days of rain, snow and mud; days of misery for the men packed in trucks as they rumbled through France and into Belgium, were prelude for the 106th's entry into battle. Inability to change clothing or footgear sopping and soggy

with icy water is not conducive to the joy of living. When such things precede the vital test, when the discomfort and misery are added to the uncertainty of battle, the men undergoing them must be of tempered caliber, men so inured to the rigors of discipline they subordinate personal matters for teamwork. And the combat teams of the 106th, unfortunately, were not yet of that caliber; the Division was paying for the frequent drain on it for replacements, with constant influx of new personnel.[21]

Awaiting the officers and men of the 106th was the ominously quiet section of the Allied line referred to as the "Ghost Front" by those combat-weary soldiers who were manning it. If it lived up to its name, it might be just the place for the new unit filled with new replacements to learn the ropes and ease itself into combat. Jones must have hoped so as his unit was trucked wearily toward the weakest part of the entire line.

The "Golden Lions" of the 106th Infantry Division began taking over the 22-mile wide section of the Ardennes front from the veteran 2nd Infantry Division on 10 December, accomplishing most of the handover on 11 December in accordance with the VIII Corps Letter of Instruction. Although the third and final infantry regiment (the 424th) did not complete its occupation of the southernmost part of the division sector until 12 December, Jones assumed responsibility for the area at 1900 hours, 11 December 1944.[22] He had barely 4 days before the main effort of the German attack slammed into his green, untried unit.

CLARKE'S CAREER

THE BEGINNINGS

Bruce C. Clarke's path to the crossroads at St.-Vith differed in many ways from that Jones had followed. Clarke was several years younger, a former enlisted soldier, West Point graduate, and engineer-turned-tanker. Perhaps most important, he had fought his way across the battlefields of France to reach the beleaguered Belgian town. In the critical early hours of the fight to hold St.-Vith, Clarke's combat leadership (and Jones' inexperience) would prove decisive.

In 1918, the year after Alan Jones was commissioned an infantry lieutenant out of college, the 17-year-old Clarke sought out a recruiting sergeant in Watertown, NY, and enlisted in the US Army.[23] The former farmboy signed enlistment papers and drew his first uniform at Fort Slocum, NY, in April 1918. Eager to see combat before the war ended, Clarke must have been disappointed that he remained in the United States in training for the final few months of the war.[24] This taste of military life seemed to please him, however, for Clarke retained a military connection after he was mustered out of the Regular Army:

> I had been an enlisted man in the Army in 1918, long enough to complete basic training. In 1920, I joined a New York National Guard artillery battalion in Buffalo, New York (the 106th Field Artillery Battalion). I rose to Corporal. From there I applied to take the competitive exam of the National Guard for West Point. I passed and entered on July 1, 1921 in the Class of 1925.[25]

Clarke did well at West Point, both academically and militarily, serving in cadet leadership positions in 3 of his 4 years there. Almost as soon as his Plebe (freshman) year was completed, Clarke was chosen a Cadet Corporal and served in that rank for the next 2 years. In his final year, he was a Cadet Captain and company commander--among the highest-ranking cadets in his class. He progressed well enough to tutor some of his classmates who were having problems, and he graduated high enough (33 of 248) to earn his first choice of branch. Clarke chose the Corps of Engineers and was commissioned in that branch on graduation day, 12 June 1925.[26]

Newly commissioned (and newly wed) 2LT Clarke reported to the 29th Engineer Topographic Battalion at Fort Humphreys, near Washington, D.C., and assumed duties as a platoon leader. He spent the next year learning the responsibilities of a small-unit leader and familiarizing himself with the tools and equipment of a junior officer in the Engineers.[27] More importantly, Lieutenant Clarke began in earnest a study of leadership, commandership, and soldiership, which became a consuming passion for the rest of his life. Beginning here and continuing through each successive unit, Clarke turned his assignments into "leadership laboratories" in which he tested his ideas on leadership and commandership and sought to draw lessons for improvement in his next unit. He wrote later of these early experiences and some of the lessons he learned about small unit leadership:

> I had fixed in my mind...principles in handling men. Many years ago I wrote we cannot produce outstanding units from the ordinary run of personnel unless we train, coach, and develop our squad leaders, platoon sergeants and platoon leaders to look well after the men in their units and mold them into proud and winning teams under the direction of good commandership from above...The key words are *teams* and *motivation*.[28]

Clarke must have impressed his superiors with his early performance, for after only a year in his first army unit he was selected to attend Cornell University and complete a degree in civil engineering. He accomplished that academic mission and returned to the military post in summer 1927. For the remainder of that summer Clarke commanded the Engineer School Colored Detachment, then attended the Engineer Officer's Advanced Course. He remained on post after completing the Advanced Course, and returned for duty in his old unit, the "29th Topo" through 1928 and into 1929. LT Clarke's next posting was to the 3rd Engineer Regiment in Schofield Barracks, HI.[29]

In Hawaii, Clarke mixed "line" duties as a platoon leader, with one of the few staff assignments of his career during the 3-year tour in the islands. He served for a time as the regimental supply officer of his engineer regiment, but predictably, the lessons he carried with him from Hawaii continued to be those of leading and motivating soldiers. In 1932, he witnessed an example of "motivation" for the unit's annual qualification rifle range in which the company first sergeant won the top award (and the lion's share of $85 from the company fund). Clarke wondered how such a system motivated the "Bolos" (soldiers who shot so poorly they failed to qualify with their weapon). He wrote later about this:

> Awards that motivate only the top men are of little value in raising the ability of a unit. It takes awards to motivate the lower third to do that. A unit is measured by the ability of the lower third personnel in it to carry their part of the load.[30]

Upon his return from Hawaii, Clarke became the junior member of the Reserve Officer Training Corps (ROTC) detachment at the University of Tennessee. Because ROTC duty was commonplace among the officers in the pre-World War II army, assignments of 4 years or even longer to civilian schools was not uncommon. So, like many others, including Bradley and Middleton, Clarke took up his post as assistant professor of military science and tactics.[31]

In addition to his military duties, which included serving as the detachment's adjutant and administrative officer, Clarke refereed football games, coached the university wrestling team, and in his spare time studied for and obtained a law degree from LaSalle Extension University. He recorded later that, although he had no intention of practicing law, the LL.B. "balanced my education."[32]

After 4 years of ROTC duty, Clarke was ordered to the Galveston Engineer District on the Texas coast in 1936. Clarke continued to perform in an outstanding manner, putting his civil engineering training to work. He described his duties:

> I was...in charge of surveying the rivers of Texas for Congress for navigation, flood control, water power and water conservation. I created a new organization of 50 professional engineers, surveyors, draftsmen and field crews covering practically the whole state of Texas. During the next three years we submitted over 40 reports to Congress on Texas.[33]

Although Clarke (now captain) had been away from a troop assignment for 7 years, his record must have been viewed as superior by engineer branch, for he was selected to attend the Command and General Staff School in 1939. His was to be the last class until after WWII. When CPT Clarke reported to Fort Leavenworth to begin the Staff School, the standard 9-month course of instruction was in effect. However, with Europe at war and Marshall frantically trying to retrieve the American Army from decades of unpreparedness and neglect, Clarke's class was cut to 5 months, and the Staff School, closed for the duration of the war. On 1 February 1940, Clarke graduated. It was the last Army school he ever attended.[34]

Clarke's next assignment was the most important one of his career because it began his association with the branch in which he would achieve his greatest successes and in which he would make his greatest battlefield contributions. Clarke was assigned to Brigadier General Adna R. Chaffee's newly formed 7th Mechanized Brigade at Fort Knox, KY. His association with the fledgling US Armored Force had begun.

Clarke was ordered to organize the 47th Engineer Troop (Mechanized) and serve also as Brigadier General Chaffee's brigade engineer in this largely experimental armored brigade. By April 1940, Clarke's troop of two lieutenants and 91 enlisted engineers was in Louisiana with Chaffee's 7th Mechanized Brigade conducting war game maneuvers against the 1st Infantry Tank Brigade from Fort Benning, GA.[35] Much rode on the outcome of these maneuvers, for a separate American armored force was still only an idea of visionaries like Chaffee. The infantry still officially owned all the tanks.

The result of the maneuvers was a smashing victory for Chaffee's armored brigade, validating his theories. No small part of the victory was due to Clarke's innovative and creative use of his engineer troop. He demonstrated to Chaffee that he understood perfectly the aggressive, slashing tactics that a powerful armored force could use to overwhelm a less mobile enemy—the same tactics the Germans were unleashing against the Anglo-French forces.[36] On 1 July 1940, Chief of Staff Marshall officially created the American armored force and activated the 1st and 2nd Armored

Divisions. For the armored force engineer, Chaffee chose
Clarke.[37]

Clarke, still a junior officer, was actually the "acting"
armored force engineer, commander of the 1st Armored
Division's 16th Armored Engineer Battalion, and division
engineer. Eventually, senior officers would arrive to bump
Clarke out of these jobs requiring higher rank. Before this
happened, Chaffee appointed Clarke to serve on the board
that developed the first Table of Organization and
Equipment for the armored division. Chaffee's guidance was
that the armored division be "a balanced team of combat
arms and services...of equal importance and equal
prestige"[38]—good guidance, since the eventual result was the
versatile, mobile, yet powerful armored divisions that led the
race across France and the battlefields of Europe in 1944 and
1945.

With the outbreak of real war in Europe, events
proceeded at a fast pace. Clarke listed his duties and
assignments over the next year and a half:

> Follow[ing] in rapid order was duty as Armored Force
> Engineer; Commanding Officer of 16th Engineer Battalion,
> 1st Armored Division; official observer with the British 1st
> Armoured Division that had come out of Dunkirk; orders
> to Pine Camp [New York] to create the 24th Armored
> Engineer Battalion [4th Armored Division]; Chief of Staff,
> 4th Armored Division during Major General (Henry W.)
> Baird's and Major General [John S.] "P" Wood's time as
> Division Commanders...I went from Captain in February
> 1940 to Major, Lieutenant Colonel and Colonel on 1
> February 1942—a two year period.[39]

The unit Clarke helped prepare for war in the pine
barrens of New York was to become one of the most famous
of the entire war in the European Theater of Operations.
Once it was unleashed on the Germans after the Normandy
breakout, it led the way in the Allied race across France. In
the process, the 4th Armored Division helped create the
legend of George Patton as a genius of armored warfare.
Commanding the vanguard and leading the way was COL
Clarke.[40]

THE 4TH AND 7TH ARMORED DIVISIONS

For more than 2 years, the 4th Armored Division had trained long and hard in the snows of Pine Camp, at the blistering Mojave Desert Training Center and the proving ground of the Tennessee maneuvers. Under its aggressive, dynamic commander, Major General John S. "P" Wood, the division was molded into a superb fighting organization. Unlike the unfortunate 106th Infantry Division, the 4th Armored was not picked apart to provide replacements, and it entered combat as a well-trained team of men who had been working together for many months.[41] Clarke had helped oversee the long months of training as the division Chief of Staff. In that position, he learned much about leadership, commandership, training and morale from Wood (and his predecessor Baird). As the division entered combat, Clarke took command of one of its principal fighting elements, Combat Command A. He would lead its triumvirate of tanks, artillery, and armored infantry from Normandy to Lorraine in an American blitzkrieg of unequalled power and mobility.[42]

Clarke's commander, "P" Wood, was a big, athletic, inspirational leader whose enthusiasm and drive seemed almost limitless. Wood established himself as one of the premiere division commanders in Europe as he drove the 4th Armored Division farther and faster than anyone thought possible once the St.-Lô breakout sprung his unit from the hedgerows of Normandy. The division's official history describes the unit's operating mode:

> Under General Wood, the Fourth Armored's style of fighting was set...It was a daring, hardriding, fast shooting style. The division's front was as wide as the roads down which it sped. The recon men out front kept going until they hit resistance too hot to handle. Teams of tanks and armored infantrymen swung out smoothly in attack formation under the protective fire of the quickly emplaced artillery. The division broke the enemy or flowed about them, cutting the German lines of communication and splitting apart the units.[43]

In the lead was Clarke and the soldiers of Combat Command A. Although the division's race across France was initially delayed by a brief (and ultimately futile) diversion west into Brittany in an attempt to capture intact some badly needed port facilities, by early August Wood had Clarke and the rest headed east.[44] Within the month, Clarke had driven his command across the Seine and had closed up on the Moselle River at Commercy. The rapid advance had covered about 1,000 miles. The 4th Armored sent 11,000 German prisoners to the rear, losing about 1,100 of its own from all causes.[45] Unfortunately, by the end of August, all along the Allied line, fuel supplies dried up because the advance had been so successful. By supreme effort, including the phenomenally successful "Red Ball Highway," a few days later supplies of fuel flowed once again. Unfortunately, the brief respite gave the Germans enough time to regain their balance and stiffen their defenses by the time the 4th Armored, including Clarke's Combat Command A, began to roll.[46] Clarke's objective was to cross the Moselle River and cut off the German forces holding out in the fortress city of Nancy. He succeeded in a smashing victory for Combat Command A and the rest of the 4th Armored. Clarke later referred to the encirclement of Nancy, including the subsequent tank battles in the vicinity near Arracourt, as his "greatest victory"[47] (despite his much-heralded success later at St.-Vith). Indeed, the operations of Clarke's Combat Command A, the 4th Armored, and its parent unit, the XII Corps, around Nancy and Arracourt are still studied at the Command and General Staff College as early examples demonstrating the principles of modern airland battle maneuver warfare. This is a lasting tribute not only to Clarke's skill as an armored warfare tactician but also to his demonstrated battle commandership.[48]

Of importance to this study is the way the conduct of the fighting around Arracourt resembled the later German attacks (and Clarke's defense) at St.-Vith. A study prepared by CGSC's Combat Studies Institute describes that fighting:

The Fifth Panzer Army...bypassed Lunéville and was moving north to strike at CC'A's exposed position around

Arracourt. The battle that resulted was one of the largest armored engagements ever fought on the Western Front...CC'A' held Arracourt with an extended tank infantry engineer outpost line supported by tanks, tank destroyers and artillery. At 0800 on 19 September [1944], company sized elements of the 113th Panzer Brigade penetrated the outposts...of CC'A's salient. Two tank destroyer platoons and a medium tank company engaged the panzers in a running fight that extended into the vicinity of CC'A's headquarters where a battalion of self-propelled 105-mm howitzers took the panzers under point-blank fire. The Germans discovered that the fog, which gave them tactical surprise and protected them from U.S. aircraft, worked to their disadvantage by negating the superior range of their tank guns. As the fighting surged back and forth through the fog, CC'A's tank and tank destroyers utilized their mobility to outmaneuver and ambush the large panzers...Colonel Clarke unleashed two medium tank companies on a sweep that took the panzers in flank and rear...According to the Germans, the panzer assault..cost them fifty precious tanks and accomplished nothing....From 20 to 25 September, the Fifth Panzer Army fed the 111th Panzer Brigade and the understrength 11th Panzer Division into a series of attacks against the Arracourt position. Each assault followed the pattern set on 19 September. The panzers attacked under the cover of fog only to be disorganized by CC'A's mobile defense.[49]

The account reads like a dress rehearsal of the later fighting at St.-Vith. The weather, tactics, equipment, and even the enemy unit involved, the 5th Panzer Army, commanded by General von Manteuffel, were the same or similar to the later, larger battle in the Ardennes. The outcomes were also similar, as the Americans scored a great success against the attackers. The entire 4th Armored Division, including Clarke's Combat Command A, which bore the brunt of the fighting, toted up an impressive 281 German tanks destroyed, 3,000 enemy killed, and another 3,000 taken prisoner against 626 friendly casualties.[50] Clarke was clearly doing exceptionally well in this particular "leadership laboratory."

Although Clarke had ably demonstrated his readiness for

a promotion by his superb battlefield performance, he would have to leave the 4th Armored in order to receive it. Armored divisions were allotted one brigadier general and one major general (the division commander). The 4th already had their brigadier general, Holmes Dager (commanding Combat Command B). Clarke was reassigned to another armored division where he could receive the star he had earned. On 1 November 1944, Clarke reported to the 7th Armored Division, a part of General William Simpson's Ninth Army in Holland, as the new commander of Combat Command B—a unit that was having problems.[51] As Clarke said, "The 7th Armored Division was in bad shape on 1 November 1944."[52]

Reflecting in the third person in postwar memoirs, he went on to describe what confronted him and his old friend, the also newly appointed division commander, Brigadier General Robert Hasbrouck, as they arrived at the 7th Armored:

> When Clarke went from the 4th Armored Division to the 7th Armored Division on 1 November 1944, General Hasbrouck and he replaced generals who were relieved, reduced to Colonel, and ordered home. They found a division that had been under the command of a former infantry officer who did not understand [the correct] employment of armored forces. He had three fixed combat commands. Their composition never changed. All three were normally engaged in the classic "two up, one back" formation. There was little flexibility and the battalions were inadequately maintained, physically and mentally depleted, and about 50 percent effective.[53]

Hasbrouck and Clarke reorganized the unit along the proper lines, making it a flexible, mobile organization like the 4th. They initiated an intensive training program to instill confidence and competence into the leadership at all levels. There was nothing wrong with the soldiers in the 7th, but the unit as a whole had suffered from poor "generalship and commandership" from the top. After 6 weeks of intensive training, Clarke and Hasbrouck were beginning to see some positive results. Clarke's promotion to general finally arrived on 7 December 1944,[54] 9 days before the Ardennes attack.

ATTACK AT ST.-VITH

As newly promoted BG Clarke continued to train Combat Command B, 7th Armored Division, in Holland and mold it into an effective fighting force, Jones was attempting much the same thing with his 106th Infantry Division in Belgium (appendix H). But while Clarke had nearly 6 months of recent combat leadership to draw upon, Jones had none. In fact, none of Jones' subordinate unit senior commanders had any worthwhile recent combat experience.[55] Further, while Clarke had 6 weeks to work with the 7th while it sat out of the combat line, Jones had only 4 days to season his troops as they manned a huge sector in the Ardennes front. This woefully inadequate period of preparation, so closely following the long and tiring journey across the Atlantic, the Channel, and then Belgium left Jones' division obviously unprepared for the German attack in mid-December.

The 106th Division's sector was probably the most difficult to defend of all sectors in Middleton's over-extended VIII Corps line. Impossibly wide for a single division to defend, it meandered for some 22 miles along the broken terrain of the German-Belgian border. Although his right (southern) flank rested in a somewhat defensible area of "innumerable watercourses" and "jumbled hills" near the 28th Infantry Division's positions, Jones' left (northern) flank abutted the V Corps-VIII Corps boundary in the Losheim Gap, the region's classic invasion route.[56] To his front, Jones was constrained to place the bulk of his combat power on the high plateau of the Schnee Eifel, with those particular positions extending into the Siegfried Line.[57]

To defend what amounted to an 8-mile deep, 22-mile wide salient into the German lines, Jones had the following: an infantry division of nine battalions of riflemen; two squadrons of cavalry (the attached 14th Cavalry Group); five battalions of field artillery; one battalion of tank destroyers; one battalion of antiaircraft artillery; and (potentially) the fires of nine battalions of VIII Corps field artillery units that were in the vicinity. In all, Jones had about 14,000 of his own soldiers, to which he added about 1,000 cavalrymen and another 1,200 or so from the tank destroyers, anti-aircraft artillery, and other attached support troops.[58] Given the extent of the sector, this total of approximately 16,000 troops was hardly a formidable force.

Jones' headquarters was in a school in the town of St.-Vith itself. Described as "an average Belgian town, with a population of a little over 2,000,"[59] it had sufficient billets to hold a division headquarters and associated support troops. More importantly, it sat at the center of a road net that tied together the roads that ran around the barrier of the Schnee Eifel plateau 12 miles to the east. Six roads crossed at the St.-Vith hub, then connected to the road nets running to the north (Malmedy), south (Bastogne), and west (Vielsalm). Like Bastogne, 25 miles to the south, St.-Vith constituted a major chokepoint for any attack through the Ardennes[60]—that is, if it could be successfully defended.

Jones may have been lacking in combat experience, but he knew enough to be uncomfortable with the defensive positions his units had been obliged to take up. The 106th had been ordered to relieve the 2nd Infantry Division in place, occupying each of the 2nd's pillboxes and positions. The bulk of Jones' combat power, the 422nd and 423rd Infantry Regiments, held these positions. They were too exposed for Jones' liking, because a determined German thrust to either flank of the plateau could put the two regiments in danger of being surrounded and cut off.[61] Jones' superior, Middleton, didn't like the exposed positions on the Schnee Eifel for the same reasons and felt the same; in fact, on his own initiative had earlier withdrawn units of the 2nd Infantry Division from some of the most exposed of the Siegfried Line positions and had the pillboxes destroyed.[62] Nevertheless, most of the positions on the plateau remained, now manned by Jones' men.

The 4 days prior to the launching of the German offensive were relatively quiet ones in the 106th Division's sector. The unit After Action Report describes the division's activities for each of the days in three short sentences. Typical is this entry for 13 December 1944:

Defensive positions maintained and improved in all sectors. Enemy activity during period consisted of artillery fire and minor patrol activity. Seven infantry battalions and one squadron of cavalry [reinforced] engaged during period.[63]

But if the lack of significant enemy activity lulled Jones and his unit into thinking the so-called "Ghost Front" would mercifully live up to its name, they soon lost this illusion.

16 DECEMBER

At 0530 hours on 16 December, US artillery forward observers looked east as "the whole horizon erupted" before their eyes. For 45 minutes, nearly 2,000 artillery pieces and mortars of all types and calibers (up to giant 14-in guns) kept up a sustained barrage that blasted front line positions, interdicted road junctions, and cut wire lines between headquarters and forward units.[64] All along the 80-mile Ardennes front, units were pounded with tons of shells in preparation for the German assault. Before the guns had stopped their barrage, German infantry, supported by panzers, advanced against the American positions.

Despite many of the wire lines being cut, the 106th headquarters received enough reports of ground action to indicate the attack was a general assault all along their over-extended line. The 422nd and 423rd Regiments both reported enemy attacks early in the day, and the lightly armed cavalry troops of the 14th Cavalry Group in the Losheim Gap were being pushed back by spirited attacks.[65] Some of the 14-in shells fell in St.-Vith, and while they did little damage, they helped lend credence to the subordinate units' battle reports.[66]

Jones' headquarters, which had barely had time to establish itself as a functioning division command entity since it arrived in St.-Vith, must have quickly become overwhelmed by the countless reports of numerous German attacks on virtually all of its deployed units throughout the morning hours of that first day. Nevertheless, Jones and his staff reacted to the increasing number of assaults by ordering units from the division's meager reserve forces to each of the threatened areas and by keeping Middleton and the VIII Corps staff informed of the developing (and deteriorating) situation.

By 1145 hours, one of the 424th's battalions in division reserve had been released to the regiment to help hold its line, and at 1200 hours one of the division's engineer companies had to be committed as infantry to block further penetrations of the 423rd's sector. Jones threw in most of the rest of his reserve forces later in the afternoon as other areas were threatened. The 422nd committed its regimental reserve in the morning but needed help from the division reserve by 1700 hours.[67] The 32nd Reconnaissance Squadron was brought up from group reserve to help the hard-pressed 14th Cavalry Group, which was quickly "unravelling."[68]

Middleton, Jones' boss, tried to help his subordinate when it became obvious that the German assault was a serious threat, but even the corps commander had few assets in reserve to influence the action. He released a large portion of his precious armored reserve at 1120 hours that morning when he assigned Combat Command B, 9th Armored Division, to the 106th. But the badly needed armored combat command, still at Faymonville in the V Corps sector to the north, would take several hours to reach St.-Vith.[69] Nevertheless, Jones set his staff to work developing a counterattack plan using this unit.[70] He would use it, of course, to try to keep his two regiments on the plateau from being surrounded. The immediate question facing Jones, however, was whether to pull back those two regiments and their supporting units while he still could.

This was the single most important question Jones would address in his entire career, and his decision would decide the ultimate fate of his unit. The combat inexperienced Jones received scant help in making his decision from his battle-hardened corps commander, Middleton. Instead of _ordering_ Jones to withdraw the bulk of his division from the exposed positions, Middleton left the final decision to his new subordinate. After a confusing and controversial phone conversation on the evening of 16 December, each man thought the other had agreed to just the opposite course of action—Middleton thought Jones was pulling the units back, but Jones believed his corps commander had approved his decision to leave them in place. This disaster was nearly catastrophic for the entire American defense of the Ardennes, for Jones had made the wrong decision. By leaving the units in place, he destroyed his division.[71]

17 DECEMBER

Jones' decision to keep the units in place on the plateau may have rested on his expectation of an early morning arrival of Combat Command B, 7th Armored (appendix I), on 17 December. He hoped to use the tanks and armored infantry to keep the roads to the east open and therefore keep the Germans out of St.-Vith.[72] But when the 7th Armored had not arrived by 0930 hours, 17 December, Jones had to take some action to stop the enemy from rapidly closing on the St.-Vith hub. Like Middleton was doing at Bastogne, Jones turned to his only remaining reserve force—combat engineers.

Jones and his staff gave the mission of delaying the enemy and defending St.-Vith to Lieutenant Colonel Tom Riggs, the big, ex-football star from the University of Illinois who commanded the 81st Engineer Combat Battalion--the 106th's division engineer unit. Riggs described how he received his critical mission:

> My orders to command a task force for the defense of St.-Vith were issued by Maj. Gen. Jones in the division CP at about 0930 on 17 December. We had just finished a division staff meeting focused on the lack of any resistance to the German advance in the northern sector defended by the 14th Cav. Gp. A German tank and infantry force was reported to be moving west on the Schoenberg-St.-Vith road. Col. Baker, chief of staff of the 106th, helped to designate and notify the attachment to the task force of [VIII] corps units: 168 Engr. Cbt Bn. and a platoon from the 820 Tank Destroyer Battalion.[73]

By dispatching Riggs' patchwork force (it included the division's band) to defend the approaches to St.-Vith, Jones (described at this time by Riggs as "an increasingly frustrated man") had fortunately taken the correct action to prevent the hard-pressed crossroads from being overrun. Riggs' force was completely destroyed over the next few days, but it kept the enemy out of St.-Vith during the critical hours before help arrived.[74]

While Jones was desperately trying to assess the overall situation and do what he could to patch up his punctured front, events were occurring elsewhere that would ultimately prevent the destruction of the 106th Division from destroying the overall defense. As Jones and his staff tried to keep their heads and react appropriately in the unfamiliarity of combat and the chaos of the overwhelming attack, Eisenhower had assessed the situation and concluded that Middleton needed help. He alerted the 7th Armored Division to move to the Ardennes to give Alan Jones some much needed (and combat-experienced) assistance.

On the evening of 16 December, Clarke was about to start out on a much-deserved rest trip to Paris when his division commander contacted him from the command post. Clarke later recalled what happened:

> At 2000 I received a telephone call from General Robert W. Hasbrouck, Commanding General, 7th Armored Division, saying that the division had received orders to march immediately south to Bastogne to report to the Commanding General of the VIII Corps. What we were to do when we got to Bastogne was unknown. He told me that the division would march as soon as road clearances could be obtained. General Hasbrouck directed that I proceed immediately to Bastogne and report to [General Middleton] to get information on the situation. My combat command would lead the division on its march of 60 to 70 miles south.[75]

Clarke grabbed his Operations Officer, Major Owen Woodruff, and set off immediately with two enlisted drivers.

The trip south to the VIII Corps headquarters at Bastogne was a miserable one in the fog over icy roads, but at 0400 hours the next morning, 17 December, Clarke found the VIII Corps Commander calmly reading in his headquarters van at Bastogne.[76] Middleton then made his greatest single contribution to the defense of St.-Vith when he calmly told Clarke, "Alan Jones is having some trouble at St.-Vith--grab something to eat and a little sleep and go to him...if he needs help give it to him."[77] By dispatching the 7th Armored to bolster Jones, Middleton ensured the vital crossroads would become a chokepoint for the German drive and not a funnel into the Allied rear.

The situation in the 106th's area was growing worse by the minute as Middleton spoke with Clarke, but the corps commander's natural calmness and understated directive failed to convey the true situation to the armored commander. Clarke, who arrived at St.-Vith about 1030 hours, was appalled to find that confusion and chaos were rampant within Jones' headquarters staff.[78] As Clarke sought out Jones to learn what was happening, he directed Woodruff to find out all he could from the 106th's staff. Years later Woodruff described the panicked situation:

> The 106th Division Headquarters was set up in a school building in St.-Vith. I was told the G-3 section was located on the top [3rd] floor of the building. [Clarke] told me to find out what the situation was while [he] conferred with General Jones. Unfortunately, as I was going up the stairs to the 3rd floor the G-3 section was coming down the stairs with bits and pieces of their equipment. The room that had contained the operation maps and other paraphernalia...was disintegrating. The operations sergeant was busy burning classified documents and otherwise destroying the maps with their acetate covers. I asked him what they were doing and he said something about the Germans are almost here and we are getting out. I tried to talk to anyone who would stand still long enough to answer a question...I never found anyone from the G-2 section to talk to...the net result of this chaos was my failure to obtain any detailed information and I never was able to find a map with troop dispositions...We acquired little or nothing in the way of information from the 106th Division staff.[79]

Meanwhile, Clarke had found Jones in his office, told him who he was, and asked to be briefed on the situation as it was known.   Jones seemed extremely agitated and apprehensive, especially since his son, Lieutenant Alan Jones, Jr., was serving as a staff officer in one of the cutoff regiments.[80] When Jones told Clarke as much as he knew—a major German attack had surrounded his two regiments on the Schnee Eifel and was pressing in on St.-Vith from three sides—the armored commander knew it was a "serious breakthrough." Clarke also concluded that the 106th's overall knowledge of the situation (both enemy and friendly) was "very hazy."[81]

Jones urged Clarke to attack to the east to relieve his cutoff troops, but when Clarke asked to speak to the surrounded commanders to coordinate the operation, the division commander said he couldn't reach them by wire or radio (although intermittent radio contact was maintained until nearly the end).[82] Jones and his staff had also neglected to appoint one overall commander for the two surrounded regiments; this would not only make it difficult to work with them from the point of view of any counterattack, but would also plague the efforts of the units themselves to coordinate their attempts to break out on their own. Moreover, the 106th had prepared no counterattack plan, offering the weak excuse that the VIII Corps had not issued its directive to prepare one until the day before the German assault[83]—not a convincing excuse from a unit that had expressed grave concern over its exposed regiments since the day it took over its sector. Earlier, on 16 December, the 106th staff had begun to plan a counterattack using Combat Command B, 9th Armored, after that unit was attached to them that day, but instead sent the 9th's tankers to the southern part of the 106th's sector on the mistaken belief the 7th Armored was arriving early on 17 December.[84] Judging from the 106th staff's chaotic state when Clarke arrived, it seems unlikely that they would have been able to coordinate a successful counterattack for the 9th Armored late on 16 or early 17 December even if they had tried.

It soon became painfully evident to Clarke that the 106th couldn't maintain enough control of the panicked traffic on its roads even to ensure the rapid arrival of Clarke's desperately needed combat command. Clarke's Combat Command B, 7th Armored, was inching its way over narrow roads clogged with fleeing vehicles in an agonizingly slow crawl towards St.-Vith. It began to look as if the rapidly advancing German columns from the east would arrive at St.-Vith before the tankers and armored infantrymen could force their way into town from the west.[85]

As Jones' staff continued to pack up and move their operation westward, the 106th Division commander remained in his office, fretting over the impossible predicament his unit found itself in, but seeming to exercise little control over any efforts to salvage the situation. Clarke said that he never observed anyone from Jones' staff (including Colonel Baker, his Chief of Staff) make any attempt to contact Jones for instructions, directives, or advice, nor did he notice that Jones called for any staff officer. Clarke remembered that, "General Jones was apparently in a state of apprehension, and he kept remarking...about his son who was a Lieutenant in one of the surrounded battle groups (regiments). It, of course, bothered him."[86]

At about 1300 hours Clarke witnessed an incident upsetting to him. Jones received a call from his corps commander, Middleton, inquiring as to the situation in St.-Vith. As the shocked armored commander listened in disbelief, Jones told his superior that, "in general, things are looking up...Clarke is here [and] has troops coming...We are going to be all right." After he had hung up, Clarke confronted Jones to ask him why he had not told his corps commander the truth about the situation. Jones explained, "General Middleton had enough troubles already."[87] To Clarke this deliberate misrepresentation of the actual situation was inexcusable, whatever its motivation and regardless of how upset Jones was over the plight of his division and his son.

The two men continued their vigil in Jones' office, awaiting the arrival of Clarke's troops and hoping the fresh tanks and troops would get there before the Germans. These troops were still on the road from Vielsalm, pushing eastward against the tide of fleeing vehicles surging west. Around 1400 hours, hearing "what seemed like small arms firing from the east"[88] the two commanders went to the third

floor to investigate. From that vantage point they thought
they could detect German soldiers coming out of the woods
to the East. This seemed to be the last straw for Jones. As
Clarke reported, Jones turned to him and said, "You take
command, I'll give you all I have."[89] It was then that Jones
made his sardonic quip that he'd set a record for "losing a
division quicker than any commander in the US Army."[90]
Jones quit his responsibilities at 1430 hours on 17 December
and, according to Clarke "apparently his headquarters had
quit before that."[91] Alan Jones' attempts to influence the
outcome of the defense of St.-Vith and save his overwhelmed
unit thus ended in chaos and despair. Bruce Clarke now
assumed that mission, and the odds appeared poor.

LEADERSHIP IN A MOBILE DEFENSE

The situation confronting Clarke at 1430 hours on the
afternoon of 17 December 1944 was discouraging from the
armored commander's point of view. He had precious little
armor and very few other troops to command, let alone to
lead on a successful defense of the St.-Vith crossroads. On
his left flank (north), the 14th Cavalry Group was being
scattered by overpowering panzer and grenadier assaults. To
his front, the bulk of the 106th Division (two regiments) was
surrounded on the Schnee Eifel plateau with little prospect
of a successful breakout. The right flank (south), defended
by the 106th's remaining infantry regiment (the 424th
Infantry) supported by Bill Hoge's Combat Command B, 9th
Armored, was only in slightly better shape[92] but it soon got
a boost from the 112th Infantry Regiment of the 28th
Infantry Division when that unit was pushed into the St.-
Vith area by the force of the German thrust toward
Bastogne.[93] Protecting the immediate approaches to St.-Vith
was Tom Riggs' pathetically small force of combat engineers,
bandsmen, and other support troops. It seemed unlikely that
the hard-pressed engineer officer could keep the Germans
out of town much longer.

Clarke could expect no staff support from the 106th
division to help him control the battle, as Jones' staff was
scurrying westward. Even Clarke's operations officer, Major
Woodruff, was unavailable to help him plan a defense—he

was futilely trying to direct chaotic traffic at the crossroads in town.[94]

During the chaos, a lieutenant colonel wearing the crossed cannons of a field artillery officer approached Clarke:

> General, I'm Roy Clay. I have a separate battalion of self-propelled 105's, the 275th Armored Field Artillery. We've got some ammunition left and we're ready to work. 'God bless you, Clay!' [Clarke replied,] 'You're all the artillery we've got. Head out the ridge east of town and support those two engineer companies dug in there.'[95]

This was the first good news Clarke had received since leaving Holland; Clay's offer to stay and fight was heartening as well as badly needed. A few other units (and bits and pieces of units) had also chosen to fight it out rather than join the retreat. In that regard, Clay's story is an instructive example of how some of these units managed to get to St.-Vith and continue to fight.

16 DECEMBER

Clay's gunners (attached to the 106th Division Artillery) had begun the battle as the only artillery in direct support of the 14th Cavalry Group defending the division's left flank in the Losheim Gap. When the German barrage began at 0530 hours on 16 December, shells hit the 275th's five forward observation posts, manned 24 hours a day to provide maximum coverage to the thinly spread cavalry troopers. Although the shelling severed all wire communications with the frontline elements, the forward observers switched to their radios to contact the battalion fire direction center and quickly received effective fire on the masses of enemy troops attacking along the entire front.[96]

As the German assault infantry and armored vehicles pushed the cavalrymen before them, they quickly cut off and surrounded most of the forward observation posts, but the observer parties continued to call in mission after mission, sometimes directing rounds onto their own positions. Clay's 275th fired furiously all through that long day and into the night, expending the equivalent of two complete basic loads

Disaster on the Schnee Eifel

in less than a day. Firing more than 4,000 rounds in less than 24 hours, gun crews reported that water poured down the muzzles to cool the weapons emerged only as steam through the breech, and heat-blistered paint peeled from the barrels. Frantic calls for assistance to the 106th and 99th Division Artilleries went unanswered, as those units were busy responding to German assaults on their own supported units. Finally, the 106th Division Artillery Commander, Brigadier General Leo McMahon, called the 275th and said, "You're on your own. Good luck."[97] No help at all could be expected through "normal" channels.

The lightly armed cavalry troopers were no match for the German assault waves. By 1530 hours, the 275th found itself on the front line with no infantry support between it and the enemy. Withdrawing in two columns to a less exposed position, the battalion continued to answer calls for fire.[98]

17 DECEMBER

The 14th Cavalry Group, disorganized and confused by the furious onslaught, frustrated Clay's gunners for much of 17 December by refusing to allow them to fire toward the east, fearing that cutoff American troops could be killed in the shelling. This situation ended in the afternoon on 17 December when the battered and dazed 14th Cavalry Group was forced to withdraw for the last time and finally disintegrated as an effective fighting force.[99]

This situation led to Clay's dramatic offer to Clarke and his approaching Combat Command B, 7th Armored. Clay recalled, "No one had to tell me I was under Clarke's command. I assumed it."[100] For the next 2 critical days, Clay's 275th Armored Field Artillery Battalion constituted the entire artillery support for Clarke's troopers manning the St.-Vith roadblock--a stand that gained Clay's gunners a Presidential Unit Citation. This battalion, and units like it that drifted into the St.-Vith salient, provided the help Clarke desperately needed to patch together a viable defense.[101]

Shortly after Clarke dispatched Clay to provide much-needed support to Rigg's tiny force, portions of the 7th

Armored began to trickle into St.-Vith. Troop B, 87th Cavalry Reconnaissance Squadron, was the first 7th Armored unit to force its way through the packed roads. Clarke immediately sent it to fall in on Riggs' left flank. As other units arrived, they too were moved to defensive positions ringing the eastern approaches to the town. The 38th Armored Infantry Battalion, the 23rd Armored Infantry Battalion, the 31st Tank Battalion, and the 33rd Armored Engineer Battalion were all in the St.-Vith vicinity by midnight, and most were in combat hours before that.[102] Clarke recorded how he disposed his forces and organized the defense:

> As [the combat command] arrived, which continued until after dark, I sent help to LTC Riggs, established a direct fire force with my tank destroyer company, established a counter-attack force of 2 tank companies and sent troops forward to the northwest and southeast locations of St.-Vith with instructions to stop the Germans. My small staff and I were up all night getting the situation organized.[103]

While the armored units were trickling into St.-Vith on the afternoon and evening of 17 December, General Hasbrouck, the 7th's commander, arrived in town in the late afternoon. After a brief meeting alone with Alan Jones, who was still in St.-Vith, Hasbrouck briefed Clarke on how he saw the mission.[104] Clarke, of course, was to stop the Germans from entering St.-Vith, or delay them for as long as possible. Hasbrouck, commanding the entire 7th Armored Division, would attempt to do the same for the whole northern sector. From his headquarters in Vielsalm, west of St.-Vith, Hasbrouck and the 7th Armored Division staff planned and conducted the defense of that portion of the VIII Corps line formerly held by the 106th Infantry Division. Hasbrouck had Clarke and his Combat Command B defending St.-Vith. To Clarke's north, Combat Command R, 7th Armored, protected the left flank of the division. Bill Hoge's Combat Command B, 9th Armored, along with the 424th Infantry Regiment of the 106th and the 28th Division's 112th Infantry Regiment, was fighting to the south of St.-Vith on the division's right flank. Hasbrouck placed his remaining combat command, Combat Command A, southwest of St.-Vith where it could respond to any breakthroughs as division reserve.[105] But the key to the entire 7th Armored's defensive line was Clarke's command at the St.-Vith hub.

Drawing on his considerable combat experience and, it would seem, recalling the lessons of the successful tank battles around Arracourt, Clarke prepared to conduct a mobile defense of the St.-Vith area. This entailed not just resisting each German attack with a brittle crust of tanks and infantrymen, but also meeting each of those thrusts by counterpunching with a mobile, powerful tank reserve. And unlike besieged Bastogne, where a chiefly infantry force held a thin line while surrounded, Clarke was willing to give ground, when necessary, to maximize the delay inflicted on the enemy. Such defensive tactics were meant to capitalize on the speed and power of his armored forces, not simply to hold terrain.[106]

17-18 DECEMBER

Commencing the night of 17-18 December and continuing with little respite through the next week, Combat Command B, 7th Armored, and its attached units reacted to assault after assault by German panzer and grenadier forces determined to take St.-Vith. Clarke, who got little sleep until his unit finally withdrew from the St.-Vith pocket on 23 December, closely controlled American reactions to the enemy attacks and stayed nearly constantly on the move to threatened areas.[107] This report of the action of 18 December, prepared by the US Army Armor School after the war, gives a good account of how Clarke's mobile defense reacted to the German attacks throughout this period:

The Germans continued their 'squeeze play' on the St.-Vith area during the cold, misty morning [of 18 December] when at 0800 they hit CC'B' with a well-coordinated attack by infantry supported by tanks. From the north the attack moved in on Hunningen and from the east against the line across the Schoenberg road. Hunningen was lost temporarily but an aggressive counterattack was mounted by CC'B', using three medium tank companies and one tank destroyer company...The crossroads was recaptured at a cost to the Germans of seven tanks and one armored car destroyed and over 100 infantry killed. On the east, CC'B' restored the line with a counterattack by two medium tank companies after initial penetrations had been made. Such counterattacks, carried out by CC'B' with aggressiveness and determination, were characteristic of the defense of St.-Vith and must have caused the Germans to think the defenders were in greater strength than was the case.[108]

In fact, the German 5th Panzer Army commander, von Manteuffel, told Clarke after the war that he thought his German forces had engaged an armored *corps* at St.-Vith and not merely a brigade-sized element. Clarke explained to the German commander that, instead of facing an American tank corps, "You were seeing the same tanks over and over again...in different places...our mobile reserve."[109] Such a defense required at least two conditions: a steady flow of fuel and ammunition, and the ability to trade ground for time. Therefore, if Clarke's troops became surrounded like the defenders at Bastogne, his mobile defense would grind to a halt and become ineffective.

20-22 DECEMBER

By 20 December, the defenders of the St.-Vith salient held "the easternmost position of any organized nature in the center sector of the Ardennes battleground,"[110] but their situation was becoming tenuous as the German attack swept around them on both sides. The 6th Panzer Army in the north had penetrated miles to the west of St.-Vith (although restricted to a narrow corridor by American units holding the Elsenborn Ridge). Von Manteuffel's 5th Panzer Army was 25 miles southwest of St.-Vith, driving westward.[111] Although the German spearheads to the rear of Clarke had not yet linked up, that seemed to be only a matter of time. Soon the decision would have to be made either to withdraw Clarke's forces from the St.-Vith salient or let them become surrounded.

On the night of 21 December the overpowering German forces finally battered their way into St.-Vith itself, pushing

Clarke's defenders out of the nearly destroyed town. The Americans, however, retained control of the surrounding area and continued effectively to deny unrestricted use of the road network to the German columns.[112] In fact, allowing the enemy into the town turned into something of an advantage for the defenders since the "traffic jam thus created" effectively knotted the roads, and by midmorning 22 December "the flood of [enemy] vehicles streaming into St.-Vith was out of control."[113] For several hours the German columns could move neither forward nor backward. Stalled within the St.-Vith traffic grid, they seemed, ironically, the victims of their own success. Although Clarke and his subordinate commanders appreciated the respite, they knew it couldn't last forever, and that the enemy columns would soon continue their westward advance. By 1100 hours on 22 December, Combat Command B was again being hard pressed by enemy units exiting the St.-Vith traffic jam.[114] Clarke was holding, but just barely.

Despite the success Combat Command B's mobile defense was having around St.-Vith, the prospect of fighting surrounded inevitably arose as the overpowering German attacks whittled down Clarke's outnumbered forces. The defensive lines of the area between Vielsalm and St.-Vith, east of the Salm River, were slowly forming into a goose egg shape, but an exit across the river remained open. With German pressure increasing, it wouldn't stay open much longer, and encirclement loomed. Clarke's refusal to allow his forces to be encircled (and turning his tanks into "iron pillboxes") was vigorously supported by Hasbrouck. It nearly got them both relieved of command.[115]

The success of the 5th Panzer Army's attack had effectively cut off the northern sector of the VIII Corps line from General Middleton's control. To counter this, Eisenhower had given command of the northern half of the bulge to Field Marshal Montgomery on 20 December, leaving Bradley with control of the area from Bastogne south. As a result of this command rearrangement, at 2230 on 20 December, the 7th Armored in the St.-Vith area came under command of Major General Matthew Ridgway's XVIII Airborne Corps, then being rushed from a "theater reserve"

position to the threatened sector.[116] Ridgway, a paratrooper
used to fighting surrounded, was not inclined to approve any
withdrawal. On 22 December matters had come to a head.
Ridgway wanted the 7th to remain east of the Salm River in
the "fortified goose-egg" and fight surrounded.[117]

To a paratrooper, fighting encircled by the enemy is not
unusual; in fact, it's how they normally start most battles
after their "vertical insertion." Because of his previous
airborne infantry combat experience, Ridgway thought, not
illogically, that Clarke's forces could continue to resist within
the goose egg, supplied through the Allied-controlled skies.
After all, the 101st Airborne was exercising this exact tactic
at the other critical roadblock, Bastogne. Why, Ridgway
wondered, couldn't the 7th Armored do the same thing in the
St.-Vith area? Hasbrouck answered Ridgway's question in a
message received at XVIII Airborne Corps headquarters at
1150 on 22 December, outlining several reasons why Clarke's
troops (and the other defenders, including Hoge's Combat
Command B, 9th Armored) should be withdrawn to safety
across the Salm River: restricted supply lines, attack from
enemy artillery from all sides, an inadequate road net to
fight a mobile defense, imminent loss of existing supply
sources, and a force only 50 percent effective after nearly a
week of combat. Primarily, the differences between the 7th
Armored at St.-Vith and the relatively fresh 101st Airborne
at Bastogne were the seriously attrited condition of the
tankers (after a week's fighting) and the necessity for the
armored unit to fight a mobile defense rather than simply
endure a static seige. As a dramatic postscript to his
message, Hasbrouck added that he had just received word of
renewed heavy attacks against Clarke's troops.[118]   Time
was short.

Ridgway remained unconvinced. A charter member of
the "airborne club," he knew neither Hasbrouck nor Clarke
and suspected their motives. As far as he knew, they could
be as panicked as some of the other officers he had met since
the battle started, giving up on an otherwise salvageable
situation. Further complicating matters, Alan Jones and the
106th Division staff (by now reduced to commanding their
own 424th Infantry Regiment and exercising loose control

over Hoge's Combat Command B, 9th Armored, and the 112th Infantry Regiment of the 28th Division) were sending Ridgway mixed and confusing signals about the situation. Ridgway went to Hasbrouck's command post to see for himself. What he got was more frustration. Although Hasbrouck once again laid out all the right reasons for withdrawal, Jones (much to Hasbrouck's disgust) seemed to change his earlier opinion and agree with Ridgway that an encircled defense was possible.[119] The corps commander, now seemingly more than ever needing to see for himself, grabbed Hasbrouck and headed for Clarke's command post. He left Jones behind.

Ridgway desperately wanted someone who knew what the actual situation was to tell him what he really wanted to hear—that is, the goose-egg defense was practicable. He wouldn't hear it from Clarke, however. Clarke told him his force was only about 40 percent effective, and would soon become combat ineffective it if wasn't withdrawn and reconstituted.[120] Even now the strong-willed corps commander was unconvinced and would remain so until someone he knew and trusted told him his plan wouldn't work. Fortunately for the battle-weary St.-Vith defenders, Ridgway had known Bill Hoge since their cadet days at West Point and therefore trusted him to tell the absolute truth about the condition of the defense. Hoge, who was still en route to Clarke's command post, spoke to Ridgway on the radio and set up a rendezvous. The two old friends met by the side of the road, and Ridgway finally realized that Hasbrouck and Clarke had been presenting the true picture. Hoge confirmed all that the 7th Armored tankers had related.[121]

While the two men were meeting, however, the order for Clarke and the other defenders to withdraw behind the Salm was being received at 7th Armored headquarters. Field Marshal Montgomery, now Ridgway's senior commander at 21 Army Group Headquarters, had independently evaluated the viability of continuing the defense east of the Salm (with the help of his "phantom" communication-liaison officers visiting many US command posts) and concluded, "They can come back with all honor...They put up a wonderful show."

CONTACT RES COMD
7TH
ARMD RODT

NO
CONTACT

HINDERHAUSEN

KROMBACH

NEUBRUECK

ST.-VITH

CONTACT
CCB
9TH ARMD GALHAUSEN

CONTACT
CCB
9TH ARMD WIESENBACH

CONTACT CCB
9TH ARMD

— 1 — NIGHTFALL 17 DEC 44
— 2 — NIGHTFALL 19 DEC 44
— 3 — NIGHTFALL 21 DEC 44
— 4 — DAYLIGHT 22 DEC 44
— 5 — EVENING 22 DEC 44
— 6 — 0700 23 DEC 44 WHEN
         WITHDRAWAL STARTED

SUCCESSIVE LINES IN
THE DEFENSE OF ST.-VITH

YARDS 1000 500 0 1000 2000 3000 4000

METERS 1000 500 0 1000 2000 3000 4000

(SOURCE DEPT OF ARMY, US ARMY ARMOR SCHOOL, *THE BATTLE AT ST -VITH, BELGIUM, 17 - 23 DECEMBER 1944*)

Defense of St.-Vith

At 1500 on 22 December, 7th Armored received a message from XVIII Airborne Corps headquarters stating that the "request of CG, 7th Armored Division, for withdrawal had been approved."[122] This (plus the talk with Hoge) forced Ridgway to accept the withdrawal. It also forced Ridgway to realize that something would have to be done formally about Jones before his contradictory actions, now issuing from Vielsalm, further complicated the situation. Upon his return to Vielsalm, Ridgway held a closed meeting with Jones, Hasbrouck, and the corps deputy Chief of Staff, Colonel Quill. Ridgway had Quill write out an order relieving Jones of his command.[123] Although the 106th Division unit history reports that Ridgway made Jones his Deputy Corps Commander in an effort to clarify the genuinely confusing command situation, this seems to be only polite fiction, meant to salve hurt feelings. Ridgway had had enough of Jones' equivocating and could not afford to subsidize any further mistakes. Later that same night, Jones was medically evacuated after collapsing with a heart attack.[124] The nightmare was over for the former 106th Division commander. For Clarke, however, it hung on through that long night.

The news that permission had been granted for Combat Command B, 7th Armored, and the other defenders in the goose egg to withdraw across the Salm to safety was received with somewhat mixed emotions at Clarke's headquarters. Receiving permission to withdraw was one thing; actually disengaging in the midst of a desperate fight and getting safely across the river would be difficult. In fact, unless the temperature dropped enough to sufficiently freeze the sticky mud that threatened to bog down his armored vehicles, Clarke might be literally stuck on the east side of the river.

23 DECEMBER

Mercifully, the weather turned cold late that night. The soggy ground froze sufficiently to support the tanks and armored vehicles and allow them to initiate a fighting withdrawal under pressure.[125] However, Clarke encountered relentless enemy attacks all around the rapidly shrinking perimeter. As the long hours of darkness slowly slipped away, enemy forces in contact kept Clarke from breaking clear completely. Finally, at 0500 on 23 December, Hasbrouck sent a message informing Clarke and the others in the goose egg that "it will be necessary to disengage, whether circumstances are favorable or not, if we are to carry out any kind of withdrawal with equipment."[126] Beginning with Hoge's Combat Command B, 9th Armored, at 0700, the defenders began to disengage. Under the protective fires of Clay's 275th Armored Field Artillery Battalion and other artillery units that had gotten across the river during the night, and with a pickup covering force of a tank company, an infantry company, and a tank destroyer company guarding the rear, Clarke and the rest moved safely across the Salm on 23 December.[127]

The movement back across the Salm, a maneuver that would not have been easy even in peacetime, was accomplished in a surprisingly smooth and organized manner—despite the fact that Clarke, once more, was called on to play traffic cop. Clarke and the remnants of Combat Command B, 7th Armored, moved into an assembly area near Xhoris by 2300. They were instructed to refuel, rearm, and prepare for action in the morning.[128]

ANALYSIS OF BATTLE LEADERSHIP

It is tempting, but neither fair nor illuminating, to conclude that Clarke was a success and Jones a failure. Such an approach doesn't do justice to either man and would obscure many lessons that could be drawn from a careful and thoughtful analysis of the action. Of course, Clarke's leadership created a successful mobile defense from a rapidly disintegrating situation, just as Jones' leadership failures contributed in large measure to the confused and panicky situation in St.-Vith. These conclusions, however, tell only part of the story and do little to instruct students of the fighting as to how Clarke's and Jones' demonstrated battle leadership influenced the outcome of the St.-Vith defense. To accomplish that, one must look beyond the superficial and examine their leadership in the context of their experience, their units, their tactical situations—and fate. Above all, it should be recognized that Jones was certainly more victim than failure in the events leading up to and culminating in the destruction of his unit at the St.-Vith crossroads. Clearly, he and his green division were the victims of adverse circumstances over which they had no control. Some of these circumstances read like a listing of the weaknesses of the entire US Army in World War II.

Infantry replacement shortages probably had the greatest impact on the performance of the 106th Infantry Division in its short-lived combat stint. By April 1944, Jones and the other leaders of the "Golden Lions" had built a combat team of infantrymen who had lived and trained together for over a year. They knew and trusted each other, and the key leadership positions at all levels were filled with trained and proven performers. The replacement shortage caused the War Department to grab infantrymen from any source available and the 106th was stripped of over 60 percent of its riflemen, wiping out the division's small unit leadership.[129] Although the 106th had been brought up to strength by the time of its deployment to Europe, these new men (most with noninfantry backgrounds) had not been fully trained or completely integrated, and none could replace the lost key leaders in the short time available. To make matters worse, the drain and fill was stretched out over the entire spring and summer of 1944, causing what would seem to the 106th's leaders as a continual state of disruption and turmoil—a terrible training environment. There seems to be little that Jones or any member of his staff could have done to alleviate this problem except, as they did, to train and integrate the newcomers as quickly as possible.[130]

Once Jones and his division arrived in Belgium, they were again the victims of circumstance--the Supreme Command's decision to attack along a broad front. This decision (along with the national strategy to abandon the earlier proposal to field 200 US Army divisions and settle for only 89) resulted in an exceptionally thin Allied line, so thin that the only "strategic reserves" available to SHAEF when the Ardennes offensive began were the two airborne infantry divisions, recuperating from the MARKET-GARDEN fiasco.[131] The effect of all this on the 106th Division, therefore. was to mandate that it hold an active section of the long Allied line, instead of completing its training within the theater of operations but safely behind the lines. Moreover, it had but 4 days in its assigned sector of that line and was still getting settled when the attack started. Although the high command had intentionally given the new 106th the quietest section of the entire front, such good intentions backfired when the full force of the German assault slammed into that very sector. Instead of the safest part of the line, it turned out to be the most dangerous.

Even within the Ardennes line itself, Jones' sector was arguably the worst to try to defend, given the restrictions placed on the unit from its higher headquarters. Unfortunately, the 106th had to contend with a corps boundary, a flank sitting astride a principal invasion route (the Losheim Gap), and a large portion of its unit confined to an exposed position on the Schnee Eifel plateau. In addition, it had been constrained to occupy defensive positions selected and prepared by another unit.[132] Although the leaders at First Army and VIII Corps must have had some misgivings about the overall dispositions and preparedness to fight of the 106th Division, it seems that no one really believed the untried unit would actually be attacked on the "Ghost Front." Had Jones been plugged into the line at any other point outside the Ardennes, he may have had sufficient time to season his troops and prepare them better for their first combat. It seems unarguable that the 106th would not have been destroyed had it not been shoved into the path of a powerful offensive that no one thought even a remote possibility. Eisenhower, Bradley, and all the rest of the high command must share the blame for being totally fooled by the timing, location, and intensity of the German attack. Later claims by Bradley and others of a "calculated risk" notwithstanding, the Allies were surprised by the Ardennes attack, and the chief victims of that surprise were Jones and his division.[133]

A further vulnerability of the 106th, shared with each of the other infantry divisions in World War II, was the lack of tanks as part of the permanent organization of the infantry division. McNair's "lean and mobile" vision for the wartime army he created led him to include within the "standard" infantry division only those formations it would always need, regardless of where in the world it fought. Tanks and other specialized units or equipment were to be assigned from "pools" when the tactical situation warranted.[134] In Europe, it was realized too late that the tactical situation nearly *always* warranted the attachment of some armor, and by the end of the war, nearly every infantry division had at least a tank battalion more or less permanently attached.[135] As a standard infantry division, however, the 106th was not expected to be fighting enemy armor for some time and had no tank units assigned to it when the attack began (apart from the lightly armored 14th Cavalry Group). The speed and power of even a tank company might have significantly helped Jones in the early stages of the battle. Its presence would certainly have provided Jones a powerful force to maneuver against what was, at least initially, an infantry-heavy German attack.

Alan Jones deserves no blame for any of these situations and could have done nothing to prevent or alleviate them, given the time available and the circumstances then existing. If these conditions are set aside, however, how did Jones help or hinder his crippled unit? Given the awful circumstances they found themselves in, how did the actions and decisions he and his staff made affect the outcome of the fighting? What were the characteristics of Alan Jones' battle leadership and how did they affect the conduct of the fight for St.-Vith?

One can argue that Jones could have done much more to restore the shattered morale of his staff by maintaining calmness within his rapidly deteriorating headquarters. Observers of Jones during that critical period described his demeanor as "extremely agitated and apprehensive," and that outwardly he appeared to be "an increasingly frustrated man."[136] In contrast to the calm, unflappable coolness of his corps commander in Bastogne, Middleton, Jones' personal leadership during the hours of greatest crisis seemed to visibly lack these traits. Clarke reported that Jones gave the impression that his knowledge of the situation was hazy,[137] and that he appeared to be consumed with worry about his son who was serving in one of the surrounded regiments.

Clarke later related that Jones returned again and again to the concern for his lost son and sometimes seemed to be thinking of little else.[138]   This concern of a father for the safety of his son is certainly understandable, but when that father is also responsible for the safety of 16,000 other sons, he has a duty to ensure those men perceive their commander as a competent and confident leader.   By his inability to project outwardly that competence and confidence, regardless of his reasons, Jones denied his staff and soldiers that image and unintentionally fired their panic.   As the division commander—the man all the "Golden Lions" looked to for inspiration and support in this crisis—Jones should have steeled his nerves and at least outwardly have shown a confidence-inspiring image.   When his nerve failed Jones, it also failed those around him.   This lack of a calm steadfastness was probably one of the biggest failures of his battle leadership at St.-Vith.

Jones' failure in personal leadership exacerbated his apparent weakness in organizational leadership—that is, a commander's ability to influence the unit's total performance by directing and focusing the efforts of the unit staff toward a common goal.[139]   One day into battle found the 106th Division staff in turmoil.   Panic had set in, and no one seemed to be in charge.   By the time Woodruff arrived, he found the entire staff frantically abandoning its headquarters and effective control already lost.   Clarke reported that no staff officer came to see Jones and that he did not send for one during one of the most critical phases of the battle; this serves to confirm that events had moved beyond Jones' ability to influence, much less control, his division.[140]

Outside, in the crowded streets of St.-Vith, near-total chaos reigned with no apparent attempt at traffic control. For a unit supposedly pinning all its hopes of rescue for its trapped regiments on the early arrival of the 7th Armored, these conditions seem unacceptable.   The 106th's staff appears to have been completely unprepared either to receive the promised reinforcements or to utilize them properly once they arrived.   Taken altogether, this points to a near complete breakdown of organizational leadership and a clear failure to maintain control of the staff, primary responsibilities of a division commander and his chief of staff. How much of this failure should be attributed to Jones and how much to his chief of staff, Colonel Baker, is not possible to ascertain, but it is the division commander who has final responsibility for the performance of his staff.

Jones' battle leadership at St.-Vith also seemed to be crippled by a lack of decisiveness at critical times. In several instances, it seemed as if Jones didn't know what needed to be done, let alone how to go about doing it. The lack of a counterattack plan to rescue his trapped regiments, the failure to appoint one overall commander to coordinate the attempted breakout of those regiments, and missing the opportunity to try a linkup with them using Hoge's Combat Command B, 9th Armored, when it became available are all examples of missed opportunities and botched chances. As Clarke observed upon his arrival in St.-Vith on 17 December, Jones seemed content to remain in his office and worry about the situation instead of trying to make something happen to change it. Later on, when Ridgway sought Hasbrouck's and Jones' opinions about defending the "fortified goose-egg," Jones exasperated both men by vacillating from one position to the other, remaining the only local commander to recommend what would have been the most disastrous action, defending the goose egg. This last example of indecision was too much for the dynamic and decisive Ridgway—he relieved Jones shortly thereafter.[141]

When reviewing Jones' actions, it may be possible that he was even then suffering the preliminary symptoms of his impending cardiac seizure a few days later. Extreme depression, confusion, apprehension, and an inability to make decisions are all typical manifestations of this condition, which could have certainly been brought on by the incredible stress Jones was under. If true, it may go a long way toward explaining Jones extreme agitation and confused state of mind when Clarke arrived.

But the instance of indecision by Jones that had the single greatest impact on the destruction of his division should actually not have been Jones' decision at all. This decision, of course, was the one to pull back the exposed regiments on the Schnee Eifel plateau before they became surrounded. This decision should rightfully have been made by Jones' corps commander, Middleton. The VIII Corps commander was an experienced, battle-hardened veteran of campaigns in Sicily, Italy, and France who had an Army-wide reputation as an expert tactician. Moreover, Middleton had expressed concern about the exposed nature of the Schnee Eifel positions well prior to the attack, and he admitted later that he knew the 106th was not up to the standards required to stop the German assault.[142] Middleton claimed he was deferring judgment to the man on the spot, Jones. Jones, however, inexperienced and new to the area, could not have made as informed and tactically sound a decision as the experienced Middleton. By making no decision, Jones left them in place, thereby dooming the troops to being surrounded and captured. However, it is Middleton's failure to order the regiments to be withdrawn, leaving Jones to decide, that must bear the principal blame.

Amid the mistakes made by Jones and his staff during this critical time, there are at least three bright spots in their performance. First, Jones' use of his rather small reserve forces early on the first day of the assault was the right response to the threat, as it was then developing. The 106th Division headquarters seems to have quickly realized the massive extent of the enemy attack and wasted no time in releasing reserves for use against each threatened sector. In this regard, they seem to have been ahead of their counterparts at VIII Corps headquarters in divining the German intention and reacting quickly to it, showing none of the command inertia that seemed prevalent later on. While their reactions were undoubtedly helped by the slowness of the German attack to develop its full force, their actions nonetheless were correct.

A second positive note in the gloom was Jones' dispatch of Riggs and his small force of engineers and support troops to defend the eastern approaches to St.-Vith on the morning of 17 December.[143] No positive action Jones took during the entire battle was more important to its overall success than when he ordered this tiny group to deploy and attempt to keep the enemy away from the vital crossroads. Though born of desperation, it nevertheless prevented St.-Vith from being overrun and allowed Clarke and Combat Command B, 7th Armored, to get into position to conduct their mobile defense. Much like Middleton was doing in front of Bastogne with his corps engineers, Jones had recognized that he had to use this engineer-turned-infantry roadblock to buy some much-needed time. It worked.

The final example of good battle leadership displayed by Jones was, ironically, his voluntarily handing over of that leadership to Clarke. Whatever Jones' state of mind was by 1430 on 17 December, he retained enough appreciation of the overall situation to realize that the junior Clarke, who would soon have his fresh armored combat command in the fight at St.-Vith, could better conduct the kind of defense necessary if he alone were in charge. Although the offer startled and surprised Clarke, it made good sense from Jones' point of view and probably was key in making Clarke's mobile defense possible. By this time in the battle, Jones may have realized his greatest contribution was simply to get out of the way.[144]

Clarke turned out to be just the right man in exactly the right place to salvage a creditable defense from a deteriorating situation. This propitious circumstance—part luck, part design—gave the combat-experienced armored commander a perfect opportunity to become one of the genuine heroes of the Battle of the Bulge. Clarke quickly seized upon that opportunity and never faltered.

Two other commanders made crucial decisions that sent Clarke and his unit to the vital crossroads: Eisenhower and Middleton. Ike's quick assessment of the scope of the German attack led to his directive to Bradley on 16 December that got Clarke on the road to Bastogne later that same night.[145] Once at VIII Corps headquarters, he received Middleton's understated directive to "go to [Jones]...if he needs help, give it to him."[146] The two senior men had sent him to the right place, but once he got to St.-Vith, Clarke was on his own.

In later years, Clarke frequently wrote and remarked that two of the primary skills of a commander were to know what needed to be done, and then have some idea of how to go about accomplishing it. Clarke's battle leadership during the defense of St.-Vith is one of the best examples of the practical application of these skills which one can find. With no advance knowledge of the situation at St.-Vith, and practically no definitive orders or directives from higher authority, Clarke organized, conducted, and commanded a superb mobile defense of one of the most critical portions of the Ardennes battlefield.

What should be done about the confused and desperate situation confronting Clarke when he arrived at Jones' headquarters was by no means obvious. Jones, naturally enough, was fixated solely on rescuing his trapped regiments on the Schnee Eifel plateau and pleaded with Clarke for a counterattack to free his units without delay,[147] but was unable to put him in contact with the leadership of the surrounded units or provide any details Clarke could use to coordinate a counterattack. With German troops threatening the outskirts of St.-Vith while Clarke's command was still trying to fight its way through, it may have occurred to observers of the situation that the sensible course of action would have been to abandon St.-Vith altogether. Establishing a more defensible line along the west side of the Salm River, anchored around Vielsalm, had some immediate advantages.

Clarke, however, rejected any course save a vigorous defense of what he quickly realized was a vital road hub. As an experienced armored commander who had fought his way across France, he knew that denying the enemy free and unrestricted use of the extensive road net around St.-Vith was the best way to slow, if not stop, a sweeping mechanized assault.

Because much of the impenetrability of the Ardennes is actually due to its poor road network, denying an invader free use of the few good roads couldn't help but slow his advance. Clarke surely must have agreed with Middleton's postwar statement about not having to be a genius to know that St.-Vith and Bastogne were critical points during the Battle of the Bulge.[148] Trained early in his career as a topographic engineer, Clarke had learned to appreciate terrain and its effect on the battlefield. Clarke realized the importance to the German drive of the St.-Vith road hub and in maintaining combat mobility and the momentum of attack.[149]

Clarke's extensive experience as a combat commander in the battles across France the previous summer—especially, it seems the Arracourt tank battles—showed him the value of capitalizing on the mobility and flexibility of his armored unit to create a mobile defense. Later he described how he conducted this defense:

> My mission was to stop or slow down the [enemy advance] until more U.S. troops could be assembled west of the Salm River. My combat command, which was a flexible organization now [compared to its weak organization prior to 1 November 1944] varied as the division commander added and took away battalions as he needed them to take care of the division's crises. My basic tactic was to keep my units mobile with a mobile counterattack force of two companies of tanks, and to give ground as necessary so as not to lose my command or any portion of it.[150]

These are nearly exactly the same tactics Clarke had used to repel Manteuffel's 5th Panzer Army attacks at Arracourt the previous September; the success they demonstrated there must have convinced Clarke they would work at St.-Vith. Now that he and Hasbrouck had reorganized the 7th Armored along the more flexible, mobile lines of the extremely successful 4th Armored Division (in which they had both held commands), Clarke had just the right weapon he needed to carry out the type of mobile defense he realized was necessary. The final element needed for Clarke to prosecute the fighting in the manner he knew was necessary was for him to be given free reign in conducting it. Jones did that at 1430 hours on 17 December when he told Clarke, "You take over; I've got nothing left."[151]

Not every commander in Clarke's position that afternoon would have been eager to be placed in charge of what appeared to be a rapidly disintegrating, losing cause. But one of Clarke's most dominant leadership characteristics, clearly demonstrated here, was a supreme and total self-confidence. Anyone who knew Clarke had to realize early on that he never doubted his own abilities, nor was he ever shy about stepping forward to take charge or expressing his opinion about any military subject. Never a braggart, he had a forceful and dynamic personality that frequently caused others to defer to him. Clarke inspired confidence in his staff and his soldiers and always seemed to exude optimism and competence. In this, he seems to have projected just the opposite image that Jones was then projecting. Given the state of affairs in St.-Vith at that time, such confidence and optimism were sorely needed.

Clarke's conduct of the defense of St.-Vith is not, however, without criticism. Some have charged that his battle leadership caused mistakes that had serious consequences for the 106th Division. Primarily, these issues revolve around the surrounded regiments on the Schnee Eifel plateau and attempts to rescue them.

The first such criticism to emerge is the charge that the "late arrival"[152] of Clarke's Combat Command B, 7th Armored Division, was instrumental in dooming the surrounded regiments of the 106th Division to capitulation. Those who make this claim point out that Jones' corps commander, Middleton, had personally told Jones that the 7th Armored was scheduled to arrive at St.-Vith by 0700 hours on 17 December, thereby causing Jones to base his rescue plans on that information.[153] When Clarke's unit failed to arrive until late on the afternoon of that day, it was too late to save Jones' trapped units. This, they say, was the single, crucial mistake which ultimately forced the units to give up. Dupuy, in his book, *Lion in the Way*, a defense of the 106th, writes, "One comes right back to the point that the nonarrival of Combat Command B, 7th Armored Division, at 7:00 A.M. that morning was the crux of the situation."[154] Because Clarke was the commander of the unit ordered to support Jones at St.-Vith, he must be responsible.

Examination of this criticism, however, fails to show where any blame for the timing of the arrival of the 7th Armored Division could be Clarke's. Indeed, the announced arrival time of the 7th Armored Division at St.-Vith (0700 on 17 December) seems to be unreasonably early. The unit had to march almost 70 miles over icy roads, clogged with fleeing vehicles, across the path of the German offensive. Historian

Russell Weigley observed, "Anyone believing this (arrival time) was not looking carefully at his maps."[155] Even though Middleton was merely passing on to Jones the First Army staff's information that the 7th Armored would "arrive at 0700 and close at 1700,"[156] it seems incredible that even the inexperienced 106th Division staff could believe the entire 7th Armored could travel from Holland in so short a time and be prepared to launch an immediate attack. At any rate, there seems to be nothing in all of this that can be attributed directly to Clarke's leadership. He went to St.-Vith when ordered and was told his combat command would be sent after him. When he got to St.-Vith, he quickly radioed for his unit to join him. The fact that it took several more hours to force its way through the fleeing traffic to get to the crossroads would appear more Jones' fault than Clarke's.

The second criticism of Clarke's leadership also deals with the trapped regiments: why did he not attack to relieve them? Those who make this criticism claim that Clarke missed a great opportunity to save the surrounded units by failing to counterattack quickly toward Schoenberg late on 17 December (or early on 18 December at the latest). Had he done so, they argue, the thin crust of German units bottling up the Americans on the plateau could have been pierced and the units relieved. This could have averted the disastrous surrender and freed about 8,500 troops to join the St.-Vith defense.

Much of this same ground, of course, has been covered earlier while discussing the leadership actions taken by Jones. Jones, after failing to decide to pull the two regiments off of the plateau (and, of course, failing to receive an order by Middleton to do so), was desperately hoping Clarke could quickly attack and break through to them. But Jones not only had no plan to accomplish this, he couldn't even coordinate such an attack with his cutoff troops. He had failed to appoint one overall commander within the pocket and had earlier missed the chance to force a linkup using Bill Hoge's Combat Command B, 9th Armored. Clarke's observations support the view of the 106th's ill preparedness; he said, "The 106th made no advance preparations for maps or gasoline which we [CCB, 7th Armored] had need for, at once, after our 80-mile march."[157]

Apparently, Jones, too, must have begun to realize that an attack to relieve the units was impossible, for Clarke reported, "At no time on 17 December did anyone, including General Jones, speak to me of attacking toward the east after the loss of communications with the troops there."[158]

After Jones gave command of the St.-Vith defense to Clarke, the armored commander had his hands full throwing his units into battle as they arrived and frantically reacting to each of the German attacks. Clarke made what is probably the best summing up of his part of the whole issue concerning the surrounded regiments when he said, "I was too busy from 4:30 P.M. on December 17th to pay too much attention to them."[159] Given the circumstances then existing, it is hard to imagine how even the entire 7th Armored could have rescued those doomed units. The only way they could have been saved was for Jones (or, more likely, Middleton) to have pulled them back earlier.

Clarke's leadership has also been criticized from the position that, since he was junior to Jones, he was automatically under Jones' command from the time he and his unit arrived in St.-Vith, and should, therefore, have reacted to Jones' orders. If he had, these critics claim, he would have launched the counterattack to save the trapped regiments, as Jones ordered. Dupuy's account repeatedly refers to Clarke's unit as being "attached" to the 106th, and treats the combat command as if it were operating under Jones' command and control during most of the fighting.[160] In reality, the command arrangements were confused and convoluted. Middleton contributed to the confusing command arrangements by failing to appoint an overall commander, choosing instead to merely ask Hasbrouck and Jones to cooperate and "carry the ball for me up there."[161]

It has always been Clarke's stated position that he remained under Hasbrouck's command throughout the fighting. He insists that he was never under Jones' command because his combat command was never formally attached to Jones' division. Clarke points out that he and his division were given oral orders simply to report to

Middleton at Bastogne, and he, personally, was merely told by the VIII Corps commander to "give Alan Jones some help if he needs it." Clarke claims that he represented his division commander as an "advance party" for the 7th Armored and was never ordered to serve under Jones.[162] Furthermore, because Jones seemed clearly to be overwhelmed by the events and handed over the defense to Clarke, the point seems a moot one. Nevertheless, it cannot be denied that the command situation (throughout the fighting and withdrawal from St.-Vith) remained one of confusion.

Perhaps the best face that can be put on this whole issue is to remember that Clarke, when command of the St.-Vith defense was thrust upon him by an overwhelmed Jones, accepted the challenge without hesitation. Such an interpretation, it seems, compliments both men's battle leadership. Dupuy's assertion that, somehow, Jones and the 106th staff retained command and effective control of that defense (including directing the efforts of Clarke's combat command) is fiction, regardless of who was the ranking officer.

A final criticism of Clarke's battle leadership concerns the defense of the so-called "fortified goose egg." Recall that when Ridgway's command was enlarged to include the 7th Armored Division as well as the other units in the St.-Vith area, he was extremely reluctant to give up any more ground than absolutely necessary. He was firmly against allowing the St.-Vith defenders to withdraw across the Salm River when that question arose on 22 December. Ridgway, used to fighting surrounded, thought that Clarke and the other units to the east of the Salm could defend the goose-egg perimeter while fighting encircled.[163] Neither Clarke nor Hasbrouck thought their armored units could fight long while surrounded. Hasbrouck stressed his reasons for thinking this in a message to Ridgway on 22 December. They seemed solid enough for the tankers. But for Ridgway, such talk was defeatism. He genuinely questioned Clarke's motives for arguing for a withdrawal and suspected the combat commander was losing his nerve. Ridgway, who knew neither Clarke nor Hasbrouck, thought that the tankers' leadership lacked firmness and resolve. Clarke, however, had good reasons for counseling withdrawal in this situation. He recalled his tense meeting with his new corps commander:

> I don't believe that Ridgway had any [hidden] purpose except that he did not know how to use an armored division. He wanted me to dig in and hold ground. He didn't understand the maneuverability of an armored unit. We [Clarke and Hasbrouck] were against it because of the logistics situation. Our division wouldn't last long cut-off, no more than a day. When Ridgway showed the plan to me I said, 'I've been fighting day and night for about a week, and I'm nearly out of gasoline, ammunition and rations.' He said, 'That is a problem for you tankers' and walked away and left me. He [Ridgway] had no knowledge or apparent interest in, an armored division.[164]

The situation was resolved in favor of Clarke and Hasbrouck when Montgomery, now in overall command in the north, overruled Ridgway and ordered the St.-Vith defenders to withdraw "with all honor."[165] Despite the favorable outcome, the incident was probably the closest Clarke came to being relieved of command—an outcome that would have been a tragic injustice.

"TO PREVENT THE CONFUSION FROM BECOMING DISORGANIZED"

It is impossible not to compare the battle leadership of Jones and Clarke. It hardly seems fair, however, to compare the inexperienced Jones with the combat-proven Clarke. But war isn't fair, and inexperienced leaders aren't provided with some handicap designed to put them on an equal footing with experienced ones. Despite the numerous disadvantages Jones was forced to confront, he (and Clarke, too) had to attempt to command to the limit of his ability at St.-Vith and provide the best defense he was capable of coaxing out of his staff and troops. One measure to gauge the success of a battle commander's leadership in such a defense can be found in Bruce Clarke's observation:

> The job of a commander in a battle when attacked by an overwhelming force is to prevent the confusion from becoming disorganized, and to eliminate command and staff inertia so that the reaction to crises can be swift and effective.[166]

Clarke recognizes that, at best, combat is a confusing and chaotic environment, even when things seem to be going right. The challenge to any leader's exercise of command is to bring enough order out of the chaos to force his will on the enemy through the combat power of his unit.

It can never be precisely determined if the 106th Infantry Division would have been destroyed had a more experienced commander been at its head, or if it was already doomed because of the terrible circumstances of its introduction to combat. It can be said that Jones' battle leadership failed to provide the kind of steady, decisive stewardship that would have given his division the fighting chance it desperately needed. His personal state and the condition of his staff by midmorning of 17 December show clearly that Jones was overcome by the stresses and demands of intense combat. The best epitaph on Jones' battle leadership is provided by Charles Whiting in his postmortem on the 106th, *Death of a Division*. Whiting's examination of Jones' situation and his performance reveals not merely a failed commander, but a man who was "a casualty of the battle just as surely as if he had been struck by a bullet."[167]

Clarke, on the other hand, salvaged a great victory from what seemed a lost cause by taking charge at the critical point of the battle and by conducting a mobile defense which succeeded in delaying the German attack for a week. He not only prevented the confusion from becoming disorganized, he turned that confusion against his enemy. Clarke's battle leadership in the defense of St.-Vith was characterized by many positive aspects: Without much guidance he knew what needed to be done; drawing on his combat experience, he knew how to go about doing it; he projected self-confidence and competence which inspired his staff and troops; and, perhaps above all, he saw it through to a successful ending.

Although the full impact and importance of Clarke's successful battle leadership at St.-Vith have not been widely publicized over the past 49 years, usually taking a back-seat to the more famous siege at Bastogne, students of the Ardennes fighting are coming to realize more and more the value of the St.-Vith defense and to appreciate its critical relationship to the entire campaign. Historian Russell Weigley, for example, writes:

> The St.-Vith defense...epitomized the American's application everywhere in the Ardennes of their army's tactical doctrine for countering just such a breakthrough...constrict the avenue of the enemy's advance. But more, perhaps than any other of the many defensive stands in the Ardennes...it was the battle of St.-Vith that bought the time required by Allied generalship to recapture control of the battle.[168]

For Clarke, the primary architect of that successful battle, that's not a bad verdict.

NOTES

1. William D. Ellis and Thomas J. Cunningham, Jr., *Clarke of St.-Vith: The Sergeant's General* (Cleveland: Dillon-Liederbach 1974), 13. This is the only full-length book about General Bruce C. Clarke and his long, distinguished career. It was written with General Clarke's cooperation and assistance. The book is somewhat episodic, containing mainly Clarke's reminiscences of what took place. Although it is an adequate portrayal of Clarke's career, it doesn't contain much independent verification of the general's recounting of events, and is never critical of Clarke's actions. Alan Jones' quote about losing his division was made to Clarke about midday on 17 December 1944, while the two men waited in Jones' office at St.-Vith for Clarke's troops to arrive.

2. Hugh Cole, *The United States Army in World War II. European Theater of Operations. The Ardennes: The Battle of the Bulge* (Washington, DC: GPO, 1965), 170. According to Cole in his official history, "The number of officers and men taken prisoner on the capitulation of the two regiments and their attached troops cannot be accurately ascertained. At least seven thousand were lost here and the figure is probably closer to eight or nine thousand. The amount lost in arms and equipment, of course, was

very substantial. The Schnee Eifel battle, therefore, represents the most serious reverse suffered by American arms during the operations of 1944-45 in the European Theater."

3. United States War Department, *Army List and Directory, 1891-1943* (Washington, DC: GPO, 1891-1943). Information concerning Alan Jones' background and early career (prior to 1944) was taken primarily from this multi-volume source, which is an official listing of assignments, unit addresses, promotions, and schooling for all officers serving in the US Army between 1891 and 1943. There are no other published references available for Jones' early career. Unless otherwise cited, all information regarding Jones' background was derived from this source; Charles Whiting, *Death of a Division* (New York: Stein and Day, 1981), 29-30, 143-144. Whiting's chronicle of the destruction, in its first combat, of Jones' inexperienced division contains some brief references, neither extensive nor detailed, to the 106th Infantry Division's commander's early career.

4. Russell F. Weigley, *Eisenhower's Lieutenants: The Campaigns of France and Germany 1944-1945* (Bloomington: Indiana University Press, 1981), 2. Professor Weigley's excellent history of the development, organization, and European operations of the US Army in World War II aptly points out that, "Historically, the American army was not an army in the European fashion, but a border constabulary for policing unruly Indians and Mexicans." The rapid demobilization that has historically (until recently) characterized the American approach to war, operated in full swing after the end of World War I. From a high of 3.6 million men in 1918, the Army was slashed to 137,000 by 1922. Bradley and Blair, *A General's Life*, 46-48.

5. Martin Blumenson, *Patton: The Man Behind the Legend 1885-1945* (New York: Berkley Books, 1987) 69, 145. Patton was one of the few officers who enjoyed a comfortable lifestyle, independent of his Army pay. Blumenson points out that, "During the Depression, [Patton's] horses and polo ponies had provoked resentment among some officers whose families were barely getting by on reduced pay scales...." Perhaps Patton's normally high standard of living caused him to be less than enthusiastic about his own prospects of serving in the Philippines when he wrote that he "would probably have to serve a tour of duty in the Philippines, an obligation for every officer. With the insurrection there at an end and the islands quiet, he considered possible assignments better suited to his aims."

6. Bradley and Blair, *A General's Life*, 69-70.

7. J.D. Morelock, "General Jacob L. Devers: Commonsense Commander," *Forward Observer* 3 (December 1988): 10. Much of the curricula of the Field Artillery School at Fort Sill had been recently updated and revitalized by its Director of Gunnery, then Major Jacob L. Devers, by the time Jones attended classes there. Devers, who became the 6th Army Group commander in Europe in World War II, was a forward-thinking, extremely capable commander who had a major impact on the Army during and after the war. A favorite of Marshall, Devers finished General Adna Chaffee's work by fielding our World War II Armored Force between 1941 and 1943. He ended the war as senior in rank to Bradley and his equal as army group commander. This overlooked and underrated soldier has never received the credit he deserves for his many significant contributions.

8. Bruce C. Clarke, "The Revolution in Army Organization, Tactics and Equipment in the Period 1940-1945," unpublished lecture notes, 15 March 1982. In a lecture given to the Corps of Cadets at West Point, Clarke pointed out many of the "great things" directed by General George C. Marshall to change the army and prepare it to fight World War II. One of these was to "do away" with the powerful position of the Chiefs of Branches (except for the Corps of Engineers) in 1940. The Branch Chiefs were very influential in the Army between the wars and substantially controlled the careers of the officers in their branches.

9. US War Department, *Army List and Directory*.

10. Clarke, "Revolution in Army Organization". Clarke points out several of the significant changes Marshall introduced into the Army as Chief of Staff immediately prior to America's entry into the war. These included: creation of the modern Armored Force; reorganization of Army divisions; nearly complete motorization, with all horse-drawn equipment eliminated; overall rapid expansion of Army manpower; elimination of outdated branches and concepts; and staffing the War Department and Army Staff with bright, promising, capable officers he had earlier identified.

11. US War Department, *Army List and Directory*.

12. Weigley, *Eisenhower's Lieutenants*, 10-11. Weigley describes McNair as, "The most influential single architect of the American ground forces in preparation for the European war...[He was] from March 1942 commander of the Army Ground Forces...[and]...a bantam, efficient, decisive, even-opinionated artilleryman whose career as a staff officer and instructor and lack of field and combat experience did not temper his assurance that he knew what was good for troops in combat. McNair's passion

was to keep the American army lean and mobile."

13. US War Department, *Army List and Directory*.

14. Ambrose, *Eisenhower*, 43-153; Bradley and Blair, *A General's Life*, 36-113. The career patterns of Eisenhower, Bradley, and Jones show striking similarities, but the most important element the three have in common is their becoming known to George Marshall. That alone was sufficient to propel their rapid rise, provided they had favorably impressed Marshall. Had they not so impressed him, Marshall surely would have relegated them to history's dustbin.

15. US War Department, *Army List and Directory*; R. Ernest Dupuy, *St. Vith: Lion in the Way—The 106th Infantry Division in World War II* (Washington, DC: Infantry Journal Press, 1949), 5-6; Whiting, *Death of a Division*, 30.

16. Dupuy, *Lion in the Way*, 5.

17. Ibid., 7.

18. Ibid., 5-7. Dupuy explains, "It was a sound theory [division training concept]. Unfortunately its preceptors did not take into account the abnormally large casualty lists which would call for replacements, nor did they realize that Army Service Forces would mount to an empire within and without the United States; an empire of sound, able-bodied men, fit for combat but placed in non-combatant positions and hence unavailable for conflict. Nor did they see the unwarranted but prevalent impression which rose during the early summer of 1944 that the war would soon be over." Dupuy may be too hard on the Army Service forces in his polemic attack. Modern armies require huge "tails" to permit the armies' "teeth" to strike the enemy. Eisenhower, in fact, felt that too much teeth and not enough tail hampered his campaign in North Africa, contributing to the Kasserine Pass debacle. Ike saw his austere logistic support network in North Africa as "strained" and doubted it could support more troops on the critical Tunisian front than were already there, although many more were needed. Martin Blumenson, *Kasserine Pass* (New York: Jove Books, 1983), 1-80. Dupuy's inference that the dregs and castoffs of an army are sufficient to run the complete logistical support systems for sophisticated, modern war machines is a parochial prejudice that modern armies can no longer afford. Good people are required in all branches.

19. Cole, *Ardennes*, 140; Dupuy, *Lion in the Way*, 6-7.

20. Whiting, *Death of a Division*, 26-27; Dupuy, *Lion in the Way*, 7-9, Cole, *Ardennes*, 140.

21. Dupuy, *Lion in the Way*, 9; Whiting, *Death of a Division*,

26.

22. US Department of the Army, *VIII Corps Letter of Instruction, 7 December 1944*; Charles B. MacDonald, *Company Commander* (New York: Bantam, 1982), 104-105. MacDonald, an historian as well as participant in the Battle of the Bulge, was assigned to the 2nd Infantry Division, east of St.-Vith, when it was relieved by the 106th Division on 11 December 1944. MacDonald reports that, "They [106th Division soldiers] were overjoyed at the prospect of seeing their first combat in such ideal defensive positions, and they showed little fear of the thinly spread lines."; Dupuy, *Lion in the Way*, 9-15; Whiting, *Death of a Division*, 27; Cole, *Ardennes*, 140.

23. Bruce C. Clarke, "The Creating of an Outstanding Battalion in 1941-1942," unpublished manuscript, 9 pages, undated. Clarke describes his background in this paper and relates many incidents that formed his early experiences. The paper culminates in a description of how he organized and trained his engineer battalion in the 4th Armored Division in 1941 and 1942; Ellis and Cunningham, *Clarke of St.-Vith*, 285.

24. Ellis and Cunningham, *Clarke of St.-Vith*, 286; Clarke, "Creating an Outstanding Battalion," 2.

25. Clarke, "Creating an Outstanding Battalion," 2.

26. Ambrose, *Eisenhower*, 43-52; Bradley and Blair, *A General's Life*, 30-35. Clarke seems to have done better than both Eisenhower and Bradley during his 4 years at West Point. While Clarke was a cadet captain and company commander, Bradley was only a cadet lieutenant, and Ike had demerit problems for most of his cadetship. Clarke's class rank (33/248) was higher than both Bradley (44/164) and Ike (61/164). Clarke was the only one of the three to receive his first choice of commissioning branch (Engineers). Ike, who wanted Cavalry, and Bradley, who preferred Engineers or Field Artillery, settled for Infantry; Clarke, "Creating an Outstanding Battalion," 2.

27. Clarke, "Creating an Outstanding Battalion," 2.

28. Ibid., 4.

29. Ibid., 2.

30. Bruce C. Clarke, "How to Motivate Soldiers," unpublished Manuscript, 2 pages, undated. This incident had a lasting impact on Clarke, and he frequently repeated it to emphasize the improper way to motivate soldiers. His company commander in this incident, however, was more motivated to win the Regimental Commander's Trophy than to encourage good marksmanship among his troops; Clarke, "Creating an Outstanding Battalion," 2.

31. Clarke, "Creating an Outstanding Battalion," 2-3.

32. Bruce C. Clarke, "The Violation of Regulations and Channels of Communications Can Be Justified," unpublished manuscript, 2 pages, 14 March 1987. During the ROTC assignment, Clarke was confronted with a situation which he called, "a great crisis to me." Apparently, "an ambitious [senior] officer without ethics" wished Clarke out of the way and convinced the university athletic council to request that Clarke ask for a transfer. Clarke refused and, after much soul-searching, reported the incident to his branch chief in Washington. The incident was resolved in Clarke's favor, and the senior officer resigned. Nonetheless, Clarke received a written reprimand from his ROTC Corps Area commander for "bypassing official channels."; Clarke, "Creating an Outstanding Battalion," 2.

33. Clarke, "Creating an Outstanding Battalion," 3.

34. Bruce C. Clarke to J.D. Morelock, 12 June 1985. Clarke was unimpressed with the course of instruction at Fort Leavenworth (although he had high regard for the school commandant, General McNair). Clarke wrote, "In 1939-1940 [CGSC] was so far behind the times that General Marshall closed it on 1 February 1940. I hope it is better." Clarke demonstrates Leavenworth's backwardness by relating a story he titles, "How an Early Bird Got an 'F'." It explains how Clarke exasperated his instructors by using tanks in an unorthodox (for then) and imaginative attack in a map exercise. He was awarded a failing grade but delights in recalling that he used the exact same tactics with phenomenal success in his dash across France in 1944. "Patton gave me an 'A'" he used to say; Clarke, "Creating an Outstanding Battalion," 3.

35. Bruce C. Clarke, "The Corps of Engineers in the Armored Force, 1940-45," unpublished manuscript, 5 pages, 1986; Clarke, "Creating an Outstanding Battalion," 3.

36. Bruce C. Clarke, "Carrying Out Orders," *EurArmy* 23 (August 1984). Clarke appears to have been extremely valuable and instrumental in Chaffee's victory over the 1st Infantry Tank Brigade in these maneuvers. He relates that, when Chaffee realized how Clarke's engineers had prepared the way to victory for his armored force, "He [Chaffee] broke down and shed a few tears. He said, 'Clarke, we are going to win!'" Chaffee's victoryand the overwhelming success of Hitler's panzers against France and Britain persuaded Marshall to create the US Armored Force, separate from Infantry branch; Chaffee was its first chief. Clarke, "Armored Force." 1-2.

37. Clarke, "Armored Force," 2-3.

38. Clarke, "Carrying Out Orders"; Clarke, "Armored Force," 3.

39. Clarke, "Creating an Outstanding Battalion," 3.

40. Hanson W. Baldwin, *Tiger Jack* (Fort Collins, CO: Old Army Press, 1979), 187. Also known as "Patton's Best," the 4th Armored Division has been called the finest unit in Europe in World War II. It spearheaded Patton's Third Army across France, led the relief of Bastogne on 26 December 1944, and fought its way across Germany. Clarke commanded Combat Command A, 1 November 1943 to 31 October 1944 during its most successful combat.

41. Baldwin, *Tiger Jack*, 113-118.

42. Kenneth Koyen, *The Fourth Armored Division: From the Beach to Bavaria* (Watertown, NY: Hungerford-Holbrook, 1949), 19; Nat Frankel and Larry Smith, *Patton's Best: An Informal History of the 4th Armored Division* (New York: Jove, 1984), 14-15; Weigley, *Eisenhower's Lieutenants*, 438, asserts that the 4th was "probably been the best of the armored divisions," and that its commander, General Wood, "was so evidently one of the best of the division commanders--perhaps the very best."

43. Koyen, *Fourth Armored Division*, 19.

44. Martin Blumenson, *The United States Army in World War II. European Theater of Operations. Breakout and Pursuit* (Washington, DC: US Government Printing Office, 1961), 359. 365-367; Weigley, *Eisenhower's Lieutenants*, 179-180.

45. US Department of the Army, *4th Armored Division, Armor in the Exploitation. The 4th Armored Division Across France to the Moselle River*, May 1949, 6; Dr. Christopher R. Gabel, *The 4th Armored Division in the Encirclement of Nancy* (Fort Leavenworth: Combat Studies Institute, 1986), 8-10, characterizes the 4th Armored's drive across France as a 700-mile long pursuit.

46. Hugh Cole, *The United States Army in World War II. European Theater of Operations. The Lorraine Campaign* (Washington, DC: US Government Printing Office, 1950), 16,84. Although the sweep across France had been spectacularly successful, the offensive sputtered to a halt all along the broad front as the fragile, over-extended supply system broke down at the end of August 1944. The lull gave the Allied forces a chance to rest tired men and repair worn equipment, but it also allowed the Germans to once more demonstrate their remarkable capacity to regenerate forces and rejuvenate worn-out units.

47. Gabel, *Encirclement of Nancy*, 12-14; Cole, *Lorraine*

Campaign, 84; Interview with Bruce C. Clarke, 13 April 1985. Clarke used the phrase "my greatest victory" to describe the conduct of operations during the Arracourt tank battles and the battles' successful conclusion in this interview.

48. US Department of the Army, US Army Command and General Staff College, *Battle Analysis Student Resource Packet. The Arracourt Tank Battles (The Lorraine Campaign 5 September-19 December 1944)* (Fort Leavenworth, KS, 1983). These tank battles are studied as part of the overall Lorraine Campaign during the Battle Analysis phase of the USACGSC core instruction. This packet is from the 1983-84 academic year.

49. Gabel, *Encirclement of Nancy*, 19-21.

50. Harry Balish, "The Battle of Nancy: A Double Envelopment," *Military Review* 29 (January 1950): 17, calls the Nancy-Arracourt fighting "one of the finest armored actions of the war."; Gabel, *Encirclement of Nancy*, 21-23, characterizes the whole Nancy-Arracourt campaign as "a brilliant episode in the annals of the 4th Armored Division."

51. Baldwin, *Tiger Jack*, 188-189; Bruce C. Clarke, "Rehabilitation of Troops in Battle," unpublished manuscript, 1 page, 15 June 1986; Bruce C. Clarke, "Clarke's Transfer," unpublished manuscript, 5 pages, undated, describes Clarke's transfer from the 4th to the 7th Armored Division: "General Patton's recommendation for Colonel Clarke's promotion to Brigadier General was approved in late October 1944 and a position...opened up in the 7th Armored Division, Ninth U.S. Army...Brigadier General Robert Hasbrouck and Colonel Clarke were both ordered to the 7th Armored in Holland on 1 November 1944 to replace...two [relieved] general officers...General Wood drove Colonel Clarke to Nancy in his jeep and saw him off for Holland in an L-4 Liaison plane...It was a sorrowful parting; they were a team."

52. Bruce C. Clarke to J.D. Morelock, 12 August 1986.

53. Clarke, "Clarke's Transfer," 5.

54. Ibid. Clarke also points out that, "these same men and units [7th Armored Division] won a Presidential Unit Citation in battle only a few weeks later."

55. Dupuy, *Lion in the Way*, 5-7. Officers who did have combat experience, such as the Assistant Division Commander, General Herbert Perrin, and the 423rd Regimental Commander, Colonel Charles Cavender, had gotten it during World War I, over 20 years earlier; Cole, *Ardennes*, 140; Whiting, *Death of a Division*, 28.

56. Cole, *Ardennes*, 140-142; Dupuy, *Lion in the Way*, 9-11.

57. US War Department, *106th Infantry Division After Action Report, December 1944*, 27 January 1945; *VIII Corps Letter of Instruction*, 7 December 1944; Dupuy, *Lion in the Way*, 9-11; Whiting, *Death of a Division*, 26-29; Cole, *Ardennes*, 140-145.

58. *106th Division After Action Report*; Dupuy, *Lion in the Way*, 12; Whiting, *Death of a Division*, 26-31.

59. Cole, *Ardennes*, 148, 272.

60. Dupuy, *Lion in the Way*, 9-11; Whiting, *Death of a Division*, 31; Cole, *Ardennes*, 272-273, makes an interesting point about the importance of the St.-Vith road network. Cole says that, although the hub at St.-Vith was important, it was not initially on the planned axis of any of the main armored thrusts. However, the Germans came to realize that St.-Vith "had to be taken early in the game" to ensure isolation of the Schnee Eifel plateau, to cover the extensive German supply lines behind each thrust, and to feed reinforcements laterally into the main attacks.

61. Dupuy, *Lion in the Way*, 16; Whiting, *Death of a Division*, 28-29; Cole, *Ardennes*, 140-142; Weigley, *Eisenhower's Lieutenants*, 448-449.

62. Cole, *Ardennes*, 140.

63. *106th Division After Action Report*.

64. Charles Whiting, *Ardennes: The Secret War* (New York: Stein and Day, 1984), described the intensity of the opening barrage: "Suddenly the complete length of the Ghost Front erupted in fire and flame. The whole weight of the artillery of three Armies, ranging from 16-inch railway guns to 3-inch mortars, descended upon the startled Americans...holding the line...The great attack had started at last! For one solid hour [sic] the great barrage continued, cutting telephone links, destroying front-line pillboxes, smashing foxholes, turning the American first-line positions into a smoking, churned-up lunar landscape. Then abruptly it ceased. For a few minutes there was a stunned silence as the men in the line, the survivors, attempted to collect themselves, faces ashen, unspoken questions in their wide, wild eyes." Although this description seems melodramatic, the barrage truly was powerful and severed most land-line communications.

65. *106th Division After Action Report*; Dupuy, *Lion in the Way*, 21-25; Whiting, *Death of a Division*, 37-43; Cole, *Ardennes*, 151-158.

66. Cole, *Ardennes*, 272.

67. *106th Division After Action Report*; Dupuy, *Lion in the Way*, 21-23; Cole, *Ardennes*, 150-160.

68. Dupuy, *Lion in the Way*, 23.

69. *106th Division After Action Report*; Cole, *Ardennes*, 273.

70. Cole, *Ardennes*, 272-275; Dupuy, *Lion in the Way*, 22.

71. Frank J. Price, *Troy H. Middleton: A Biography* (Baton Rouge: LSU Press, 1974), 216, lets Middleton off the hook too easily by allowing Jones to take all the blame. Despite the foulup on the switchboard and the other confusion reigning during that critical time, it was Middleton's responsibility as Jones' experienced senior to order the regiments withdrawn; Dupuy, *Lion in the Way*, 23-24; Whiting, *Death of a Division*, 51-53; Cole, *Ardennes*, 275; Weigley, *Eisenhower's Lieutenants*, 451.

72. Cole, *Ardennes*, 275; Dupuy, *Lion in the Way*, 22-25; Weigley, *Eisenhower's Lieutenants*, 451.

73. Thomas J. Riggs, Jr., to Bruce C. Clarke, 28 January 1986, 2.

74. Riggs to Clarke, 28 January 1986; John Hanlon, "Tom Riggs' Remarkable World War II Odyssey," *Providence Sunday Journal*, 29 December 1985. Riggs' story is a fascinating one and reads like a Hollywood adventure script. Knocked unconscious by German mortar fire on 22 December, Riggs was captured and sent to a POW camp in Germany. About 10 days later he was transferred to a camp in occupied Poland. One month later, Riggs escaped and headed east towards the advancing Russians. He finally met Polish partisans who led him to a Soviet tank unit. Riggs remained with the tankers for 10 days, observing their fighting and steady push towards Berlin. His Soviet tank commander finally sent him east to Warsaw in preparation for eventual repatriation. For 10 days in Warsaw, Riggs helped construct a displaced persons camp, but then hopped a ride on a Russian train to Odessa, 750 miles away on the Black Sea. He talked his way onto a British tanker bound for Istanbul, then hitched another ride on a freighter to Port Said, Egypt. There he managed to talk his way onto one more ship and eventually made it to Naples, Italy. Riggs turned himself over to US military authorities, but had to force his way through red tape to get back to his old outfit, the 81st Engineer Battalion, which was refitting in France. He finished the war building POW cages in the Ruhr area of Germany where he processed over a million German POWs. Cole, *Ardennes*, 273. Although Cole credits the bulk of the engineer defensive effort east of St.-Vith to the 168th Combat Engineer Battalion (an VIII Corps unit), Riggs claims his 81st Engineer Battalion bore the brunt of the fighting. Riggs says, "The CO of the 168 Engrs. reported at the defense line east of St.-Vith

[and] described his battalion as being at 50% strength...he further stated that he was not an enthusiastic supporter of the secondary infantry responsibility for combat engineers. Thus it did not surprise me to receive less than a company from this battalion."

75. US Department of the Army, US Armor School, *The Battle at St.-Vith, Belgium, 17-23 December 1944*, 1949, 4; Bruce C. Clarke, "Move to Saint Vith, 16-18 December 1944," unpublished manuscript, 4 pages, undated.

76. Ellis and Cunningham, *Clarke of St.-Vith*, 7-8; Armor School, *Battle at St.-Vith*, 4; Clarke, "Move to Saint Vith," 1.

77. Bruce C. Clarke, "The Battle for St.-Vith: Armor in the Defense and Delay," *Armor* 83 (November-December 1974): 40; Clarke interview, 13 April 1985.

78. Bruce C. Clarke, "Defense of St.-Vith," interview by the author, 10 November 1987, tape recording. Clarke said, "My detailed description of [Jones] on the 17th and 18th of December [1944] would be unbelievable...Jones was constantly concerned about his son. It was a mistake to have him in his division."

79. Owen E. Woodruff, Jr., to Bruce C. Clarke, 27 January 1987.

80. US War Department, *Army List and Directory*. Jones' son, Alan W. Jones, Jr., graduated from the US Military Academy in 1943. Commissioned in the infantry, he was assigned to the staff of the 423rd Infantry Regiment in his father's 106th Infantry Division. When the German attack surrounded that unit on the Schnee Eifel plateau on 17 December 1944, 1st LT Jones was with his unit. He was captured on 20 December and spent the duration of the war in a prisoner-of-war camp in Hammelburg, Germany.

81. Clarke, interview, 10 November 1987; Armor School, *Battle at St.-Vith*, 4; Clarke, "Move to Saint Vith," 2.

82. Woodruff to Clarke, 27 January 1987; Armor School, *Battle at St.-Vith*, 7-9; Ellis and Cunningham, *Clarke of St.-Vith*, 13.

83. Dupuy, *Lion in the Way*, 16-17; Clarke, interview, 10 November 1987.

84. Cole, *Ardennes*, 272-275; Whiting, *Death of a Division*, 80; Dupuy, *Lion in the Way*, 23.

85. Ellis and Cunningham, *Clarke of St.-Vith*, 13; Clarke, interview, 10 November 1987. About noon on 17 December Clarke witnessed a bizarre scene when the 14th Cavalry Group commander, Colonel Mark Devine, burst into Jones' office claiming to have been "chased into the building by a Tiger tank!" When Jones hesitated, Clarke suggested the distraught cavalryman go to

Bastogne and report the situation to his corps commander, Middleton. Devine stared at Clarke and Jones, then rushed out of the room. Neither man saw him again during the battle.

86. Clarke, "Move to Saint Vith," 2; Clarke, interview, 10 November 1987; Alfred D. Chandler, Jr., et al., eds. *The Papers of Dwight David Eisenhower, The War Years*, vol. 4 (Baltimore: Johns Hopkins Press, 1970), 2335. Eisenhower recognized the "abnormal strains" placed upon a division commander in active combat and sent several "home for a rest." Ike wrote to Marshall (5 December 1944) that these strains "are really more than any one man should be called upon to bear...Corps, Army and Army Group commanders stand up well. They are in the more fortunate middle area where their problems involve tactics and local maintenance, without on the one hand having to burden themselves with politics, priorities, shipping and maquis, while they are spared the more direct battle strains of a Division commander." He also fully appreciated the additional "shock and stress" of division commanders like Stroh and O'Daniel, who had both lost only sons in the war.

87. Clarke, interview, 10 November 1987; Clarke, "Move the Saint Vith," 2. Later Clarke wrote that Jones had "deliberately lied" to Middleton and charged he continued to lie over the next few days to cover it up. Despite Jones misrepresentation to his corps commander, it seems that it could have little impact on the fighting at St.-Vith. By then, Middleton had no control over the events occurring at the beleaguered crossroads and was unable to influence the action there in any case. It did, of course, cause Clarke to lose much respect for the harassed Jones.

88. Clarke, "Move to Saint Vith," 2.

89. Ibid.

90. Ellis and Cunningham, *Clarke of St.-Vith*, 13; Clarke, "Move to Saint Vith," 2; Clarke, interview, 10 November 1987.

91. Woodruff to Clarke, 27 January 1987; Armor School, *Battle at St.-Vith*, 9.

92. Armor School, *Battle at St.-Vith*, 6-9; Whiting, *Death of a Division*, 80; Cole, *Ardennes*, 275-278.

93. Robert F. Phillips, *To Save Bastogne* (New York: Stein and Day, 1983), 150; Dupuy, *Lion in the Way*, 105.

94. Woodruff to Clarke, 27 January 1987; Clarke, "Move to St.-Vith," 3.

95. Roy Udell Clay, interview by author, 12 March 1986; Clarke interview, 13 April 1985; Armor School, *Battle at St.-Vith*, 9; Ellis and Cunningham, *Clarke of St.-Vith*, 97-98. Clay and his men fought hard to stay in the battle when they could easily have

joined in the general retreat. Indeed, later that day a staff officer suggested to Clay that the unit retire westward because "Everybody else is retreating." Clay refused, saying, "We came here to fight the enemy and the way I see it, from this position we can fire in just about any direction and kill Germans."

96. Roy U. Clay, *Curbstone: The History of the 275th Armored Field Artillery Battalion in World War II* (Jackson, TN: Richerson, 1978), 10-18. Clay reports that his forward observer parties stuck by their posts during the assaults, and many were surrounded. Under the cover of darkness, however, most were able to avoid the German units and slip back through enemy lines, rejoining their battalion; Roy U. Clay, interview by author, 23 and 26 February 1986; Cole, *Ardennes*, 149; Clay, interview, 12 March 1986.

97. John S.D. Eisenhower, *The Bitter Woods* (New York: G.P. Putnam's Sons, 1969), 198; Price, *Middleton*, 215; Roy U. Clay, interview by author, 23 and 26 February 1986. MacMahon, the 106th Division Artillery commander, could do little else but wish Clay and his gunners "good luck." The entire overextended front was exploding and MacMahon had all he could handle just trying to piece together some support for his own hard-pressed regiments.

98. Clay, interviews, 23 February and 12 March 1986. The cavalry troopers retired behind the artillerymen without notice twice during that first terrible day. Clay's gunners were able to occupy new firing positions with little trouble, however, each time this happened. Splitting the battalion into two columns, each using a different route, and moving at staggered intervals reduced the risks and facilitated the retrograde operation. At one point, each column had to cross a bridge over the Our River which was being interdicted by German artillery. After observing the air bursts for some minutes, however, battalion officers discovered that the rounds were arriving with such regularity, that both units were able to cross untouched simply by anticipating the intervals. Methodical "Prussian logic" gone awry, it appears.

99. Clay, *Curbstone*, 10-18; Clay, interviews, 26 February and 12 March 1986. Clay reports that this was the most frustrating part of the entire battle. The roads in front of them were choked with German troops and vehicles, but Clay's gunners were prohibited from firing for several crucial hours that day. To make matters worse, COL Devine, the panicky commander of the 14th Cavalry Group, ordered Clay to emplace his M7, 105-mm, self-propelled howitzers along likely avenues of approach for German armor, intending, apparently, to forsake completely the howitzer's primary role and utilize Clay's guns as nothing more

than tank destroyers. Finally, Clay could take no more and set off to locate BG MacMahon to resolve the matter. Circumstances overcame events, however, for by the time Clay arrived at the command post in St.-Vith, Clarke's troops were on the way into town. With the cavalry group virtually destroyed as an effective fighting force, Clay's next assignment was obvious to him--support Clarke.

100. Clay, interview, 12 March 1986.

101. Armor School, *Battle at St.-Vith*, 9; Cole, *Ardennes*, 279.

102. Riggs to Clarke, 28 January 1986; Armor School, *Battle at St.-Vith*, 9-10.

103. Clarke, "Move to Saint Vith," 3.

104. Ibid.

105. Armor School, *Battle at St.-Vith*, 10-12; Cole, *Ardennes*, 275-280.

106. Clarke, interviews, 13 April 1985 and 10 November 1987.

107. Clarke, interview, 10 November 1987, described some of his actions during that time by relating, "I had no defensive *lines* but had strong defensive *areas*. The defense was very flexible...I constantly imagined where the next crisis or crises would take place, and decided ahead of time what to do if they did." Regarding his personal supervision of events, "I never had my clothes off until 23 December. I visited units [in my jeep and] my driver tied me to my seat with rope so I could sleep and not fall out."

108. Armor School, *Battle at St.-Vith*, 12.

109. Ellis and Cunningham, *Clarke of St.-Vith*, 329.

110. Cole, *Ardennes*, 393.

111. Ibid.

112. Armor School, *Battle at St.-Vith*, 21.

113. Cole, *Ardennes*, 411.

114. Ibid., 412.

115. Clarke, interview, 10 November 1987; Cole, *Ardennes*, 412; Armor School, *Battle at St.-Vith*, 22-25.

116. *7th Armored Division After Action Report*, 95-96.

117. Cole, *Ardennes*, 410-413; Whiting, *Death of a Division*, 137-141.

118. Cole, *Ardennes*, 412-413; *7th Armored Division After Action Report*.

119. Whiting, *Death of a Division*, 138.

120. Clarke, interview, 10 November 1987; Whiting, *Death of a Division*, 139.

121. Robert W. Hasbrouck to Bruce C. Clarke, undated.

Hasbrouck wrote of the "fortified goose-egg" idea that "Montgomery...saved us from Ridgway's crazy idea of leaving us in the woods east of Vielsalm as an 'island of resistance' to fight back to back...Both Ridgway and Bradley thought any withdrawal was disgraceful. Fortunately, Montgomery appreciated the value of a withdrawal on occasion. That saved the 7th Armored Division."; Whiting, *Death of a Division*, 140-141.

122. Cole, *Ardennes*, 411-413; Whiting, *Death of a Division*, 142; Armor School, *Battle at St.-Vith*, 25-26.

123. Whiting, *Death of a Division*, 142.

124. US War Department, *Army List and Directory*, shows that Alan W. Jones was medically retired from active duty on 31 October 1945, in the retired rank of major general; Whiting, *Death of a Division*, 143.

125. Ellis and Cunningham, *Clarke of St.-Vith*, 133.

126. Cole, *Ardennes*, 415; Armor School, *Battle at St.-Vith*, 25.

127. Cole, *Ardennes*, 415-422; Armor School, *Battle at St.-Vith*, 25-26; Clarke, interview, 10 November 1987; Clay, interview, 12 March 1986.

128. Armor School, *Battle at St.-Vith*, 26; Clarke, interview, 13 April 1985.

129. Dupuy, *Lion in the Way*, 7, reports that "The worst of this damage was the fact that key men were being seized. These drafts of strength were accomplished under rigorous screening which insisted on taking the best, only the best...In their place came groups from Army Specialized Training Program, from the Army Air Forces, the Army Ground Forces Replacement Depots, and volunteers for infantry...from anti-aircraft and coast artillery units...with a sizeable complement from military police and Army Service Forces units."

130. US War Department, *12th Army Group Report of Operations, G-1 Section*, 1948. It appears the replacement problem was never really solved in time to influence the conduct of the European fighting. Reports contained in the G-1 files for Bradley's 12th Army Group show correspondence concerning ways to try to eliminate the problem throughout the final months of the war.

131. Weigley, *Eisenhower's Lieutenants*, 458.

132. *VIII Corps Letter of Instruction, 7 December 1944.*

133. Bradley and Blair, *A General's Life*, 354.

134. J.D. Morelock, "Senior Leadership: The Crucial Element of Combat Power" (Master of Military Art and Science thesis, 1984), 15-19.

135. Ibid.. 16.

136. Riggs to Clarke, 28 January 1986; Whiting, *Death of a Division*, 80.

137. Clarke, "Move to Saint Vith," 2.

138. Clarke, interview, 10 November 1987.

139. Morelock, "Senior Leadership," 5.

140. Clarke, "Move to Saint Vith," 3.

141. Whiting, *Death of a Division*, 142.

142. Cole, *Ardennes*, 140; Price, *Middleton*, 268.

143. Riggs to Clarke, 28 January 1986.

144. Clarke, interview, 10 November 1987; Whiting, *Death of a Division*, 80. Dupuy, predictably, is silent on this entire issue, apparently satisfied to pretend it never occurred.

145. Weigley, *Eisenhower's Lieutenants*, 458.

146. Clarke, "Battle for St.-Vith," 40; Clarke, interview, 13 April 1985.

147. Armor School, *Battle at St.-Vith*, 9; Clarke, "Move to Saint Vith," 2.

148. Franklin Institute, *Art and Requirements of Command, Generalship Study* 2 (Philadelphia: Systems Sciences Department, Franklin Institute, 1967), 15.

149. Clarke, interview, 10 November 1987. Clarke did not need Hasbrouck to reiterate the fact that denying the important St.-Vith crossroads to the Germans was key to slowing the attack in their sector. In fact, the armored division commander's orders to Clarke were only "to stop or slow down the German advance and he [Hasbrouck] would support me with the rest of the division."

150. Ibid.

151. Clarke, "Move to Saint Vith," 2.

152. Dupuy, *Lion in the Way*, 65.

153. Cole, *Ardennes*, 274-275.

154. Dupuy, *Lion in the Way*, 100.

155. Weigley, *Eisenhower's Lieutenants*, 451.

156. Cole, *Ardennes*, 274-275.

157. Clarke, interview, 10 November 1987.

158. Woodruff to Clarke, 27 January 1987; Clarke, interview, 10 November 1987.

159. Clarke, interview, 10 November 1987.

160. Dupuy, *Lion in the Way*, 76.

161. Eisenhower, *Bitter Woods*, 286.

162. Clarke, interview, 10 November 1987; Clarke, "Move to Saint Vith," 2.

163. Matthew B. Ridgway, *Soldier: The Memoirs of Matthew B. Ridgway (As Told to Harold H. Martin)* (New York: Harper and

Brothers, 1956); Cole, *Ardennes*, 411-413; Whiting, *Death of a Division*, 138-143.

164. Clarke, interview, 10 November 1987.

165. Cole, *Ardennes*, 413; Armor School, *Battle at St.-Vith*, 25.

166. Clarke, interview, 10 November 1987. Clarke's "confusion," of course, is simply Clausewitz' "friction" put another way. It's merely a different way of stating Clausewitz' dictum that, in war, even the simplest things are difficult to accomplish.

167. Whiting, *Death of a Division*, 144. It's undoubtedly also true that untrained generals and untrained units tend not to perform very well in their first combat.

168. Weigley, *Eisenhower's Lieutenants*, 490. Bruce C. Clarke continued to rise in rank through the postwar years becoming one of the Army's most celebrated combat commanders and trainers. At the close of World War II he was assigned to General Jacob Devers' Army Ground Forces command where he was instrumental in creating the post-war Army professional military education system. During the last year of the Korean War, the then lieutenant general commanded the X Corps (whose units included the 7th Infantry Division fighting for Pork Chop Hill). Promoted to full General, Clarke commanded US Army Europe and Seventh Army during the Berlin crisis in the early 1960s. General Clarke retired from active service in 1963 but continued to write about and advise senior Army leaders on leadership and command the remainder of his life. Dwight Eisenhower once paid tribute to Clarke by remarking, "The US Army has had two great trainers—Baron von Steuben and Bruce Clarke." General Clarke died in March 1988.

7. Heroes and Victims

The best of the US combat commanders had their share of failures, and even the unluckiest ones, those most victimized by the unexpected German offensive, experienced some measure of success. Combat is an incredibly confusing and obscure environment, and the waging of war is an imprecise science that, if it follows any law, seems most faithful to the Law written by the mythical Murphy. Sorting out the "good" leaders from the "bad" is no easy task; they are often two manifestations of the same commander's leadership. Further, simply pointing out the successes and failures of American battle leadership in this watershed battle begs an overall assessment. History demands an attempt at a comprehensive accounting and a fair appraisal of the performance of each senior US leader.

"SUCCESS ON THE BATTLEFIELD SPEAKS FOR ITSELF"

The shortest and simplest answer to the question of an overall assessment of American battle leadership in the Ardennes is perhaps best summed up by a quote from historian Martin Blumenson's recent reflective essay on Eisenhower and his top lieutenants: "Success on the battlefield speaks for itself."[1] That is, because the ultimate test of the effectiveness of battle leadership is battlefield victory, American commanders in the Ardennes are judged to be successful leaders. Such an analysis, however, slights the really outstanding leadership accomplishments of the US commanders.

It cannot be denied that failures in American leadership led to a situation that permitted Hitler to organize and launch his great offensive against a sector of the line so weakened that German battlefield success seemed highly probable.[2] This leadership failure and the resulting German strategic surprise were later compounded by the inability of the Allies to launch a timely, coordinated counteroffensive that could have trapped and destroyed the bulk of German troops in the bulge. Both of these leadership failures represented serious lapses in battle command on the Allied, principally American, side of the battle line. To these two failures at the strategic level must be added the biggest leadership failure of the battle at the tactical level—the mass surrender of two regiments of the 106th Infantry Division.[3]

Examining the actual conduct of the battle once the German attack began, however, yields an overwhelmingly positive assessment of how American battle leadership fought that campaign. Although American senior commanders were responsible for the one-sided conditions in the Ardennes through their actions in the months preceding the attack, they nevertheless responded to the assault in a timely fashion with solid, effective, competent leadership that proved successful in gaining control of the battle and winning it. Their actions at the operational and tactical level combined to overcome the strategic blunders and turn a potentially disastrous situation to the Allies' favor.

Eisenhower may have invited the German riposte in the Ardennes in the first place with his insistence on general offensives all along the line, but he largely redeemed the situation by reacting to counter quickly, then defeat, the German attack.[4] If he failed to motivate Montgomery to launch a timely counterattack on the north of the bulge, the 100,000 (or more) precious combat troops the Germans lost in the battle were, nonetheless, unavailable to confront Ike's armies during the subsequent battles for Germany.[5]

Similarly, Bradley's uncharacteristic failure to exert aggressive, positive command of his army group at the beginning of the battle was effectively offset by Eisenhower's more active role in the actual conduct of the fighting. For once forsaking his habitual hands-off approach to the exercise of battle command, Ike intervened early and appropriately to create the conditions leading to the defeat of the German offensive.[6] Patton's aggressive development and execution of the American counterstroke from the south more than made up for Bradley's lack of a firm hand at the helm of 12th Army Group. Patton really didn't need the help anyway.[7]

It was Patton again, along with his West Point classmate, Simpson, and some outstanding subordinate commanders at the corps, division, and regimental levels who created battlefield success when Hodges' failures and bad decisions threatened to doom First Army. With Simpson rapidly flooding First Army area with reinforcements, Patton striking swiftly to relieve Bastogne, and solid subordinate commanders like Middleton, Gerow, Hasbrouck, Cota, Barton, Fuller, and Clarke stubbornly frustrating every enemy move, Hodges' army not only survived, it ultimately triumphed, despite the First Army commander's poor leadership.[8]

Mistakes of leadership and command at the tactical level, including the horrendous disaster that befell the 106th Infantry Division, also tended to be redeemed by the successes of American battle leadership in the Ardennes. Even though Middleton and Jones failed to save the 422nd and 423rd Infantry Regiments of Jones' 106th Division from encirclement and surrender on the Schnee Eifel in front of St.-Vith, Clarke's masterful mobile defense of the area with his combat command of the 7th Armored Division and attached units largely compensated for the loss of the infantrymen. Further, despite the Germans' rapid rush through the Losheim Gap, the Americans' stalwart defense of the commanding Elsenborn Ridge stymied the enemy's ability to exploit the rupture. It seems clear that when the leadership successes and failures of this battle are closely examined—when the actions and command decisions of the senior American commanders and their resulting impact on the battle's outcome are weighed and measured on the scales of victory and defeat—American battle leadership was a tremendous success.

The senior leaders like Eisenhower, Simpson, Patton, and Middleton actually *won* this greatest land battle in US history; they didn't merely survive it. Their battle leadership in the Ardennes was not that of military incompetents or amateurs who didn't know their jobs. Ike and the other successful American commanders showed they knew exactly what had to be done, and they quickly set about doing it. On balance, American battle leadership in America's greatest land battle proved decisively successful.

WHAT MAKES THE MAN?

It is interesting to analyze how these successful battle leaders developed the leadership skills they used to win the Battle of the Bulge. Obviously, they did not suddenly spring onto the battlefields of World War II Europe as full-blown military geniuses. They all had to study and learn their trade, then practice it before they could become successful battle leaders, and they had all engaged in the systematic study of warfare, in one form or another, their whole adult lives.

With few exceptions, these leaders attended a progressively higher series of schools and professional military education courses, alternating with ever more demanding command and staff officer assignments. Through these alternating line and school duties, they gained a background of knowledge and professional skill leading to positions of ever-increasing responsibilities. Once the war began, they gained combat experience and learned valuable lessons in combat command on the battlefields of North Africa, Sicily, and France.[9]

The meek, the incompetent, and the troublesome were, for the most part, weeded out on those same battlefields, their places taken by others who, having been similarly prepared, were moved up from subordinate commands or were impatiently waiting in the wings for their own chance.[10] They all learned the basics of their trade between the World Wars in service schools like the Command and General Staff School, the War College, and the Army Industrial College.[11] They supplemented the basics with practical knowledge gleaned from a variety of command and staff assignments in troop units spread over the globe in such places as the Philippines, Hawaii, the Canal Zone, and the United States.[12] While still junior officers, they challenged their ingenuity and broadened their perspectives and experience in other varied duties such as organizing and running the Civilian Conservation Corps, teaching ROTC and coaching college football, or managing an engineer district the size of Texas.[13] They served apprenticeships to the famous (like Marshall and MacArthur) and the near famous (like Fox Conner and Adna Chaffee), and they continued to learn.[14] And throughout their careers, they interacted with and learned from each other, growing as leaders.[15] When the lucky few were chosen from the pack and given command during the war, the competent ones gained valuable combat experience they put to good use in positions of ever-increasing responsibility.

But while their background and preparation seem common and straightforward, the actual process used to <u>select</u> them for important commands is less so. The key is not how the men learned their trade and practiced their profession in the years between the World Wars, but the process Marshall and his intimates used to select the lucky ones for higher command. However inappropriate such a personal sponsorship system seems today, it was a definite institution at that time.[16]

Many of the key men leading the battle in the Ardennes had been personally chosen by George Marshall for plum assignments and were "sponsored" by him through part of their careers. They were identified by the Chief of Staff early on, and he kept track of their progression, selecting the ones he considered most promising for important positions as the war clouds in Europe gathered.[17] Later, he secured their promotions to high command, then collaborated with them in selecting other promising officers to fill key positions when those assignments opened up.[18] However, these leaders, fortunate in their timing to be in the right place at the right time to be noticed by Marshall, were probably not the only capable, competent officers in the US Army. Their backgrounds seem relatively common and so unremarkable that their Marshall connection seems the only thing setting them apart from their contemporaries. Blumenson points this out when he explains the "hitch" in the Marshall method:

> The Marshall method of identifying and rewarding first-rate officers was a system within a system. It worked well so far as it went. For every person entered in Marshall's notebook, there were probably a dozen, perhaps more, who were every bit as good as the ones he listed. The others were simply unfortunate because they failed to come within Marshall's orbit or ken....How many excellent individuals were slighted simply because of their bad luck of never meeting or working with Marshall is, of course, a matter of conjecture.[19]

The very fact that the careers of Eisenhower, Patton, Simpson, and others prior to World War II were unremarkable, ordinary, and similar to those of their contemporaries is itself a testament to the system which produced them. There probably were a number of other "Ikes" and "Brads" who, if they had been touched by Marshall and received the call to leadership, could have produced a great victory as Ike did. Blumenson, pondering what the American Army of that war would have looked like if Marshall had not been leading it, concluded that, "Most likely, some of our heroes of World War II would have had different names."[20]

This conclusion not only brings the legends down to mortal size, it also reduces pondering on how our World War II leaders were produced.

In the end, however they were chosen, and whether they were good leaders or bad, heroes or victims, most of these combat leaders of the American Army in northwest Europe found themselves in the Ardennes that terrible December to face what became one of the greatest tests of their battle leadership the war would produce. In this final exam in battle leadership that called on all their experiences over the decades leading up to the Battle of the Bulge, it seems clear that the majority of them passed this test so well as to bear emulation.

NOTES

1. Martin Blumenson, "Eisenhower Then and Now: Fireside Reflections," *Parameters* 21 (Summer 1991):29.

2. Forrest C. Pogue, "The Supreme Allied Command in Northwest Europe, 1944-1945," *Essays in History and International Relations*, ed. Dwight E. Lee and George McReynolds (Worcester, MA: Clarke University Press, 1949), 172-173; Jacques Nobécourt, *Hitler's Last Gamble* (New York: Schocken Books, 1967), 84, 130, 284; Russell F. Weigley, *Eisenhower's Lieutenants: The Campaign of France and Germany, 1944-1945* (Bloomington, IN: Indiana University Press, 1981), 463-464; David Eisenhower, *Eisenhower: At War, 1943-1945* (New York: Random House, 19986), 555.

3. John Toland, *Battle: Th Story of the Bulge* (New York: Random House, 1959), 53; Hugh M. Cole, *The United States Army in World War II. European Theater of Operations. The Ardennes: The Battle of the Bulge* (Washington, DC: Office of the Chief of

Military History/GPO, 1965), 170, 274-275, 331; Weigley, *Eisenhower's Lieutenants*, 451; Frank J. Price, *Troy H. Middleton: A Biography* (Baton Rouge: LSU Press,1974), 216.

4. Pogue, "Supreme Command," 175, 178, 192; Nobécourt, *Last Gamble*, 77-78; Weigley, *Eisenhower's Lieutenants*, 458.

5. Basil H. Liddell Hart, *The Other Side of the Hill* (London: Cassell, 1951), 465; Weigley, *Eisenhower's Lieutenants*, 574. Liddell Hart condemns the offensive by writing, "The Ardennes offensive carried to the extreme of absurdity the military belief that 'attack is the best defense.' It proved the 'worst defense'--wrecking Germany's chances for further serious resistance." There were tough battles yet to come, including the bitter Rhineland Campaign, but Hitler had used up his last major mobile reserves in the Ardennes.

6. D.K.R. Crosswell, *The Chief of Staff: The Military Career of General Walter Bedell Smith* (New York: Greenwood Press, 1991), 294-296.

7. Martin Blumenson, *Patton: The Man Behind the Legend, 1885-1945* (New York: Berkeley Books, 1987), 246-252; Omar N. Bradley and Clay Blair, *A General's Life: An Autobiography of General of the Army Omar N. Bradley* (New York: Simon and Schuster, 1983), 367-368; Weigley, *Eisenhower's Lieutenants*, 498-506, 519-527.

8. The listed commanders are Major General Troy Middleton, VIII Corps; Major General Leonard Gerow, V Corps; Major General Robert Hasbrouck, 7th Armored Division; Major General Norman Cota, 28th Infantry Division; Major General Raymond Barton, 4th Infantry Division; Colonel Hurley Fuller, 110th Infantry Regiment (28th Infantry Division); and Bruce C. Clarke, CCB, 7th Armored Division.

9. Robert H. Berlin, "United States Army World War II Corps Commanders: A Composite Biography," *The Journal of Military History* 53 (April 1989): 149, 162; Martin Blumenson, "America's World War II Leaders in Europe: Some Thoughts," *Parameters* 19 (December 1989): 4; J. Lawton Collins, *Conversations with General J. Lawton Collins* (Ft. Leavenworth, KS: US Army Command and General Staff College, 1983), 5-6. Berlin hypothesizes that the interwar officers "developed common professional skills and abilities" gained through schools, service with troops, and as instructors or on staffs.

10. Blumenson, "America's World War II Leaders," 4. Blumenson writes that, once the war began, the "early battles...proved out the real leaders and shook out the duds."

11. Robert H. Berlin, "Dwight David Eisenhower and the Duties of Generalship," *Military Review* 70 (October 1990): 17; E. M. Flanagan, Jr., "A Force of Professionals," *Army* 42 (March 1992): 57; Berlin, "Corps Commanders," 155; Collins, *Conversations*, 3-4; Blumenson, "America's World War II Leaders," 8. Blumenson describes the professional military education of the era: "Successful officers usually proceeded through a progression of educational institutions. First came the Military Academy at West Point or college work with the ROTC, both leading to a commission. Then arrived the advance branch schooling at Fort Benning for Infantry, Fort Sill for Artillery, Fort Belvoir for the Engineers, and the like. Next came the course variously titled but eventually called the Command and General Staff College at Fort Leavenworth, which was regarded generally as the most important school assignment for all officers, the prerequisite, it was said, for promotion to high rank and major responsibility. Finally, the top of the educational pile was the Army War College." Collins, like many of the top World War II leaders, a student and instructor in this school system, related, "I am a great believer in the Army school system. The thing that saved the American Army--no question about it in my judgment--was this school system, the entire school system....The school system made an army for us. I've said I'd give up a division before I'd give up one of our schools." Flanagan, reporting on the results of a questionnaire he circulated to "between the wars"-era retired generals, wrote that one response summed up the consensus. It said, "The answer to your question can be summed up in three words: Schools, schools, and schools."

12. Stephen E. Ambrose, *Eisenhower: Volume One, Soldier, General of the Army, President-Elect, 1890-1952* (New York: Simon and Schuster, 1983); Bradley and Blair, *A General's Life*; Blumenson, *Patton*; Price, *Middleton*; Thomas R. Stone, "General William Hood Simpson: Unsung Commander of US Ninth Army," *Parameters* 11 (February 1980); Weigley, *Eisenhower's Lieutenants* and *History of the United States Army* (New York: MacMillan, 1967); Crosswell, *Chief of Staff*; Cole C. Kingseed, "Eisenhower's Prewar Anonymity: Myth or Reality?" *Parameters* 21 (Autumn 1991); Berlin, "Corps Commanders." Virtually all of the interwar regular officers alternated line, staff, and school assignments to one degree or another. Some, like Bradley and Middleton, spent more time in schools (both as student and instructor) than did others, but they all held a wide variety of troop and staff duties in field units and headquarters throughout the period between the two World Wars. Troop units were spread over the entire United States, from large

posts, like Forts Benning and Sill, to small ones, like Fort Dodge (Iowa) and Fort Screven (Georgia). Overseas troop and staff duty was often highlighted by tours in the Philippines, Hawaii, or Panama—all usually sought after because, despite the isolation from the States, a high standard of living was possible, even on an Army officer's meager pay. Berlin, examining the interwar careers of the 34 officers who commanded corps during the war, wrote, "Command of troop units was a desirable assignment for officers during the interwar period because it could result in highly beneficial officer efficiency reports...[and, thus] twenty-two of the thirty-four officers gained extensive command experience during the interwar period. As their experience grew, they usually led successively larger units, moving from company to battalion to regiment." Berlin continues that "staff assignments during the interwar period var[ied] from regimental staff duty to service on the General Staff in Washington where twenty of the future corps commanders served." "Often," Berlin writes, "these staff assignments were long tours of duty lasting from three to five years."

13. Bruce C. Clarke, "Creating an Outstanding Battalion in 1941-1942," unpublished; Bradley and Blair, *A General's Life*, 71-72; Kingseed, "Eisenhower's Anonymity," 88-96.

14. Richard M. Ketchum, "Warming Up on the Sidelines for World War II," *Smithsonian* 22 (September 1991): 102; Kingseed, "Eisenhower's Prewar Anonymity," 90-96; Ambrose, *Eisenhower*; Bradley and Blair, *A General's Life*; Blumenson, *Patton*; Weigley, *Eisenhower's Lieutenants*; Berlin, "Duties of Generalship," 16-17. Bradley's service under Marshall and Eisenhower's assignment as an assistant to MacArthur in the Philippines are well-known examples of apprenticeships to famous or to-be-famous leaders. Ike's mentorship by General Fox Conner or Bruce Clarke's close service under General Adna Chaffee are less well known, but were extremely influential in forming these officers' interwar experiences. Ketchum points out the role played by the famous 1941 maneuvers in helping Marshall shape the face of American Army leadership at the beginning of the war. He writes, "Many officers' careers were made, others' broken" by the war games. "Of 42 army, corps and division commanders who participated in the Louisiana maneuvers, only 11 got significant combat assignments during World War II." Ketchum records that Marshall's collaborator in creating the American Army of World War II, General Lesley J. McNair, said in the wake of the maneuvers, "A lot of these Generals who want to fire their Chief of Staff ought to fire themselves....We're going to start at

the top and work down. We've got some bum Generals...but we're going to weed them out. Have we the bright young Majors and Captains to replace them? Yes."

15. Roger H. Nye, "Whence Patton's Genius?" *Parameters* 22 (Winter 1991-1992): 60-73; Kingseed, "Eisenhower's Prewar Anonymity," 89-90; Berlin, "Duties of Generalship," 16; Blumenson, "America's World War II Leaders," 9; Collins, *Conversations*, 3. Many of the World War II leaders interacted personally and professionally throughout the period, to each others' mutual benefit. Indeed, one salutary benefit of bringing officers together in a school environment is so that they may interact and learn from each other. The contacts made while attending the Army's schools are often the most important lasting effects of the experience. Eisenhower's and Patton's collaboration and publishing of articles on the future of mechanized warfare in the early 1920's is a well-known example of personal and professional interaction, and mutual intellectual stimulation. Nye highlights the importance of a "lifetime program of professional reading" which should not be overlooked as an influence on the future careers and professional development of the World War II leaders. He identifies Patton's extensive library and lifetime habit of reading as one manifestation and source of his military genius. Blumenson supports this conclusion by writing, "George Patton grew professionally through his reading, a 'monumental self-study he charted for himself.'" Blumenson, however, expands this beyond Patton by continuing, "He was hardly alone. Quite a few officers strove for knowledge and [their] development gained professional competence by more or less systematic reading. They also interacted with like-minded officers of their generation, all 'intelligent, stimulating men...studying their profession' individually and in small groups, off duty and at the service schools." When Collins was asked how he prepared himself for war, he answered, "To some considerable extent, by reading military history. I told my own son, 'If you really want to learn your trade, you couldn't do any better than studying Freeman's book on Robert E. Lee'....I read military history, and I got a good deal out of the good ones." While he was forming and training the Ninth Army staff, Simpson re-read *Lee's Lieutenants* as a refresher course in the timeless elements of command and leadership, and recommended that his staff do the same. Eisenhower read all aspects of military history in earnest while serving under Fox Conner in the Canal Zone, and "Conner," writes Berlin, "guided Eisenhower in his reading of military literature from Civil War officer memoirs to Carl von Clausewitz's *On War*." Berlin relates that "Eisenhower recalled

that 'life with General Conner was a sort of graduate school in military affairs and the humanities.'"

16. Crosswell, *Chief of Staff*, 31-68; Berlin, "Corps Commanders," 156, 166; Weigley, *History of the US Army* and *Eisenhower's Lieutenants*. Berlin, writing of the 34 corps commanders, but, nonetheless, speaking of the experiences of all the senior American commanders in the war, records, "Their professional military education, experience in a variety of positions, and operational knowledge combined with combat leadership prepared them to serve the army ably at war." Berlin also refers to this question when he notes the comments of Ernest Harmon, outstanding commander of the 1st and 2nd Armored Divisions in World War II: "A military historian recently asked me how the United States, indifferent and even contemptuous of the military in peacetime, had been able to produce a group of generals proficient enough to lead armies successfully against German might....I am now convinced that the intensive and imaginative training at the Command and General Staff College had a great deal to do with it." It seems obvious that the American senior leaders who commanded the US Army in Europe in World War II were prepared for this task by a combination of professional military education in schools, alternating with command and staff assignments, and supplemented by challenging duties, extensive reading and self-study, professional and personal interaction, and apprenticeships to senior officers. The issue that remains less clear is the manner in which these officers were *selected* to hold the positions they held during the war. Relying on Marshall's "little black book" is not a "system" per se, and, at least in some cases, put the wrong man in a critical position. It certainly discriminated against those who did not come in contact with Marshall and probably overlooked some otherwise outstanding leaders.

17. Morris Janowitz, *The Professional Soldier* (New York: Free Press-Macmillan), 296-297; Blumenson, "America's World War II Leaders," 5; Daniel P. Bolger, "Zero Defects: Command Climate in First US Army, 1944-1945," *Military Review* 71 (May 1991): 64-67. Janowitz describes the "Marshall Method": "Just as Marshall's appointment represented a departure from seniority appointment, so he, in turn, was vigorous in recruiting officers for higher command. His personal appointments filled central staff positions in Washington and manned key posts in the military structure for the European Theater....Many of these officers were deeply influenced by Marshall's leadership, and came to reflect his sentiments. For years, Marshall, like other aspiring officers, had

been keeping lists of officers whose talents had impressed him, and whom he intended to select as commanders, if he were appointed Chief of Staff, or in a position to influence the selection of commanders. Being an innovator, he selected for his list men who were energetic and who had demonstrated ability at problem-solving by his standards." Blumenson points out the importance of the "Benning connection": "Particularly lucky were those who had been with Marshall at the Infantry School at Fort Benning between 1927 and 1932, when he was Assistant Commandant. Outstanding students and faculty members were especially well-regarded and in his good graces. They had proved their potential for heavy responsibility, and Marshall looked after them during the war. They were generally excellent in discharging their duties, and they flourished and rose in rank and in authority." Bolger puts a darker spin on the "Marshall Connection" by pointing out that the "frosty, reserved Marshall" was a "tester rather than a teacher" or helpful coach, and that a single mistake on the part of even a promising subordinate could "finish" him in Marshall's book. "Once a man failed," Bolger writes, "Marshall rarely granted a second chance." Bolger proposes that this "Marshall legacy" led to his chosen commanders, such as Bradley and Hodges, creating a hostile and brutal command climate in the First Army.

18. Stephen E. Ambrose, *The Supreme Commander: The War Years of General Dwight D. Eisenhower* (Garden City, NY: Doubeday and Co., 1970), 597; Crosswell, *Chief of Staff*, 298-299; Stone, "Simpson," 81. Once Marshall had selected a commander, it sometimes proved difficult to remove him, even if the commander performed poorly in combat. After Eisenhower relieved the hapless, troublesome, and inept Lloyd Fredendall from command of II Corps after he had bungled the battle of Kasserine Pass in February 1943, Marshall still tried, from time to time, to get Eisenhower to take him back in a combat command assignment. Ike declined. Nevertheless, despite his well-deserved relief from command, Fredendall was promoted to lieutenant general and given command of the Second Army, a training command, for the duration of the war--all at Marshall's insistence.

19. Blumenson, "America's World War II Leaders," 94.

20. Kingseed, "Eisenhower's Pre-war Anonymity, 87-98; Blumenson, "America's World War II Leaders," 94. Kingseed casts reasonable doubt on the supposed anonymity of Eisenhower in the last years leading up to America's entry into World War II and, by implication, the "unremarkableness" of Ike's career. He writes: "Few if any officers of Eisenhower's generation matched his

versatile record of unsurpassed skill in administration, management, command, staff work, and communications. And what is perhaps more important, this record was known to the people who mattered before the United States entered World War II." Blumenson has correctly pointed out that we will never know just how good those officers waiting in the wings were.

APPENDIXES

APPENDIX A

Chain of Command, Allied Expeditionary Force
February 1944
(Forrest Pogue, *Supreme Command*, 54)

APPENDIX B

SHAEF Headquarters, 6 June 1944
(Forrest Pogue, *Supreme Command*, 67)

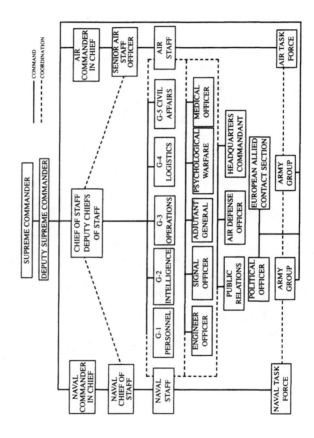

APPENDIX C

Operational Allied Chain of Command, May 1945
(Forrest Pogue, *Supreme Command*, 454)

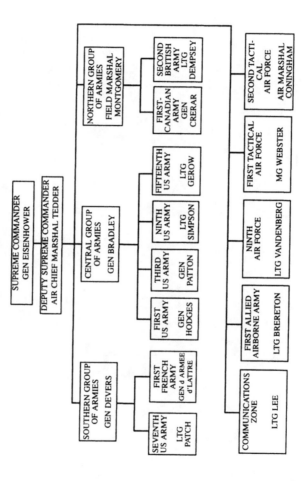

SUPREME COMMANDER
GEN EISENHOWER

DEPUTY SUPREME COMMANDER
AIR CHIEF MARSHAL TEDDER

SOUTHERN GROUP OF ARMIES
GEN DEVERS

SEVENTH US ARMY
LTG PATCH

FIRST FRENCH ARMY
GEN d ARMEE d'LATTRE

CENTRAL GROUP OF ARMIES
GEN BRADLEY

FIRST US ARMY
GEN HODGES

THIRD US ARMY
GEN PATTON

NINTH US ARMY
LTG SIMPSON

FIFTEENTH US ARMY
LTG GEROW

NORTHERN GROUP OF ARMIES
FIELD MARSHAL MONTGOMERY

FIRST CANADIAN ARMY
GEN CRERAR

SECOND BRITISH ARMY
LTG DEMPSEY

COMMUNICATIONS ZONE
LTG LEE

FIRST ALLIED AIRBORNE ARMY
LTG BRERETON

NINTH AIR FORCE
LTG VANDENBERG

FIRST TACTICAL AIR FORCE
MG WEBSTER

SECOND TACTICAL AIR FORCE
AIR MARSHAL CONINGHAM

APPENDIX D

Ardennes Command Arrangement
from 20 December 1944

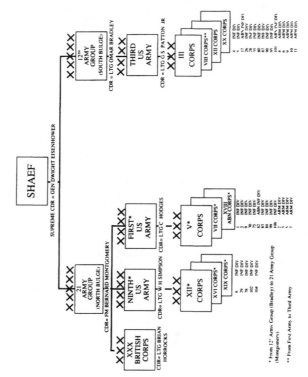

SHAEF
SUPREME CDR = GEN DWIGHT EISENHOWER

21 ARMY GROUP (NORTH BULGE)
CDR = FM BERNARD MONTGOMERY

12TH ARMY GROUP (SOUTH BULGE)
CDR = LTG OMAR BRADLEY

XXX BRITISH CORPS
CDR = LTG BRIAN HORROCKS

NINTH* US ARMY
CDR = LTG W H SIMPSON

FIRST* US ARMY
CDR = LTG C HODGES

THIRD US ARMY
CDR = LTG G S PATTON JR

XII* CORPS
XVI CORPS*
XIX CORPS*

V* CORPS
VII CORPS*
XVIII ABN CORPS**

III CORPS
VIII CORPS*
XII CORPS
XX CORPS

* From 12" Army Group (Bradley) to 21 Army Group (Montgomery)

** From First Army to Third Army

Appendix E

12th Army Group, 16 December 1944

12TH ARMY GROUP (XXXXX)
CDR = LTG OMAR N BRADLEY
ASGD STRENGTH = 815,087

FIRST ARMY (XXXX)
CDR = LTG COURTNEY HODGES
ASGD STRENGTH = 341,659

THIRD ARMY (XXXX)
CDR = LTG GEORGE S PATTON JR
ASGD STRENGTH = 257,518

NINTH ARMY (XXXX)
CDR = LTG WILLIAM H SIMPSON
ASGD STRENGTH = 188,825

V CORPS (XXX)
2 INF DIV
8 INF DIV
78 INF DIV
99 INF DIV
CC B 9 ARM DIV

VII CORPS (XXX)
1 INF DIV
9 INF DIV
83 INF DIV
104 INF DIV
3 ARM DIV
5 ARM DIV

VIII CORPS (XXX)
4 INF DIV
28 INF DIV
106 INF DIV
9 ARM DIV ( )

III CORPS (XXX)
26 INF DIV

XII CORPS (XXX)
35 INF DIV
80 INF DIV
87 INF DIV
4 ARM DIV
6 ARM DIV

XX CORPS (XXX)
5 INF DIV
90 INF DIV
95 INF DIV
10 ARM DIV

XIII CORPS (XXX)
84 INF DIV
102 INF DIV
7 ARM DIV

XVI CORPS* (XXX)

XIX CORPS (XXX)
29 INF DIV
30 INF DIV
2 ARM DIV

* On 16 December 1944, XVI Corps had no divisions assigned to it. Its strength, 9,549, consisted of headquarters, service, and assorted, non-divisional combat troops

369

APPENDIX F

First Army, 16 December 1944

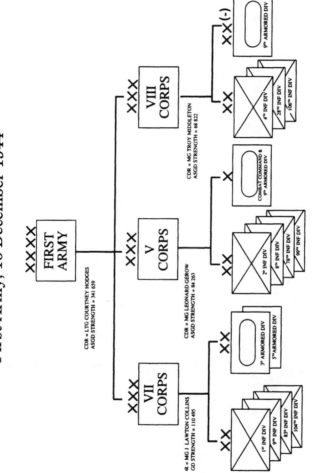

APPENDIX G

VIII Corps, 16 December 1944

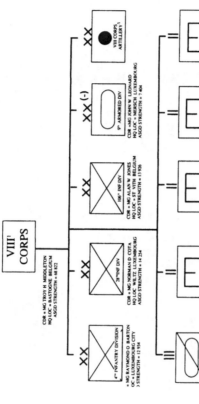

1 Primarily infantry-heavy VIII Corps had 242 M4 (SHERMAN) medium tanks and 185 tank destroyers available

2 Combat Command B, 9th Armored Division, was temporarily attached to V Corps in support of that unit's recently begun attack on the Roer River Dams, Combat Command R was held as a corps reserve by MG Middleton, only Combat Command A occupied a portion of the front line,

3 VIII Corps units totaled 394 pieces (105mm and larger)

APPENDIX H

106th Infantry Division, 16 December 1944

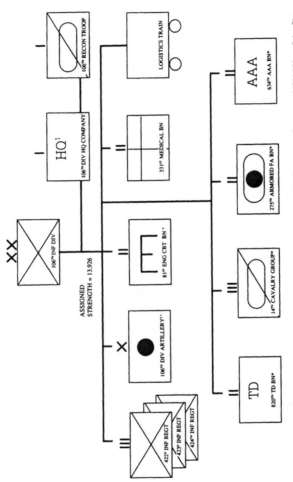

1 106ᵗʰ INF DIV Special Troops included   106ᵗʰ Signal Company, 806ᵗʰ Ordance Company, 106ᵗʰ Quartermaster Company, and 106th Military Police Platoon

2 106ᵗʰ Divartry included   3 x 105 Howitzer Battalions (589, 590, 591 FA), 1 x 155 Howitzer Battalion (592 FA)

3 In addition to organic and attached artillery units, VIII Corps had positioned Nine Corps Artillery battalions in the 106ᵗʰ Division Sector (174ᵗʰ, 333ᴿᴰ, and 402ᴺᴰ Field Artillery Groups)

4 On 15 Dec, VIII Corps attached the 168ᵗʰEngineer Combat Battalion, which answered to Commander, 81ˢᵗ Engineer Combat Battalion

* Indicates attached units not organic to 106ᵗʰ Infantry Division   Overall strength about 18,000

APPENDIX I

Combat Command B, 7th Armored Division
17-23 December 1944

Not counting casualties, Combat Command B probably controlled about 5,000 men.

Attached to Combat Command B from 106ᵗʰ Infantry Division or VIII Corps on or after 17 December 1944

APPENDIX J

German Order of Battle, 16 December 1944

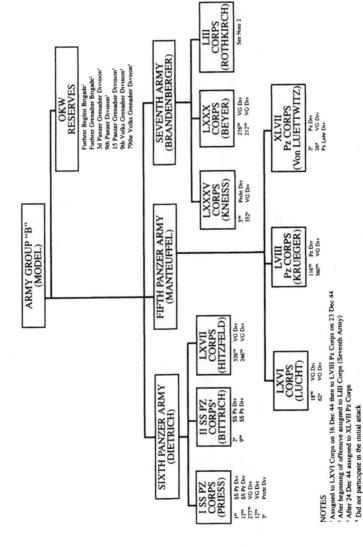

ARMY GROUP "B"
(MODEL)

OKW RESERVES

Fuehrer Begleit Brigade[1]
Fuehrer Grenadier Brigade[1]
3d Panzer Grenadier Division[1]
9th Panzer Division[1]
15 Panzer Grenadier Division[1]
9th Volks Grenadier Division[1]
79the Volks Grenadier Division[1]

SIXTH PANZER ARMY
(DIETRICH)

I SS PZ CORPS
(PRIESS)

1st   SS Pz Div
12th   SS Pz Div
277th VG Div
12th   VG Div
3r   Prcht Div

II SS PZ CORPS[4]
(BITTRICH)

2nd   SS Pz Div
9th   SS Pz Div

LXVII CORPS
(HITZFELD)

326th VG Div
246th VG Div

FIFTH PANZER ARMY
(MANTEUFFEL)

LXVI CORPS
(LUCHT)

18th   VG Div
62d   VG Div

LVIII Pz CORPS
(KRUEGER)

116th Pz Div
560th VG Div

XLVII Pz CORPS
(Von LUETTWITZ)

2nd   Pz Div
26d   VG Div
Pz Lehr Div

SEVENTH ARMY
(BRANDENBERGER)

LXXXV CORPS
(KNEISS)

5th   Prcht Div
352d   VG Div

LXXX CORPS
(BEYER)

276th VG Div
212th VG Div

LIII CORPS
(ROTHKIRCH)

See Note 2

NOTES

[1] Assigned to LXVI Corps on 16 Dec 44 then to LVIII Pz Corps on 23 Dec 44
[2] After beginning of offensive assigned to LIII Corps (Seventh Army)
[3] After 24 Dec 44 assigned to XLVII Pz Corps
[4] Did not participate in the initial attack

(Source: Dept of Army, US Army Armor School, *The Battle at St-Vith, Belgium, 17-23 December 1944*)

APPENDIX K

Principal Personalities

Field Marshal Sir Harold Alexander. (British) Commander of British troops in North Africa during the last phases of the Tunisian campaign. Was Eisenhower's ground commander (Army Group) for the Sicily invasion. Later assumed Supreme Allied Command of the Mediterranean Theater of Operations.

Lieutenant General Kenneth A.N. Anderson. (British) Commander of British First Army during the Allied Tunisian campaign, 1942-1943.

General of the Army Henry H. (Hap) Arnold. (American) Beginning in 1938, was head of Army Air Forces; served in this capacity throughout the war. One of the members of the Combined Chiefs of Staff.

Major General Raymond O. Barton. (American) Commander of 4th Infantry Division during the Battle of the Bulge.

General of the Army Omar N. Bradley. (American) Brought to North Africa to assist Eisenhower in overseeing ground war in 1943. II Corps commander in Sicily invasion; First Army commander during Normandy invasion; 12th Army Group commander 1944-1945 in Europe; operational commander for largest number of US troops in history (1,300,000).

General der Panzertruppen Erich Brandenberger. (German) Commander of German 7th Army during the Ardennes Offensive. This primarily infantry force was to guard the offensive's left flank.

Lieutenant General Lewis H. Brereton. (American) Commanded several numbered Air Forces in Pacific and in Europe. Later Commander-in-Chief First Allied Airborne Army in Europe, 1944-1945.

Field Marshal Sir Alan Brooke. (British) Chairman, British Chiefs of Staff committee. Chief of the Imperial General Staff for most of World War II.

Captain Harry C. Butcher. (American) Naval officer who served as Eisenhower's aide, keeping a detailed diary throughout the European war.

Major General Adna R. Chaffee. (American) Armored Corps champion in the years prior to WWII. Commanded the experimental 7th Mechanized Brigade during the 1940 Maneuvers, helping to validate theories of mechanized warfare and garner support for a separate US armored force. Commanding General of 1st US Armored Corps, 1940-1941. Died of cancer August 1941, at age 56, on eve of US entry into the war.

General Mark W. Clark. (American) Commander of Fifth Army during the Italian campaign. Later commanded 15th Army Group in Italy.

Brigadier General Bruce C. Clarke. (American) Commander of Combat Command `A', 4th Armored Division, leading unit of Patton's Third Army during the "race across France," summer 1944. Commander of Combat Command `B', 7th Armored Division at St.-Vith, Belgium, during the Battle of the Bulge.

Lieutenant Colonel Roy U. Clay. (American) Commander of 275th Armored Field Artillery Battalion at St.-Vith, Belgium during the Battle of the Bulge.

Lieutenant General J. Lawton Collins. (American) Aggressive, energetic commander of VII Corps. Led breakout at St.-Lô.

Air Marshal Sir Arthur Coningham. (British) In North Africa commanded First Tactical Air Force; later commanded Second Tactical Air Force in Europe.

Major General Fox Conner. (American) Pershing's Operations Officer in World War I. "Discovered" Eisenhower in 1920, mentored him, and rescued his career in 1920's-1930's. Commanded 20th Infantry Brigade in Panama with Eisenhower as Executive Officer, 1922-1924.

Major General Norman D. Cota. (American) Commander of 28th Infantry Division during the battle of the Huertgen Forest and the Battle of the Bulge.

General Henry D.G. Crerar. (Canadian) Chief of Canadian General Staff. Later division, corps, then First Canadian Army commander in Europe.

Admiral Sir Andrew Cunningham. (British) Commander of British Naval Forces in Mediterranean; Eisenhower's naval component commander for TORCH landings.

Admiral Jean-Francois Darlan. (French) Deputy Premier of Vichy government under Marshal Petain. In exchange for support of Allies, appointed leader of French forces in North Africa after TORCH landings by Eisenhower.

Charles De Gaulle. (French) Commander of Free French forces, 1940-1945.

Major General Sir Francis De Guingand. (British) Montgomery's Chief of Staff in the Eighth Army in North Africa and 21st Army Group in Europe.

Lieutenant General Sir Miles Dempsey. (British) Corps commander of British forces in Tunisia and Sicily; British Second Army commander in Europe.

General Jacob L. Devers. (American) Commander-in-Chief of European Theater of Operations in 1943; commanding general of North African Theater in 1943-1944; later Deputy Supreme Allied Commander in Mediterranean Theater; commanded 6th Army Group in Europe, August 1944-1945.

Colonel Mark Devine. (American) Commander of the 14th Cavalry Group during the first days of the Battle of the Bulge.

Colonel-General (SS) Josef "Sepp" Dietrich. (German) Early Hitler Nazi crony who became commander of 6th SS Panzer Army during the Ardennes Offensive. Responsible for German main attack, but his units became bogged down causing momentum of attack to shift to Manteuffel's Fifth Panzer Army.

Major General Lloyd R. Fredendall. (American) Commanded II Corps during TORCH landings and subsequent operations in Tunisia. Relieved of command after Kasserine Pass loss; returned to United States and commanded Second Army (training unit).

Colonel Hurley Fuller. (American) Commander of the 110th Infantry Regiment (28th Infantry Division) during the Battle of the Bulge. Captured when Clervaux is overrun.

Lieutenant General Leonard T. Gerow. (American) Commanded V Corps in Europe, 1944-1945. Later commanded Fifteenth Army in Europe, 1945.

Major General Ernest N. Harmon. (American) Eisenhower's special representative to II Corps immediately after the debacle at Kasserine Pass; thereafter, commander of the 1st and 2nd Armored Divisions, 1942-1945.

Brigadier General Robert W. Hasbrouck. (American) Commander of the 7th Armored Division during the Battle of the Bulge.

General Courtney H. Hodges. (American) Commander of First Army in Europe, 1944-1945.

Brigadier General William M. Hoge. (American) Commander of Combat Command `B', 9th Armored Division during the Battle of the Bulge. Later, as 9th Armored Division commander, sees his unit capture the bridge over the

Commander of Combat Command 'B', 9th Armored Division during the Battle of the Bulge. Later, as 9th Armored Division commander, sees his unit capture the bridge over the Rhine at Remagen.

Major General Clarence R. Huebner. (American) Commanded 1st Infantry Division from Sicily through D-Day to end of Battle of the Bulge. Assumed command of V Corps at conclusion of Ardennes campaign.

Major General Alan W. Jones. (American) Commander of the 106th Infantry Division during the Battle of the Bulge. Two-thirds of his division surrendered outside of St.-Vith, marking the largest capitulation of US troops in the European Theater.

Marshal Alphonse Juin. (French) Commander-in-Chief of French forces in North Africa, 1943.

Major General William B. Kean, Jr. (American) Chief of Staff for First US Army, 1944-1945, serving in that position under both Bradley and Hodges.

Fleet Admiral Ernest J. King. (American) Chief of Naval Operations, 1941-1945.

General Jean de Lattre de Tassigny. (French) Commander-in-Chief of French First Army, 1944-1945.

Lieutenant General John C.H. Lee. (American) Commanded the Communications Zone (Comm 'Z') in Europe 1944-1945.

Air Chief Marshal Sir Trafford Leigh-Mallory. (British) Commanded Fighter Command, 1942-1943; Commander-in-Chief of Allied Expeditionary Air Force, SHAEF, 1943-1944.

General of the Army Douglas MacArthur. (American) Army Chief of Staff, 1932-1935. Oversaw buildup of Philippine Defense Force, 1935-1941. Supreme Allied

General der Panzertruppen Hasso von Manteuffel. (German) Outstanding Panzer commander. Commanded Fifth Panzer Armee during the Ardennes Offensive. Achieved greatest success of any German commander during the Battle of the Bulge.

General of the Army George C. Marshall. (American) Chief of Staff of US Army, 1939-1945. Known as "Architect of Victory" for his influence on winning World War II. Later Secretary of Defense and Secretary of State.

Brigadier General Anthony C. McAuliffe. (American) Acting commander of the 101st Airborne Division during the Battle of the Bulge. Senior commander of forces in Bastogne during the siege. Famous for "Nuts!" reply to German surrender demand.

General Lesley J. McNair. (American) Commander of Army Ground Forces, 1942-1944. Created much of the doctrine, organization, and structure of US Army of World War II. Killed during the carpet bombings of St.-Lô in July 1944.

Major General Troy H. Middleton. (American) VIII Corps commander in Europe, 1944-1945. Commanded units attacked during the Battle of the Bulge and oversaw defense, counterattack.

Feldmarschal Walter Model. (German) Pro-Nazi commander of Army Group B, 1944-1945. Ardennes Offensive Panzer Armies under his Army Group's Command.

Field Marshal Sir Bernard Montgomery. (British) Commanded Eighth Army in North Africa. Defeated Rommel at El Alamein. Led attack during Sicily invasion; Allied ground commander during Normandy invasion and commanded 21st Army Group in Europe 1944-1945.

Brigadier General James E. Moore. (American) Chief of Staff for Ninth US Army 1944-1945, under Simpson.

Lieutenant General Sir Frederick E. Morgan. (British) Deputy Chief of Staff for SHAEF 1944-1945.

Admiral Lord Louis Mountbatten. (British) Supreme Allied Commander in Southeast Asia 1944-1945.

Lieutenant General Alexander Patch. (American) Seventh Army commander 1944-1945.

General George S. Patton, Jr. (American) Commanded ground forces during TORCH landings (western area). II Corps commander in Tunisia (after Fredendall relief); Seventh Army commander in Sicily campaign; Third Army commander in Europe 1944-1945. Spearheaded Allied breakout from Normandy and pursuit across France.

Ernie Pyle. (American) War correspondent famous for living with troops and reporting the G.I. story. Killed during battle of Okinawa.

Major General Elwood R. Quesada. (American) Ninth Tactical Air Force commander 1944-1945.

Admiral Sir Bertram Ramsay. (British) Sicily Task Force commander; Commander-in-Chief of Allied Naval Forces.

Lieutenant General Matthew Ridgway. (American) 82nd Airborne Division Commander in Sicily and Italy. Later XVIII Airborne Corps commander in Europe 1944-1945.

Lieutenant Colonel Thomas J. Riggs, Jr. (American) Commander of 81st Engineer Combat Battalion at St.-Vith during the Battle of the Bulge.

Colonel William B. Roberts. (American) Commander of Combat Command `B', 10th Armored Division during the Battle of the Bulge.

Major General Walter Robertson. (American) Commander of 2nd Infantry Division during the Battle of the Bulge.

Feldmarschal Erwin Rommel. (German) Commander of Afrika Korps 1941-1943. Defeated by Montgomery at El Alamein 1942. Won tactical victory against Americans at Kasserine Pass 1943. Commander of Army Group B in France, 1943-1944. Implicated in plot to kill Hitler, kills self, July 1944.

Feldmarschal Gerd von Rundstedt. (German) Commander-in-Chief of Army Group West 1942-1944.

Lieutenant General William H. Simpson. (American) Commanded the Ninth Army in Europe 1944-1945. Part of Montgomery's 21st Army Group, December 1944 to April 1945. First Allied troops to reach Elbe River, April 1945.

Lieutenant General Walter Bedell Smith. (American) Eisenhower's Chief of Staff at AFHQ and SHAEF 1942-1945.

General Carl A. Spaatz. (American) Commander of United States Strategic Air Forces in Europe 1944-1945.

Henry L. Stimson. (American) Secretary of War 1941-1945.

Major General Kenneth W.D. Strong. (British) SHAEF G-2, 1943-1945.

Air Chief Marshal Sir Arthur Tedder. (British) Air commander in Middle East Theater, then Mediterranean Theater. Deputy Supreme Allied Commander for SHAEF 1944-1945.

Major General Orlando Ward. (American) Commander of 1st Armored Division during the Kasserine Pass debacle, Tunisia, 1943.

Major General J.F.M. Whiteley. (British) Intelligence and operations advisor to Eisenhower in SHAEF 1943-1945.

General Sir Henry Maitland Wilson. (British) Supreme Allied Commander in Mediterranean Theater of Operations

1943-1945.

Major General John S. "P" Wood. (American) Commander of 4th Armored Division 1942 to December 1944. Unit spearheaded the Normandy breakout and subsequently led the "race across France" in the summer of 1944 as Patton's Third Army's lead unit.

SELECTED BIBLIOGRAPHY

BOOKS

Ambrose, Stephen E. *Eisenhower: Volume I. Soldier, General of the Army, President-Elect, 1890-1952.* New York:. Simon and Schuster, 1983.

——. *The Supreme Commander: The War Years of General Dwight David Eisenhower.* Garden City, NY: Doubleday and Company, 1969.

Baldwin, Hanson W. *Tiger Jack.* Fort Collins, CO: Old Army Press, 1979.

Barnett, Correlli, ed. *Hitler's Generals.* New York: Grove Weidenfeld, 1989.

Bender, Mark C. *Watershed at Leavenworth: Dwight D. Eisenhower and the Command and General Staff College.* Fort Leavenworth, KS: US Army Command and General Staff College, 1990.

Berlin, Robert H. *US Army World War II Corps Commanders: A Composite Biography.* Fort Leavenworth, KS: Combat Studies Institute, 1989.

Blumenson, Martin. *Eisenhower.* New York: Ballantine Books, Inc., 1972.

——. *Kasserine Pass.* New York: Jove Books, 1983.

——. *Patton: The Man Behind the Legend, 1885-1945.* New York: Berkley Books, 1987.

——. *The Patton Papers II: 1940-1945.* Boston: Houghton Mifflin, 1974.

——. *The United States Army in World War II. European Theater of Operations: Breakout and Pursuit.* Washington, DC: Office of the Chief of Military History/GPO, 1961.

—— and James L. Stokesbury. *Masters of the Art of Command.* Boston: Houghton Mifflin, 1975.

Bradley, Omar N., and Clay Blair. *A General's Life: An Autobiography by General of the Army Omar N. Bradley.* New York: Simon and Schuster, 1983.

Bradley, Omar N. *A Soldier's Story.* New York: Henry Holt, 1951.

Breuer, William B. *Operation Dragoon: The Allied Invasion of the South of France.* New York: Jove Books, 1987.

Bryant, Arthur. *Triumph in the West.* Garden City, NY: Doubleday, 1959.

Butcher, Harry C. *My Three Years With Eisenhower: The Personal Diary of Captain Harry C. Butcher, USNR.* New York: Simon and Schuster, 1946.

Carver, Sir Michael, ed. *The War Lords: Military Commanders of the Twentieth Century.* Boston: Little, Brown and Company, 1976.

Chandler, Alfred D., ed. *The Papers of Dwight David Eisenhower, The War Years.* Vols. I-V. Baltimore: Johns Hopkins Press, 1970.

Clausewitz, Carl v. *On War.* Edited and translated by Michael Howard and Peter Paret. Princeton, NJ: Princeton University Press, 1976.

Clay, Roy U. *Curbstone: The History of the 275th Armored Field Artillery Battalion in World War II.* Jackson, TN: Richerson, 1978.

Cole, Hugh M. *The United States Army in World War II. European Theater of Operations: The Ardennes: The Battle of the Bulge.* Washington, DC: Office of the Chief of Military History/GPO, 1965.

——. *The United States Army in World War II. European Theater of Operations: The Lorraine Campaign.* Washington, DC: Office of the Chief of Military History/GPO, 1950.

Collins, J. Lawton. *Lightning Joe: An Autobiography.* Baton Rouge: LSU Press, 1979.

——. *Conversations with General J. Lawton Collins.* Fort Leavenworth, KS: US Army Command and General Staff College, 1983.

Conquer: The Story of the Ninth Army, 1944-1945. Nashville, TN: Battery Press, 1980.

Craven, Wesley Frank, and James Lea Cate. *The Army Air Forces in World War II. Europe: Argument to V-E Day,*

January 1944-1945. Washington, DC: Office of Air
Force History/GPO, 1983.

Crookenden, Napier. *Battle of the Bulge 1944.* New York:
Scribner's, 1980.

Crosswell, D.K.R. *The Chief of Staff: The Military Career
of General Walter Bedell Smith.* New York: Greenwood
Press, 1991.

Dunleavy, T.M., ed. *Generals of the Army and the Air
Force.* 1954.

Dupuy, R. Ernest. *St. Vith: Lion in the Way--The 106th
Infantry Division in World War II.* Washington, DC:
Infantry Journal Press, 1949.

Eggenberger, David. *An Encyclopedia of Battles.* New
York: Dover Books, 1985.

Eisenhower, David. *Eisenhower: At War, 1943-1945.* New
York: Random House, 1986.

Eisenhower, Dwight D. *Crusade in Europe.* Garden City,
NY: Doubleday and Company, 1948.

Eisenhower, John S.D. *The Bitter Woods.* New York: G.P.
Putnam's Sons, 1969.

Ellis, John. *The Sharp End: The Fighting Man in World
War II.* New York: Charles Scribner's Sons, 1980.

——. *Brute Force: Allied Strategy and Tactics in the Second
World War.* New York: Viking Books, 1990.

Ellis, William D., and Thomas J. Cunningham. *Clarke of
St. Vith: The Sergeant's General.* Cleveland: Dillon-
Liederbach, 1974.

Fest, Joachim C. *The Face of the Third Reich.* New York:
Penguin, 1979.

Frankel, Nat, and Larry Smith. *Patton's Best: An Informal
History of the 4th Armored Division.* New York: Jove
Books, 1984.

Franklin Institute. *Art and Requirements of Command.*
Vol. 1, *Summary Report*; Vol. 2, *Generalship Study.*
Philadelphia: Systems Science Department of the
Franklin Institute, 1967.

Gabel, Christopher R. *Seek, Strike, and Destroy: US Army
Tank Destroyer Doctrine in World War II.* Fort
Leavenworth, KS: US Army Command and General
Staff College, 1985.

——. *The US Army GHQ Maneuvers of 1941.* Washington, DC: Center of Military History/GPO, 1991.

——. *The 4th Armored Division in the Encirclement of Nancy.* Fort Leavenworth, KS: US Army Command and General Staff College, 1986.

Galland, Adolf. *The First and the Last: The Rise and Fall of the German Fighter Forces, 1938-1945.* New York: Ballantine Books, 1957.

Greenfield, Kent R., ed. *Command Decisions.* Washington, DC: Office of the Chief of Military History/GPO, 1960.

Greenfield, Kent R. *The United States Army in World War II. The Army Ground Forces: The Organization of Ground Combat Troops.* Washington, DC: Historical Division, GPO, 1947.

——. *American Strategy in World War II: A Reconsideration.* Malabar, FL: Robert Kreiger Publishing, 1982.

Harrison, Gordon A. *The United States Army in World War II. European Theater of Operations: Cross-Channel Attack.* Washington, DC: Office of the Chief of Military History/GPO, 1951.

Hogg, Ian V. *Artillery 1920-1963.* New York: Arco Publishing, 1980.

——. *The Encyclopedia of Infantry Weapons of World War II.* New York: Thomas Y. Crowell Company, 1977.

Howard, Michael, ed. *The Theory and Practice of War.* Bloomington: Indiana University Press, 1965.

Howe, George F. *The United States Army in World War II. Mediterranean Theater of Operations: Northwest Africa: Seizing the Initiative.* Washington, DC: Office of the Chief of Military History/ GPO, 1957.

Howitzer, The. 1909 ed. West Point, NY: US Military Academy, 1909.

——. 1912 ed. West Point, NY: US Military Academy, 1912.

——. 1915 ed. West Point, NY: US Military Academy, 1915.

Irving, David. *The War Between the Generals.* New York: Congdon and Lattes, 1981.

Janowitz, Morris. *The Professional Soldier*. New York: Free Press-Macmillan, 1960.

Jessup, John E., Jr., and Robert W. Coakley. *A Guide to the Study and Use of Military History*. Washington, DC: GPO, 1979.

Keegan, John, ed. *Churchill's Generals*. New York: Grove Weidenfeld, 1991.

Keegan, John. *Six Armies in Normandy: From D-Day to the Liberation of Paris*. New York: Penguin Books, 1982.

Kennett, Lee. *G.I.: The American Soldier in World War II*. New York: Warner Books, 1987.

Killen, John. *A History of the Luftwaffe*. New York: Bantam Books, 1987.

Koyen, Kenneth. *The Fourth Armored Division: From the Beach to Bavaria*. Watertown, NY: Hungerford-Holbrook Company, 1949.

Lamb, Richard. *Montgomery in Europe 1943-1945*. London: Buchan and Enright, 1983.

Lee, Dwight E., and George McReynolds, eds. *Essays in History and International Relations*. Worcester, MA: Clark University Publishing, 1949.

Leinbaugh, Harold P., and John D. Campbell. *The Men of Company K: The Autobiography of a World War II Rifle Company*. New York: Bantam Books, 1987.

Lewin, Ronald. *Churchill as Warlord*. New York: Stein and Day, 1973.

Liddell Hart, Basil H. *The Memoirs of Captain Liddell Hart*. London: Cassell and Company, 1965.

———. *The Other Side of the Hill*. London: Cassell and Company, 1951.

MacArthur, Douglas. *Reminiscences*. New York: McGraw-Hill, 1964.

MacDonald, Charles B. *The Battle of the Huertgen Forest*. New York: Jove Publications, 1984.

———. *A Time for Trumpets: The Untold Story of the Battle of the Bulge*. New York: Bantam, 1985.

———. *Company Commander*. New York: Bantam, 1982.

———. *The Mighty Endeavor: The American War in Europe*. New York: Quill-William Morrow, 1986.

——. *The United States Army in World War II. European Theater of Operations: The Last Offensive.* Washington, DC: Office of the Chief of Military History/GPO, 1973.

——. *The United States Army in World War II. European Theater of Operations: The Siegfried Line Campaign.* Washington, DC: Office of the Chief of Military History/GPO, 1973.

Mahon, John K. *History of the Militia and the National Guard.* New York: Macmillan Publishing Co., 1983.

Marshall, S.L.A. *Bastogne: The First Eight Days.* Washington, DC: The Infantry Journal Press, 1946.

——. *Men Against Fire: The Problem of Battle Command in Future War.* Gloucester, MA: Peter Smith, 1947.

Matloff, Maurice. *The United States Army in World War II. The War Department: Strategic Planning for Coalition Warfare, 1943-1944.* Washington, DC: Office of the Chief of Military History/GPO, 1953.

Matthews, Lloyd J., and Dale E. Brown, eds. *The Challenge of Military Leadership.* Washington, DC: Pergammon Brassey's, 1989.

Merriam, Robert E. *Dark December.* Chicago/New York: Ziff-Davis, 1947.

Meyer, Harold J. *Hanging Sam: A Military Biography of General Samuel T. Williams.* Denton, TX: University of North Texas Press, 1990.

Mick, Allen H., ed. *With the 102nd Infantry Division Through Germany.* Nashville, TN: Battery Press, 1980.

Military History and Publications Section, The Infantry School. *Infantry in Battle.* Washington, DC: Infantry Journal, Inc., 1959.

Mitchell, Ralph M. *The 101st Airborne Division's Defense of Bastogne.* Fort Leavenworth, KS: Combat Studies Institute, 1986.

Montgomery, Bernard Law. *The Memoirs of Field-Marshal the Viscount Montgomery of Alamein, K.G..* New York: Signet Books, 1958.

Nobécourt, Jacques. *Hitler's Last Gamble.* New York: Schocken Books, 1967.

Palmer, Robert R., Bell I. Wiley, and William R. Keast. *The United States Army in World War II: The Army Ground*

Forces. The Procurement and Training of Ground Combat Troops. Washington, DC: Office of the Chief of Military History/GPO, 1948.

Paret, Peter, ed. *Makers of Modern Strategy: From Machiavelli to the Nuclear Age.* Princeton: Princeton University Press, 1986.

Perrett, Geoffrey. *There's A War To Be Won: The United States Army in World War II.* New York: Random House, 1991.

Phillips, Robert H. *To Save Bastogne.* New York: Stein and Day, 1983.

Pogue, Forrest C. *The United States Army in World War II. European Theater of Operations: The Supreme Command.* Washington, DC: Office of the Chief of Military History/GPO, 1954.

Price, Frank J. *Troy H. Middleton: A Biography.* Baton Rouge: LSU Press, 1974.

Reed, Prentiss B., Jr. *Personal Leadership for Combat Officers.* New York: McGraw-Hill, 1943.

Ridgway, Matthew B. *Soldier: The Memoirs of Matthew B. Ridgway (As Told to Harold H. Martin).* New York: Harper and Brothers, 1956.

Saied, Kemal. *Thunderbolt Odyssey: P-47 War in Europe.* Tulsa, OK: Stonewood Press, 1989.

Sebree, Edmund B., ed. *Leadership at Higher Levels of Command as Viewed by Senior and Experienced Combat Commanders.* Monterey, CA: U.S. Army Leadership Research Unit, 1961, "William H. Simpson," by Alvan C. Gillem, Jr.

Smith, Walter Bedell. *Eisenhower's Six Great Decisions (Europe 1944-1945).* New York: Longmans, Green and Company, 1956.

Steward, Hal D. *Thunderbolt: The History of the Eleventh Armored Division.* Nashville, TN: Battery Press, 1981.

Stokesbury, James L. *A Short History of World War I.* New York: William Morrow, 1981.

Toland, John. *Battle: The Story of the Bulge.* New York: Random House, 1959.

——. *The Last 100 Days.* New York: Random House, 1965.

United States Command and General Staff College.

Dwight D. Eisenhower: The Professional Soldier and the Study of History. Fort Leavenworth, KS: US Army Command and General Staff College, 1990.

Van Creveld, Martin. *Fighting Power: German and U.S. Army Performance 1939-1945*. Westport, CT: Greenwood Press, 1982.

——. *Supplying War: Logistics From Wallenstein to Patton*. New York: Cambridge University Press, 1977.

Van Gelder, Lawrence. *Ike: A Soldier's Crusade*. New York: Universal Publishing, 1969.

Weigley, Russell F. *The American Way of War: A History of U.S. Military Strategy and Policy*. New York: Macmillan, 1973.

——. *Eisenhower's Lieutenants: The Campaign of France and Germany 1944-1945*. Bloomington, IN: Indiana University, 1981.

——. *History of the United States Army*. New York: Macmillan, 1967.

Whitaker, W. Denis, and Shelagh Whitaker. *Rhineland: The Battle to End the War*. New York: St. Martin's Press, 1989.

Whiting, Charles. *Death of a Division*. New York: Stein and Day, 1981.

——. *Ardennes: The Secret War*. London: Century Publishing, 1984.

Wilmot, Chester. *The Struggle for Europe*. New York: Harper and Brothers, 1952.

Young, Desmond. *Rommel: The Desert Fox*. New York: Quill, William Morrow, 1950.

Government Documents

US Department of the Army. *Annual Reports of the Commandant. The General Service Schools, 1923-24 to 1927-28*. Fort Leavenworth, KS: General Service School Press, 1924 to 1928.

——. Clarke, General Bruce C. *St. Vith: Counteroffensive*. Industrial College of the Armed Forces, April 1975.

——. Fontenot, Major Gregory. *The Lucky Seventh in the Bulge: A Case Study for the Airland Battle*. MMAS thesis, Command and General Staff College, 1985.

—. Morelock, Major Jerry. *Senior Leadership: The Crucial Element of Combat Power*. MMAS thesis, Command and General Staff College, 1984.

—. Nelson, Major Dale. *The Ardennes, 1944--The Defensive Battles*. MMAS thesis, Command and General Staff College, 1981.

—. Armor School. *The Battle at St- Vith, Belgium*. 1949.

—. Armor School. *Campaigns and Battles—Germany 1944, Armor in the Defense, Armor on a Corps Boundary, Ardennes*. 1944.

—. Army Ground Forces. AGF Extracts, *106th Division Artillery Lessons Learned*. 1945.

—. Army Ground Forces. AGF Board Report--Engineer Notes.

—. Command and General Staff College. *Battle of the Bulge Bibliography*. 20 November 1973.

—. Center for Military History. *American Armies and Battlefields in Europe*. Washington, DC: GPO, 1992. (Reprint of 1938 edition prepared by the American Battle Monuments Commission.)

—. Center for Military History, German Army Operations in the Ardennes (5 documents translated from the German), Dietrich, Wagner, Manteuffel.

—. Center for Military History. *Main Reasons for Failure of the Ardennes Offensive*. 17 pages translated from the German.

—. General Orders No. 11. 27 April 1981.

—. 12th Army Group, Report of Operations (Final After Action Report). Multiple Volumes. Washington, DC: Superintendent of Documents, 1948.

—. 12th Army Group. *G-1 Daily Summaries*. 1944.

—. First Army, *Road Net Used for Regrouping Army Moves*. 17-26 December 1944 (16 Maps).

-. Ninth U.S. Army. *Corps and Divisions Under Ninth U.S. Army in European Theater of Operations*. 1 September 1944-15 June 1945.

-. Ninth U.S. Army. Army Service Forces, Report No. 169, *Command and Staff Procedures*, 31 July 1945.

-. Ninth U.S. Army, Administrative Instructions, 30 November 1944.

——. Ninth U.S. Army, After Action Report, 1-15 May 1945

——. Ninth U.S. Army, After Action Report, December 1944, January-May 1945.

——. Ninth U.S. Army, *Ninth Army Engineer Operations in Rhine River Crossings*, 30 June 1945.

——. V Corps, After Action Report, December 1944.

——. VIII Corps, *Report on the Artillery with the VIII Corps in the Reduction of Brest, 22 August-19 September 1944.* Command and General Staff School.

——. VIII Corps, *American Intelligence on German Counteroffensive*, December 1944.

——. VIII Corps, After Action Report, 1 July 1944-May 1945.

——. VIII Corps, Field Order No. 9, 1 August 1944.

——. VIII Corps, Field Order No. 10, 2 August 1944.

——. VIII Corps, Field Order No. 12, 29 December 1944.

——. VIII Corps, Field Order No. 1, 2 January 1945.

——. VIII Corps, Operations Instructions, 19 August-29 December 1944.

——. VIII Corps, Operations Memorandum No. 3, *Operations in the Ardennes.*

——. VIII Corps, Operations Memoranda No. 20-25, 3 February-25 February 1945.

——. VIII Corps, Letters of Instruction, August 1944-1 January 1945.

——. VIII Corps, *Attack of a Fortified Zone*, 9 October 1944, European Theater of Operations.

——. 4th Armored Division, *Armor at Bastogne*, Armored School, Student Research Report, May 1949.

——. 4th Armored Division, *Armor in the Exploitation, 4th Armored Division Across France to the Moselle River*, Armored School, Student Research Report, May 1949.

——. 4th Armored Division, *Armor versus Mud and Mines, 4th Armored Division in the Sarre-Moselle Area*, Armored School, Student Research Report, 1950.

——. 4th Armored Division, Army Ground Forces, *Tactics and Administration, Armored Division*, War Department Observers Board Draft Report, ETOUSA, June 1945.

—. 4th Armored Division, *Operation of CC'A', 4th Armored Division, Normandy Beachhead to the Meuse River, 28 July-31 August 1944*, Lt. Col. H.C. Pattison, Command and Staff College, 1946-47.

—. 4th Armored Division, *Establishment and Defense of the Nancy Bridgehead*, September 1944.

—. 4th Armored Division, Armor in the Exploitation, Armored School, Student Research Report, May 1950.

—. 4th Armored Division, After Action Report, September-October 1944, European Theater of Operations.

—. 4th Armored Division, After Action Report, 17 July-31 August 1944, European Theater of Operations.

—. 4th Armored Division, After Action Report, 1-30 November 1944, European Theater of Operations.

—. 4th Armored Division, *Relief of Bastogne, 20 December 1944-1 January 1945*.

—. 4th Armored Division, *Lorraine Campaign Combat Interviews*, 9 November-10 December 1944.

—. 4th Armored Division, Memorandum for Commander, Third U.S. Army, 2 October 1944.

—. 4th Armored Division, Training Memorandum to Unit Commanders, 23 September 1944.

—. 7th Armored Division, *Battle Honors, Distinguished Unit Citation--7th Armored Division*, 27 June 1947.

—. 7th Armored Division, After Action Report, September 1944 to May 1945, Summary of Operations, Administrative and Statistical Summary.

—. 7th Armored Division, After Action Report, December 1944, *Battle of St. Vith, Belgium, 17-23 December 1944*.

—. 7th Armored Division, After Action Report, September 1944 to May 1945, Report of Division Artillery.

—. 28th Infantry Division, Unit Report, July 1944-April 1945.

—. 28th Infantry Division, After Action Report, July 1944-May 1945, Division Artillery.

—. 28th Infantry Division, *Operations of 1st Battalion, 110th Infantry Regiment, 16-18 December 1944*.

—. 28th Infantry Division, *Operations of 112th Infantry Regiment, 1944*.

———. 28th Infantry Division, *History of 3rd Battalion, 112th Infantry Regiment, July 1944-April 1945*.

———. 106th Infantry Division, Report of Action Against the Enemy, 7 December 1944-9 May 1945.

———. 106th Infantry Division, After Action Report, December 1944.

———. 106th Infantry Division, After Battle Report, 424th Infantry Regiment, ending 31 December 1944.

———. 106th Infantry Division, After Action Report, December 1944, January-May 1945, Report of the DivArty.

———. 32nd Armored Cavalry Reconnaissance Squadron, Action Against the Enemy, 1 January 1945.

———. 275th Armored Field Artillery Battalion, Unit Report 30 November-31 December 1944.

———. Field Manual (FM) 22-100, *Military Leadership*. Washington, DC: Department of the Army, 1983.

———. Field Manual (FM) 100-5, *Operations*. Washington, DC: Department of the Army, 1982.

Periodicals and Articles

Albright, John. "Introducing 'P' Wood—4th Armored Division." *Armor* 81 (January-February 1972): 24-29.

Ambrose, Stephen E. "Eisenhower's Legacy." *Military Review* 70 (October 1990): 4-14.

Baldwin, Hanson W. "'P' Wood of the 4th Armored." *Army* 18 (January 1968): 45-54.

Balish, Harry. "The Battle of Nancy: A Double Envelopment." *Military Review* 29 (January 1950): 16-23.

Berlin, Robert H. "United States Army World War II Corps Commanders: A Composite Biography." *The Journal of Military History* 53 (April 1989): 147-167.

———. "Dwight David Eisenhower and the Duties of Generalship." *Military Review* 70 (October 1990): 15-25.

Blumenson, Martin. "The Decision to Take Brest." *Army* 10 (March 1960): 44-48.

———. "America's World War II Leaders in Europe: Some Thoughts." *Parameters* 19 (December 1989): 2-13.

——. "Eisenhower Then and Now: Fireside Reflections." *Parameters* 21 (Summer 1991).

Bolger, Daniel P. "Zero Defects: Command Climate in First U.S. Army, 1944-1945." *Military Review* 71 (May 1991): 61-73.

Bradin, James W. "28th Infantry Division: The Forgotten Pennsylvanians." *Army* 37 (August 1987): 62-67.

Clarke, Bruce C. "The Battle for St. Vith: Armor in the Defense and Delay." *Armor* 83 (November-December 1974): 39-40.

——. "Carrying Out Orders." *EurArmy* 23 (August 1984): 1-2.

Dunleavy, T.M. "General William Hood Simpson." *Generals of the Army and the Air Force* 2 (June 1954): 19-21.

Dupuy, R. Ernest. "'Beat Monty' Spirit Helped U.S. Forces Crush Germany." *Army-Navy Journal* 99 (7 April 1962): 18-19.

Flanagan, E.M., Jr. "A Force of Professionals." *Army* 42 (March 1992): 56-57.

Gabel, Christopher R. "The 1941 Maneuvers." *Military Review* 71 (August 1991): 88-89.

Grow, Robert W. "Mobility Unused." *Military Review* 32 (February 1953): 18-24.

Hanlon, John. "Tom Riggs' Remarkable World War II Odyssey." *Providence Sunday Journal* (29 December 1985).

Harris, Boyd M. "A Perspective on Leadership, Management and Command." *Military Review* 64 (February 1984): 48-57.

Ketchum, Richard M. "Warming Up on the Sidelines for World War II." *Smithsonian* 22 (September 1991): 88-103.

Kingseed, Cole C. "Eisenhower's Prewar Anonymity: Myth or Reality?" *Parameters* 21 (Autumn 1991): 87-98.

Lattimer, Philip W. "When the Black Panthers Prowled." *Army* 42 (January 1992): 44-46.

McLain, Raymond S. Edited by Albert N. Garland. "One of the Greatest: A Study in Leadership." *Military Review* 49 (December 1969): 18-27.

Morelock, J.D. "General Jacob L. Devers: Commonsense Commander." *Forward Observer* 3 (December 1988-February 1989).

———. "Death in the Forest: Close Support During the Battle of the Bulge." *Field Artillery Journal* (September-October 1986):8-14.

Nye, Roger H. "Whence Patton's Genius?" *Parameters* 22 (Winter 1991-1992): 60-73.

Raymond, Allen D., III. "The Battle of St. Vith." *Armor* 73 (November-December 1964): 5-11.

Stone, Thomas R. "General William Hood Simpson: Unsung Commander of the U.S. Ninth Army." *Parameters* 11 (February 1981): 44-52.

———. "1630 Comes Early on the Roer." *Military Review* 53 (October 1973): 3-21.

UNPUBLISHED MATERIAL

Clarke, Bruce C. "The Revolution in Army Organization, Tactics, and Equipment in the Period 1940-1945." Lecture notes, 15 March 1982.

———. "Clarke's Transfer." undated.

———. "The Corps of Engineers in the Armored Force, 1940-1945," 1986, Ms.

———. "The Creating of an Outstanding Battalion in 1941-1942."

———. "How to Motivate Soldiers."

———. "The Move to St. Vith, Belgium, 16-18 December 1944."

———. "The Rehabilitation of Troops in Battle." 15 June 1986.

———. "The Violations of Regulations and Channels of Communications Can Be Justified." 14 March 1987.

———, to J.D. Morelock, 12 June 1985.

———, to J.D. Morelock, 12 August 1986.

Clay, Roy U., to J.D. Morelock, 23 February 1986.

———, to J.D. Morelock, 26 February 1986.

Cole, Hugh M., to J.D. Morelock, 4 September 1990.

Eddy, Manton S. "Diary—Activities of General Eddy, 24 March 1944 and 3 June 1944 to 23 May 1945." Fort Benning, GA: US Army Infantry Museum.

Hasbrouck, Robert W., to Bruce C. Clarke, undated.

Hummel, Louis, to Kathryn Hoffert, 4 March 1918.

Morelock, J.D. "Senior Leadership: The Crucial Element of Combat Power." Master of Military Art and Science thesis, 1984.

Riggs, Thomas J., to Bruce C. Clarke, 28 January 1986.

Stone, Thomas R. "He Had the Guts to Say No: A Military Biography of General William Hood Simpson." Ph.D. diss., Rice University, 1974.

Woodruff, Owen E., Jr., to Bruce C. Clarke, 27 January 1987.

OTHER SOURCES

Blumenson, Martin. "Breakout and Pursuit." S.L.A. Marshall Lecture, US Army Command and General Staff College, Fort Leavenworth, KS, 13 March 1984.

Clarke, Bruce C. Interview by author, 13 April 1985. McLean, VA.

——. Interview by author, February 1986, Carlisle Barracks, PA.

——. "The Defense of St. Vith." Interview by author, 10 November 1987.

Clay, Roy U. Interview by author, February 1986, Carlisle Barracks, PA.

——. Interview by author, 12 March 1986, Carlisle Barracks, PA.

Eisenhower, Dwight D. "Command in War." Lecture, National War College, Fort McNair, Washington, D.C., 30 October 1950.

Garrett, Eugene. "The Malmédy (Baugnez Crossroads) Massacre." Interview by author, November 1987 (tape recording).

Harris, Boyd M. Interview by author, 9 September 1983, Fort Leavenworth, KS.

Pogue, Forrest C. "Over the Beaches: D-Day." S.L.A. Marshall Lecture, US Army Command and General Staff College, Fort Leavenworth, KS, 17 January 1984.

——. Interview by author, 18 January 1984, Fort Leavenworth, KS.

Services Cinema Corporation, Producer. *The Ardennes Offensive 1944*. United Kingdom, London: Ministry of Defence. 1979. Film.

INDEX

AUTHOR

Jerry Morelock is a colonel in the US Army. Currently he is the Chief, Russia and Republics Branch, European Division, J-5, Office of the Joint Chiefs of Staff. He has been selected as the Director, Combat Studies Institute at the Army Command and General Staff College.

He is a graduate of the US Military Academy at West Point, and holds an MS from Purdue University and a Master of Military Art and Science from the US Army Command and General Staff College. Colonel Morelock is also a distinguished graduate of the Industrial College of the Armed Forces, where, as a Research Fellow, he wrote this study.

Colonel Morelock's previous positions have included battery commander in the United States and Viet Nam, tactical officer at West Point, and battalion commander in Germany. As a military historian he won the 1984 Arter-Darby Military History Writing Award for excellence in professional scholarship, and the 1986 US Field Artillery Association History Writing Contest. Colonel Morelock was also chosen as a Distinguished Essayist in the 1991 Chairman, Joint Chiefs of Staff, Strategy Essay competition.

Printed in the United States
122861LV00004B/7-30/A